Environmental Sustainability in Asian Logistics and Supply Chains

Xiaohong Liu
Editor

Environmental Sustainability in Asian Logistics and Supply Chains

Springer

Editor
Xiaohong Liu
Business School
Central University of Finance and Economics
Beijing
China

This book is supported by Beijing Natural Science Foundation (9162015) and Central University of Finance and Economics.

ISBN 978-981-13-0450-7 ISBN 978-981-13-0451-4 (eBook)
https://doi.org/10.1007/978-981-13-0451-4

Library of Congress Control Number: 2018940632

Printed on acid-free paper

This Springer imprint is published by the registered company Springer Nature Singapore Pte Ltd.
The registered company address is: 152 Beach Road, #21-01/04 Gateway East, Singapore 189721, Singapore

Preface

With the increasing global awareness of the significance of environmental protection, Asia has witnessed a significant trend toward greening logistics and supply chains. Asia is the largest and the most populous continent in the world, and in recent years, it has enjoyed the fastest economic growth. Nevertheless, although economic progress has brought prosperity to Asian economies and societies, it has created concomitant environmental problems. To date, the byproducts of this booming economy include a notable contribution to the greenhouse effect, considerable air and water pollution, the overuse of natural resources, and the production of hazardous waste, resulting in substantial widespread environmental degradation in Asia. Moreover, as the most significant production and consumer base in terms of economic globalization, Asia plays a crucial role in global supply chain management (SCM). Thus, the development of environmentally sustainable supply chains is in high demand, to preserve the local and global environment.

Inspired by this observation, this book, entitled "Environmental Sustainability in Asian Logistics and Supply Chains", addresses issues relating to logistics and supply chains from the perspective of Asian environmental sustainability. It brings together selected presentations from the *12th International Congress on Logistics and SCM Systems (ICLS2017)* held in Beijing, China, August 20–23, 2017. The congress was organised by the Business School, Central University of Finance and Economics and the International Federation of Logistics and SCM Systems (IFLS). It included submissions from researchers covering a variety of topics relating to green and sustainable logistics and supply chains in the Asian context, such as green logistics and environmental impact, green SCM and firm performance, green operations and optimization, the sustainability of supply chains, carbon measurement of logistics, and corporate social responsibility. To effectively disseminate the most significant findings from this successful symposium and stimulate further research in this field, the authors of key presentations were invited to contribute full chapters for inclusion in this book. The research contained within utilises both empirical studies and math modeling research. It is anticipated that the book will prove a valuable resource for both academics and practitioners wishing to deepen their knowledge in the field of Asian logistics and supply chains in respect of environmental sustainability.

The preparation and publication of this book would not have been possible without the support of the Central University of Finance and Economics and the International Federation of Logistics and SCM Systems (IFLS). Therefore, I would like to take this opportunity to express my sincere appreciation to them both. In particular, I am grateful to the board of the IFLS for their valuable contribution to the book:

Honorary Chairman: Prof. Karasawa, Yutaka, Kanagawa University, Japan

Chairman: Prof. Kachitvichyanukul, Voratas, Asian Institute of Technology, Thailand

Senior Vice Chairman: Prof. Wu, Yen-Chen Jim, National Taiwan Normal University, Taiwan

Vice Chairmen: Prof. Lai, Kin Keung, City University of Hong Kong, China; Prof. Liu, Xiaohong, Central University of Finance and Economics, China; Prof. Rim, Suk-Chul, Ajou University, Korea; Prof. Wakabayashi, Keizo, Nihon University, Japan; Prof. Tsai, Kune-Muh, National Kaohsiung First University of Science & Technology, Taiwan

I would like to thank all the authors for submitting their full chapters as requested, and to express my gratitude for their valuable contributions to the book. I also wish to gratefully acknowledge and recognise the important contribution of the reviewers of the manuscripts. Finally, special thanks go to the staff at Springer for their kind support of the editorial work.

Beijing, China
January 2018

Xiaohong Liu

Contents

Part I
Empirical and Conceptual Research

An Analysis of Energy-Related CO_2 Emissions from China's Logistics Industry

Xiaohong Liu, Alan C. McKinnon and Ning Wei

Abstract China's logistics industry has developed rapidly in recent years. As the level of logistical activity has grown so has the sector's carbon footprint. The measurement and control of these logistics-related CO_2 emissions is of vital importance to the nation's energy and climate change strategies. This paper reports the results of an analysis of these emissions over the period 2000–2015 using two decomposition techniques, i.e. Environmental Kuznets curve (EKC) and the Logarithmic Mean Divisia Index (LMDI). In absolute terms, the amount of CO_2 emissions from China's logistics industry rose sharply and exhibited a cubic relationship with GDP rather than the more typical EKC curve. On the other hand, the ratio of CO_2 emissions to energy consumption for China's logistics industry was found to be declining. From the perspective of energy usage, two factors, energy intensity and energy structure, are identified as being the main contributors to the decrease in CO_2 emission intensity, with energy intensity dominating. On the basis of these research results, the paper discusses ways of further reducing the CO_2 emission intensity of China's logistics industry.

Keywords Logistics industry · CO_2 emission intensity · Energy intensity Energy structure · Environmental Kuznets curve · Logarithmic Mean Divisia Index

X. Liu (✉)
Business School, Central University of Finance and Economics, Beijing, China
e-mail: xliu@cufe.edu.cn

A. C. McKinnon
Kühne Logistics University, Hamburg, Germany

N. Wei
Horizon Research Consultancy Group, Beijing, China

X. Liu (ed.), *Environmental Sustainability in Asian Logistics and Supply Chains*,
https://doi.org/10.1007/978-981-13-0451-4_1

1 Introduction

Logistics is concerned with the movement, storage and handling of materials as they move from raw material source, through the production system to points of final consumption. It is widely recognised that logistics plays a vital role in economic development and corporate strategy. In China, the expansion of logistics has been closely coupled with economic growth. According to the report released by China Federation of Logistics and Purchasing (CFLP) on China logistics annually, in 2016, the total revenue of China's logistics industry reached 7.9 trillion RMB Yuan, an annual increase of 4.6%, and representing a 10.6% share of GDP. Some estimates put its share as high as 15% [4]. Given its major contribution to the growth of the country's economy and society, China's logistics industry has been regarded by the Chinese government as one of the ten 'restructuring and revitalization industries' since 2009.

The exceptionally rapid growth of logistical activity in China, particularly the movement of freight, has placed a heavy burden on the environment. For example, the number of commercial road vehicles grew by 49% between 2009 and 2016 and the amount of freight moved (expressed in 2389.1 billion tokm) by 64%. The huge increase in road freight traffic has been responsible for much of the exacerbation of air quality and congestion problems over this period. The focus of this paper, however, is on another externality-namely CO_2 emissions from the fossil fuel consumed by logistics operations.

The Chinese government made a commitment in 2009 to cut national CO_2 emissions per unit of GDP, (i.e. carbon intensity), by 40–45% of 2005 levels by 2020. Numerous studies have analysed trends in China's carbon emissions and the potential for reducing them (e.g. [18, 22, 23, 28, 33, 38, 41, 42]), though, none has as yet attempted to calculate emissions from the logistics industry. This has been an important omission as the logistics sector accounts for 10–15% of Chinese GDP, is energy intensive, a major emitter of CO_2 and expected to make a significant contribution to meeting the 2020 national carbon intensity target. The omission can be partly explained by the heterogeneity of logistics services and the lack of clear boundaries between "logistics" and other industries. In addition to those businesses whose main activity is logistics, for many others, such as manufacturers and retailers, it is an ancillary activity and so, in national accounting, often subsumed within other sectors. This complicates the measurement of logistics-related emissions. Indeed, to date only one attempt has been made to carbon footprint logistical activities at a global level [40] and, to our knowledge, none at a national level. Data limitations have confined the analysis discussed in this paper to emissions from businesses classified as having 'transportation, storage and postal services' as their primary activity. These businesses will be referred to collectively as the logistics sector or logistics industry.

The present study has four objectives:

(1) To quantify total CO_2 emissions from China's logistics industry;
(2) To analyse the relationship between these logistics emissions and economic development and energy consumption;
(3) To examine the structure and intensity of the CO_2 emissions from China's logistics industry;
(4) To identify the main ways of reducing the carbon intensity of Chinese logistics.

The remainder of the paper is structured as follows. Section 2 reviews relevant literature, on the inter-relationship between logistics activities, energy use and CO_2 emissions. Section 3 describes the research methodology employed in this study. It outlines the data sources and the two measurement techniques used, one constructing the Environmental Kuznets curve (EKC) and the other calculating the Logarithmic Mean Divisia Index (LMDI). Section 4 presents the research results, including estimates of the total energy consumption and CO_2 emissions of China's logistics industry and the corresponding energy- and carbon-intensity values. Section 5 offers suggestions for cutting logistics-related emissions in China and summarises the main conclusions.

2 Literature Review

2.1 Logistics Activities, Energy Use and CO_2 Emissions

The nature of the environmental impact of logistics is related to functional operations (e.g. transport, warehousing), energy consumption, emissions and the infrastructures over which they operate.

The implementation of logistics activities requires a proportional amount of energy. The consumed energies are used in logistics operations, such as transport, warehousing, and material handling. Among these activities, transport is the largest contributor to energy consumption. It is reported transport accounts for approximately 25% world energy demand for about 61.5% of all the oil used each year [29].

While consuming large quantities of energy, logistics activities generate numerous pollutants such as CO_2, SO and noise, which have substantially damaged ecological systems. According to World Economic Forum [40], logistical activities account for roughly 5.5% of total global GHG emissions. Of those logistics activities, the fundamental function, i.e. freight transport, accounts for 80–90% of logistics-related carbon emissions and is regarded as one dominant source of emission of most pollutants [26]. At the corporate level, as reported by Davis [8], 80–90% of the emission savings comes from transport and the remainder comes from warehousing. The sustainability of logistics has become one core issue in logistics service provisions.

2.2 *Carbon Assessment of Logistics*

Much of the research on this subject has focused on the carbon auditing of individual companies' logistics operations. Different approaches and methodologies have been used for measuring CO_2 emissions from freight transport (e.g. [5, 27]) and warehousing operations [30]. As freight transport typically represents around 85–90% of total logistics-related CO_2 emissions [40], emissions from this source overwhelmingly dominate the calculation. At the corporate level, efforts have been made to harmonise data collection and analysis methodologies, emission factors and reporting standards [13].

Less attention has been paid to the measurement of carbon emissions from logistical activities at a national level. Most studies conducted at this level have been confined to freight movement and, in some cases, particular modes of freight transport (e.g. [11, 35]). In a study of the carbon footprinting of road haulage operations in the UK, McKinnon and Piecyk [27] found that many different approaches could be adopted, each yielding widely varying estimates. National-level assessments of CO_2 emissions from freight transport in other countries have used differing data sources and methods of calculation (e.g. [10, 21]). An important distinction can be made between top-down and bottom-up approaches.

The top-down approach uses high-level input-based measures, in this case macro-level estimates of the fuel/energy purchased by or supplied to companies in particular sectors. It then applies energy-based emission factors to these aggregated estimates of energy consumption. However, as noted by McKinnon [25], the classification of energy use by sector and sub-sector can make difficult to differentiate logistics-related energy consumption with sufficient accuracy. Failure to differentiate vehicle type at the point of fueling in statistical accounting often makes it difficult to split energy consumption between freight and passenger vehicles.

The bottom-up approach uses output-based measures derived from estimates of the actual amount of work done by the logistics sector. In the case of freight transport, this work can be measured by physical units such as tonne-kms or vehicles-kms, metrics which, in some countries are regularly tracked by government transport surveys. Average conversion factors can then applied to translate these transport variables into energy consumption and CO_2 emissions. Kamakaté and Schipper [19] and Eom et al. [11] adopted this bottom-up approach in their analyses of trends in the energy intensity of trucking operations in various countries including Australia, France, Japan, the United Kingdom, United States and Korea, but not China.

Ideally, where sufficient data exists, both top-down and bottom-up analyses should be conducted to permit cross-validation.

3 Research Methodology

3.1 Top-Down Approach and Data Sources

Given data availability in China, this study adopts the top-down approach to assess CO_2 emissions from logistics industry. The data used in this study are mainly from two sources:

(a) *China Statistical Yearbook*
(b) *China Energy Statistical Yearbook*

Although the Chinese government and various non-governmental organizations have been steadily increasing the amount of data collected on logistical activities over the past decade, the National Statistics Yearbook does not separately identify logistics as business sector. It does, however, publish data on 'transportation, storage and postal services' which can be considered to roughly approximate to the 'logistics industry'. For example, Song et al. [34] used data from this statistical category to measure the amount of energy consumed by the 'logistics service industry'. The latest published energy data for this category relates to 2015. Energy data was also obtained for this category from the National Statistics Yearbook for 2000, as allowing this to be used as the base year for the analysis.

3.2 Techniques of Measurement

As explained earlier, logistics emission trends over the period 2000–2015 were analysed using two techniques, Environmental Kuznets curve (EKC) hypothesis and the Logarithmic Mean Divisia Index (LMDI).

The EKC hypothesis, which was proposed by Grossman and Krueger [14], indicates a strong statistical relationship between environmental quality and per-capital income. According to the EKC hypothesis, environmental quality initially worsens with the increases in per-capita income but then improves after an Income Turning Point (ITP); at high income levels economic growth leads to environmental improvement. The EKC is shaped like as an inverted U shape. The EKC hypothesis implies that it is possible for countries simultaneously to enjoy higher income and improved environmental quality. For example, by using a reduced-form approach, Schmalensee et al. [31] found clear evidence of an "inverse U" relationship with a within-sample peak between CO_2 emissions (and energy use) per capita and per-capita income. Through the estimation of EKC, López-Menéndez et al. [24] analysed the impact of economic growth on CO_2 emissions by using data from 27 EU countries during the period 1996–2010. The EKC hypothesis applied in the present study aims to indicate the inter-relationship between CO_2 emissions from China's logistics industry and economic development.

LMDI is a refined decomposition method which ensures decompositions with identically null residual terms. LMDI was first introduced by Ang and Choi [2] and further developed by Ang and Liu [3]. Given its theoretical and practical advantages, it has become one of the most popular decompositional methodologies in the last decade. A growing number of studies have used the LMDI method to decompose energy and CO_2 emissions trends in the transport sector. For example, Wang et al. [39] used it to analyse total transport-related CO_2 emissions in China while Sorrell et al. [35] applied the technique to decompose energy use in the UK road freight sector. The LMDI method used in this paper is to assess the contribution made by different factors to changes in CO_2 emissions from China's logistics industry.

4 Empirical Results and Discussion

4.1 *Growth of China's Logistics Industry, Energy Use and CO_2 Emissions*

Table 1 and Fig. 1 show in absolute terms the annual growth of value-added, energy consumption and CO_2 emissions in China's logistics industry between 2000 and 2015.

Table 1 Growth of China's logistics industry, energy use and CO_2 emissions

Year	Value added (Billion Yuan)	Energy consumption (Million TCE)	CO_2 emissions (Million Tonnes)
2000	616.19	112.42	58.13
2001	687.13	116.13	59.63
2002	749.43	123.13	63.47
2003	791.48	141.16	71.93
2004	930.65	166.42	85.36
2005	1066.88	183.91	95.11
2006	1218.63	202.84	104.42
2007	1460.51	219.59	113.46
2008	1636.76	229.17	116.10
2009	1652.24	236.92	118.68
2010	1878.36	260.68	130.16
2011	2184.20	285.36	140.85
2012	2376.32	315.25	156.13
2013	2604.27	348.19	168.65
2014	2850.09	363.36	174.11
2015	3048.78	383.18	182.18

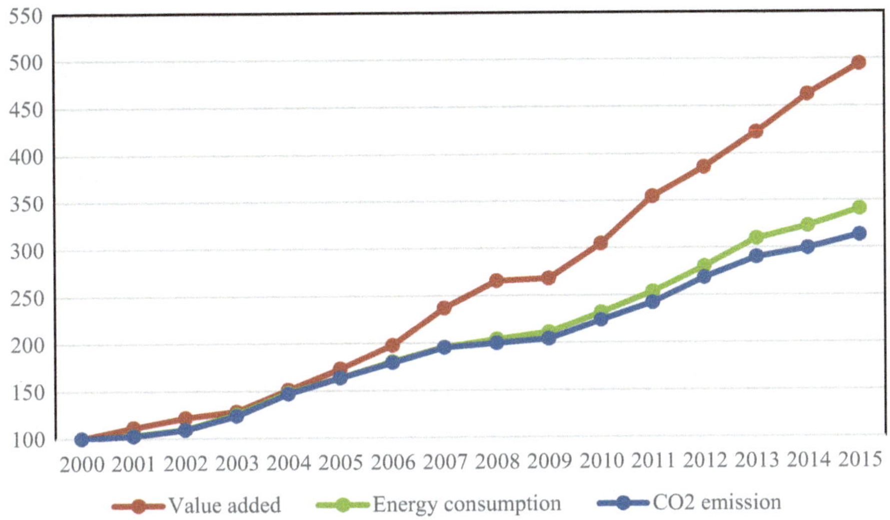

Fig. 1 Changes of annual growth of China's logistics industry, energy consumption and CO_2 emission. *Notes* The vertical axis shows index values with the 2000 values set at 100. *Data sources* China Statistical Yearbook; China Energy Statistical Yearbook

It is noted that the CO_2 emissions are calculated building upon the energy consumption. The calculation is divided into two steps: the first step is to estimate the amount of CO_2 emissions based on each energy source consumed by China's logistics industry in terms of the final energy consumption, coal equivalent coefficient and the carbon emission coefficients. The second step is to estimate the total amount based upon the individual energy source. It is exhibited in Eq. (1):

$$C = \sum_i C_i = \sum_i \alpha_i \beta_i E_i \tag{1}$$

where C denotes the total CO_2 emissions annually, i denotes energy source i; C_i denotes the amount of CO_2 emissions related to energy source i; α_i denotes the CO_2 emission coefficient of energy source i, namely, CO_2 emissions per unit of energy consumed; β_i denotes coal equivalent coefficient of energy source i, namely, the amount of coal equivalent converted by per unit of energy. E_i denotes the energy consumption by energy source i annually. The amount of CO_2 emissions by consuming per unit of energy source i is the CO_2 emission coefficient of energy source i multiply coal equivalent coefficient of energy source i. The *China Energy Statistical Yearbook* contains statistics on eight types of energy consumed by China's logistics industry: coal, gasoline, kerosene, diesel, fuel oil, liquefied petroleum gas, natural gas and electricity. Total CO_2 emissions are therefore calculated based upon the sum of the eight energy sources. The CO_2 emission coefficients (α_i) and the coal equivalent coefficient (β_i) are collected from the IPCC [17] and *China Energy Statistics Yearbook* respectively.

Table 1 and Fig. 1 show how the value-added, energy consumption and CO_2 emissions for the logistics sector changed between 2000 and 2015. Over this period, the value of outputs from the Chinese logistics sector grew 4.9 times, significantly faster than the sector's 3-fold increase in energy consumption and CO_2 emissions. All three trends increased steadily over this period. The global recession of 2008–2010, which dampened the level of activity across the Chinese economy, temporarily interrupted the strong growth trend that the logistics sector was exhibiting. The growth of logistics-related energy consumption and CO_2 emissions also slackened over this period.

4.2 Relationship Between Logistics-Related Carbon Emissions and Economic Growth

This relationship was examined using a regression analysis:

$$Y = a + bX + cX^2 + dX^3 + \varepsilon \tag{2}$$

where Y denotes the amount of CO_2 emissions emitted by China's logistics industry, X denotes per capita GDP, a, b, c, d are parameters of the model, ε is stochastic error. The relationship between CO_2 emissions from China's logistics industry and per capita GDP is defined by the values of a, b, c, d. Table 2 presents the tested results of the analysis showing the degree of fit with three different functions: linear, quadratic and cubic.

The different shapes of curve correspond to differing values for the a, b, c, and d parameters [9]:

(1) $b \neq 0$, $c = 0$, $d = 0$, linear relationship;
(2) $b > 0$, $c > 0$, $d = 0$, quadratic curve, a U shaped curve;
(3) $b > 0$, $c < 0$, $d = 0$, quadratic curve, an inverted U-shaped curve;
(4) $b \neq 0$, $c \neq 0$, $d \neq 0$, cubic curve, N-shaped curve.

The coefficient of determinations (R-square values) of the three models (0.981, 0.982, 0.993) are close to 1, which indicates the goodness if fit is good. Of the three

Table 2 Model summary and parameter estimates

Equation	Model summary					Parameter estimates			
	R Square	F	df1	df2	Sig.	Constant (a)	b	c	d
Linear	0.981	735.689	1	14	0.000	2869.519	43.075		
Quadratic	0.982	359.729	2	13	0.000	2182.241	51.127	−0.019	
Cubic	0.993	580.953	3	12	0.000	-4224.204	165.877	−0.616	0.001

Notes The independent variable is per capital GDP; the dependent variable is CO_2 emission from China's logistics industry

models, the adjusted R^2 of the cubic equation model is the largest one (0.993), which shows the best fitness. Apart from this, the *p*-values of the parameters the cubic equation models are less than (sig.) 0.01,passing *t-test*, namely, all these parameters are statistically significant. The constant of the quadratic equation curve does not pass the *t-test* and hence is not statistically significant. The parameters of the linear equation model are significant, but its R^2 is smaller than that of the cubic equation mode. Therefore, of these three models, the cubic equation model is significant and best fitness.

$$\begin{aligned} & Y = -4224.204 + 165.877X - 0.616X^2 + 0.001X^3 \\ & R^2 = 0.993 \quad F = 580.953 \quad Sig. = 0.000 \end{aligned} \tag{3}$$

X represents per capital GDP; Y corresponds to CO_2 emissions per capital GDP. A fitted diagram between CO_2 emissions and per capital GDP is presented in Fig. 2, in which the curve shows a general upward trend though fluctuation.

Based on the fitted result, the relationship between CO_2 emissions from China's logistics industry and per capital GDP followed a cubic curve between 2000 and 2015 and not the classic inverted U-shaped curve postulated by the EKC model. The growth of logistics emissions appears to be accelerating relative to GDP per capita growth. This suggests that China is at a stage in its development when the level of logistics activity is rising sharply and the pressures on the logistics sector to curb energy use and CO_2 emission are relatively weak. The main priority is to

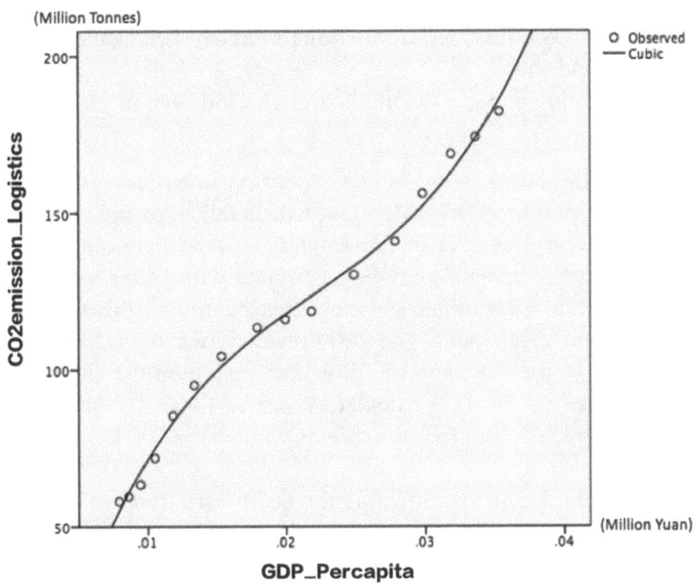

Fig. 2 Logistics CO_2 and per capita GDP (Cubic curve)

expand the capacity of the sector to handle the rapid increases in the volume of goods transported, handled and stored. There is a danger, however, that in this rapid growth phase, opportunities to install more energy- and CO_2-efficiency systems and practices are possibly being missed and may prove to be expensive to retrofit at a later stage in the logistics development process.

The relationship between economic growth and logistics-related CO_2, however, provides only a crude indicator of the sector's environmental performance. To gain a better understanding of its CO_2 generating properties, it is necessary to analyse two other ratios: (i) logistics carbon emissions to added value by the logistics sector and (ii) logistics CO_2 to logistics energy consumption. Trends in these intensity values are discussed in the next section.

4.3 CO_2 Emission Intensity of China's Logistics Industry

In the present study, CO_2 emission intensity is defined as CO_2 emissions per unit of value added in China's logistics industry and calculated as in Eq. (4):

$$K_t = \frac{C_t}{Y_t} \tag{4}$$

where

K_t represents the level of CO_2 emission intensity of China's logistics industry in t year (unit: kg CO_2 per RMB Yuan);
C_t represents the CO_2 emissions from China's logistics industry in year t (unit: hundred thousand tons);
Y_t represents the value added of China's logistics industry in year t (unit: billion RMB Yuan)

Figure 3 shows the changes in the CO_2 emission intensity of China's logistics industry during the period 2000–2015. Overall, it fell by roughly a third having experienced a temporary reversal of the downward trend between 2002 and 2004 and in 2009. The earlier reversal may be associated with China's accession to the WTO in 2001 and macro-economic policies released around this time to stimulate domestic demand and investment. The 2009 reversal, which was relatively minor, may be attributable to the effects of the global recession on the China economy in general and logistics sector in particular. In recessions, declining demand for logistics services typically reduces the average utilisation of freight vehicles and warehousing.

In order to identify the factors affecting the downward trend in logistics' carbon intensity, an LMDI analysis was used. The focus of this analysis was the relationship between CO_2 emissions and energy consumption in the Chinese logistics sector. Two factors are therefore considered: energy structure and energy intensity. Energy structure measures the relative dependence of the logistics sector on

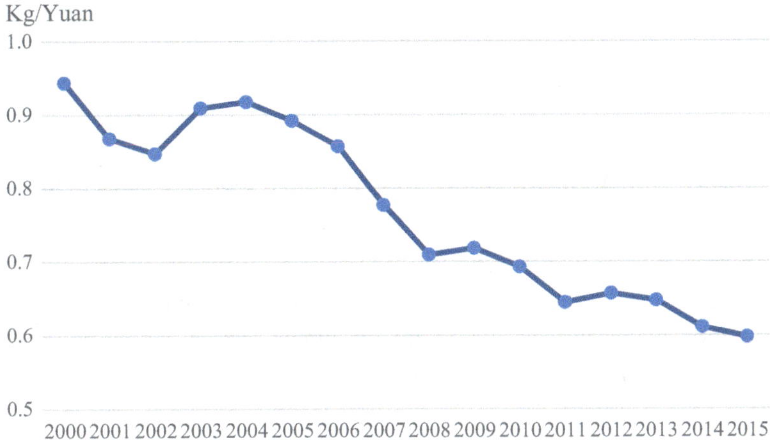

Fig. 3 CO_2 emission intensity of China's logistics industry (2000–2015)

different types of energy which vary in their carbon content. The structure effect takes account of the change in the proportions of different types of energy consumed. The energy intensity is a measure of energy consumed per unit of value added. The intensity effect measures changes in the ratio of total energy used to total value added. The LMDI model investigating the change of CO_2 emission intensity is given as the following in Eq. (5):

$$\mathrm{C}^{\mathrm{t}} = \sum_i C_t^i = \sum_i \frac{C_t^i}{E_t^i} * \frac{E_t^i}{E_t} * \frac{E_t}{Y_t} * Y_t \tag{5}$$

C^{t} represents the total CO_2 emissions from China's logistics industry in year t (unit: million tons);

C_t^i represents the CO_2 emissions from the use of energy source i by China's logistics industry in year t (unit: million tons);

E_t^i represents the amount of the energy source i consumed by China's logistics industry in year t (unit: million tce);

E_t represents the total energy consumed by China's logistics industry (unit: million tce);

Y_t represents the value added by China's logistics industry in year t (unit: hundred million).

The equation can be further rewritten as the following:

$$\frac{\mathrm{C}^{\mathrm{t}}}{\mathrm{Y}_{\mathrm{t}}} = \sum_i \frac{C_t^i}{E_t^i} * \frac{E_t^i}{E_t} * \frac{E_t}{Y_t} \tag{6}$$

Combing Eqs. (5) and (6):

$$K_t = \frac{\mathrm{C^t}}{\mathrm{Y_t}} = \sum_i \frac{C_t^i}{E_t^i} * \frac{E_t^i}{E_t} * \frac{E_t}{Y_t} \tag{7}$$

Assume $M_t^i = \frac{C_t^i}{E_t^i}$, M_i represents the CO_2 emissions from the consumption of per unit of energy source i., namely, the CO_2 emission coefficient for energy source i (α_i). Assume $S_t^i = \frac{E_t^i}{E_t}$, then S_i represents the percent of the consumption of energy source i accounting for the total energy consumption by China's logistics industry, reflecting the change of energy structure. Assume $I_t = \frac{E_t}{Y_t}$, I_i represents the energy consumption of China's logistics industry per unit of output, reflecting the energy intensity.

Equation (7) can therefore be rewritten as the following:

$$K_t = I_t \sum_i M_i S_i \tag{8}$$

We use the LMDI approach to decompose CO_2 emissions changes of China's logistics industry into carbon emission coefficient, energy structure and energy intensity. Assuming K_0 represents CO_2 emission intensity in the base year, with the LMDI method, we divide the cumulative changes in CO_2 emissions in year t into the summation of different factors' cumulative changes:

$$\Delta K_{t0} = K_t - K_0 = \Delta K_M + \Delta K_S + \Delta K_I + \Delta K_{rd} \tag{9}$$

$$\Delta H_{t0} = \frac{K_t}{K_0} = H_M * H_S * H_I * H_{rd} \tag{10}$$

In Eq. (9), ΔK_{t0} represents the total change of CO_2 emission intensity for China's logistics industry for the year t compared to the base year 0; ΔK_M, $\Delta K_{S,}$ ΔK_I and ΔK_{rd} represent individual factors influencing the change of CO_2 emission intensity for China's logistics industry; ΔK_{rd} is a residual term. In Eq. (10), ΔH_{t0} represents the ratio of CO_2 emission intensity for logistics industry for the year t compared to the base year 0; $H_{M,}$ $H_{S,}$ H_I and H_{rd} represent the extent to which individual factors influence the change of CO_2 emission intensity, H_{rd} is a residual term. Overall, ΔK_M and H_M represent CO_2 emission intensity factor of energy; ΔK_S and H_S represent energy structure, while ΔK_I and H_I represent energy intensity. As M_t^i denotes CO_2 emissions per unit energy consumption in year t, it is a constant, hence $\Delta K_M = 0$, $H_M = 1$.

Given that *China Statistics Yearbook* doesn't provide the values for 1999, the present study assumes 2000 as the base year for calculation. The result is presented in Table 3. The following Fig. 4 exhibits the contribution of energy structure and energy intensity to CO_2 emission intensity of China's logistics industry.

As shown in Fig. 4, overall, the trend of CO_2 emission intensity is declining. The change of energy intensity tends to be the same as that of CO_2 emission

Table 3 Decomposition analysis of energy-related CO_2 emission intensity by LMDI for China's logistics industry

Year	ΔK_{t0}	H_{t0}	ΔK_S	H_S	ΔK_I	H_I
2001	−0.0755	0.9199	−0.0063	0.9930	−0.0692	0.9264
2002	−0.0963	0.8979	−0.0027	0.9970	−0.0936	0.9006
2003	−0.0345	0.9634	−0.0136	0.9855	−0.0209	0.9777
2004	−0.0260	0.9724	−0.0075	0.9920	−0.0185	0.9803
2005	−0.0518	0.9451	0.0001	1.0002	−0.0519	0.9450
2006	−0.0864	0.9084	−0.0040	0.9956	−0.0824	0.9125
2007	−0.1664	0.8236	−0.0006	0.9993	−0.1658	0.8242
2008	−0.2339	0.7521	−0.0168	0.9797	−0.2171	0.7676
2009	−0.2248	0.7617	−0.0261	0.9688	−0.1987	0.7862
2010	−0.2503	0.7347	−0.0284	0.9656	−0.2219	0.7609
2011	−0.2984	0.6837	−0.0365	0.9546	−0.2619	0.7163
2012	−0.2862	0.6966	−0.0341	0.9578	−0.2521	0.7273
2013	−0.2957	0.6865	−0.0513	0.9368	−0.2444	0.7329
2014	−0.3324	0.6476	−0.0582	0.9267	−0.2742	0.6988
2015	−0.3457	0.6335	−0.0635	0.9195	−0.2822	0.6889

Note At constant prices in 2000

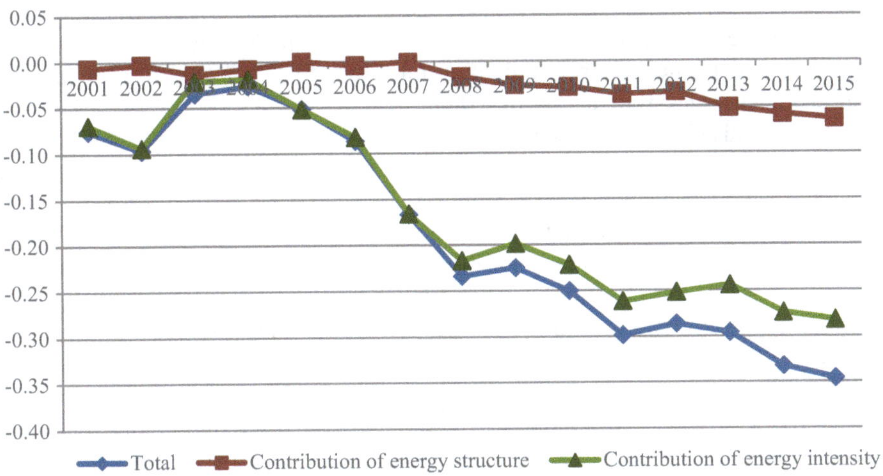

Fig. 4 Contribution of energy structure and energy intensity to CO_2 emission intensity of China's logistics industry

intensity. This result indicates that the change of CO_2 emissions is primarily derived from energy intensity. The curve of energy structure is stable, slightly fluctuating along the horizontal axis. This also indicates that energy structure has marginally affected the change of CO_2 emission intensity. In addition, Fig. 4 also shows that, since 2007, the influence of energy structure on CO_2 emission intensity starts and gradually increases.

5 Conclusions and Policy Suggestions

This paper analyses the CO_2 emissions from China's logistics industry during the period 2000–2015. By employing the EKC and LMDI techniques, the results reveal that the amount of CO_2 emissions in China's logistics industry increased continuously during this phase, while CO_2 emission intensity decreased. The relationship between the CO_2 emissions from China's logistics industry and per capital GDP exhibited a cubic curve, not the typical EKC inverted U-shape curve. The decline in energy intensity was the main determinant of the decrease in CO_2 emission intensity, whereas energy structure contributed only marginally to the change. For instance, energy intensity of China decreases to 57% from 2000 to 2015, however, the extent to which energy intensity declined in the China's logistics sector (31.1%) was only half that of the national economy as a whole. This suggests that it may be possible to accelerate energy efficiency improvements in the logistics sector.

China's freight transport intensity is relatively high and will continue to rise for the foreseeable future driven by the growth in demand from sectors such as energy and construction and the lengthening of freight hauls in inter-province transport [15]. SDSN & IDDRI [32], nevertheless argue that there is likely to be a substantial reduction in freight transport intensity by 2050. They are more much pessimistic about the prospects for achieving large reductions in the energy intensity of freight transport (toe per ton-kilometer traveled) and the CO_2 intensity of freight transport energy (tCO_2 emitted per toe) by then. In the short to medium term it is important for China to get onto a carbon reduction trajectory that will lead to the required level of logistics decarbonisation by 2050.

Several initiatives are already underway to cut emissions from the freight transport sector. Although they are strongly motivated by the need to improve local air quality, their contribution to cutting carbon emissions is also emphasised in policy documents. These initiatives can be traced back to a World Bank-funded green trucking project in Guangzhou in 2018 which was scaled-up to a provincial level across Guangdong in 2011. This piloted several measures designed to cut energy use and emissions in the trucking sector, including the use of articulated vehicles to offer a 'drop and hook' capability, adopting new truck technologies and establishing new information platforms to enhance load-matching. The success of this project encouraged the launch of a China Green Freight Initiative in 2012 which is more broadly-based and national in scale. This initiative, which is managed by China Road Transport Association (CRTA), the Research Institute of Highway (RIOH) of the Ministry of Transport, and Clean Air Asia, promotes the application of the avoid/shift/improve (ASI) approach to the decarbonisation of freight movement. More recently, the Smart Freight Centre [37], the German development agency GIZ [12] and US Rocky Mountain Institute [1] have all been active in raising awareness of energy/emission-reducing measures and running demonstration projects. They have shown, for example, how improved management of tyres, driver training and load matching schemes can yield significant reductions in the carbon intensity of Chinese trucking. Several studies have also examined the carbon benefits of switching to lower carbon fuels [6, 20], electrifying the vehicle fleet and powering it with lower carbon electricity [36].

The emission reduction targets for the main transport modes contained in the 12th Five Year Plan (FYP) in 2012 has given the implementation of these green freight initiatives greater urgency, particularly as a separate reduction targets have been set for the movement of freight by road. This FYP set a target to reduce energy consumption and CO_2 emissions per road tonne-km between 2005 and 2020 by respectively 16 and 20% [7]. The Plan estimates that the potential exists to cut the energy intensity of freight movements by road and water by 11%, by structural optimisation; 12% by managerial actions and by an unspecified amount through the application of new technology. No data is yet available on the extent to which the FYP decarbonisation targets for these freight transport modes are being met.

In the meantime, regulatory changes and plans demonstrate a strong governmental commitment to decarbonise the road freight sector. In 2014, China became only the second country in the world to introduce fuel economy standards for new trucks. The ICCT [16] suggests that Stage 3 of these standards will tighten 'vehicle consumption limits for tractors, trucks and coaches by an average of 21.7–27.2% when using Stage 1 limits as the baseline'.

There is no doubt that, at a macro-level, there is a strong political commitment to decarbonising freight transport operations in China and that the bottom-up efforts of various agencies at provincial and city levels and are providing strong support. It remains to be seen, however, if current initiatives will be sufficient to decarbonise logistics operations as a whole by a large enough margin for the country to meet its COP21 carbon reduction targets.

Acknowledgements This study is supported by Beijing Natural Science Foundation (9162015).

References

1. Agenbroad, J., Mullaney, D., & Wang, Z. (2016). *Improving efficiency in Chinese trucking and logistics*. Rocky Mountain Institute. www.rmi.org/improving_efficiency_in_Chinese_trucking_and_logistics. Accessed May 5, 2017.
2. Ang, B. W., & Choi, K. (1997). Decomposition of aggregate energy and gas emission intensities for industry: A refined Divisia index method. *The Energy Journal, 18*(3), 59–73.
3. Ang, B. W., & Liu, F. L. (2001). A new energy decomposition method: Perfect in decomposition and consistent in aggregation. *Energy, 26*, 537–548.
4. Anon. (2016). China aims to reduce logistics costs. *China Daily*, 27th August.
5. Auvinen, H., Clausen, U., Davydenko, I., Diekmann, D., Ehrler, V., & Lewis, A. (2014). Calculating emissions along supply chains—Towards the global methodological harmonization. *Research in Transportation Business and Management, 12*, 41–46.
6. Bin, Y., Jie, T., & Qiang, L. (2012). Feasibility analysis of renewable energy powered tourism island—Hainan, China. *Journal of Renewable and Sustainable Energy, 4*(6), 83–127.
7. Clean Air Asia. (2013). *China Green Freight Policy and Institutional Analysis Report*. Beijing: Final Report for the World Bank.

8. Davis, H. W., & Company. (2007). Logistics cost and service. *Presentation on the Annual Conference of the Council of Supply Chain Management Professionals (CSCMP)*, Philadelphia, the USA.
9. Dinda, S. (2004). Environmental Kuznets Curve hypothesis: A survey. *Ecological Economics, 49,* 431–455.
10. Eng-Larsen, F., Lundquist, K.-J., Olander, L.-O., & Wandel, S. (2012). Explaining the cyclic behavior of freight transport CO_2-emissions in Sweden over time. *Transport Policy, 23,* 79–87.
11. Eom, J., Schipper, L., & Thompson, L. (2012). 'We keep on truckin': Trends in freight energy use and carbon emissions in 11 IEA countries. *Energy Policy, 45,* 327–341.
12. GIZ. (2017). *Green Freight in Asia in the Context of the Sustainable Development Goals' GIZ, Bonn/Eschborn*. http://transportandclimatechange.org/wp-content/uploads/2017/03/10th-EST-Background-Paper_Green-Freight-in-Asia-in-the-Context-of-the-SDGs.pdf. Accessed June 10, 2017.
13. Global Logistics Emissions Council. (2016). *GLEC framework for logistics emissions methodologies*. http://www.nucms.nl/tpl/smart-freight-centre/upload/GLEC_4pager_DIGITAL.pdf. Accessed January 20, 2017.
14. Grossman, G., & Krueger, A. (1995). Economic environment and the economic growth. *Quarterly Journal of Economics, 110,* 353–377.
15. Hao, H., Wang, H., & Ouyang, M. (2012). Fuel consumption and life cycle GHG emissions by China's on-road trucks: Future trends through 2050 and evaluation of mitigation measures. *Energy Policy, 43,* 244–251.
16. ICCT. (2016). *Stage 3 china fuel consumption standard for Commercial heavy-duty vehicles*. http://www.theicct.org/sites/default/files/publications/HDV%20Stage%203%20Fuel%20Consumption%20Standard_ICCT_20160708.pdf. Accessed June 2, 2017.
17. IPCC. (2006). IPCC guidelines for National Greenhouse Gas Inventories. In H. S. Eggleston, L. Buendia, K. Miwa, T. Ngara, & K. Tanabe (Eds.), *National Greenhouse Gas Inventories programme*. Japan: IGES.
18. Jalil, A., & Mahmud, S. F. (2009). Environment Kuznets curve for CO_2 emissions: A cointegration analysis for China. *Energy Policy, 37,* 5167–5172.
19. Kamakaté, F., & Schipper, L. (2009). Trends in truck freight energy use and carbon emissions in selected OECD countries from 1973 to 2005. *Energy Policy, 37,* 3743–3751.
20. Liaquat, A. M., Kalam, M. A., Masjuki, H. H., & Jayed, M. H. (2010). Potential emissions reduction in road transport sector using biofuel in developing countries. *Atmospheric Environment, 44,* 3869–3877.
21. Liimatainen, H., & Pollanen, M. (2009). Trends of energy efficiency in Finnish road freight transport 1995–2009 and forecast to 2016. *Energy Policy, 38*(12), 7676–7686.
22. Lin, B., & Lei, X. (2015). Carbon emissions reduction in China's food industry. *Energy Policy, 86,* 483–492.
23. Liu, L., Fan, Y., Wu, G., & Wei, Y. (2007). Using LMDI method to analyze the change of China's industrial CO_2 emissions from final fuel use: An empirical analysis. *Energy Policy, 35,* 5892–5900.
24. López-Menéndez, A. J., Péerez, R., & Moreno, B. (2014). Environmental costs and renewable energy: Re-visiting the Environmental Kuznets Curve. *Journal of Environmental Management, 145,* 368–373.
25. McKinnon, A. C. (2007). *CO_2 Emissions from Freight Transport in the UK*. Commission for Integrated Transport, London. Archived at: http://webarchive.nationalarchives.gov.uk/20110304133323/, http://cfit.independent.gov.uk/pubs/2007/climatechange/index.htm. Accessed December 6, 2016.
26. McKinnon, A. C. (2010). Green logistics: The carbon agenda. *LogForum, 6*(1), 1–9.
27. McKinnon, A. C., & Piecyk, M. (2009). Measurement of CO_2 emissions from road freight transport: A review of UK experience. *Energy Policy, 37*(10), 3733–3742.

28. Ouyang, X., & Lin, B. (2015). An analysis of the driving forces of energy-related carbon dioxide emissions in China's industrial sector. *Renewable and Sustainable Energy Reviews, 45,* 838–849.
29. Rodrigue, J. P., Comtois, C., & Slack, B. (2013). *The geography of transport systems* (3rd ed.). London.: Routledge.
30. Rüdiger, D., Schön, A., & Dobers, K. (2016). Managing greenhouse gas emissions from warehousing and transshipment with environmental performance indicators. *Transportation Research Procedia, 14,* 886–895.
31. Schmalensee, R., Stoker, T. M., & Judson, R. A. (1998). World carbon dioxide emissions: 1950–2050. *The Review of Economics and Statistics, 80*(1), 15–27.
32. SDSN & IDDRI. (2014). Pathways to deep decarbonization 2014 report, SDSN & IDDRI.
33. Shaw, D., Pang, A., Lin, C., & Hung, M. (2010). Economic growth and air quality in China. *Environmental Economics and Policy Studies, 12,* 79–96.
34. Song, M., Wang, S., Jiang, Z., Yang, J., & Wang, Y. (2012). Will environmental logistics be promoted by changing industrial structure? A quantitative analysis from 1978 to 2007 in China. *Supply Chain Management: An International Journal, 17*(1), 15–14.
35. Sorrell, S., Lehtonen, M., Stapleton, L., Pujol, J., & Champion, T. (2009). Decomposing road freight energy use in the United Kingdom. *Energy Policy, 37*(8), 3115–3129.
36. Tang, J., Ye, B., Lu, Q., Wang, D., & Li, J. (2014). Economic analysis of photovoltaic electricity supply for an electric vehicle fleet in Shenzhen, China. *International Journal of Sustainable Transportation, 8*(3), 202–224.
37. Wang, B., Song, H., & Li, S. (2016). *Smart Freight Centre in China.* http://www.nucms.nl/tpl/smart-freight-centre/upload/Green%20Trucks%20China%202016.pdf. Accessed March 5, 2017.
38. Wang, C., Chen, J., & Zou, J. (2005). Decomposition of energy-related CO_2 emission in China: 1957–2000. *Energy, 30,* 73–83.
39. Wang, W. W., Zhang, M., & Zhou, M. (2011). Using LMDI method to analyze transport sector CO_2 emissions in China. *Energy, 36*(10), 5909–5915.
40. World Economic Forum. (2009). *Supply chain decarbonization. The role of logistics and transport in reducing supply chain carbon emissions.* http://www3.weforum.org/docs/WEF_LT_SupplyChainDecarbonization_Report_2009.pdf. Accessed October 22, 2016.
41. Yin, X., Chen, W., Eom, J., Clarke, L. E., Kim, S. H., Patel, P. I., et al. (2015). China's transportation energy consumption and CO_2 emissions from a global perspective. *Energy Policy, 82,* 233–248.
42. Zhang, Y., & Da, Y. (2015). The decomposition of energy-related carbon emission and its decoupling with economic growth in China. *Renewable and Sustainable Energy Reviews, 41,* 1255–1266.

Identifying Green Assessment Criteria for Shipping Industries

Taih-Cherng Lirn, Christina W. Y. Wong, Kuo-Chung Shang and Ya-Ting Li

Abstract This study empirically identifies critical assessment criteria used by tramp shipowners and container shipowners in Taiwan, and how they perceived the importance of the criteria to their operations. Through an extensive literatures review, twelve green performance indicators are categorized into four underlying assessment criteria, namely shipowners' green policy, cooperation between green shipping stakeholders, reverse logistics management, and green design and promise. An Analytical Hierarchical Process (AHP) approach was employed to pairwisely compare the degree of importance of these major green assessment criteria and used by the shipping industry. Further analysis by ranking the weight of each of the four major criteria indicated that shipowners' green design and promise is the most important criteria in the shipowners' context, followed by, shipowners' green policy, cooperation among shipping stakeholders, and reverse logistics management. Differences between container shipowners' and tramp shipowners' perceptions on the importance level of the twelve green performance indicators are found. This study advances knowledge by empirically and theoretically validates the degree of importance of green shipping assessment criteria. Institutional theory has greater importance on shipowners' green practices than the stakeholders theory does.

T.-C. Lirn (✉)
Department of Shipping and Transportation Management, National Taiwan Ocean University, Keelung, Taiwan
e-mail: tedlirn@mail.ntou.edu.tw

C. W. Y. Wong
The Institute of Textiles and Clothing, The Hong Kong Polytechnic University, Hung Hom, Hong Kong

K.-C. Shang
Department of Transportation Science, National Taiwan Ocean University, Keelung, Taiwan

Y.-T. Li
Taiwan International Port Corp, Kaohsiung, Taiwan

X. Liu (ed.), *Environmental Sustainability in Asian Logistics and Supply Chains*,
https://doi.org/10.1007/978-981-13-0451-4_2

Keywords Green assessment · Green shipping · Tramp shipping
Container shipping · Institutional theory · Stakeholders theory · Resource-based view (RBV)

1 Introduction

Although consumers are increasingly willing to pay more for green products and they view green performance as one of the most important criteria in selecting their service providers [51, 61], many shipowners were not keen to employ green management practices in providing freight service before the 1990s. Environmental costs can account for as much as 20% of corporate capital expenditures in pollution intensive industries [26]. Olavarrieta and Ellinger [48] review resource-based theory and indicate a distinctive logistics capability is a source of sustainable competitive advantage and superior performance. How to view environmental protection and green logistics as a form of corporate resource and capability to enhance its competitiveness and efficiency is become a popular trend. Previous literatures have indicated shipping firms allocate resources to help protect the environment in order to gain cost, service, and environmental advantages [33, 34, 55], [6]. For example, cutting emissions by 50% may mean that dramatically less marine bunker is needed in the shipping industry. Lu et al. [38] examine the relationships between corporate social responsibility (CSR) and organisational performance in container shipping in Taiwan, they found the 'community involvement and environment' and 'disclosure' dimensions have positive effects on financial performance of a shipping company. In short, most literatures are either employ RBV to study the relationship between logistics performance and their green performance. None of any previous study focused on identifying green assessment criteria for shipping industry which is very important if ocean carriers intend to improve their green performance and consequently their overall financial performance.

2 Green Shipping Literature Reviews

There are four major criteria in the green shipping performance criteria, including shipowners' green policy, cooperation between shipping stakeholders, reverse logistics management, and green design and promise. Thus the literature reviews section has reviewed the related previous publications in sequence accordingly.

1. Shipowners' green policy
   (1) Green business plan;

(2) Voluntary EP certification;
(3) Regular environmental protection practice.

2. Cooperation between shipping stakeholders

(1) Green procurement;
(2) Green delivery service;
(3) Green promotion.

3. Reverse logistics management

(1) Recycling recyclables;
(2) Waste disposables.

4. Green design and promise

(1) Green operation;
(2) Emission reduction;
(3) Environmental protection participation;
(4) Complying with green regulations.

While study suggests that most of the SO_2 emissions are generated by shipping fleet rather than by the land-based sources, and it is estimated that about 15% of the anthropogenic NO_x emissions and 7% of the SO_2 emissions are due to shipping [8, 20]. It is reported that tramp ships and container ships using poor quality marine bunker are the major carbon and particulate matters emitters in the shipping industry which are responsible for approximately 60,000 cardiopulmonary and lung cancer deaths annually [42, 46]. By studying the European shipping industry and its corporate social responsibility (CSR), Fafaliou et al. [21] reveal that only shipping companies that are either subsidiaries of international conglomerates or owned by shipowners who are personally aware of the corporate benefits of being socially responsible would be conscious of their environmental impact. Several researches indicate that there can be significant trade-offs between the environmental benefits and economic benefits [35, 52]. According to the European Commission's report in 2013, EU-related emissions from shipping are expected to increase further by 51% by 2050 compared to 2010-levels. Thus it is important for the maritime transport sector to reduce CO_2 emissions by 40% in 2050 compared to 2005 levels in order to reduce its environmental impact [6].

Many shipping stakeholders are increasingly worried that shipping activities damage the environment and increase resource consumption. In the mean time, port authorities using pricing strategies, access regulations, and concession policy as green management tools to ask shipowners and terminal operators to ensure the consistent improvement of their economic competitiveness and environmental quality [36]. Acciaro et al. [1] proposes a successful innovation framework for environmental sustainability of seaports and also indicates only those innovations that meet stakeholders' economic and environment requirements have chances to succeed in the port and shipping industries. The system dynamics technique is used to simulate the impact of efficient ship operation on the improvement of fuel consumption of a ship at sea and her operating costs, CO_2 emissions and externalities [47]. As a result, increasing number of shipping companies and academicians develops and implements green shipping theories and practices to address the environmental concerns of shippers with hope to attract the use of their freight services. Recently, adoption of green management technology is becoming one of the major tools that shipping companies use to compete in the era of global warming.

Knowing the importance of shipowners' performance due to green freight service criteria can help the shipowners allocate their valuable resources in implementing green practice. This can also provide an insights to governance for government agencies to improve their national shipowners' green performance, and to help international organizations (e.g. International Maritime Organization and Marine Environmental Protection Committee[1]) and port states[2] to make appropriate environmental protection guidelines to regulate cargo vessels' green performance. This research aims to examine the green performance assessment criteria identified in the literature, their performance impact, and compare differences between container shipowners and tramp shipowners on the assessment criteria.

2.1 Development of Green Shipping Campaign

One of the pioneering campaigns on green shipping is launched by Norwegian shipowners and research institutes that aim to reduce gas emission (NO_x and SO2) and solid waste dumping into the ocean from ships. Emission from ship not only pollutes the air but also endangers the residents' health in the port community [6] and results in the global climate change [31]. An increasing numbers of researches findings indicated ships are moving polluted waters from one port to another. For example, grey water from the engine room, sewage water in the bilge, washing water from cargo hold cleaning in the tramp ships, oily waste water, and ballast water with hazardous bacteria and marine living organisms. Uncontrolled ballast water discharge might endanger the survival of indigenous marine micro organism and spread disease [16, 31, 33]. The U.S.A. has suffered from many fairway blockings by the zebra mussels brought by the uncontrolled ballast water from the visiting ships and the US government spent $3.1 billion USD on port water

[1]According to the United States Coast Guard, the Marine Environment Protection Committee (MEPC) is a committee of the International Maritime Organization (IMO). The committee meets every 9 months to develop international conventions relating to marine environmental concerns including ship recycling, controlling emissions, and invasive species.

[2]Port state is the state to implement the inspection on both its national and foreign ships visiting the state's ports by PSC officers (inspectors) for the purpose of verifying that the competency of the master and officers on board, and the condition of the ship and its equipment comply with the requirements of international conventions (e.g. SOLAS, MARPOL, STCW, etc.). Thus both flag states and port states can regulate the green performance of ocean shipowners.

treatment system in order to remove the problem. Thus Michigan State firstly punishes ships calling Michigan ports without onboard ballast water treatment system $25,000 USD since 2007. IMO also promulgates BWM (ballast water management) convention in 2004 to control ballast water and sediment. Marine Environment Protection Committee (MEPC) of IMO addresses implementation issues and three guidelines on ballast water management treaty to eradicate the global spread of harmful organisms in ships' ballast water [16, 45, 52]. Global efforts on protecting the marine environments are endowed by the United Nations Convention on the Law of the Sea and the MRRPOL 73/78 Convention.

2.2 *Measurement of Green Shipping Performance*

Although green consumption and green marketing are popular business research topics, the extant literature on green ports and port operators and on green shipping management are scarce [12, 39, 50]. Psaraftis and Kontovas [52] identifies three measures to reduce the greenhouse gas emission from ships: technical measures, market-based instruments, and operational options. The technical measures include designing the fuel-efficient ship hulls, using fuel-efficient marine engine and propeller, alternative fuel (fuel cell and bio-fuel), cold-ironing during berthing, scrubber, wind-sail (e.g. by Beluga Shipping). The market-based measures include emission trading system (ETS), and carbon levy scheme. ETS allocates certain amount of carbon emission quota to each shipowner and the shipowner can trade it. On the contrary, the carbon levy is solely charged to the shipowners by the Hong Kong government. The operation measures include using economic/ecological steaming speed, optimal routing, and fleet management. The Singapore Shipowners Association also suggests government to charge the bunker levy to support the introduction of an International Compensation Fund (ICF) and the upgrading of the ship design and building technology.

Lai et al. [33] indicates six measures shipowners can use to improve their green performance: company policy and procedure, shipping documentation, shipping equipment, shipping collaboration, shipping material, and shipping design for compliance. American Association of Port Authorities (AAPA) list eleven factors to measure the green performance of a port: air pollution, wet land conservation, fishery resources conservation and endangered species protection, waste water and rain water discharge, traffic jam, noise and light hazard, culture heritage and historical sites preservation, land and water pollution from oil spill, gas emitted from chemical tanks and fumigation, unregulated solid and hazardous waste dumping, and earth and land erosion.

Recent studies on green shipping performance criteria and framework are largely qualitative [34, 62]. These studies identify four factors influencing green performance of a shipowner, including: shipowners' green policy, cooperation between GSM stakeholders, reverse logistics management, and green design and promise. Table 1 summarizes the indicators reflecting these factors which are previously reported in the literature.

3 Research Methodology

3.1 Sample

Survey target respondents were the executives of major shipowners in Taiwan and were selected based on review of their corporate profiles on their websites. Shipowners were chosen to participate in the study if they have implemented or plan to implement green shipping practices, or their executives have delivered speeches on green shipping management (GSM). It is found that the shipowners with green shipping practices were mostly large shipowners and are listed in major stock exchanges in Taiwan. Thirteen leading container shipowners and seven major tramp shipowners in Taiwan were targeted to respond to the survey. The portfolios of the respondents are shown in the following table (Table 2).

3.2 Research Techniques

To understand the perceived importance of the assessment criteria and the performance of shipping companies of each criterion, two techniques were employed: the Analytic Hierarchy Process (AHP) technique and the Importance and Performance Analysis (IPA) technique. The AHP technique is firstly used to find the weight in terms of the importance of the green performance criteria, followed by the use of the IPA to illustrate the level of importance of the indicators.

The AHP technique is a popular Multi-Criteria Decision Method (MCDM) that is used to simplify a complicated system by constructing a hierarchic structure and help evaluate the performance of alternatives to be chosen [28]. A hierarchy can be composed of three levels: criterion, sub-criterion, and alternatives. An AHP structure should follow the homogeneity axiom such that the elements being compared should not differ from each other too much in terms of their degree of importance [22]. Application of traditional statistics to analyze the survey responses simply does not meet the requirement of central limit theorem and the normal distribution. There is no requirement on the minimum number of respondents when the AHP technique is employed to make an empirical analysis. There are three procedures in implementing the AHP technique: decomposition, comparative judgments, and hierarchic composition or synthesis of priorities. The pairwise comparison between each sub-criterion and criterion needs to satisfy a transitivity

Table 1 Green shipping performance criteria and sub-criteria

Criteria/ Sub-criteria		Previous literatures														
		Krozer and Kothuis [31]	Bailey and Soloman [6]	Clarke [15]	Fafaliou et al. [21]	Bernal et al. [10]	Le Rossignol [37]	David and Gollasch [16]	Franc [23]	MARINTEK [42]	Alvik et al. [2]	Eyring et al. [19]	Sonak et al. [57]	Chang et al. [12]	Hall [25]	Tzannatos [59]
Shipowners' green policy (Criterion A)	Green business plan (A1)	*	*		*				*		*	*	*			*
	Voluntary EP certification (A2)	*			*						*		*			
	Regular EP practices (A3)								*							
Cooperation between shipping stakeholders (Criterion B)	Green procurement (B1)	*	*		*		*					*				
	Green delivery service(B2)	*	*		*											
	Green promotions (B3)				*											
Reverse logistics management (Criterion C)	Recycling recyclables (C1)	*				*		*	*					*		
	Waste disposables (C2)	*	*			*		*								

(continued)

Table 1 (continued)

Criteria/Sub-criteria		Previous literatures														
		Krozer and Kothuis [31]	Bailey and Soloman [6]	Clarke [15]	Fafaliou et al. [21]	Bernal et al. [10]	Le Rossignol [37]	David and Gollasch [16]	Franc [23]	MARINTEK [42]	Alvik et al. [2]	Eyring et al. [19]	Sonak et al. [57]	Chang et al. [12]	Hall [25]	Tzannatos [59]
Green design and promise (Criterion D)	Green operation (D1)	*	*	*		*	*		*		*	*				*
	Emission reduction (D2)	*	*						*	*	*	*	*		*	*
	EP participation (D3)				*		*									
	Complying with green regulations (D4)		*	*	*						*	*	*	*		*

Criteria/Sub-criteria		Previous literatures														
		Psaraftis and Kontovas [52]	Lai et al. [33]	Enshaei and Mesbahi [18]	Gregson et al. [24]	Kontovas and Psaraftis [30]	Lun [39]	Lai et al. [34]	Melin and Rydhed [44]	Osberg [49]	Balland et al. [7]	Bengtsson et al. [9]	Hoffman et al. [25]	USCG [60]	Yang et al. [64]	Poulsen et al. [53]
Shipowners' green policy (Criterion A)	Green business plan (A1)	*	*				*					*		*	*	
	Voluntary EP certification (A2)	*					*	*								
	Regular EP practices (A3)	*					*	*							*	

(continued)

Table 1 (continued)

Criteria/Sub-criteria		Previous literatures														
		Psaraftis and Kontovas [52]	Lai et al. [33]	Enshaei and Mesbahi [18]	Gregson et al. [24]	Kontovas and Psaraftis [30]	Lun [39]	Lai et al. [34]	Melin and Rydhed [44]	Osberg [49]	Balland et al. [7]	Bengtsson et al. [9]	Hoffman et al. [25]	USCG [60]	Yang et al. [64]	Poulsen et al. [53]
Cooperation between shipping stakeholders (Criterion B)	Green procurement (B1)	*					*			*		*			*	
	Green delivery service(B2)							*							*	
	Green promotions (B3)							*							*	
Reverse logistics management (Criterion C)	Recycling recyclables (C1)	*			*		*									
	Waste disposables (C2)	*														
Green design and promise (Criterion D)	Green operation (D1)	*		*			*			*		*		*	*	
	Emission reduction (D2)	*	*			*	*		*		*		*	*		
	EP participation (D3)	*					*	*		*					*	
	Complying with green regulations (D4)		*	*	*		*	*							*	*

Note EP (Environmental Protection)
*Found in the study

Table 2 Affiliations of surveyees and respondents

	Types of respondents	Questionnaire posted	Questionnaire responded	Responding rate (%)
Ocean shipowners	Container shipowners	13	8	61.5
	Dry tramp shipowners	7	5	71.4
	Total	20	13	65

Source This research

relationship but a perfect transitivity relationship is not required. When a transitivity relationship does not exist, the consistency index (C.I.) and consistency ratio (C.R.) are employed to test the degree of consistency of the respondent's responses. The C. I. and C.R. values are less than 0.1 if the respondent's responses are perceived to be consistent. AHP allows inconsistency. A higher than usual inconsistency ratio will result because of the extreme judgments necessary; thus, one can accept the inconsistency ratio even though it is greater than 10% under an extreme judgments scenario [22].

Martilla and James [43] were the first to propose the IPA technique to analyze automobile dealers' services and customers' patronage to the dealers' services. Service attributes with a high degree of importance and a low degree of customer satisfaction were suggested to invest resources by the car dealers to retain their customers' patronage. Although Sampson and Showalter [54] indicate that importance is a dynamic construct that changes as perceptions of performance change, the IPA technique is still a useful tool for social science research to identify performance criteria that require an immediate improvement. By using the median or the mean value of the degree of importance and performance as the origin point of a matrix, four quadrants are formed in the IPA matrix: keep up the good work, concentrate here, low priority, and possible overkill [43].

4 Results of Analyses

Based on the resource-based view of a firm, green shipping practices can be helpful to improve the shipping companies' overall performance [34]. To investigate the green performance measurement of shipping companies, a set of four green performance criteria with a total of twelve green indicators were used to design the questionnaire.

In early 2011, questionnaires were posted to the 20 targeted shipowners based in Taiwan, and 13 of them responded, resulting in a response rate of 65%. Of these 13 valid responses, 8 of them are container shipowners and 5 of them are tramp shipowners. Respondents included executives from eight container shipowners and five tramp shipowners. The degree of importance of these twelve sub-criteria and the four green performance criteria perceived by the ocean container shipowners and tramp shipowners are depicted in Table 3.

The threshold value 0.1 of the C.I. and the C.R. were employed to decide whether the respondents' replies were acceptable to proceed with the hierarchical analysis. Once a response was found above 0.1, the authors reviewed the replies from the respondent to find whether there was an inconsistent response. The respondents were contacted again to ask about the conflicting answers. The authors have to carefully explain where the confliction arises. If a respondent perceives 'shipowners' green policy is three times more important than the 'cooperation among shipping stakeholders', and (s)he also perceives 'shipowners' green policy' is three times more important than the 'reverse logistics management', then the degree of importance between 'Cooperation among shipping stakeholders' and 'reverse logistics management' should be the same. The respondents then have to correct at least one of the conflicting answers and the problem was resolved.

Based on the findings, from the ocean shipowners' viewpoints, none of the four green shipping performance criteria is located in the 'concentrate here' quadrant of Fig. 1. Of the four green shipping performance assessment criteria, ocean shipowners perceived 'green design and promise' as the most important (with 39.3% of glob*al weight) as shown in* Table 4.

Among the three indicators in the 'green design and promise' criterion,, with an importance weight of 48.5%, 'complying with green regulations' is perceived by container shipowners to be the most important one, with 18.9% of global weight (see Table 4). As the Chinese proverb says, 'Law is the minimum standard of ethics, and ethics is the upmost standard of law'. Complying with the international green shipping regulations is one of the most important performance indicators because a violation of regulations not only damages the shipowner's reputation, but also means they need to pay a large sum of penalty. For example, in 2005, the container shipping company Evergreen Marine Corp. paid $25 million to the U.S. Department of Justice(DoJ) as the largest-ever penalty for concealing vessel pollution [3]. Recently, the Italian Carbofin S.PA. agreed to plead guilty and pay a $2.75 million criminal penalty for falsifying oil record books aboard one of its ship to US DoJ in 2014 [56].

Green business plan and emission reduction are perceived to be the second and the third most important performance indicators in evaluating container shipowners' green performance (Table 3). Many developed countries, such as the USA and Canada, have stricter environmental controls than the international regulation requires. The port states have regulations for emission control areas and SOx emission control areas, as well as a compulsory shore power supply to make the port green [3, 29]. This evidences the increasing degree of importance of vessel emission reduction for container shipowners. Only shipowners with green business plan are likely to meet the requirements from various strict PSC environmental regulations.

The tramp shipowners perceived that 'shipowners' green policy' is the most important green shipping performance criterion, with an importance weight of 44.8%. The three performance indicators of this criterion, namely green business

Table 3 Degree of importance of the criteria and indicators as perceived by ocean-going shipowners

Degree of importance								Degree of performance	IPA quadrants
Factors		Tramp shipowners		Container shipowners		All respondents		All respondents	All respondents
Criteria (Criteria weight perceived by container/tramp shipowners	Indicators	Global weight	Ranking	Global weight	Ranking	Global weight	Ranking	Score	Quadrant
Shipowners' green policy 0.263/0.448	Green business plan (GBP)	0.211	(1)	0.13	(2)	0.161	(2)	3.23	Keep up the good work
	Voluntary EP certification (EPC)	0.118	(3)	0.07	(7)	0.088	(4)	3.13	Concentrate here
	Regular EP practices (REPP)	0.119	(2)	0.063	(8)	0.083	(5)	3.03	Concentrate here
Cooperation among shipping stakeholders 0.11/0.161	Green procurement (GPROC)	0.07	(7)	0.04	(11)	0.051	10)	3.10	Low priority
	Green delivery service (GDS)	0.044	(10)	0.028	(12)	0.034	(12)	3.03	Low priority
	Green promotion (GP)	0.047	(8)	0.042	(10)	0.046	(11)	3.20	Possible overkill
Reverse logistics management 0.142/0.134	Waste disposal (WD)	0.088	(5)	0.061	(9)	0.075	(6)	3.20	Possible overkill
	Recyclables recycled (RR)	0.046	(9)	0.081	(6)	0.069	(7)	3.17	Possible overkill
Green design and promise 0.485/0.257	Green operation(GO)	0.029	(12)	0.09	(5)	0.060	(9)	3.13	Possible overkill
	Emission reduction (ER)	0.079	(6)	0.115	(3)	0.104	(3)	3.13	Concentrate here
	EP participation (EPP)	0.033	(11)	0.092	(4)	0.065	(8)	3.23	Low priority
	Complying with green regulation (CR)	0.117	(4)	0.189	(1)	0.164	(1)	3.14	Keep up the good work
Average score						0.0833		3.14	Origin point

Note Please see the Appendix 1 for the definitions of the twelve green performance indicators

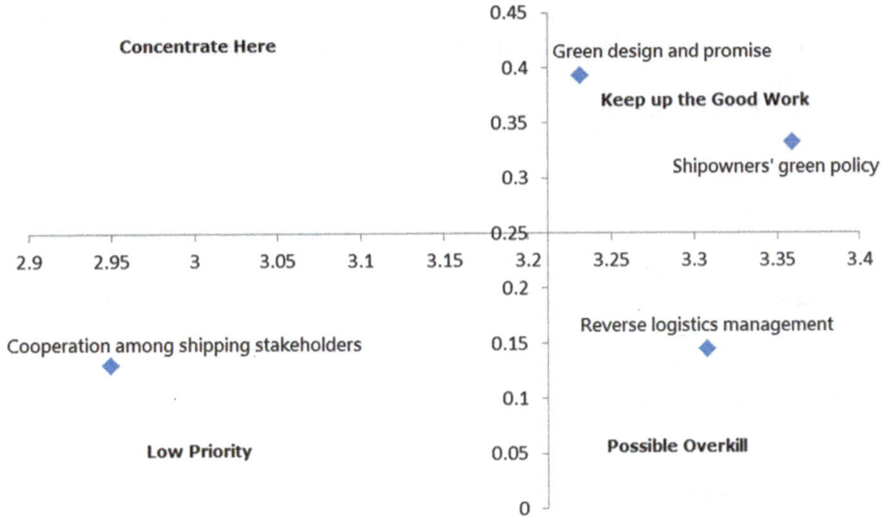

Fig. 1 Ocean shipowners' perception on the importance and performance analysis (IPA) of four major green shipping assessment criteria

Table 4 Perception on the importance and performance of the four major green assessment criteria by all Taiwan ocean shipowners

Criteria	Weight	Performance	IPA quadrants
Shipowners' green policy	0.332	3.359	Keep up the good work
Cooperation among shipping stakeholders	0.131	2.949	Low priority
Reverse logistics management	0.144	3.308	Possible overkill
Green design and promise	0.393	3.231	Keep up the good work
Average	0.25	3.212	Origin point

plan, regular environmental protection practices, and voluntary environmental protection certification, were perceived to be the three most important green shipping performance sub-criteria. Tramp shipowners were requested to pass the International Safety Management (ISM) code auditing and certification by the beginning of July 1998, and container shipowners were requested to pass the ISM external audit by mid 2002. According to the U.S. Coast Guard [60], the objectives of the ISM Code are to ensure safety at sea, the prevention of human injury or loss of life, and the avoidance of damage to the environment, in particular, to the marine environment, and to property [6].

Tramp ships are general cargo ships and tramp ships that travel around the world without any fixed service route or schedule. It is therefore very difficult for tramp shipowners to understand all ports' environmental regulations from around the world. The best practice for tramp shipowners is to adopt a green business plan to avoid violating the environmental regulations of a port state. So that tramp shipowners broadly qualify for the green shipping requirement, it is also highly desirable for them to pass the ISO14001 certification for environmental protection. Tramp shipowners are involved in many chartering activities, and a charter party often requires a contract of many pages. The charter party used in tramp shipping industry is a lengthy document and an electronic form of the documents would reduce the amount of paper used for printing. This is especially important to tramp shipowners as they rarely visit their home port, which makes ship supplies replenishment difficult.

A cross-comparison of the ranking of the importance of the twelve indicators between container shipowners and tramp shipowners reveals that both types of shipowners perceive the 'green business plan' as one of the three most important performance indicators as shown in Table 5. Most Asian ocean container shipowners' major customers are large European and American importers who purchase Asian manufacturing products using the free on board (FOB) term. These importers control the decision of freight services and ocean shipowners to move their imported cargoes, but they have to take their consumers' green expectations into consideration [14, 19]. Thus, container shipowners have to meet such customers' demands of being environmentally responsible.

Major international retailers, such as Wal-Mart and IKEA, ask their freight service providers to move their cargoes in an environmentally friendly manner [34]. Complying with environmental protection regulations and reducing emissions and liquid waste discharge from ships are two of the minimum standards that container shipowners have to achieve to satisfy the green consumers' environmental protection demands. As container ships have a faster speed than tramp vessels and consume more bunker fuel, they emit much larger amounts of CO_2, NO_x, SO_x, and PM (particulate matters). Thus, container shipowners perceived emission reduction to have a higher degree of importance than did the tramp shipowners as shown in Table 4. In addition, container shipowners move manufactured products, and as many branded manufactured products are keen to have their brand considered green, 'green design and promise' are perceived to have a higher degree of importance from container shipowners' viewpoint than that from tramp shipowners' viewpoint.

A comparison of the perceptual difference between container shipowners and tramp shipowners is depicted in Table 5. There are perceptual gaps on the importance ranking of the four criteria and twelve green performance indicators between container shipowners and tramp shipowners. In the shipowners' green policy criterion, three indicators of the shipowners' green policy dimension are ranked as the top three important indicators by tramp shipowners. On the other hand, two of the four indicators in the 'green design and promise' dimension are perceived to be the most important and the third most important green performance indicators as perceived by container shipowners in this survey.

Table 5 Perceptual gaps of importance between container shipowners and tramp shipowners

Criteria	Weight ranking		Indicators (Abbreviation)	Weight ranking	
	Container shipowners	Tramp shipowners		Container shipowners	Tramp shipowners
Shipowners' green policy	2	【1】	Green business plan (GBP)	【2】	【1】
			Voluntary EP certification (EPC)	7	【3】
			Regular EP practices (REPP)	8	【2】
Cooperation among shipping stakeholders	4	3	Green procurement (GPROC)	11	7
			Green delivery service (GDS)	12	10
			Green promotion (GP)	10	8
Reverse logistics management	3	4	Waste disposal (WD)	9	5
			Recycling recyclables (RR)	6	9
Green design and promise	【1】	2	Green operation (GO)	5	12
			Emission reduction (ER)	【3】	6
			EP participation (EPP)	4	11
			Complying with EP regulation (CR)	【1】	4

【n】 to indicate the most important criteria and the three most important indicators in evaluating the performance of the green container shipowners and the green tramp shipowners

'Green business plan' and 'complying with environmental protection regulation' are perceived by both tramp shipowners and container shipowners to be two of the top five important green performance indicators. Shipowners can publish their green business plan on their websites, popular social media websites, and in their corporate social responsibility report to allow their employees clearly to not only take note of the green policy, but also understand how to achieve the target of this green policy. Regular issue of the environmental regulation notice from the shipowners' office to their staff on board is helpful to update the seafarers' knowledge on environmental protection regulations, and finally, shipowners' fleets can follow the international environmental regulations.

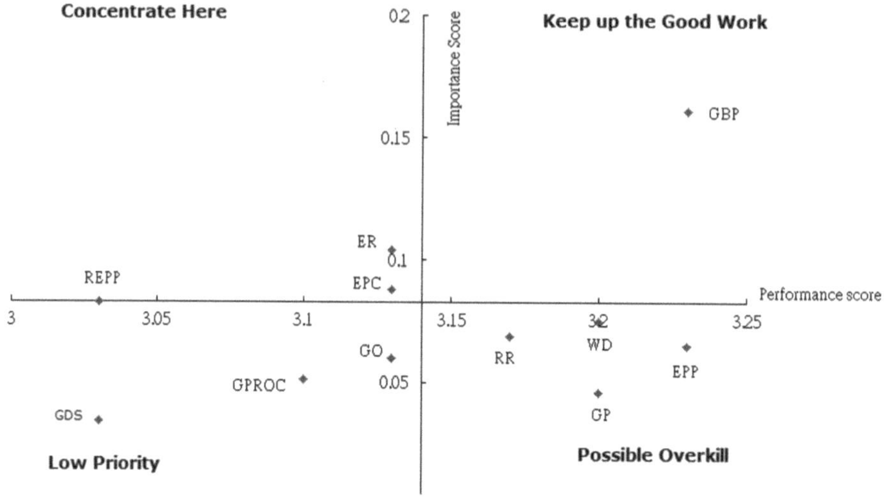

Fig. 2 Ocean-going shipowners' perception on the green shipping assessment indicators. *Note* Green business plan (GBP), voluntary EP certification (EPC), Regular EP practices (REPP), Green procurement (GPROC), Green delivery service (GDS), Green promotion (GP), Waste disposal (WD), Recyclables recycled (RR), Green operation (GO), Emission reduction (ER), EP participation (EPP), Complying with regulation (CR)

Finally, the IPA technique was employed to find the green shipping performance sub-criteria located in the critical quadrant ('concentrate here' quadrant) where the degree of importance is high but the degree of performance is low. Figure 2 shows the overall importance and performance of these twelve green shipping performance indicators of the container shipowners and tramp shipowners.

Three of the twelve indicators are located in the 'concentrate here' quadrant, which implies that the 'voluntary environmental protection certification' (EPC), 'regular environmental protection practice' (REPP), and 'emission reduction' (ER) performance indicators urgently need improvement. There is an indicator located in the 'keep up the good work' quadrant, namely, 'green business plan' (GBP) suggesting that ocean-going shipowners perform well in this performance indicator. Concerning the GBP indicator, the shipowners show that they have set up a green vision and the top management support the operation of an environmental protection monitoring system and encourage inter-departmental green cooperation in the company. Based on the EPC performance indicator, shipowners are advised to obtain the ISO14000 and ISO14001 environmental protection certification to attract and retain the patronage of large shippers. To reduce emissions (ER), ocean-going shipowners might consider acquiring the detailed information of their ships' emissions (e.g. SO_x, and NO_x emission rate per ton-miles cargo carried) and provide a carbon footprint calculator on their website. When compliance with the regulations (CR) performance indicator is considered, the shipowners have to follow the current international environmental protection regulations, for example, the

London Convention (Convention on the Prevention of Marine Pollution by Dumping of Wastes and Other Matter (LDC), 1972), MARPOL73/78 (International Convention for the Prevention of Pollution from Ships) and 2004 BWM (Ballast Water Management Convention). The 'waste disposal' (WD) indicator is located in the possible 'overkill' quadrant. This criterion includes the disposal of the sewage water and bilge water from cargo holds. Part of the resources used for this possibly 'overkill' indicator could be moved to improve the green performance of the three criterion located in the 'concentrate here' quadrant and to maintain the good performance of the abovementioned two performance indicators in the 'keep up the good work' quadrant.

5 Conclusions and Implications

5.1 Conclusions

Three contributions are made by this study. First, shipping companies should prepare for the prevalence of the green trend, but there are few extant green shipping studies that endeavor to establish a set of green shipping performance assessment criteria and indicators, and to provide constructive environmental governance and monitoring indicators to the maritime authorities. Second, the degree of importance of criteria influencing green performance of a shipping company is firstly reported by this research. Third, green performance determinants of the ocean shipowners are for the first time identified in this research.

Four criteria and twelve performance indicators are identified related to green shipping practices. Applying Analytical Hierarchical Process (AHP) and Importance-Performance Analysis (IPA) techniques, this study found the perceived importance and shipowners' performance on four major criteria and twelve indicators of green shipping management. As far as green shipping practices are concerned, shipowners perceive complying with green regulation, implementing green business plan, and following emission reduction regulation as the three most important green performance indicators. In addition, the findings indicated that there are perceptual gaps regarding the degree of importance of green assessment indicators between the container shipping sector and the tramp shipping sector. Tramp shipowners and container shipowners perceive 'implementing green business plan' and 'complying with environmental regulation' to be their most important green performance indicators, respectively. Finally, voluntary environmental protection certification (EPC), emission reduction(ER), and regular environmental practices (REPP) are perceived by all respondents to have lower degree of performance but a higher degree of importance. Shipping companies should spend more resources on these three performance indicators to effectively improve their green performance.

5.2 Implications

In general, the two leading green shipping performance indicators, 'complying with environmental protection regulation' and 'green business plan', have a global weight of 0.325 (0.164 + 0.161) in terms of the degree of their importance for all the responding ocean shipowners. This implies an ocean shipowner should firstly prepare its green business plan according to corresponding environmental protection regulations if it intends to effectively improve their green shipping practices. A theoretical implication for this finding is made as follow, institutional criteria are more important than the stakeholder criteria. Carriers' green policy indicator and green design and promise indicator are institutional theory-related. Cooperation among shipping stakeholders and reverse logistics management are stakeholders theory-related. Stakeholders theory and institutional theory are the basis of green shipping practices adoption. The previous theory *focuses on identifying stakeholder' interest and finding ways to meet their demands*, while the latter theory argues *the GSPs is the result from customers' pressure, industrial institutionalized norms, and regulatory requirements. Institutional process is coercively, mimetically, and normatively driven which results in structural isomorphism* [40]. From our survey, it is found the shipowners are more institutional theory-oriented than stake-holder oriented when they evaluate the degree of importance on various green shipping indicators. Ocean shipowners should review international green regulations and draft a green shipping policy accordingly before the other green shipping indicators can be then effectively implemented. A future structural equation modeling research could be carried out to test this proposed theoretical implication. Another theoretical implication of this research in terms of the methodology includes the combination of AHP technique with the IPA model. Container shipowners and tramp shipowners are not only different in the types of cargoes they carried, but also in the degree of importance of the green assessment indicators they perceived.

There are several practical implications of the research findings. First, there are perception gaps regarding the importance of the four criteria and the twelve green shipping performance indicators between the ocean container shipowners and tramp shipowners. Tramp shipowners perceive 'shipowners' green policy' as the most important criterion in improving their green performance. Three indicators are included in this green criterion: green business plan, regular environmental protection practices, and voluntary environmental protection certification. Although the number of ports called by tramp ships is far less than the ones of container shipowners, but these responding tramp ships have regularly loaded coal and iron ore in Australia. The extent of rigor for a tramper being checked by the Australian port state control officers is strict while the responding container shipowners most have their fleets serve within the Asian region where the PSC inspection is not as strict as the one in Australia. As a result, tramper owners realize that they have not only to comply with all green requirements but must also consistently promote and support the green business plan. Tramp shipowners should accomplish their green policy by building their own sustainability culture, obtaining voluntary EP certification, and promoting environmental protection practices. Container shipowners are regularly checked and visited by port state control inspectors. They perceive that the 'green design and promise' criterion as important in addition to the 'shipowners' green policy' criterion. A sea-shore rotating work shift as adopted by the Evergreen Marine Corporation can allow seafarers work ashore for a short period after the seafarers complete their annual seafaring employment agreements. Thus, intensive training programs on international environmental protection regulations such as International Convention for the Prevention of Pollution from Ships and Ballast Water Management Convention can be provided to the seafarers during their shore-based working shifts.

Second, slow steaming makes a greater contribution to the emission reduction on container ships than on tramp ships. The regular steaming speed of a container ship is used to be around 24 knots and their owners can reduce speed from 24 knots to as slow as 15 knots when the bunker price is very high, the market is over supply, and the ships' charter hire is very low [41], while dry tramp ships' normal sailing speed is used to be around 14 knots and can simply be reduced to as low as 9 knots [17]. The greater the speed reduction, the more the bunker consumption reduction, and thus the more the green image improvement. Green brand image could improve the green branding value [14]. In a container ship, there are hundreds or even thousands of shippers who load their cargo on board, but there might be only one or several shippers in a dry tramp ship. Therefore the branding value of container shipowners and their corporate images are more conspicuous than those of tramp shipowners. With so many shippers to deal with, container shipowners should invest more resources than tramp shipowners to improve their environmental protection practices and thus their corporate images. Complying with green regulation without being punished by port states is a fundamental necessity not to damage a container shipowners' image. 'Participation in non-profit oriented environmental protection organizations (such as 'North American Marine Environment Protection Association' and 'Taiwan Association of Marine Pollution Control') and 'the creation of green corporate culture' by including a green vision in the corporate development plan are found important to improve shipowners' green image.

Third, cooperation among shipping stakeholders in terms of green delivery service is perceived to have the lowest degree of importance to the green shipping criteria assessment. Green delivery service by using eco-packaging and green promotion by providing carbon footprint calculators to the shippers are two of the three indicators in the cooperation among shipping stakeholders criteria and are not perceived important by the shipowners. Therefore shipowners are suggested to outsource these two non-core services to the other third logistics service providers.

Green operation which involved innovational issue is experiencing continuing development in the ocean shipping industry [5, 63]. Performances of green product innovation and green process innovation were positively correlated to the corporate competitive advantage [13]. Thus, future studies may attend to two issues: The shipowners' green innovation and their corporate performance. A comparative study of the perceptual gaps on the criteria and sub-criteria influencing the green shipping performance between global container shipowners and major shippers is also highly encouraged in future research.

Acknowledgements The authors would like to thanks for the insightful comments from the reviewers of the IFSPA2015 proceedings which greatly improve the quality of this manuscript and the financial sponsorship from the Taiwan's Ministry of Science and Technology under the project number 98-2410-H-327-041—that made this research possible.

Appendix Questionnaire and the Definition of the Twelve Sub-criteria Shown in the Questionnaire

Criteria	Sub-criteria	Description
Carriers' green policy (Criterion A)	A1. Green business plan	In ocean carriers with vision and corporate culture of sustainability, senior management support the EP monitoring and cooperation between departments
	A2. EP certification	Carriers endeavor to obtain EP certification, e.g., the ISO 14001 certification
	A3. Regular EP practices	Carriers employ ICT technology to reduce typos and avoid using hard copy reports. Promoting environmental protection and energy conservation activities
Cooperation among GSP stakeholders (Criterion B)	B1. Green procurement	Evaluating suppliers' green performance before inviting them to tender for the procurement bidding. For example, eco-friendly containers, eco-ship, and low-sulfur bunker
	B2. Green delivery service	Cooperation between shippers and carriers for the freight movement, for example, using eco-friendly packaging material and freight shipped by eco-containers
	B3. Green promotion	Disclosing corporate EP information and green marketing to the public, for example, publishing corporate eco-reports, providing carbon footprint calculators to the shippers
Reverse logistics (Criterion C)	C1. Waste disposal	Processing the ships' waste appropriately, which includes sewage water treatment, cargo holds washing water containing the remnants of any dry cargo material, ballast water operation, and scrapping of old ships
	C2. Recyclables recycled	Selling the redundant equipment, facilities, and recyclable oil sludge in a ship's sludge tanks

(continued)

(continued)

Criteria	Sub-criteria	Description
	C3. Green operation	Having an operation plan to reduce energy consumption and to increase energy efficiency, which includes economic sailing speed (eco-speed), appropriate ocean routing plan, and using shore power supply
Green design and promise (Criterion D)	D1. Emission reduction	Reducing carbon footprint and sulfur emissions during shipping activities
	D2. EP participation	Participating in EP societies and EP non-profit organizations, and EP activities
	D3. Complying with regulations	Following international regulations, e.g., MARPOL73/78 and 2004 BWM ("International Convention for the Control and Management of Ships' Ballast Water and Sediments") conventions and regulations

References

1. Acciaro, M., Vanelslander, T., Sys, C., Ferrari, C., Roumboutsos, A., Giuliano, G., et al. (2014). Environmental sustainability in seaports: a framework for successful innovation. *Maritime Policy & Management, 41*(5), 480–500.
2. Alvik S., Eide M. S., Endresen, Ø., Hoffmann, P., & Longva, T. (2010). *Pathways to low carbon shipping-abatement potential towards 2030*, DNV, Editor. Høvik.
3. Anonymous. (2010, October 04). Evergreen buys energy-saving reefer units. *Cargonews Asia.*
4. Anonymous. (2012, June 18). Rotterdam switches on shore-based power for ships. *Cargonews Asia.*
5. Azzone, G., & Noci, G. (1998). Seeing ecology and "green" innovations as a source of change. *Journal of Organizational Change Management, 11*(2), 94–111.
6. Bailey, D., & Solomon, G. (2004). Pollution prevention at ports: Clearing the air. *Environmental Impact Assessment Review, 24*(7/8), 749–774.
7. Balland, O., Ove, E. S., & Fagerholt, K. (2012). Optimized selection of air emission controls for vessels. *Maritime Policy & Management, 39*(4), 387–400.
8. Beecken, J., Mellqvist, J., Salo, K., Ekholm, J., Jalkanen, J.-P., Johansson, L., et al. (2015). Emission factors of SO_2, NO_x and particles from ships in Neva Bay from ground-based and helicopter-borne measurements and AIS-based modeling. *Atmospheric Chemistry and Physics, 15*(9), 5229–5241.
9. Bengtsson, S., Fridell, E., & Andersson, K. (2012). Environmental assessment of two pathways towards the use of biofuels in shipping, *Energy policy, 44*, 451–463.
10. Bernal, J. L., Miguélez, J. R. P., Sanz, E. N., & de la Ossa, E. M. (1999). Wet air oxidation of oily wastes generated aboard ships: Kinetic modeling. *Journal of Hazardous Materials, 67*(1), 61–73.
11. Chang, C. C., & Wang, C.-M. (2012). Evaluating the effects of green port policy: Case study of Kaohsiung harbor in Taiwan. *Transportation Research Part D: Transport and Environment, 17*(3), 185–189.
12. Chang, Y. C., Wnag, N., & Durak, O. S. (2010). Ship recycling and marine pollution. *Marine Pollution Bulletin, 60*(9), 1390–1396.

13. Chen, Y. S., Lai, S. B., & Wen, C. T. (2006). The influence of green innovation performance on corporate advantage in Taiwan. *Journal of Business Ethics, 67*(4), 331–339.
14. Chen, Y. S. (2010). The drivers of green brand equity: Green brand image, green satisfaction, and green trust. *Business Ethics, 93*(2), 307–319.
15. Clarke, A. C. (2006). *Towards a future maritime policy for the Union: A European vision for the oceans and seas: How inappropriate to call this planet earth when it is quite clearly ocean*. Brussels: Commission of the European Communities.
16. David, M., & Gollasch, S. (2008). EU shipping in the dawn of managing the ballast water issue. *Marine Pollution Bulletin, 56*(12), 1966–1972.
17. Devanney, J. (2011). *Speed limits versus slow steaming*. www.c4tx.org/ctx/pub/spd_limit.pdf. Accessed on September 16, 2014.
18. Enshaei, H., & Mesbahi, E. (2011). Development of a methodology for estimation of ballast water operation in UK ports. *Maritime Policy and Management, 38*(7), 691–703.
19. Eyring, V., Isaksen, I. S. A., Berntsen, T., Collins, W. J., Corbett, J., Endresen, O., et al. (2010). Transport impacts on atmosphere and climate: Shipping. *Atmospheric Environment, 44*(37), 4735–4771.
20. European Environment Agency. (2002). *Annual European Community CLRTAP emission inventory 1990–2000*. Technical Report 91_report_2002_73/en, 2002.
21. Fafaliou, I., Lekakou, M., & Theotokas, I. (2006). Is the European shipping industry aware of corporate social responsibility? The case of the Greek-owned short sea shipping companies. *Marine Policy, 30*(4), 412–419.
22. Forman, E. H., & Selly, M. A. (2002). *Decision by objectives*. Singapore: World Scientific Publishing Company.
23. Franc, P. (2014). Mitigating maritime transport emissions: Diversified effects between European short sea and deep sea shipping. In: *Transport Research Arena (TRA) 5th Conference: Transport Solutions from Research to Deployment*. Paris, France.
24. Gregson, N., Grang, M., Ahamed, F., Akhter, N., & Ferdous, R. (2010). Following things of rubbish value: End-of-life ships, "chock-chocky" furniture and the Bangla-deshi middle class consumer. *Geoforum, 41*(6), 846–854.
25. Hall, J. W. (2010). Assessment of CO_2 and priority pollutant reduction by installation of shoreside power. *Resources, Conservation and Recycling, 54*(7), 462–467.
26. Hart, S. L., & Ahuja, G. (1996). Does it pay to be green? An empirical examination of the relationship between emission reduction and firm performance. *Business Strategy and the Environment, 5*(1), 30–37.
27. Hoffmann, P. N., Eide, M. S., & Endresen, Ø. (2012). Effect of proposed CO_2 emission reduction scenarios on capital expenditure. *Maritime Policy & Management, 39*(4), 443–460.
28. Ishizaka, A., Balkenborg, D., & Kaplan, T. (2011). Does AHP help us make a choice? An experimental evaluation. *Journal of the Operational Research Society, 62*(10), 1801–1812.
29. Knowler, G. (2012, June 04). Shippers pay the cost of slow steaming lines. *Cargonews Asia*.
30. Kontovas, C., & Psaraftis, H. (2011). Reduction of emissions along the maritime intermodal container chain: Operational models and policies. *Maritime Policy and Management, 38*(4), 451–469.
31. Krozer, J. K. M., & Kothuis, B. (2003). Demonstration of environmentally sound and cost-effective shipping. *Journal of Cleaner Production, 11*, 767–777.
32. Lampe, M., & Gazda, G. M. (1995). Green marketing in Europe and United States. *International Business Review, 4*, 295–312.
33. Lai, K. H., Cheng, T. C. E., & Tang, A. (2010). Green retailing: Factors for success. *California Management Review, 52*(2), 6–31.
34. Lai, K.-H., Lun, V. Y. H., Wong, C. W. Y., & Cheng, T. C. E. (2011). Green shipping practices in the shipping industry: Conceptualization, adoption, and implications. *Resources, Conservation and Recycling, 55*(6), 631–638.
35. Lai, K.-H., Wong, C. W. Y., Lun, V. Y. H., & Cheng, T. C. E. (2013). Shipping design for compliance and the performance contingencies for shipping firms. *Transportation Research Part E, 55*(1), 74–83.

36. Lam, J. S. L., & Notteboom, T. (2014). The greening of ports: A comparison of port management tools used by leading ports in Asia and Europe. *Transport Reviews, 34*(2), 169–189.
37. Le Rossignol, M.-H. (2007). *Global terminal operators: An overview.* Washington: The Inter-American Committee on Ports (CIP) of the Organization of American States (OAS).
38. Lu, C.-S., Lin, C.-C., & Tu, C.-J. (2009). Corporate social responsibility and organisational performance in container shipping. *International Journal of Logistics Research and Applications, 12*(2), 119–132.
39. Lun, V. Y. H. (2011). Green management practices and firm performance: A case of container terminal operations. *Resources, Conservation & Recycling, 55*(6), 559–566.
40. Lun, Y. H. V., Lai, K. H., Wong, W. Y. C., & Cheng, T. C. E. (2016). *Green shipping mangement.* New York: Srpinger.
41. Maloni, M., Aliyas, J. A., & Gligor, D. M. (2013). Slow steaming impacts on ocean carriers and shippers. *Maritime Economics & Logistics, 15*(2), 151–171.
42. MARINTEK (Norwegian Marine Technology Research Institute). (2000). *Study of greenhouse gas emissions from ships.* Trondheim, Norway: MARINTEK.
43. Martilla, J., & James, J. (1977). Importance-performance analysis. *Journal of Marketing, 41*(1), 77–79.
44. Melin, A., & Rydhed, H. (2011). Swedish ports' attitudes towards regulations of the shipping sector's emissions of CO_2. *Maritime Policy and Management, 38*(4), 437–450.
45. MEPC. (2014). *IMO's environment committee addresses implementation issues as ballast water management treaty nears entry into force Marine Environment Protection Committee (MEPC).* 67th session, October 13–17, 2014. http://www.imo.org/en/MediaCentre/PressBriefings/Pages/33-mepc-67-bwm.aspx#.ViNWGn4rKM8. Accessed on October 18, 2015.
46. Millar, M. (2011). *Creating a green port culture—Leadership strategies in environmental sustainability for the port of Hong Kong.* Hong Kong: Turnkey Consulting Limited.
47. Moon, D. S.-H., & Woo, J. K. (2014). The impact of port operations on efficient ship operation from both economic and environmental perspectives. *Maritime Policy & Management, 41*(5), 444–461.
48. Olavarrieta, S., & Ellinger, A. E. (1997). Resource-based theory and strategic logistics research. *International Journal of Physical Distribution & Logistics Management, 27*(9/10), 559–587.
49. Osberg, T. G. (2011). *Gas fuelled engine installations in ships, Background, status, safety, some solutions—Interferry Barcelona.* http://www.interferry.com/2011papers/3-1Presentation_Osberg.pdf.
50. Park, J. Y., & Yeo, G.-T. (2012). An evaluation of greenness of major Korean ports: A fuzzy set approach. *The Asian Journal of Shipping and Logistics, 28*(1), 67–82.
51. Porter, M. E., & van der Linde, C. (1995). Toward a new conception of the environment-competitiveness relationship. *The Journal of Economic Perspectives, 9*(4), 97–118.
52. Psaraftis, N. H., & Kontovas, A. C. (2010). Balancing the economic and environmental performance of maritime transportation. *Transportation Research Part D, 15*(8), 458–462.
53. Poulsen, R. T., Ponte, S., & Lister, J. (2016). Buyer-driven greening? Cargo-owners and environmental upgrading in maritime shipping. *Geoforum, 68,* 57–68.
54. Sampson, S. E., & Showalter, M. J. (1999). The performance-importance response function: Observations and implications. *The Service Industries Journal, 19*(3), 1–25.
55. Sarkis, J., Zhu, Q., & Lai, K. (2011). An organizational theoretic review of green supply chain management literature. *International Journal of Production Economics, 130*(1), 1–15.
56. Schuler, M. (2014). *Italian shipping firm to pay $2.75 million fine over magic pipe pollution case.* http://gcaptain.com/italian-shipping-firm-pay-2-75-million-fine-magic-pipe-pollution-case/. Accessed on October 18, 2015.

57. Sonak, S., Pangam, P., Giriyan, A., & Hawaldar, K. (2009). Implications of the ban on organotins for protection of global coastal and marine ecology. *Journal of Environmental Management, 90*(Supplement 1), S96–S108.
58. TDSM (The dictionary for sustainable management). (2012). *True-Blue Greens*. http://www.sustainabilitydictionary.com/true-blue-greens/.
59. Tzannatos, E. (2010). Ship emissions and their externalities for the port of Piraeus–Greece. *Atmospheric Environment, 44*(3), 400–407.
60. USCG. (2012). *International safety management code*. http://www.dieselduck.ca/library/03%20regulatory/ism_info.htm. Accessed April 12, 2017.
61. van Kasteren, Y. (2008). *What are the drivers of environmentally sustainable consumer behaviour*? In T. Geer Ken, A. Tukker, & C. Vezzoli (Eds.), *Sustainability management, marketing and consumption* (pp. 173–186). The *2nd Conference of the Sustainable Consumption Research Exchange* (SCORE) *Network Proceedings*. Brussels, Belgium: Sustainable Consumption Research Exchanges (SCORE).
62. Wuisan, L., van Leeuwen, J., & van Koppen, C. S. A. (2012). Greening international shipping through private governance: A case study of the Clean Shipping Project. *Marine Policy, 36* (1), 165–173.
63. Yang, C. C., Marlow, P. B., & Lu, C. S. (2009). Assessing resources, logistics service capabilities, innovation capabilities and the performance of container shipping services in Taiwan. *International Journal of Production Economics, 122*(1), 4–20.
64. Yang, C.-S., Lu, C.-S., Haider, J. J., & Marlow, P. B. (2013). The effect of green supply chain management on green performance and firm competitiveness in the context of container shipping in Taiwan. *Transportation Research Part E: Logistics and Transportation Review, 55*(1), 55–73.

Logistics Network Design for Rice Distribution in Sulawesi, Indonesia

Rosmalina Hanafi, Muhammad Rusman, Mark Goh and Robert de Souza

Abstract This paper investigates the logistics network design for rice distribution of a 4-supplier, 3-warehouse, 14-customer distribution point network in the province of Sulawesi, Indonesia. An MIP model is formulated, with the objective of minimising the procurement, inventory, and transportation costs from supplier through to the warehouses and onto the distribution locations. Computational experiments are conducted using ILOG CPLEX Optimization Studio. Optimal solutions are found. Initial results suggest an achievement of economic and environmental sustainability through a cost reduction in the transportation cost from the supplier to the warehouses of 17.44%, and from warehouses to consumer distribution points by 5.68% respectively.

Keywords Network optimization · Rice · Indonesia

1 Introduction

Today, there is much interest and debate on the acceptability, prevalence, and practice of environmental sustainability in the context of Asian logistics and supply chains. In the literature, Marchet et el. [9] have highlighted that environmental

---

R. Hanafi · M. Rusman
Industrial Engineering Department, Hasanuddin University, Makassar, Indonesia
e-mail: malinahanafi@yahoo.com

M. Rusman
e-mail: rusman@tiunhas.net

M. Goh (✉)
NUS Business School and the Logistics Institute-Asia Pacific, National University of Singapore, 21 Heng Mui Keng Terrace, NUS, Singapore 119613, Singapore
e-mail: mark_goh@nus.edu.sg; bizgohkh@nus.edu.sg

R. de Souza
The Logistics Institute-Asia Pacific, National University of Singapore, Singapore, Singapore
e-mail: rdesouza@nus.edu.sg

X. Liu (ed.), *Environmental Sustainability in Asian Logistics and Supply Chains*,
https://doi.org/10.1007/978-981-13-0451-4_3

sustainability is a nascent area of promising research, not just because of the dearth of papers in this domain but also because of the better environmental sustainability adoption and measurement, particularly by those adopted and diffused in the West. Hence, the writing of this book chapter is timely as the interest on sustainability grows in tandem with economic development and the current climate on the need to include environmental sustainability and social sustainability in the equation of cost minimisation for Asian freight and logistics, and the overarching supply chain within developing Asian economies. In this regard, the national governments have an economic, moral and social agenda to ensure that cost efficiency is achieved at the expense of environmental and social sustainability during logistics delivery and distribution. This is especially true for the Third World countries in Asia where there is a pressing need to support and feed the growing rural communities sited faraway from the urban population centres.

As technology improves, there is a corresponding demand for better, more advanced, and more responsible logistics services. Part of the suite of the advanced logistics services would invariably include the use of smart optimisation tools and platforms to improve operational efficiency in the short term (cost) and to ensure acceptable environmental and social sustainability in the longer term. For this matter, this chapter, as part of the contribution to the book, therefore seeks to present a practical and real life case study on the logistics design of a complicated distribution network which seeks to safeguard cost sustainability, and provide social and environmental sustainability in the process. We speak of the largest developing economy in Southeast Asia and focus on a staple in the diet of many Asians, Indonesia and rice.

Rice is an essential agriculture commodity in Indonesia. As a staple food for the bulk of the population, the daily demand and consumption for rice is naturally high and almost functional in every Indonesian household diet. There is thus a need to match supply with demand well especially since the population of Indonesia is found in the main island of Java while the rice fields are further afar within Indonesia, a sprawling archipelago of 17,000 odd islands, not all of which are always nor readily accessible by road or rail transport. Air or ocean transport are unacceptable options given the high cost of transportation internationally. At the same time, the Indonesian Government has a responsibility to see to it that the poorer population residing in these remote islands are properly fed, or risk a political cost at the next elections. In this regard, the national and regional governments work closely through the relevant government agencies to ensure that social sustainability for the masses living away from the main and provincial cities is upheld through the timely and cost effective distribution of rice in an optimised way. At the same time, to maintain good political relations with her ASEAN neighbours, rice has to be delivered to feed this group of people so as to stop them from slashing and burning virgin forests to grow their own crops, at the expense of environmental pollution. Already, a major environmental issue in Indonesia is deforestation, particularly for Sulawesi.

We now turn our attention to the topic on hand, the rice distribution network for Sulawesi, Indonesia.

The Sulawesi Rice Distribution Network

Sulawesi is a major rice production point in Indonesia, ranked third after Java and Sumatra, contributing about 11% of the national rice production volume annually. In Indonesia, as like most Asian countries, rice production follows a seasonal pattern, and depends on several factors such as the rice production areas, harvest period, amount of rainfall, and the amount and quality of the fertilizer used. Given these uncertainties, the rice yield levels can vary from district to district, from region to region. At the same time, barring significant changes in the population and food consumption patterns, rice consumption follows a predictable trend as it is a staple product [4]. From a decision maker and government perspective, for obvious social, political, environmental and cost reasons, proper planning and logistics distribution is required to ensure the rice availability and accessibility, and to improve food security in the process. To be able to undertake this task effectively, a sustainable logistics network optimization design for rice distribution is called for. In the ideal, this network optimisation design must provide for the availability of alternative optimal solutions so that either all or some of the sustainability concerns are managed in the most optimal manner possible. For instance, some of the optimal solutions obtained through rigorous modelling can be cost focused while other solutions can be socially and environmentally acceptable.

The rice distribution network, as in all other agri-food networks, comprises a set of suppliers (farmers), plants (rice mills), distribution centers (DC) (warehouses), and an elaborate transportation infrastructure down to the last mile, through modality choices in transport. The challenge is bi-directional. First and foremost, new locations for the consumption (due to the transmigration of the rural population in search of better economic prospects) and hence the storage of rice (due to the changing warehousing profile) will surface. At the same time, the supply of rice is never certain in terms of the volume of rice that can be harvested each year.

Given this situation, several logistics network configuration decisions are needed on a yearly basis. For instance, which existing and new locations should be used, the number of customers/households to be served from which DCs, which suppliers should supply to which mills, and so on.

2 Literature Review

The literature has attempted to address some if not all of these things and more using a myriad of techniques and objectives. For instance, recently, Yildiz et al. [14] devised a multi-criteria method for comparing the total reliability and total cost of a network. Others such as Georgiadis et al. [5] considered the optimal design of supply chain networks that are subject to uncertain transient demand variations. Even on the issue of strategic network planning, Goetschalckx [6] has supplied some mathematical formulations to understand this challenging problem while Klibi et al. [8] reviewed the scholarly effort expended in the design of value-creating supply chain networks. The review of such literature is particularly useful in our context given the need to generate value from the rice farmers on to the socially disadvantaged recipients of the rice through the government agency responsible for administering the social service. The literature has also provided evidence of the application of robust operations management techniques to manage the supply chain issues in distribution networks. In this case, Schwarz and Weng [12] studied the impact of lead time uncertainty on the safety stock on the design of a Just-In-Time supply chain. At the same time, there are studies that have adopted an operational treatment on the network distribution problem. For instance, van Houtum et al. [13] studied the materials coordination problem in stochastic multi-echelon systems.

Indeed, the logistics network design problem has attracted much attention, simply because there is now a need to integrate the strategic issues of location and nodes risk assessment, with the tactical and operational challenges of storing, buffering, scheduling and routing of stock throughout the network, as highlighted by Nickel and Saldanha-da-Gama [10], not to mention the need to gingerly balance these objectives with social and environmental sustainability implicitly. Specific to the use of MIP on this class of problems, Kauder [7] has studied the network design problem of an automotive manufacturer, who is subject to uncertainty in the global marketplace. Further, Salema et al. [11] applied MIP to the study of a closed loop logistics network design problem, again incorporating the tactical decisions of production, storage, and distribution. Adopting this MIP approach, we will investigate the logistics design network problem of rice distribution in Makassar, South Sulawesi.

3 Problem Description

Recognising the significant role of rice in maintaining the socio-economic stability, the Indonesian government has been intervening by organizing the rice logistics business through BULOG (the State Logistics Agency). As an administrative agency, BULOG is tasked to maintain the availability, stability, and affordability of basic food. In the case of rice, BULOG maintains the national rice reserve stock, implements market operation to keep the price stable, provides and distributes rice to alleviate any rice shortage during emergency situations. BULOG has twenty six regional divisions (Divre) located in the capitals of the provinces in Indonesia. The sub-regional division (Subdivre) serves as the sub-regional logistics agency at the city/district level. The South and West Sulawesi of BULOG (BULOG Divre Sulselbar) located in Makassar is a regional division at the provincial level dedicated to serve as the main logistics centre that handles the rice logistics related activities within South and West Sulawesi, where there is a large resident population of 18 million living on the world's eleventh largest island, encompassing a land mass of 174,600 km^2 (https://en.wikipedia.org/wiki/Sulawesi). BULOG applies the over-arching policy of purchasing domestically produced and harvested rice to keep prices at the farm level and to ensure sufficient stock for domestic market consumption. BULOG also serves the public as part of its social protection program by distributing subsidized rice to the poor under the Raskin program. The Raskin program, a subsidized rice delivery program pivoted on social sustainability, is aimed at alleviating the financial challenge faced by low income households by providing rice purchased at highly subsidized prices to the poor or near poor households to fulfil their basic food needs [1]. The logistics coverage and responsibility for BULOG is shown in Fig. 1.

Put simply, BULOG purchases the grain/rice grown domestically directly from the farmers, farmer associations, and indirectly through partners. The procurement of grain/rice is conducted, using the system of Public Service Obligation (PSO) and commercial means. The Grain-Rice Processing Unit (UPGB) processes the grain/ rice and distributes the processed rice through the retailers, groceries, inter-island, inter divre/subdivre, inter-UPGB, and PSO.

The BULOG Divre Sulselbar covers 11 subregional divisions, one of which is the BULOG Sub Regional Division Makassar. Figure 2 shows the warehouse capacity of the subdivres under BULOG Divre Sulselbar.

The current logistics facilities of the BULOG Sub Regional Division Makassar include three warehouses. At the same time, the rice suppliers are found in the

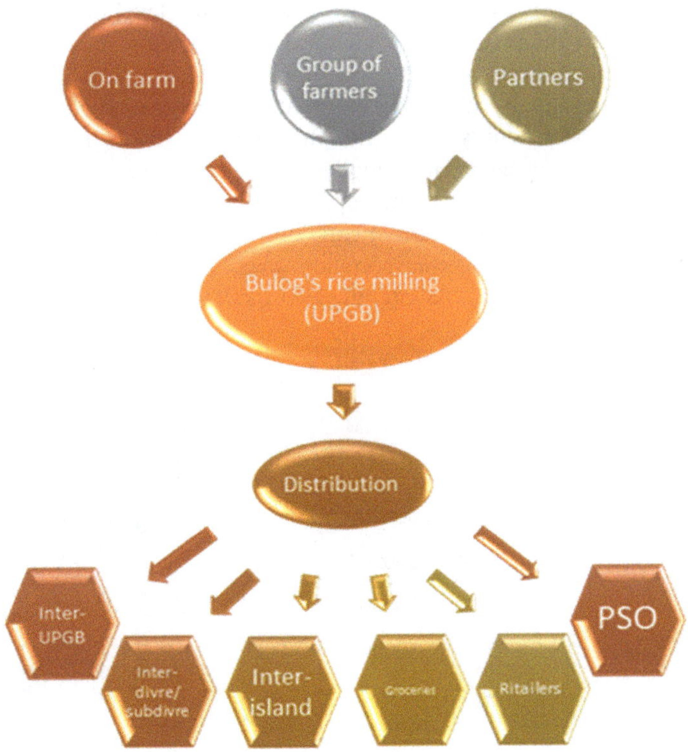

Fig. 1 Rice flows of BULOG. *Source* www.BULOG.co.id

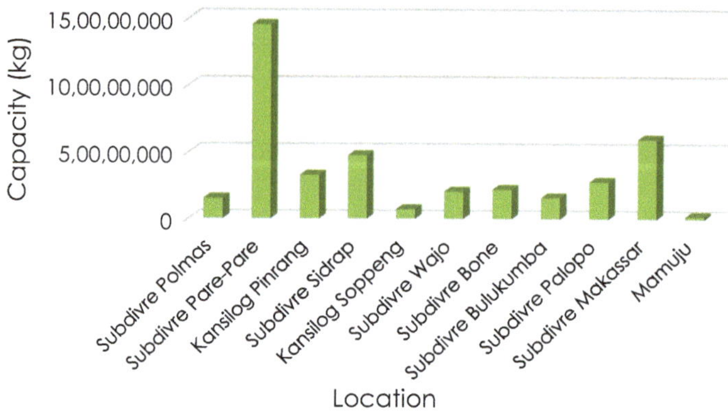

Fig. 2 Warehouse capacity of BULOG Divre Sulsebar. *Source* BULOG Divre Sulselbar

towns of Takalar, Gowa, Makassar, and Maros. The BULOG Subdivre Makassar distributes the subsidized rice intended for low income households to 14 consumer distribution points or municipalities in Makassar city itself. Figures 3 and 4 show the rice procurement and rice distribution conducted by the BULOG Subdivre Makassar in 2015, respectively. As can be seen, a higher level of rice procurement occurs during May, June, and July, which are the harvesting seasons. The overall rice distribution tends to be constant over time.

We begin our study by analysing the rice distribution network starting at a supplier. One important entity in the rice distribution network is the warehouses which act as a connector between a supplier and the consumers and the warehouse helps to store the rice supplied by the supplier to be distributed to the consumers. A quick scan and review of the current condition of rice distribution suggest that a good warehouse management, transportation, and logistics system is required to ensure an efficient flow of rice. An optimization model can be applied to reduce the

Fig. 3 Rice procurement in 2015—Makassar Subdivre. *Source* BULOG Divre Sulselbar

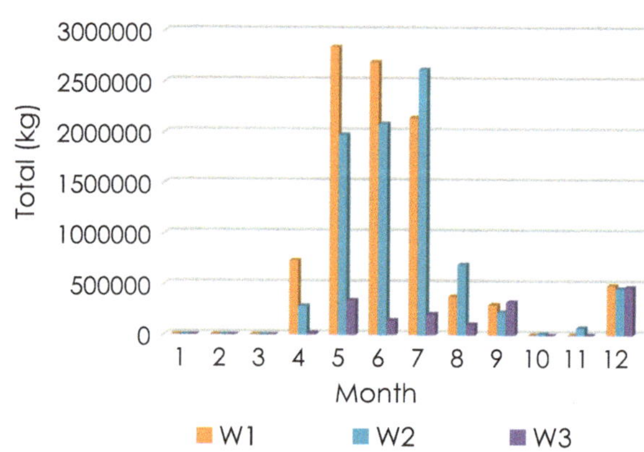

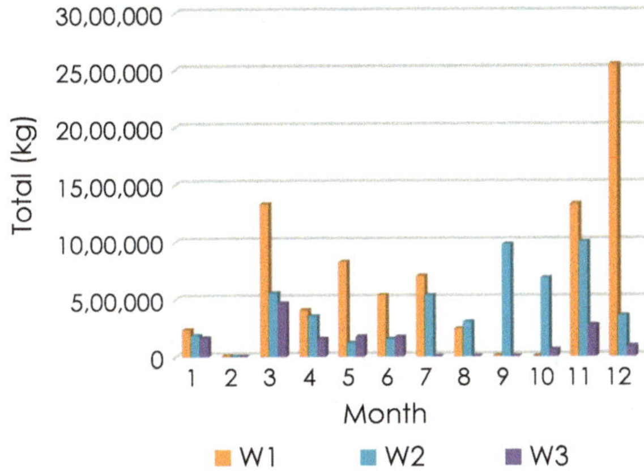

Fig. 4 Rice distribution in 2015—Makassar Subdivre. *Source* BULOG Divre Sulselbar

overall logistics costs, to ensure an efficient decision making process and improve the current service levels in the rice logistics system.

Therefore, in this study, a mathematical model is developed for BULOG Subdivre Makassar. The objective of this study is to develop an optimization model to determine the number, location and capacity of the rice distribution centres and warehouses in Makassar, South Sulawesi. Based on the results obtained, we hope to show how guidance and recommendations on how the logistics network of rice distribution in Makassar, South Sulawesi can be better managed not just in terms of cost optimality, but also for environmental and social sustainability through meaningfully exploiting the alternative optimal solutions found.

4 Solution Approach

We first analyse the current logistics processes and map the logistics distribution process for a 4-supplier, 3-warehouse, 14-customer distribution point network. The logistics network model is then re-created to accurately represent the current rice logistics system. Next, an optimal network distribution is identified and validated.

5 Problem Formulation

The problem is formulated as a Mixed Integer Problem (MIP) whose objective is to minimize the total logistics cost using the following notations and assumptions.

Assumptions:

The demand is known and given.
The transportation distances are available and known.
No stochasticity is involved in the problem studied.

Notations:

Pc_i^t	Procurement cost at supplier i in period t
Q_i^t	Quantity supplied by supplier I in period t
Tc_{ij}^t	Transportation cost per unit (kg) from supplier i to warehouse j in period t
Wc_j^t	Cost of opening a warehouse j in period t
Ifc_j^t	Inventory fixed cost at warehouse j in period t
Ivc_j^t	Inventory variable cost at warehouse j in period t
Il_j^t	Inventory level at warehouse j in period t
Tc_{jk}^t	Transportation cost per unit (kg) from warehouse j to consumer k in period t
S_{max}	Maximum amount of rice that can be supplied
$Wcap_j$	Capacity of warehouse j
D_k^t	Demand of rice at consumer location k in period t
x_{ij}^t	Amount of rice to be supplied from supplier i to warehouse j in period t
y_{jk}^t	Amount of rice to be transported from warehouse j to consumer k in period t
z_j^t	Binary variable indicating whether warehouse j to be opened or not in period t

MIP Model:
Min

$$\sum_{i\in I} Pc_i^t Q_i^t + \sum_{i\in I}\sum_{j\in J} Tc_{ij}^t x_{ij}^t + \sum_{j\in J} Wc_j^t z_j^t + \sum_{j\in J} Ifc_j^t + \sum_{j\in J} Ivc_j^t Il_j^t + \sum_{j\in J}\sum_{k\in K} Tc_{jk}^t y_{jk}^t \tag{1}$$

Constraints:

$$\sum_{j\in J} x_{ij}^t \le S_{max} \quad \forall i \in I \tag{2}$$

$$\sum_{j\in J} x_{ij}^t \ge \sum_{j\in J} y_{jk}^t \quad \forall i \in I \tag{3}$$

$$\sum_{j \in J} x_{ij}^{t} + Il_{j}^{t-1} - \sum_{j \in J} y_{jk}^{t} \leq \sum_{j \in J} Wcap_{j} \quad \forall j \in J \tag{4}$$

$$\sum_{j \in J} y_{jk}^{t} = \sum_{k \in K} D_{k}^{t} \quad \forall j \in J, \forall k \in K \tag{5}$$

$$\sum_{j \in J} x_{ij}^{t} + Il_{j}^{t-1} \geq \sum_{k \in K} D_{k}^{t} + Il_{j}^{t} \quad \forall j \in J \tag{6}$$

$$\sum_{i \in I} x_{ij}^{t} \leq Wcap_{j} \quad \forall j \in J \tag{7}$$

$$\sum_{k \in K} y_{jk}^{t} \leq Wcap_{j} \quad \forall j \in J \tag{8}$$

$$z_{j}^{t} = \begin{cases} 1, & \textit{open a warehouse} \\ 0, & \textit{otherwise} \end{cases} \tag{9}$$

$$x_{ij}^{t} \geq 0; \quad y_{jk}^{t} \geq 0; \quad Il_{j}^{t} \geq 0. \tag{10}$$

The objective function of Eq. (1) represents the costs to be minimized. These include the cost of opening a warehouse, transportation, procurement, and inventory costs. Constraint (2) denotes that the total amount of rice to be supplied from supplier i to warehouse j should be less than or equal to the maximum quantity of rice that can be supplied. Constraint (3) ensures that the total amount of rice to be supplied from supplier i to warehouse j in period t should be greater than or equal to the total amount of rice to be distributed from warehouse j to consumer k in period t. Constraint (4) indicates the balance of inventory level in which the total amount of rice to be supplied to warehouses plus the inventory level at previous period should be less than or equal to the total capacity of the warehouses plus the total amount of rice to be distributed from the warehouses to the consumers in period t. Constraint (5) enforces that the total quantity of rice to be transported from the warehouses to the consumers should be equal to the total demand of rice at the consumer locations in period t. Constraint (6) requires that the total amount of rice to be supplied to the warehouses plus the inventory level at the previous period should be greater than or equal to the consumer demand plus the inventory level in period t. Constraint (7) indicates that the total quantity of rice to be supplied from supplier i to warehouse j in period t should be less or equal with the capacity of warehouse j. Constraint (8) enforces that the total quantity of rice to be transported from warehouse j to consumer k in period t should be less than or equal to the capacity of warehouse j. Equation (9) represents a binary decision variable denoted by z_{j}^{t} which is whether to open a warehouse or not. Inequalities (10) represent the decision variables x_{ij}^{t} and y_{jk}^{t} and the non-negativity constraints on the corresponding decision variables.

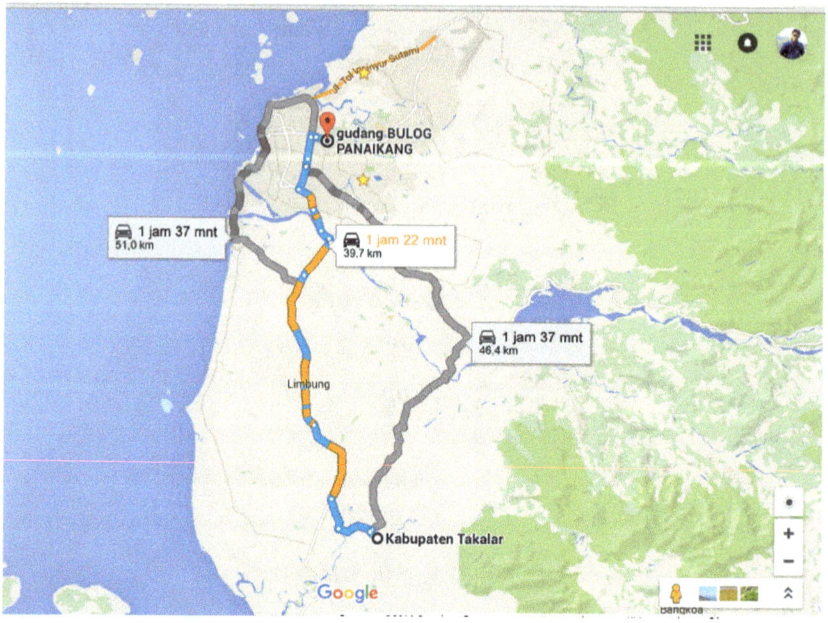

Fig. 5 Distance from a supplier to warehouse

Fig. 6 Distance from warehouse to consumer distribution point

Table 1 Quantity of rice supplied to Makassar in 2015

Supplier	Amount of rice supplied to warehouse (kg)	Distribution cost from supplier to warehouse (Rp)	Warehouse	Distribution cost from warehouse to consumer distribution point (Rp)
Makassar (S1)	720,000	1,123,200	W1	9,852,014
Takalar (S2)	4,978,990	59,299,771	W2	5,944,469
Gowa (S3)	4,274,750	31,162,928	W3	1,833,322
Maros (S4)	7,021,650	68,461,088	Total	17,629,805
Total	16,995,390	160,046,987		

Source BULOG Divre Sulselbar

Table 2 Demand of rice at consumer distribution points

No.	Consumer distribution point	Demand (kg)
1	Kec. Wajo	90,930
2	Kec. Biringkanaya	884,760
3	Kec. Bontoala	230,250
4	Kec. Makassar	707,940
5	Kec. Mamajang	337,650
6	Kec. Manggala	475,690
7	Kec. Mariso	327,525
8	Kec. Panakkukang	1,044,120
9	Kec. Rappocini	745,020
10	Kec. Tallo	1,199,940
11	Kec. Tamalanrea	342,900
12	Kec. Tamalate	1,340,820
13	Kec. Ujung Pandang	87,300
14	Kec. Ujung Tanah	535,280
	Total	8,350,125

Source BULOG Divre Sulselbar

Next, we map the route distances using Google map to determine the various transportation distances from the supplier to the warehouses and from the respective warehouse to the consumer distribution points, as shown respectively in Figs. 5 and 6. At the same time, detailed data is provided by BULOG on the amount of rice sent to Makassar and the demand of rice at the consumer distribution points as shown in Tables 1 and 2 respectively (Fig. 7).

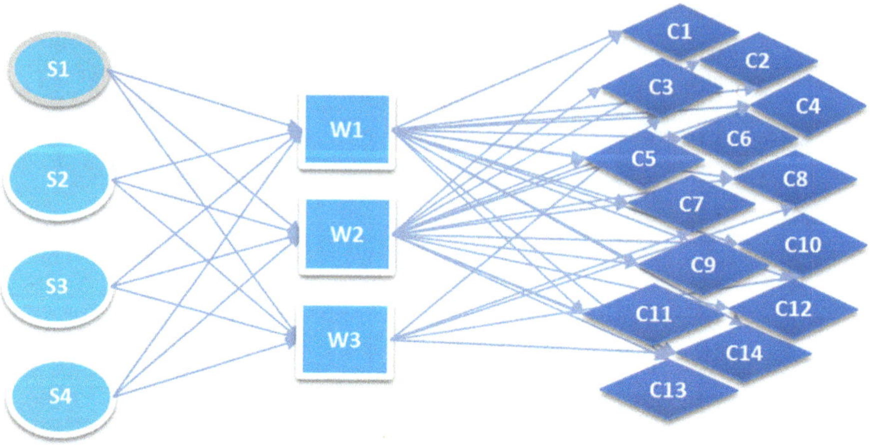

Fig. 7 Existing rice distribution network at subregional division Makassar

6 Results of Experimentation

Several computational experiments are conducted using the ILOG CPLEX Optimization Studio ver. 12.2 to test the model. The performance of the model is examined by applying different scenarios with various combinations of suppliers and warehouse capacities. Initially, a test model is generated for the analysis of the rice distribution network consisting of 4 suppliers, 3 warehouses and 14 consumer distribution points. In this test, the following warehouse capacities were applied: W1 is 21 million kg, W2 is 21 million kg, and W3 is 6 million kg. An optimal solution is obtained with a total logistics cost of Rp 81,545,340, with a CPU time of 10 s, and without having to open a new warehouse. Three optimal solutions are possible to transport the rice from supplier to warehouse and from which warehouse to supply. The results obtained are summarised in Table 3.

As can be seen from Table 3, the first solution suggests that Makassar (S1) should supply 720,000 kg of rice to warehouse W1 while the second and the third solutions indicate that Makassar (S1) should supply 720,000 kg of rice to warehouse W2. All solutions indicate that Takalar (S2) does not supply to any warehouse. The first optimal solution indicates that Gowa supplies 620,820 kg of rice to W1, 2,200,970 kg to W2, and 1,452,960 kg to W3. The second alternative optimal solution indicates that Gowa supplies 4,274,750 kg of rice only to W2. The third alternative optimal solution indicates that Gowa supplies 1,340,820 kg of rice to W1, 2,313,110 kg to W2, and 620,820 kg of rice to W3. Maros (S4) supplies only to W2 with 3,355,375 kg of rice for all solutions. Each solution also yields a different combination of rice to be distributed from the

Table 3 Quantity of rice to be transported from supplier to warehouse

Supplier	Warehouse	Amount of rice to be supplied to warehouse (kg)	Amount of rice to be supplied to warehouse (kg)	Amount of rice to be supplied to warehouse (kg)
		I	II	III
Makassar (S1)	W1	720,000	0	0
Makassar (S1)	W2	0	0	0
Makassar (S1)	W3	0	720,000	720,000
Takalar (S2)	W1	0	0	0
Takalar (S2)	W2	0	0	0
Takalar (S2)	W3	0	0	0
Gowa (S3)	W1	620,820	0	1,340,820
Gowa (S3)	W2	2,200,970	4,274,750	2,313,110
Gowa (S3)	W3	1,452,960	0	620,820
Maros (S4)	W1	0	0	0
Maros (S4)	W2	3,355,375	3,355,375	3,355,375
Maros (S4)	W3	0	0	0
Total		8,350,125	8,350,125	8,350,125

warehouses to the consumer distribution points. The solutions obtained satisfy the demand at all the consumer distribution points with a total of 8,350,125 kg. The quantity of rice to be distributed from warehouses W1, W2, and W3 to the 14 consumer demand points as given by the three solutions are presented in Tables 4, 5, and 6.

The optimized network for rice distribution is shown in Fig. 8.

Further, the optimal solution for the amount of rice to be delivered from the supplier to the warehouses suggests that the total transportation cost can be reduced by 17.44%. At the same time, the optimal amount of rice to be distributed from the warehouses to the consumer distribution points and from which warehouse to supply to a consumer distribution point has reduced transportation cost by 5.68%, as shown by Figs. 9 and 10 respectively. Clearly, the optimal solution is win-win for cost effectiveness and environmental sustainability as less fuel is now burnt. As for social sustainability, given that at least three alternative optimal solutions are found, it is possible to engineer the options of the set of alternative solutions to arrive at the most acceptable social sustainability solution. Hence, having alternative optimal solutions to play with is a win-win-win solution for BULOG in this case.

Table 4 Alternative solution I—quantity of rice to be distributed from warehouse to consumer distribution point

Warehouse	Consumer	Amount of rice to be distributed to consumer (kg)	Warehouse	Consumer	Amount of rice to be distributed to consumer (kg)	Warehouse	Consumer	Amount of rice to be distributed to consumer (kg)	Total
W1	C1	0	W2	C1	90,930	W3	C1	0	90,930
W1	C2	0	W2	C2	884,760	W3	C2	0	884,760
W1	C3	0	W2	C3	230,250	W3	C3	0	230,250
W1	C4	0	W2	C4	0	W3	C4	707,940	707,940
W1	C5	0	W2	C5	337,650	W3	C5	0	337,650
W1	C6	0	W2	C6	475,690	W3	C6	0	475,690
W1	C7	0	W2	C7	327,525	W3	C7	0	327,525
W1	C8	1,044,120	W2	C8	0	W3	C8	0	1,044,120
W1	C9	0	W2	C9	0	W3	C9	745,020	745,020
W1	C10	0	W2	C10	1,199,940	W3	C10	0	1,199,940
W1	C11	0	W2	C11	342,900	W3	C11	0	342,900
W1	C12	296,700	W2	C12	1,044,120	W3	C12	0	1,340,820
W1	C13	0	W2	C13	87,300	W3	C13	0	87,300
W1	C14	0	W2	C14	535,280	W3	C14	0	535,280

Table 5 Alternative solution II—rice to be distributed from warehouse to consumer distribution point

Warehouse	Consumer	Rice to be distributed to consumer (kg)	Warehouse	Consumer	Rice to be distributed to consumer (kg)	Warehouse	Consumer	Rice to be distributed to consumer (kg)	Total
W1	C1	0	W2	C1	90,930	W3	C1	0	90,930
W1	C2	0	W2	C2	884,760	W3	C2	0	884,760
W1	C3	0	W2	C3	230,250	W3	C3	0	230,250
W1	C4	0	W2	C4	707,940	W3	C4	0	707,940
W1	C5	0	W2	C5	337,650	W3	C5	0	337,650
W1	C6	0	W2	C6	475,690	W3	C6	0	475,690
W1	C7	0	W2	C7	327,525	W3	C7	0	327,525
W1	C8	0	W2	C8	1,044,120	W3	C8	0	1,044,120
W1	C9	0	W2	C9	745,020	W3	C9	0	745,020
W1	C10	0	W2	C10	479,940	W3	C10	720,000	1,199,940
W1	C11	0	W2	C11	342,900	W3	C11	0	342,900
W1	C12	0	W2	C12	1,340,820	W3	C12	0	1,340,820
W1	C13	0	W2	C13	87,300	W3	C13	0	87,300
W1	C14	0	W2	C14	535,280	W3	C14	0	535,280

Table 6 Alternative solution III—quantity of rice to be distributed from warehouse to consumer distribution point

Warehouse	Consumer	Amount of rice to be distributed to consumer (kg)	Warehouse	Consumer	Amount of rice to be distributed to consumer (kg)	Warehouse	Consumer	Amount of rice to be distributed to consumer (kg)	Total
W1	C1	0	W2	1	90,930	W3	C1	0	90,930
W1	C2	0	W2	2	0	W3	C2	884,760	884,760
W1	C3	0	W2	3	230,250	W3	C3	0	230,250
W1	C4	0	W2	4	707,940	W3	C4	0	707,940
W1	C5	0	W2	5	337,650	W3	C5	0	337,650
W1	C6	0	W2	6	475,690	W3	C6	0	475,690
W1	C7	0	W2	7	327,525	W3	C7	0	327,525
W1	C8	0	W2	8	1,044,120	W3	C8	0	1,044,120
W1	C9	0	W2	9	745,020	W3	C9	0	745,020
W1	C10	0	W2	10	743,880	W3	C10	456,060	1,199,940
W1	C11	0	W2	11	342,900	W3	C11	0	342,900
W1	C12	1,340,820	W2	12	0	W3	C12	0	1,340,820
W1	C13	0	W2	13	87,300	W3	C13	0	87,300
W1	C14	0	W2	14	535,280	W3	C14	0	535,280

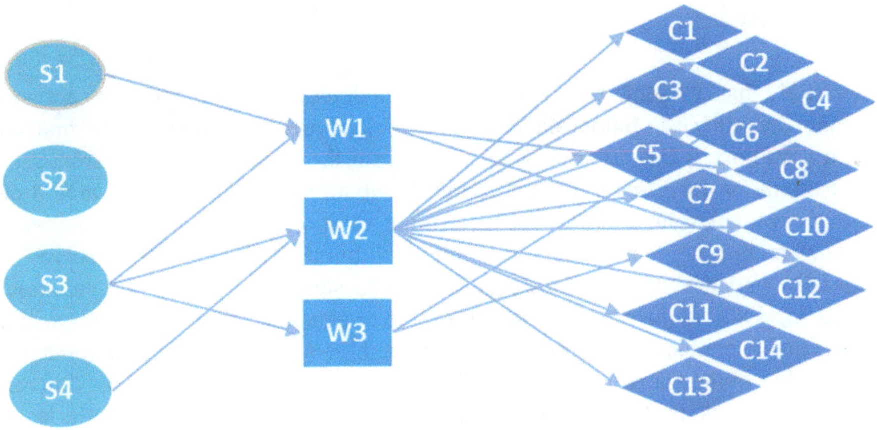

Fig. 8 Optimized rice distribution network with alternative optima

Fig. 9 Optimal amount of rice to be sent from supplier to warehouse. *Note* S Suppliers, C Customers, W Warehouses, Opt Optimal amount of rice quantity to be sent from supplier to warehouse

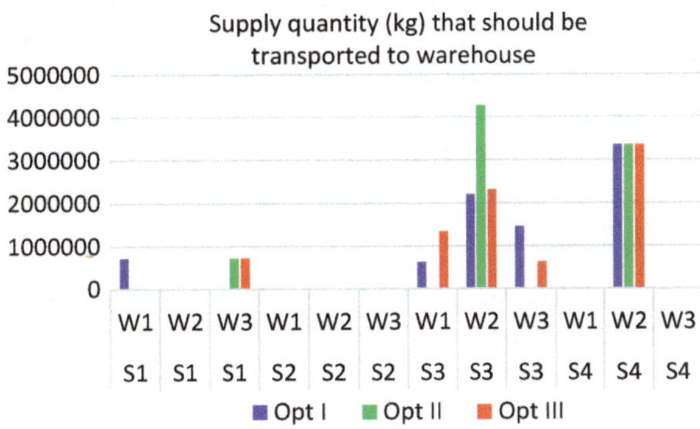

Fig. 10 Optimized amount of rice to be sent from warehouses to consumer distribution points. *Note* S Suppliers, C Customers, W Warehouses

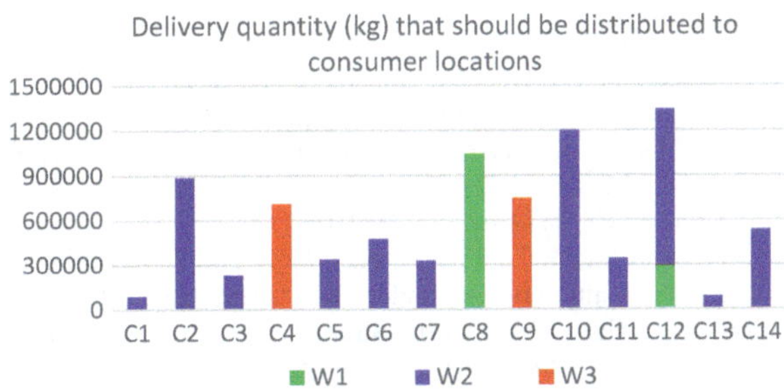

7 Conclusion

This study has presented a mathematical model of the rice logistics network problem in Sulawesi, Indonesia. The main objective of the model is to find the minimum logistics cost of transporting rice from the suppliers to the warehouses, and from the warehouses to the consumer distribution locations. At the same time, through optimal solutions, we can determine solutions which are environmental sustainable through the reduction in the fuel burnt. The problem is solved to optimality and the total logistics cost is reduced significantly. The computational results suggest that the proposed model is able to generate optimal solutions within an acceptable computational time. Although the model is presented in the context of a 3-echelon optimization model, they are generic and can be adapted for different logistics network problems within Indonesia and other developing countries in Asia, with a need to achieve cost effective solutions coupled with environmental and social sustainability

Moving forward, for future research, the proposed optimisation model can be improved and extended to include other relevant elements of logistics systems and we apply model to other logistics systems involving more upstream suppliers, warehouses, and other downstream customers. Further study will be conducted to analyse the entire network of rice logistics operations in Indonesia, and simulate the relevant aspects of rice flow from the surplus areas to the deficit areas and to also adopt a bi-level robust optimisation approach for the logistics network design solutioning.

Acknowledgements We recognise the kind assistance of the Coordinating Ministry of Economic Affairs, Indonesia in supporting the data collection effort.

References

1. Alatas, V., & Jellema, J. (2012). *Raskin Subsidized Rice Delivery*, World Bank Report, 28 pp.
2. Berger, P. D., Gerstenfeld, A., & Zeng, A. Z. (2004). How many suppliers are best? A decision analysis approach. *Omega, 32,* 9–15.
3. BULOG (n.d.), Personal communications and retrieved from www.bulog.co.id.
4. Fisher, M. L. (1997). What is the right supply chain for your product? *Harvard Business Review, March–April, 75*(2), 105–116.
5. Georgiadis, M. C., Tsiakis, P., Longinidis, P., & Sofioglou, M. K. (2011). Optimal design of supply chain networks under uncertain transient demand variations. *Omega, 39,* 254–272.
6. Goetschalckx, M. (2000). Strategic network planning. In H. Stadtler & C. Kilger (Eds.), *Supply chain management and advanced planning: Concepts, models, software and case studies* (pp. 79–95). Berlin: Springer.
7. Kauder, S., & Meyer, H. (2009). Strategic network planning for an international automotive manufacturer. *OR Spectrum, 31*(3), 507–532.
8. Klibi, W., Martel, A., & Guitouni, A. (2010). The design of robust value-creating supply chain networks: A critical review. *European Journal of Operational Research, 203*(2), 283–293.

9. Marchet, G., Melacini, M., & Perotti, S. (2014). Environmental sustainability in logistics and freight transportation: A literature review and research agenda. *Journal of Manufacturing Technology Management, 25*(6), 775–811.
10. Nickel, S., & Saldanha-da-Gama, F. (2009). Logistics network design. *OR Spectrum, 31*(3), 461–463.
11. Salema, M. I. G., Povoa, A. P. B., & Novais, A. Q. (2009). A strategic and tactical model for closed-loop supply chains. *OR Spectrum, 31*(3), 573–599.
12. Schwarz, L. B., & Weng, Z. K. (2000). The design of a JIT supply chain: the effect of lead time uncertainty on safety stock. *Journal of Business Logistics, 21,* 231–253.
13. van Houtum, G. J., Inderfurth, K., & Zijm, W. H. J. (1996). Materials coordination in stochastic multi-echelon systems. *European Journal of Operational Research, 95,* 1–23.
14. Yildiz, H., Yoon, J., Talluri, S., & Ho, W. (2016). Reliable supply chain network design. *Decision Sciences, 47*(4), 661–698.

A Basic Research for Delivery Price Yardsticks for the 3PL Industry

Angela Y. Y. Chen and Yutaka Karasawa

Abstract The current delivery cost is set at a fixed price by product volume in a specified region while in general delivery price is based on the weight, size, and distance. Therefore, in this case study, we have proposed a new price system, which is set by zone and distance, especially when considering the liter and kilometer unit price (ℓk@) as a yardstick value, to make a tentative research of this brand new method in the field. In order to evaluate this new price system, we first produced six ways to calculate the unit price system, and then one was selected. However, the possibility of a new price system is dependent on the final evaluation on the strategic judgement of the firm.

Keywords Delivery price · Strategic judgement · Supply chain management strategy

1 Introduction

This study is a basic theory with regard to setting the delivery price in a small area of Japan, by taking into consideration the distance, size, and volume of the goods. Therefore, we proposed a new price system, which has been established by zone and distance, especially when calculating the liter and kilometer unit price (ℓk@) as a standard value, which is a brand new method in the field. The purpose of this research was to propose a moderate price for a distribution center within a small area, and exactly how the distance and volume will affect the delivery unit price. Concretely, the projected firm has a number of problems of which the primary one

A. Y. Y. Chen (✉)
China University of Technology, No. 56, Sec. 3, Xinglong Road, Wunshan District, Taipei 116, Taiwan (R.O.C.)
e-mail: angelayychen@cute.edu.tw

Y. Karasawa
Kanagawa University, Yokohama, Japan
e-mail: karasawa-y@h09.itscom.net

X. Liu (ed.), *Environmental Sustainability in Asian Logistics and Supply Chains*,
https://doi.org/10.1007/978-981-13-0451-4_4

is setting a reasonable price for their customers, as the present amount is only regulated by the weight of the goods, when in actuality, the distance should also be considered. Our proposal could be seen as a positive indication as to a probable solution for the firm.

Therefore, we will use the Gravity Model to show which method is the most productive for setting a delivery price, with the fairness cost sufficient for both customers and the firm. We will also clarify how the importance of the ℓk@ as a standard value will affect the firm's management and strategy.

2 Purpose of Research

- It is necessary to set the delivery unit price as an issue of supply chain management strategy, therefore, this research will not only look at the problem of delivery unit price, but also deal with the managerial side of business strategy.
- There are two methods to decide the unit price, one is the market price method, the other is the cost plus (+) α method. This research focuses on the unit price with cost plus α method. This case study is strong local style, and there are rarely competitive companies, also the delivery price is as the selling price, not as cost.
- When comparing the setting price of the firm, which is the method of cost plus, we have introduced weight, size, volume, and distance to set the price by zone, as it is also necessary to verify the overall delivery unit price.
- The key to developing the SCM strategy is to locate the optimum delivery center, which also effects the delivery price, as there is presently no research about linkage of price setting with the setting of an optimal location.
- It is necessary to synthesis the problem of setting the delivery unit price and propose the best one.

Figure 1 shows all proposes of this research, such as motivations, purposes, evaluation methods and characters. Therefore, we have come to understand that an optimal simulation brings to the industry concerned not only a delivery cost price setting, but also a price flexibility, price competitive capability, and strategic supply chain management transformation.

3 Content of Research

3.1 Process of Evaluation by Unit Price

Since the fact that the basic element of the research is to set the unit price by zone, therefore, it is necessary to make clear how important this can be in the whole unit price research. The concept of this research process is as shown in Fig. 2.

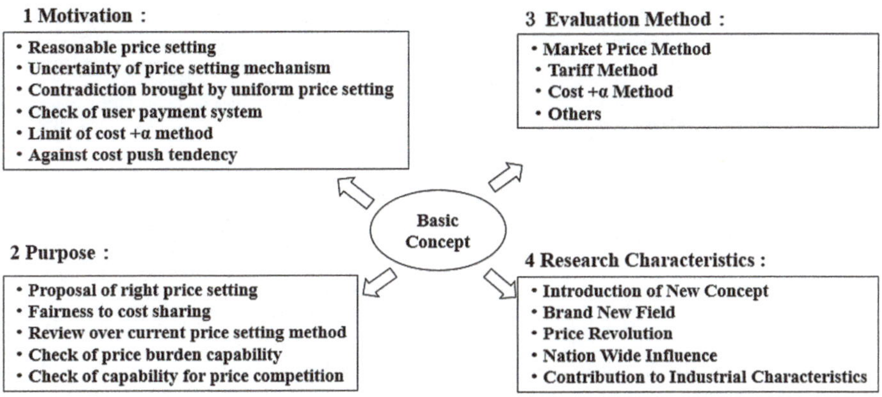

Fig. 1 Basic concept of this research. *Source* Angela Chen et al. [2], p. 136

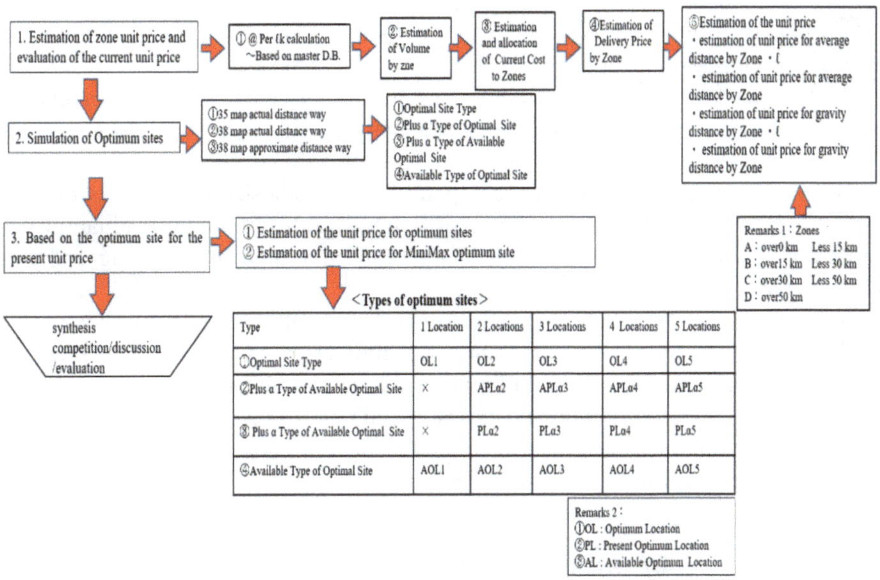

Fig. 2 Concept of the research process. *Source* Angela Chen et al. [1], p. 44

Firstly, to estimate the zone unit price and then to evaluate the current unit price, we collected one month of master data of a firm's unit price. There were about 20,000 customers, delivery transactions, and the running distance was approximately 30,000 km. From the data, we estimated the delivery volume by zone, then calculated the price by zone and goods, also estimating and calculating the average distance and gravity distance, and finally, the result of current ℓk@ is on the basis of an evaluation for the current unit price.

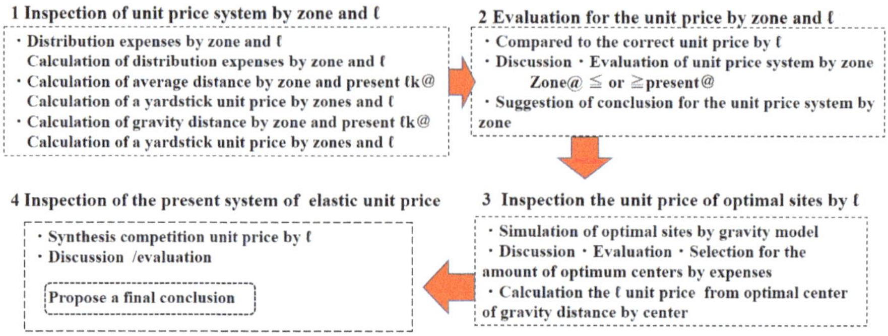

Fig. 3 The basic evaluation of unit price. *Source* Angela Chen et al. [1], p. 45

Secondly, to simulate the optimum location, we used the gravity model, and selected the area to divide into a suitable amount of several small areas by cities or counties, thereby making 41 models available by computer simulation. To evaluate the estimated results, the optimal locations were selected by the minimum and maximum optimum locations.

Thirdly, after selecting, we analyzed each optimal center, and then calculated from each center by the average distance and gravity distance. Moreover, we compared the tentative to current unit price by each zone, from each optimal center.

Fourthly, the stage of synthesis competition, to synthesize and discuss the current unit price, and unit price by zone of optimal center, the final evaluation was perceived. To suggest the maximum of the brand new unit price setting and possibility is as shown in Fig. 3.

At first, we distributed the expenses to verify the unit price system by zone and by liter base. Secondly, we distributed the unit price to calculate by liter; we evaluated the unit price by zone and by liter. There was also a consideration for the unit price by liter from optimum site types, brand new system of unit price elasticity or competitive unit price; as this can be seen as the direction of innovative business strategy in the near future.

3.2 *Inspection of the Zone Unit Price*

The research process of inspection for the unit price is as shown on bold line in Fig. 4. Concretely speaking, we used the existing customers' ordering data to produce the ordering data by each zone, we also estimated an absolute delivery distance (from delivery center to delivery place of customer) and average delivery distance (the real distance of delivery) from the present delivery system for estimating the unit price of each zone. On the other hand, to calculate the average distance and gravity distance, on the **premise** that the distance of the present zone and every 10 km' zone, secondly, assuming distance unit price, based on the present ℓk@, finally, we analyzed the suitability of the present ℓk@.

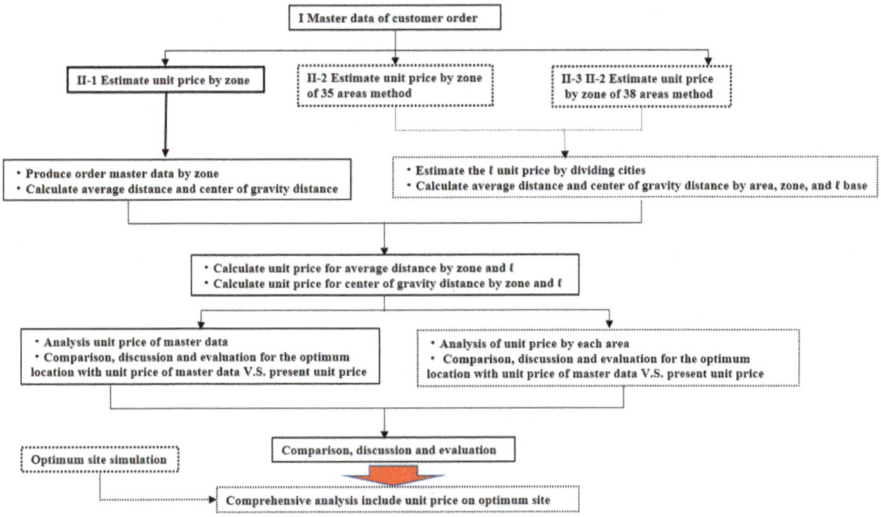

Fig. 4 The process of overall analysis by delivery unit price. *Source* Angela Chen et al. [2], p. 137

3.3 Process of Distributing Zone Price

The process of distributing by each zone and each liter was to distribute by the basic ratio of the master data of customer ordering. Firstly, we divided all delivery amounts into A, B, C, and D zones, then each zone time with each zone ratio, to calculate the total amount of each zone. Conversely, we estimated the average distance and the gravity distance within each zone. The present ℓk@ is as the standard to calculate for each unit price. Finally, we discuss the best delivery unit price to implement the evaluation (Figs. 5 and 6).

For the delivery cost and ℓk@, the total cost, the delivery cost and direct cost were respectively 0.539, 0.476 and 0.426 yen as shown in Fig. 7. It is of concern based on the ℓk@, from the cost and the distant viewpoint to estimate the unit price, and finally, we evaluate and discuss.

3.4 Basic Research Data

We used the mater data from the firm, to analyze, divide and separate them to produce the basic master data such as the ordering data of customers, distance by zone, for this research, as shown in Fig. 7.

We take into consideration the three types with this overall research. Initially, we summarized the basic numerical value from the basic master data given by the firm, as shown in Table 1. Furthermore, we analyzed and made the zone master data

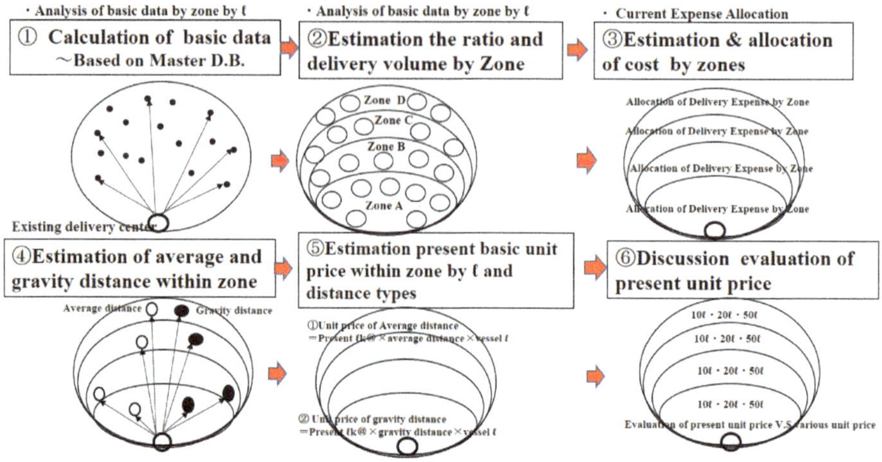

Fig. 5 Distribution delivery amount by zone and liter. *Source* Angela Chen et al. [1], p. 45

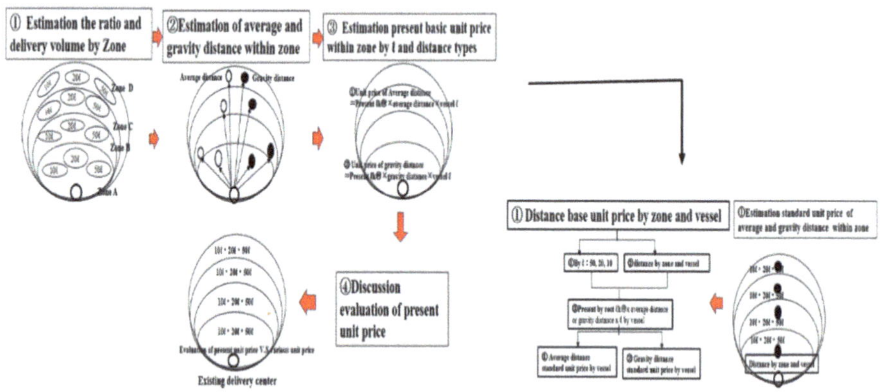

Fig. 6 The estimated method for unit price of present ℓk@ standard by liter by bottle. *Source* Angela Chen et al. [2], p. 137

from the original master data. There were 13,012 customers, and 19,040 transactions within a small area, as shown in Figs. 8 and 9. The master data of the total delivery cost means the sum of the delivery cost and a storage fee, the so-called delivery center fee. The delivery cost means the sum of the expenses between an indirect delivery fee and a direct delivery fee. The direct cost means the expense directly related to the delivery cost. Our research focuses on the unit price by zone. Due to the optimal locations directly related to the delivery cost, we will discuss the delivery unit price for this delivery center fee.

The process of calculating the cost and unit price is as follows; there are 10 steps (Table 2). Firstly, to show the character and unit price of each zone, the distributed

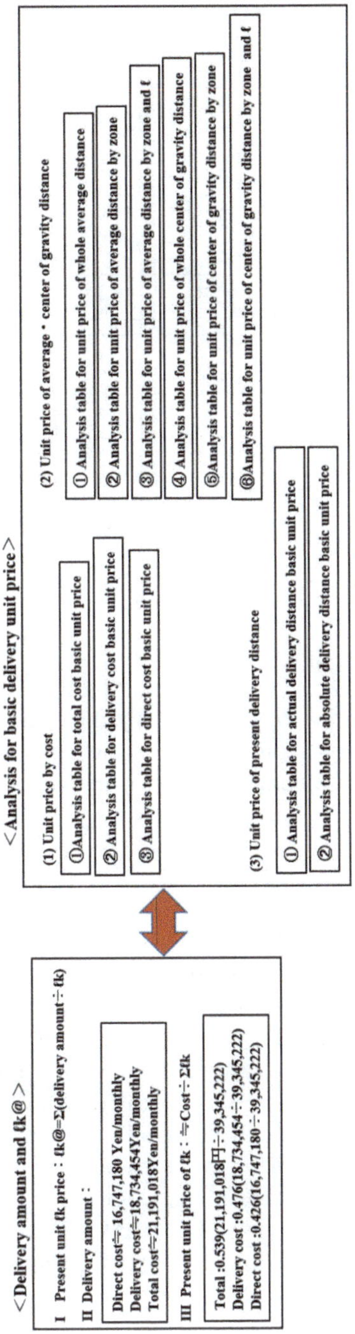

Fig. 7 Basic analysis of ℓ@. *Source* Angela Chen et al. [2], p. 138

Table 1 Basic data

1 Master Data

- Delivery Transactions : 19,040
- Customers : 13,012
- Mileage : 29,036km
- Total delivery distance : 2,052,629km
- Total Cost : 21,191,018Yen/Month
- Delivery Cost : 18,734,454Yen/Month
- Direct Cost : 16,747,180Yen/Month
- Present Price : Fix delivery fee/time
  - 10ℓ : 260Yen(ℓ@26Yen)
  - 20ℓ : 520Yen (ℓ@26Yen)
  - 50ℓ : 635Yen (ℓ@12.7Yen)
- Expenses : Omit
- Present Center : 1 Place

2 Basic Data

- Distance by Zone

(Present)	**(Approximate Distance)**
A : 0km<15km or less	0km<10km or less
B : 15km<30km or less	10km<20km or less
C : 30km<50km or less	20km<30km or less
D : over 50km	over 30km

- Present ℓk Unit price≒Cost÷Σℓk
  - Total Cost : 0.539(21,191,018÷39,345,222)
  - Delivery Cost : 0.478(18,734,454÷39,345,222)
  - Direct Cost : 0.426(16,747,180÷39,345,222)

3 Distance Master Data

Zone	bottle (ℓ)	Unit Price	ℓ@	Zone Distance<15km<30km<50km>over 50km				<10km<20km<30km> over 30km	
				Present Delivery		Present Zone Actual Distance Method		Approximate Distance method (10km different by Zone)	
				Absolute distance	Average Distance	Average Distance	Center of Gravity Distance	Average Distance	Center of Gravity Distance
A	10	260	26	8	9	5.63	7.08	3.79	5.12
	20	520	26	11	11	7.07	6.95	4.68	4.63
	50	635	12.5	10	10	6.84	6.94	4.51	4.51
Subtotal	41.2	610	14.6	11	10	6.90	6.94	4.55	4.53
B	10	260	26	22	22	22.00	22.00	0	0
	20	520	26	30	33	20.72	22.48	13.80	14.02
	50	635	12.5	32	31	21.01	21.00	14.47	14.36
Subtotal	42.3	612	14.3	32	32	20.94	20.94	14.32	14.32
C	10	260	26	40	40	40.30	40.30	28.69	26.89
	20	520	26	45	49	38.15	37.78	24.17	23.93
	50	635	12.5	52	51	35.99	35.62	23.48	23.36
Subtotal	39.1	606	15.2	49	50	36.93	36.02	23.73	23.45
D	10	260	26	64	64	64.05	64.05	42.09	42.09
	20	520	26	69	80	63.80	63.68	41.52	41.69
	50	635	12.5	79	81	63.19	63.03	40.38	40.38
Subtotal	31.6	583	17.7	72	80	63.60	63.28	41.14	40.88
(base Subtotal	10	260	26	46	43	45.06	64.05	30.83	26.86
	20	520	26	18	18	13.62	63.68	9.32	7.94
	50	635	12.5	15	15	10.26	63.03	7.02	7.00
Total	41.1	610	14.6	16	16	11.25	63.28	7.70	7.14
Zone A	41.2	610	14.6	11	10	6.90	6.94	4.55	4.53
Zone B	42.3	612	14.3	32	32	20.94	20.94	14.32	14.32
Zone C	39.1	606	15.2	49	50	36.93	36.02	23.73	23.45
Zone D	31.6	583	17.7	72	80	63.60	63.28	41.14	40.88
Total	41.1	610	14.6	16	16	11.25	10.43	7.70	7.14

Remarks:
①Average distance is calculated from master data.
②Gravity distance is calculated from latitude and longitude with the center of delivery amounts.

method by zone and ℓ, and the ℓk unit price by direct cost. Moreover, after calculating the optimal locations, combined with the unit price by using the ℓk@ (ℓ based unit price), then those numerical values are based on the data of the firm.

3.5 *Character of Zone*

To analyze the character of the zone by the distribution of the customers, delivery amount, and ℓk (liter and kilometer).

Primarily, to analyze the distribution, there are total of 13,012 customers, on the A zones area, and there are 10,519 customers for 80.8% (Fig. 10). Secondly, there are 1766 customers on the B zones area, for 13.6%, there are 354 customers, on the C zone for 2.7%, and on the D zone there are 373 for 2.9%. The figures on zone C and zone D are smaller, but zone D is in the wide area.

For the distribution of the delivery amount, zone A is for 81.8%, zone B is for 14.5%, zone C is for 2.2%, and zone D is for 1.5%. The demand for a residential building or an urbane side is more than the city side (Fig. 11).

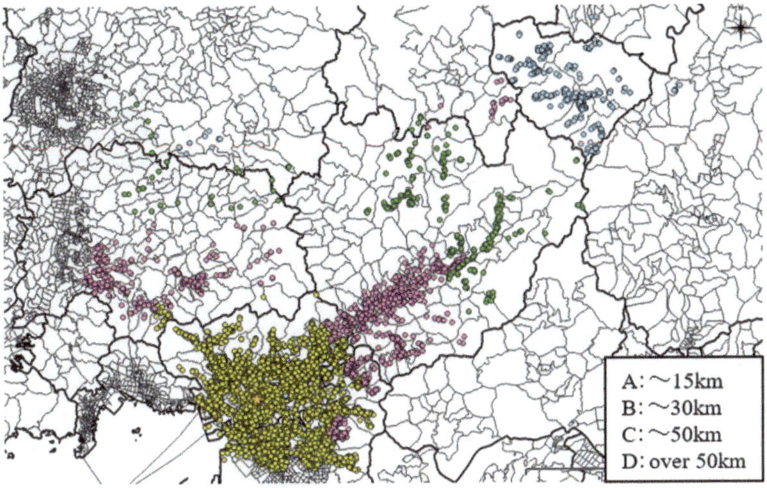

Fig. 8 Zone Customers by real distance

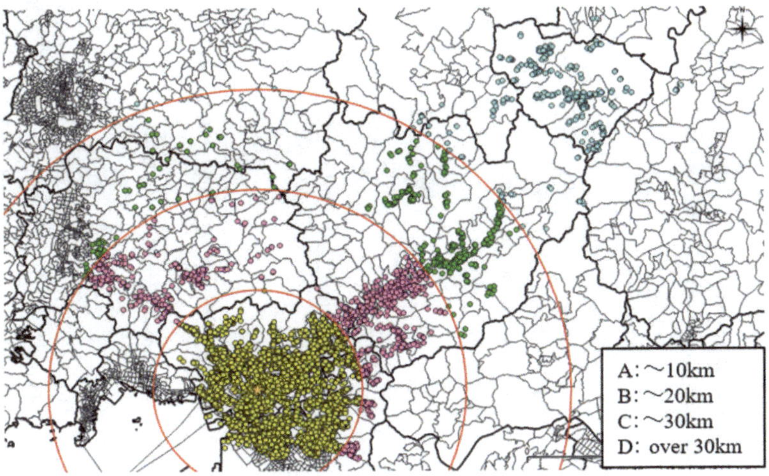

Fig. 9 Zone Customers by approximate distance

Table 2 The process of calculating the cost and unit price

1	Distribution by zone and ℓ = cost × ratio by zone and ℓ					
	Cost:					
	Total cost = 21,000,000 yen/month (delivery cost + Storage cost)					
	Delivery cost = 18,000,000 yen/month (direct delivery cost + delivery storage cost)					
	Direct cost = 16,747,180 yen/month (delivery cost = delivery fee)					
		Delivery fee				
		10 ℓ: 300 kg × 26 yen/kg = 7800 yen				
		20 ℓ: 163,860 kg × 26 yen/kg = 4260,360 yen				
		50 ℓ: 982,600 kg × 12.7 yen/kg = 12,479,020 yen				
		Total delivery income: 16,747,180 yen				
2	ℓk unit price = cost × ratio by zone and ℓ ÷ number of Bottles by each zone					
	Ex: direct cost standard of zone A					
	Bottles	① Number of bottles	② Ratio of total	③ Σℓk	④ Basic ℓk unit price ③ ÷ ①	⑤ Amount ② × 16,747,180
	10ℓ	12	0.00355	1395	49.5	594
	20ℓ	6650	4.14298	1630,066	104.3	693,833
	50ℓ	16,101	53.00572	20,855,220	551.3	8,876,964
	Subtotal (ℓ)	22,763	57.15225	22,486,681	420.5	9,571,391
	Total (direct cost)	27,875	100.0	39,345,222	–	16,747,180
3	Unit price of direct cost = cost × ratio by zone and ℓ ÷ number of bottles of each zone					
	Ex: direct cost standard of zone A					
	① Bottles	② Number of bottles	③ Delivery amount	④ Ratio of total	⑤ Basic amount ④ × direct cost	⑥ Direct cost basic unit price④ ÷ ②
	10ℓ	12	120	0.010	1752	142
	20ℓ	6650	133,000	11.598	1,942,320	292
	50ℓ	16,101	805,050	70.202	11,756,878	730
	Subtotal (ℓ)	22,763	938,170	81.810	13,700,950	602
	Total (direct cost)	27,875	1,146,760	100.0	16,747,180	–

(continued)

Table 2 (continued)

	Remarks	Cost standard of unit price does not take into account the distance, due to the delivery amount by zone, so unit price by bottle is nothing to do with the zone, is fixed price.
		The average unit price of zones are zone A is 602 yen, zone B is 618 yen, zone C is 572 yen, zone D is 461 yen
4	Standard of ℓk unit price	
		Total cost standard of ℓk unit price: 0.539 (21,191,018 yen ÷ 39,345,222) Delivery cost standard of ℓk unit price: 0.476 (18,734,454 yen ÷ 39,345,222) Direct cost standard of ℓk unit price: 0.426 (16,747,180 yen ÷ 39,345,222)
5	Standard of distance unit price	
	Formulation:	Present ℓk unit price by cost × distance × bottles by ℓ(10ℓ, 20ℓ, 50ℓ)
	(1) Average distance standard of unit price	① Average distance standard of unit price of total cost: 0.539 × Average distance × bottle(ℓ) ② Average distance standard of unit price of delivery cost: 0.476 × Average distance × bottle(ℓ) ③ Average distance standard of unit price of direct cost: 0.426 × Average distance × bottle(ℓ)
	(2) Gravity distance standard of unit price	① Gravity distance standard of unit price of total cost: 0.539 × Average distance × bottle(ℓ) ② Gravity distance standard of unit price of delivery cost: 0.476 × Average distance × bottle(ℓ) ③ Gravity distance standard of unit price of direct cost: 0.426 × Average distance × bottle(ℓ)
6	Absolute distance and delivery distance	
	Absolute distance: the real distance from delivery center to the place of customers Absolute average distance: Σ (the real distance of the delivery place ÷ the number of delivery customers) Delivery distance: Σ (the distance from delivery center to delievery place × ordering times) ÷ Σordering times Delivery averagedistance: Σ (the distance of deliverying places ÷ the number of delivery customers)	
7	The method of 50ℓ standard unit price	
	10ℓ unit price: 260 yen ≒ (625 yen × 10ℓ ÷ 50ℓ) × 2–250 yen 10ℓ unit price: 500 yen ≒ (625 yen × 20ℓ ÷ 50ℓ) × 2–520 yen	
8	The calculation of unit price by gravity distance of the optimum site	
	Calculation of unit price = total amount of delivery center ÷ average bottles Average ℓ = (10ℓ × 10ℓ (total bottles) + 20ℓ × 20ℓ (total bottles) + 50ℓ × 50ℓ (total bottles) ÷ (10ℓ total bottles + 20ℓ total bottles + 50ℓ total bottles) Average ℓ bottles = Σℓ ÷ average ℓ	

(continued)

Table 2 (continued)

9	The optimum site of the minimum fee of delivery center for calculating various cost
	The best minimum fee: 38Map real distance reasonable type of 3 places An exchange rate of total cost: 0.591 ≒ 12,515,717 yen ÷ 21,191,018 yen An exchange rate of delivery cost: 0.668 ≒ 12,515,717 yen ÷ 18,734,454 yen An exchange rate of direct cost: 0.747 ≒ 12,515,717 yen ÷ 16,747,180 yen
10	Formulation of ℓk basic unit price(ℓkB@)
	ℓk Basic unit price (ℓkB@) = (Ziℓjk ÷ Σℓk) × Ci............ ① ℓk@Basic unit price (ℓk@B@) = (Σℓk ÷ Ci) × Ziℓj............② Average distance basic unit price (AkB@) = ℓkB@ × ℓj × AKB...........③ Gravity distance basic unit price (GKB@) = ℓkB@ × ℓj × GKB...........④ But, b@: basic unit price, Ziℓjk: distance by zone and bottle liter size, ℓk: ℓk by zone and bottle size base, Ci: each type of cost amount, ℓkB@: basic unit price of liter kilometer (ℓk), AKB: Average distance, GKB: Gravity distance

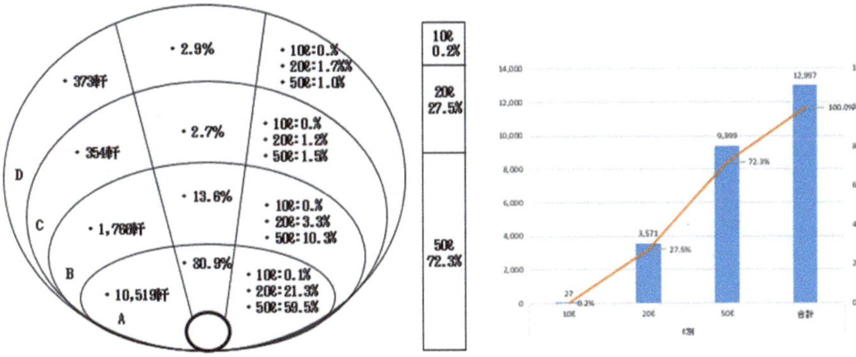

Fig. 10 Analysis of distributed customers

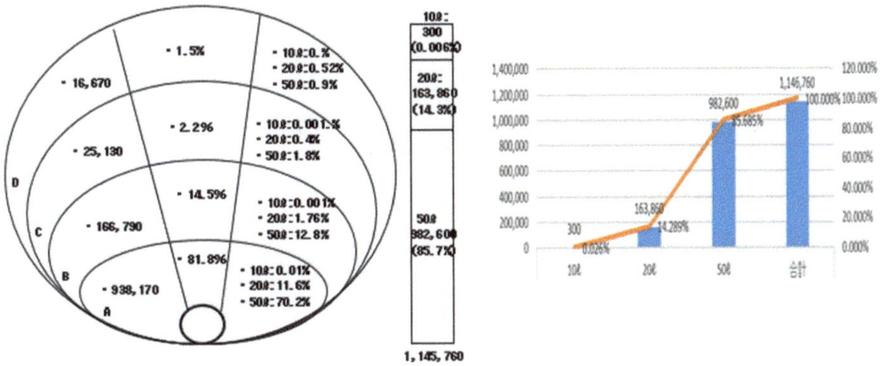

Fig. 11 Analysis of delivery amount by bottle

From the $\Sigma\ell k$ point of view, zone A is for 57.2%, zone B is for 30.6%, zone C is for 6.8%, and zone D is for 5.4%. It should be noted that the number of ℓk in the urbane area is bigger than the city side (Fig. 12).

3.6 Summary

The summary of this study for the unit price settings are as follows;

I Distribution Standard Unit Price: As $\Sigma\ell k$ construction ratio standard to distribute the amount, the determinate amount divided by order amount, and the distributed unit price is surmised.

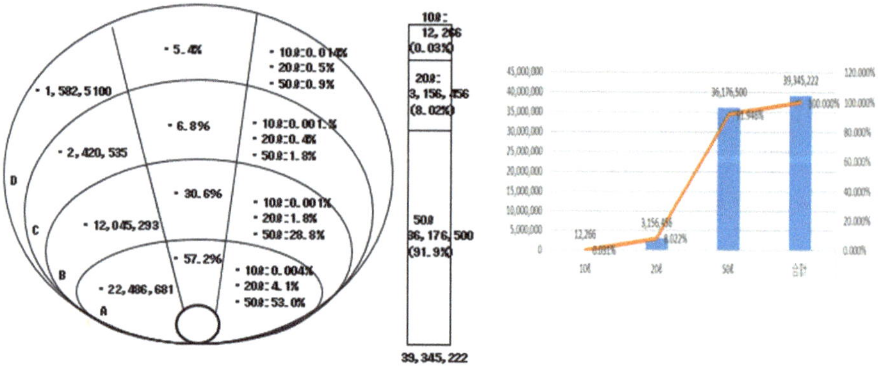

Fig. 12 Analysis of distributed $\Sigma\ell K$ by zone

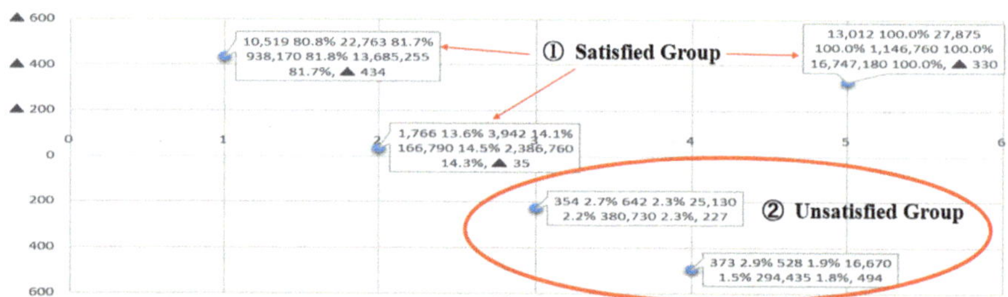

Zone	Vessel (ℓ)	Unit price	Unit price(ℓ)	Divided zone : <15km<30km<50km>Over		Difference of present delivery									
				Present Delivery		Difference of Abosolute distance unit price	Difference of Average distance unit price	Customers	%	Vessel	%	Delivery amount (L)	%	Amount	%
				Abosolute distance	Average distance										
ZoneA	41.2	610	14.6	11	10	▲ 417	▲ 434	10,519	80.8%	22,763	81.7%	938,170	81.8%	13,685,255	81.7%
ZoneB	42.3	612	14.3	32	32	▲ 35	▲ 35	1,766	13.6%	3,942	14.1%	166,790	14.5%	2,386,760	14.3%
ZoneC	39.1	606	15.2	49	50	210	227	354	2.7%	642	2.3%	25,130	2.2%	380,730	2.3%
ZoneD	31.6	583	17.7	72	80	386	494	373	2.9%	528	1.9%	16,670	1.5%	294,435	1.8%
Total	41.1	610	14.6	16	16	▲ 330	▲ 330	13,012	100.0%	27,875	100.0%	1,146,760	100.0%	16,747,180	100.0%

Fig. 13 Distribution map of absolute distance unit price by zone of customers vessels delivery volume amount

II Cost $\ell k@$ by Cost: The $\ell k@$ by cost equal (=) each cost divide (÷) present $\Sigma\ell k$.

III Present Standard $\ell k@$: Distance times (×) present standard unit price.

However, as the distance standard master data, there were two types of the present delivery distances, one was the absolute distance (shown in Fig. 13), and the other was an average of the total delivery distance.

The analysis is about the present delivery of the absolute distance unit price standard that should not only be taken into consideration for the unsatisfied group, but also needs a strategy for the satisfied group as well.

General speaking, the center of a city will have a well-infrastructure city gas, as the need for the propane gas decreases naturally, so there is a potential need to shift the business to the countryside, so it should also take into consideration a

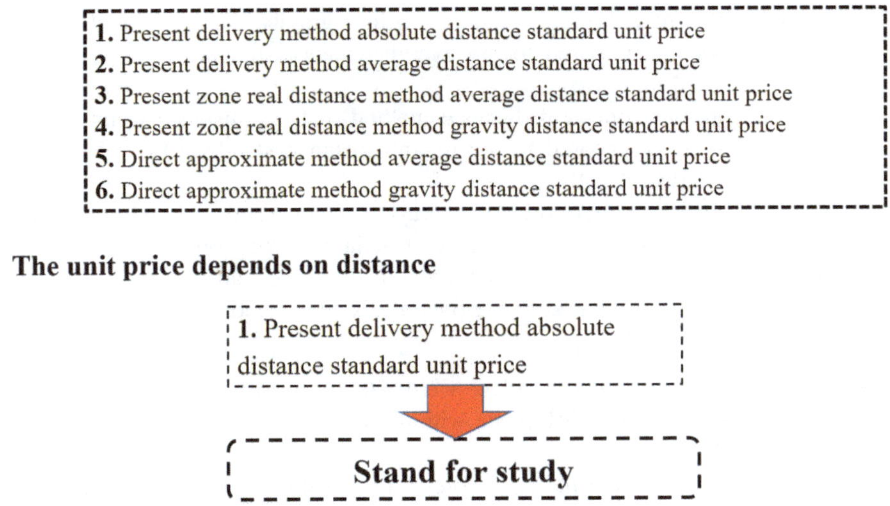

Fig. 14 Six ways to calculate the unit price

depopulated region. Strategically, it is an economical phenomenon antinomy, as we understand that it is problematic of the strategies or tactics to overcome the antinomy.

There were also two types of each of the 38 groups by real distance and direct approximate distance for the present delivery distances, which were the average distance and gravity distance. Therefore there are six ways to calculate the unit price (shown in Fig. 14),

Suggestion I:

As the standard unit price, we suggest the ℓk@ system.

Suggestion II:

This research suggested that the real distance method of gravity distance standard unit price of present zone was the best unit price setting, and should be taken into consideration in the near future, due to the fairness setting unit price by the distance and delivery amount.

Moreover, the results of ranking difference of each unit price is as follows; due to the ℓk@ being common with all methods, the decision depends on the distance, therefore, the rankings are as follows;

First place	direct approximate method gravity distance standard unit price ~ compared to the overall distance standard 7.14 km standard unit: 1
Second place	direct approximate method average distance standard unit price ~ compared to the overall distance standard 7.70 km compared unit: 1.08

Third place	present zone real distance method gravity distance standard unit price ~ compared to the overall distance standard 10.43 km compared unit: 1.61
Fourth place	present zone real distance method average distance standard unit price ~ compared to the overall distance standard 11.25 km compared unit: 1.8
Fifth place	present delivery method average distance standard unit price ~ compared to the overall distance standard 16 km compared unit: 2.49
Sixth place	present delivery method absolute distance standard unit price ~ compared to the overall distance standard 16 km compared unit: 2.49

(Remarks) fifth place and sixth place were actually from fifth place versus sixth place to eighth place versus fifth place within 13 short distance items.

Suggestion III:

This research also clarifies the price competition. When taking into consideration the potential needs of the customers, of which vary widely, the result of optimal location simulation, the rethinking of the unit price setting strategy, and then providing the best suggestion. Therefore, the price competition is as follows;

It was very clear for the present direct cost and the present unit price, the minimum was 330 yen ~ the maximum was 485 yen. Namely, the overall price competition was concretely as following the numerical values. Due to its adopted total price, the unit price was not by liter, but was reserved for overall.

- Present delivery method absolute distance standard unit price 16 km ▲330 yen
- Present delivery method average distance standard unit price 16 km ▲330 yen
- Present zone real distance method average distance standard unit price 10.43 km ▲412 yen
- Present zone real distance method gravity distance standard unit price 11.25 km ▲427 yen
- Direct approximate method average distance standard unit price 7.7 km ▲475 yen
- Direct approximate method gravity distance standard unit price 7.14 km ▲485 yen

4 Results

The drastic reform for unit price of the present delivery system is as follows;

- Market price system
- Tariff (route area price) system
- Cost plus α system
- Others.

This study investigated the delivery unit price of the same product within the same industrial business region, due to it being an area monopoly business type; we were not able to discover the competitor situation. As for the tariff (route, area price), according to the Japanese Ministry of Land, Infrastructure, Transport and Tourism and the deregulation for the Motor Truck Transportation Business Act on the Internet. The truck business was intended to put service into practice, and provide a more efficient business model adapted to meet the needs of the users, a fare and fee should be reported in advance, and thereby abolishing the operation area system, with the Acts being modified in April, 2003. Therefore, it should be noted that there were no tariff systems that had existed before. In addition, there was a tariff system in the 2001 version of a car built at that time, but it was not fitted to this milk run type (delivery route), so we only took the cost plus α system to solve the problem.

The summary of the analyzed results are as follows;

- The mono unit price by present bottle (vessel), this means one of the cost plus α type unit price strategy, but it was not appropriate.
- The distributed unit price was to distribute the ratio of the delivery amount with the present unit price, due to the estimate of the unit price by bottle, it was possible to compare simply to the present unit price, however, it was not the innovative unit price, as this was the basic extension theory of the present unit price.
- When we talked about the cost of the ℓk@, there were three types of cost, which were the direct cost, delivery cost, and total cost. The direct cost was the basic cost of the present unit price setting, the delivery cost was the cost related to delivery, and the total cost was the cost of the basic simulation for the optimum sites.

Therefore, if the distributed cost had been fixed with the distance yardstick, the result of the estimated unit price would only be in proportion to the cost. Namely, the direct cost is as a yardstick to compare to the present unit price.

- The present ℓk@ yardstick delivery unit price was the distance cost concept, and it was fair to consumers as well as being appropriate to the theory of the firm. Moreover, due to its links to an amplitude of competitive prices; it shows objectively operational numerical offers of the firm.
- As to the amplitude of the competitive unit price, it exists in the numerical theory, whether it puts it into practice or not, its dependent on the operation site, which was quite ambiguity.
- Except for the potential price competition, that was very important for the Supply Chain Management strategy to apply the simulation of optimum sites, and to innovate the management of the firm.

It is not only for the competition of the delivery unit price, but also for dealing with the drastic business operation. We will suggest the importance and necessity for the structural innovation at the end.

5 Conclusion

This study has suggested the best price setting for the home delivery field. The case study, as the problem of area delivery type was in the setting of the unit price by only the delivery amount (vessel) without considering the distance. Here, we have taken into account the delivery distance for the delivery unit price setting. On a piece type delivery unit price, which we had set by weight standard, and then set the distance by zone. The ℓk@ was as a yardstick, the brand new unit price setting method had appeared and we finally made the inspection.

We have suggested multi-methods that setting the unit price should be considerate of weight, distance, specifications, and so on. There are three denoted types; I Distribution yardstick unit price, II Cost ℓk@ by cost, and III Present yardstick ℓk@.

Our suggestions are as follows;

First of all, we proposed the ℓk@ system as a yardstick unit price.

Secondly, we suggested that here it reflects the fairness by considering the distance and delivery amount, and the present zone real distance method gravity distance standard unit price could well be the unit price setting method in the future. Due to the ℓk@ being common, the decision was dependent on the distance, the result of difference for all the unit price setting methods is as follows;

First place	direct approximate method gravity distance standard unit price ∼ compared to the overall distance standard 7.14 km standard unit: 1
Second place	direct approximate method average distance standard unit price ∼ compared to the overall distance standard 7.70 km compared unit: 1.08
Third place	present zone real distance method gravity distance standard unit price ∼ compared to the overall distance standard 10.43 km compared unit: 1.61
Fourth place	present zone real distance method average distance standard unit price ∼ compared to the overall distance standard 11.25 km compares unit: 1.8
Fifth place	present delivery method average distance standard unit price ∼ compared to the overall distance standard 16 km compared unit: 2.49
Sixth place	present delivery method absolute distance standard unit price ∼ compared to the overall distance standard 16 km compared unit: 2.49

Finally, this research had made clear the price competition, but we shall take into consideration the variations in needs as the main reason for potential requirements in the future. We have therefore suggested that the strategic price setting should also look at the result of the optimum sites simulation.

References

1. Angela, Y. Y. Chen, Sato, T., Karasawa, Y., Wakabayashi, K., & Toyotani, J. (2016a). A Basic Research on a Delivery Cost Settings to End Users Supported by the Optimum Site Selection Model, Indonesia, ICLS 2016, p. 47. Journal of the Japan Society of Logistics Systems, Vol. 15, No. 1, March, 2016
2. Angela, Y. Y. Chen, Sato, T., Karasawa, Y., Toyotani, J., & Wakabayashi, K. (2016). A Basic Research on a Delivery Cost, the Procedure of 19th Nihon Logistics System Association, pp. 136–138, June, 2016. 15.09.2009.

A Systematic Literature Review on Sustainability and Disruptions in Supply Chains

Ilias Vlachos, Luisa Huaccho Huatuco, Guljana ShakirUllah and Adriana Roa-Atkinson

Abstract The purpose of this paper is to provide the state-of-the-art of the theme: 'sustainability and disruptions in supply chains'. The main motivation for the research was to identify the level of connectivity between these apparent separate topics and identify gaps for carrying out future research. A systematic literature review was carried out, searching the World of Science database, 76 papers were selected for analysis. The main database consulted was Web of Science for the period 2000–2016. The articles were classified according to their year of publication, country/region focus of study, citation, journal name, for example. Then the tallies of each group were collected into a MS Excel file in order to do a series of analyses, plot graphs and make comparisons. The findings point out that the *International Journal of Production Economics* leads the way in terms of publishing work on this theme. Most of the published work comes from North-America and Europe, however China also features highly in the ranks. The 'sustainability' literature included topics of: positive relation between sustainable supply chain management and economic and environmental performance. The disruptions literature included topics of: information sharing, inventory management and multiple suppliers. Some scarce combination of sustainability and disruptions was found.

Keywords Sustainability · Disruptions · Supply chains

I. Vlachos (✉) · G. ShakirUllah · A. Roa-Atkinson
Leeds University Business School, University of Leeds, Woodhouse Lane,
Leeds LS2 9JT, UK
e-mail: I.Vlachos@leeds.ac.uk

G. ShakirUllah
e-mail: gul.su1992@gmail.com

A. Roa-Atkinson
e-mail: arcatkinson@yahoo.co.uk

L. Huaccho Huatuco · A. Roa-Atkinson
The York Management School, University of York, Freboys Lane,
York YO10 5GD, UK
e-mail: luisa.huatuco@york.ac.uk

X. Liu (ed.), *Environmental Sustainability in Asian Logistics and Supply Chains*,
https://doi.org/10.1007/978-981-13-0451-4_5

1 Introduction

Disruptions can have devastating effects on individuals, organisations and the wider economy which is why it is imperative that organisations evaluate their supply chain (SC) vulnerabilities. Though disruptions are varying in definition, Wilson [84] defines them as events which disturb the flow of resources in a SC, subsequently leading to an unexpected pause in the movement of goods.

Unexpected disruptions (UD), specifically low frequency and high impact UD can have substantial effect on business, environment and society at large. With the rise of a globalized economy, supply chains are becoming increasingly complex and interconnected with global sourcing on a rise [32].

Mitroff and Alpaslan [3] found, in a study conducted over two decades that from the fortune 500 companies, that only between 5 and 25% organisations were prepared to deal with disruptions. Furthermore, as this area of research is still to mature, there is little evidence of research which has combined the effects of disruptions with the three sustainability metrics: economic, environmental and social. Therefore, this paper seeks to add to research area by combining these two topics.

2 Methods

The systematic literature review methodology was employed [6]. The Web of Science database was searched with inclusion of 3* and 4* ABS journals [23]. The search term (Disruption OR disaster OR emergenc* OR cris*) AND (Sustainab* OR green OR environ* OR resilience OR robustness) AND (Measur* OR manag* OR quant*) AND (Supply OR network OR chain) was used between the years 2000–2016.

This search retrieved 1465 papers which, when refined into the research domain of social sciences resulted in 525 papers. The search was further refined into the research area of operations research management which produced 167 papers, operations research management was the most applicable grouping in the Web of Science for this paper. After this stage, the abstracts and relevant titles were examined to decide their suitability with the paper which led to 76 papers academic peer-reviewed journal articles from 28 different journals and conference papers which reflected great significance to our research paper (See Appendix). The use of conference papers demonstrates that this is a developing topic. See Fig. 1.

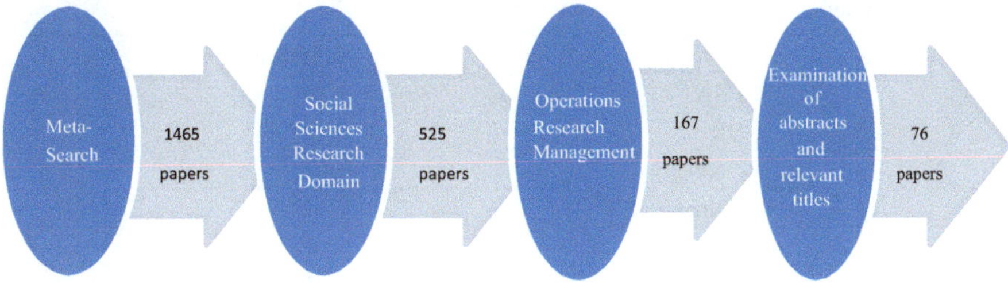

Fig. 1 Screening methodology

3 Findings

Table 1 illustrates the top ten journals where papers regarding UD and sustainability have been published. The *International Journal of Production Economics* leads the way with 16 publications, more than five times the 10th journal, i.e. *Transportation Research.* Table 2 represents the geographic variety of scholars' affiliations. The concentration of affiliations is primarily in North America (57%), followed by Europe and Australia (33%). However, publications from scholars in China, Malaysia, Philippines and Iran (10%) show that this topic is not only of interest to the Western world. Figure 2 represents keywords used by authors with risk management and SCM gaining 37 hits and 36 hits respectively while GSCM only gains 11 hits.

Table 1 Ranking of journals by number of publications

	Journal title	Publications
1	International Journal of Production Economics	16
2	Journal of Operations Management	5
3	Production and Operations Management	5
4	OMEGA—International Journal of Management Sciences	4
5	International Journal of Physical Distribution and Logistics Management	4
6	MIT Sloan Management Review	4
7	International Journal of Operations and Production Management	4
8	International Journal of Production Research	4
9	European Journal of Operational Research	3
10	Transportation Research Parts B and E	3

Table 2 Geography of scholars' affiliations by first author

	Country	Publications
1	USA	39
2	UK	8
3	Germany	7
4	China	5
5	Canada	4
6	France	3
7	Austria	2
8	Australia	1
9	Poland	1
10	Malaysia	1
11	Philippines	1
12	Switzerland	1
13	Iran	1
14	Portugal	1
15	The Netherlands	1

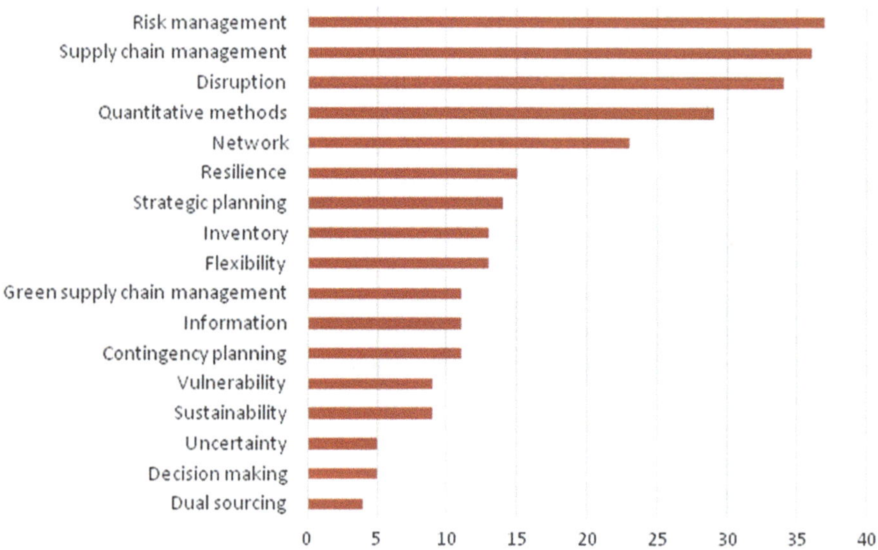

Fig. 2 Frequency of keywords used by authors

3.1 *Disruption*

Research on disruption has shifted from a short-term approach emphasising the requirement to prevent and protect an organisation against disruptions to a

Table 3 Techniques of responding to large-scale UD

Authors	Collaboration	Multiple suppliers	Information sharing	Management culture	Inventory management	Decision making
Christopher and Peck [26]	X	X	X	X	X	X
Kleindorfer and Saad [43]	X	X	X		X	X
Tang [70]	X	X				
Knemeyer et al. [46]	X	X	X	X	X	X
Schmitt and Singh [60]					X	
Chopra and Sodhi [24]		X			X	

longer-term approach, which identifies disruptions and fortifies the organisations preparedness, so that it can build resilience against these disruption risks [5].

Table 3 demonstrates the different techniques studied by researchers of responding to large-scale UD. As supply chains are becoming increasingly interconnected due to factors, such as globalisation, the effects of disruptions are increasingly extensive and can go beyond the immediate area of disruption stretching across an entire supply network. However, the entire supply network may not be visible to an organisation, therefore reducing the complexity in the supply network is ever more challenging [8, 49, 86]. There is a thorough investigation of disruptions in the literature and researchers have suggested strategies based on the source of risk, e.g. Kleindorfer and Saad [43] state that risk may arise from problems in coordinating supply and demand or from a disruption to normal events. In devising optimal strategies, studies establish strategies based on the risk status of an organisations e.g. risk-averse or risk-taking. Conceptual frameworks suggested by Kleindrofer and Saad [43] and Christopher and Peck [26] show the stages in preparing an organisation to deal with UD, such as classifying risks and documentation of procedures.

Researchers have advanced on these conceptual frameworks by developing quantitative and qualitative techniques to understand how an organisation can respond to UD, e.g. through information sharing between organisations across the entire SC for increasing resilience towards disruption [7, 27, 33, 34, 72]. Kleindorfer and Saad [43] state information sharing among partners in the SC is crucial for successful preparation and response to potential disasters, they suggest the level of investment contributed towards reliable information gathering and sharing should be based on the probability of a disruption occurring and the predicted losses if investment into information sharing was not made. Although researchers stress the importance of information sharing by stating that the unwillingness to share information causes defects in existing business models, the technicalities, such as the network through which information should be transmitted, received and stored are either limited or non-existent [2, 9].

Knemeyer et al. [46] propose a four-step proactive framework which is identified as an extension of Kleindorfer and Saad's [46] framework. Although these frameworks provide a practical guidance for organisations to improve their preparedness for an UD, they will require extensive use of resources therefore applying them in industry may be problematic as a Zurich Insurance [11] report reveals over 55% of organisations do not regularly monitor risk in their SC due to lack of time.

3.2 *Sustainability*

The literature on sustainability has shifted from being viewed as a trade-off between expenses and economic growth to being vital for an organisation in order to grow and remain competitive [4, 44]. While there has been growing research on the notion of SSCM and increasing pressures on organisations to integrate the three sustainability metrics: economic, environmental and social into their operations, little emphasis has been given to sustainability in relation to disruptions [44]. Many researchers [10, 17, 29, 88] recognise the economic and environmental aspect of sustainability while little regard is given to the social aspect. They all believe that organisations competitiveness can be improved through its internal strategy by cost reduction through the implementation of sustainable strategies. Bowen et al. [17] developed a model which included a two-phase survey conducted with public limited companies in the UK, they state that improving the 'literacy' of the purchasing personnel in an organisation can improve an organisations economic and environmental stance through the reduction of material use and waste which ultimately reducing. Adding to this, Cruz and Matsypura [29] develop a framework in their study which evidences that improved decision-making through taking into account sustainability can reduce an organisations transaction costs and waste.

3.3 *Combining Both Disruptions and Sustainability in SCs*

Although combining SCD and SCS is scarce in the literature, few researchers have recently attempted to combine both topics [1, 5, 36, 39, 56]. The papers by Hofmann et al. [39] and Gonzalez et al. [36] are published in journals whereas the remaining papers were published at conferences indicating that this topic is in its early stages. Rush et al. [56] investigate the rebuilding of sustainable communities for families and children post disruption and provide recommendations such as making assembling disaster kits which include necessities such as water and a flashlight, providing 'community safe houses' where residents can go if bad weather arises and assigning different roles to local communities if a disruption occurs. Although this paper provides recommendations for communities in case of disruptions, it has not been backed up by quantifiable evidence or testing of any sort such as simulation to check whether it would be practical in theory. Hofmann et al. [39] study how SC disruptions can arise from sustainability issues, for example, some of Apple's suppliers in China have almost destructive working conditions for their employees which presented Apple with a wave of negative publicity.

4 Discussion and Conclusions

Although the sustainability agenda is gaining traction in many corners in Operations and SCs, evidence of fully sustainable implementation (i.e. all dimensions given equal importance) is still work in progress. Furthermore, scholars and practitioners alike are in need of going beyond the Triple Bottom Line in terms of measuring sustainability performance, so new models, frameworks and methodologies should be proposed to enthuse and achieve sustainability and resilience in SCs.

Some key findings are listed below:

- The literature on disruptions is more rigorously studied with prominent frameworks provided by researchers such as Kleindorfer and Saad [43].
- Within the disruption literature, the focus of has been on using quantitative methods to investigate economic effects and service level of SC strategies in case of disruption with less emphasis on environmental and social dimensions.
- The literature regarding disruption is very much concentrated on research carried out in Western countries whereas the literature on sustainable SCM is more geographically diverse.

In concluding, this paper presents a systematic literature review that could be used for future research. Although the number of publications have steadily increased in the last few years for each separate topic, i.e. 'sustainability' and 'disruptions' in SC, there is still a gap in terms of publications combining both topics in mainstream operations and supply chain management publications. In terms of sustainability, the focus has been mainly on Economic and more recently on Environmental dimensions with less emphasis on the Social dimension. In terms of disruptions, the focus is on SCRM and various frameworks for organizations to address, mitigate and respond in the face of SC disruptions.

One of the limitations of this paper is that although a systematic literature review has been carried out, there may be publications which may have been missed out due to not being listed in Web of Science database. Moreover, the search term used may have not captured all possible synonymous terms by which scholars publish their work.

Future research avenues will consider pursuing the data collection of relevant case studies to better explore and understand the combined interaction between supply chain disruptions and sustainability. Furthermore, a survey questionnaire could be designed for managers to test some propositions deriving from the case studies.

References

1. Huaccho Huatuco, L., ShakirUllah, G., & Burgess, T. F. (2017). Supply Chain Major Disruptions and Sustainability metrics: A case study. In G. Campana, R. J. Howlett, R. Setchi, & B. Cimatti (Eds)., *Sustainable design and manufacturing 2017, smart innovations, systems and technologies* (Vol. 68, pp. 185–192). Berlin: Springer.
2. Lanza, G., Stricker, N., & Stoll, J. (2013). Innovative product-services for robust global supply chains—A viewpoint. In *Proceedings of the 17th Cambridge International Manufacturing Symposium* (14 p), Institute for Manufacturing, University of Cambridge, Cambridge, UK, 19–20 September 2013.
3. Mitroff, I., & Alpaslan, M. (2003). Preparing for evil. Harvard *Business Review.* Available from: https://hbr.org/2003/04/preparing-for-evil. Accessed on 13th June 2017
4. Pantouvakis, A., Vlachos, I., & Zervopoulos, P. D. (2017). Market orientation for sustainable performance and the inverted-U moderation of firm size: Evidence from the Greek shipping industry. *Journal of Cleaner Production, 165,* 705–720.
5. ShakirUllah, G., Huaccho Huatuco, L., & Burgess, T. F. (2014). A literature review of disruption and sustainability in supply chains. In R. Setchi, R. J. Howlett, M. Naim, & H. Seinz (Eds.), *Sustainable Design and Manufacturing 2014 Part 1, KES Transactions on Sustainable Design and Manufacturing, 1*(1), 500–511. Special Edition, Sustainable Design and Manufacturing. UK: Future Technology Press.
6. Tranfield, D., Denyer, D., & Smart, P. (2003). Towards a methodology for developing evidence-informed management knowledge by means of systematic review. *British Journal of Management, 14,* 207–222.
7. Vlachos, I. P. (2015). Applying lean thinking in the food supply chains: A case study. *Production Planning & Control, 26*(16), 1351–1367.
8. Vlachos, I. P. (2016). Reverse Logistics Capabilities impact on Firm Performance and the mediating role of business strategy. *International Journal of Logistics: Research and Applications*, pp. 424–442.
9. Vlachos, I. P., & Bourlakis, M. (2006). Supply Chain Collaboration between retailers and manufacturers: Do they trust each other? *Supply Chain Forum: An International Journal, 7* (1), 70–78.
10. Vlachos, I. P., & Malindretos, G. (2012). Market Access and Sustainability effects on regional performance: Evidence from the Messinian Region-Greece. *The Regional Science Inquiry Journal, IV*(3), 137–153.
11. Zurich Insurance. (2012). The Weakest Link: UK PLC's Supply chain. UK.

List of Articles Resulting from the Systematic Literature Review

12. Ambulkar, S., Blackhurst, J., & Grawe, S. (2015). Firm's resilience to supply chain disruptions: Scale development and empirical examination. *Journal of Operations Management, 33–34,* 111–122.
13. Azadeh, A., Atrchina, N., Salehia, V., & Shojaeia, H. (2013). Modelling and improvement of supply chain with imprecise transportation delays and resilience factors. *International Journal of Logistics Research and Applications, 17*(4), 269–282.
14. Bakshi, N., & Kleindorfer, P. (2009). Co-opetition and Investment for Supply-Chain Resilience. *Production and Operations Management, 18*(6), 583–603.
15. Barker, K., & Santos, J. R. (2010). Measuring the efficacy of inventory with a dynamic input–output model. *International Journal of Production Economics, 126*(1), 130–143.
16. Baroud, H., Ramirez, J., Barker, K., & Rocco, C. (2014). Stochastic measures of network resilience: Applications to waterway commodity flows. *Society of Risk Analysis, 34*(3), 1317–1335.

17. Bowen, F., Cousins, P., Lamming, R., & Faruk, A. (2001). The role of supply management capabilities in green supply. *Production and Operations Management, 10*(2), 174–189.
18. Burgholzer, W., Bauer, G., Posset, M., & Jammernegg, W. (2013). Analysing the impact of disruptions in intermodal transport networks: A micro simulation-based model. *Decision Support Systems, 54*(4), 1580–1586.
19. Burke, G., Carrillo, J., & Vakharia, A. (2007). Single versus multiple supplier sourcing strategies. *European Journal of Operational Research, 182*(1), 95–112.
20. Carmeli, A., & Schaubroeck, J. (2008). Organizational Crisis-Preparedness: The importance of learning from failures. *Long range planning, 44*(3), 179–196.
21. Carter, C. R., & Rogers, D. S. (2008). A framework of sustainable supply chain management: Moving toward new theory. *International Journal of Physical Distribution & Logistics Management, 38*(5), 360–387.
22. Carvalho, H., Barrosso, A., Machado, V., Azevedo, S., & Machado, C. (2012). Supply chain redesign for resilience using simulation. *Computers & Industrial Engineering, 62*(1), 329–341.
23. Chartered Association of Business Schools. (2015). *Academic Journal Guide 2015*. https://charteredabs.org/academic-journal-guide-2015/. Accessed on 2 October 2017.
24. Chopra, S., & Sodhi, M. (2004). Managing risk to avoid supply-chain breakdown. *MIT Sloan Management Review, 46*(1), 53–61.
25. Chopra, S., & Sodhi, M. (2014). Reducing the risk of supply chain disruptions. *MIT Sloan Management Review, 55*(3), 72–80.
26. Christopher, M., & Peck, H. (2004). Building the resilient supply chain. *International Journal of Logistics Management, 15*(2), 1–13.
27. Cohen, M. A., & Kunreuther, H. (2007). Operations risk management: Overview of Paul Kleindorfer's contributions. *Production and Operations Management, 16*(5), 525–541.
28. Comes, T., Hiete, M., Wijngaards, N., & Schultmann, F. (2013). An approach to Multi-Criteria decision problems under severe uncertainty. *Journal of Multi Criteria Decision Analysis, 20*(1–2), 29–48.
29. Cruz, J. M., & Matsypura, D. (2008). Supply chain networks with corporate social responsibility through integrated environmental decision-making. *International Journal of Production Research, 47*(3), 621–648.
30. Das, K., Lashkari, R., & Mehta, M. (2014). Designing a resilient supply management system for a supply chain. In Y. Guan & H. Liao (Eds.), *Industrial and Systems Engineering Research Conference (IIE Annual Conference Proceedings)* (pp. 301–310), Palais des Congrés de Montréal, Montréal, Canada, 31st May–3rd June 2014.
31. Deleris, A. L., & Erhun, F. (2005). Risk management in supply networks using Monte-Carlo Simulation. In M. E. Kuhl, N. M. Steiger, F. B. Armstrong, & J. A. Joines (Eds.), *Proceedings of the 2005 Winter Simulation Conference* (pp. 1643–1649), 4–7 December 2005, Orlando, Florida, USA.
32. Elkins, D., Handfield, R., Blackhurst, J., & Craighead, C. (2005). 18 Ways to guard against disruption. *Supply Chain Management Review, 9*(1), 46–53.
33. Fischbacher-Smith, D., & Fischbacher-Smith, M. (2012). The vulnerability of public spaces: Challenges for UK hospitals under the 'new' terrorist threat. *Public Management Review, 15*(3), 330–343.
34. Gatignon, A., Van Wassenhove, L. N., & Charles, A. L. (2010). The Yogyakarta earthquake: Humanitarian relief through IFRC's decentralized supply chain. *International Journal of Production Economics, 126*(1), 102–110.
35. Giunipero, L., & Eltantawy, R. (2003). Securing the upstream supply chain: A risk management approach. *International Journal of Physical Distribution and Logistics Management, 34*(9), 698–714.
36. Gonzalez, E. D. R. S., Maculan, N., Huatuco, L. H., Montoya-Torres, J. R., Diabet, A., Almeida, C., et al. (2015). Decision-support models and tools for helping to make real progress to more sustainable societies. *Journal of Cleaner Production, 105*, 1–13.

37. Gunasekaran, A., & Kobu, B. (2007). Performance measures and metrics in logistics and supply chain management: A review of recent literature (1995–2004) for research and applications. *International Journal of Production Research, 45*(12), 2819–2840.
38. Heckmann, I., Comes, T., & Nickel, S. (2015). A critical review on supply chain risk—Definition, measure and modelling. *Omega: International Journal of Management Sciences, 52*, 119–132.
39. Hofmann, H., Busse, C., Bode, C., & Henke, M. (2014). Sustainability-related supply chain risks: Conceptualization and management. *Business Strategy and the Environment, 23*, 160–172.
40. Jones, E., Squire, B., Autry, C., & Peterson, K. (2014). A contingent resource-based perspective of supply chain resilience and robustness. *Journal of Supply Chain Management, 50*(3), 55–73.
41. Juttner, U., & Maklan, S. (2011). Supply chain resilience in the global financial crisis: An empirical study. *Supply Chain Management: An International Journal, 16*(4), 246–259.
42. Kim, Y., Chen, Y., & Linderman, K. (2015). Supply network disruption and resilience: A network structural perspective. *Journal of Operations Management, 33–34*, 43–59.
43. Kleindorfer, P. R., & Saad, G. H. (2005). Managing disruption risks in supply chains. *Production and Operations Management, 14*(1), 53–68.
44. Kleindorfer, P. R., Singhal, K., & Van Wassenhove, L. N. (2005). Sustainable operations management. *Production and Operations Management, 14*(4), 482–492.
45. Klibi, W., & Martel, A. (2012). Modeling approaches for the design of resilient supply networks under disruptions. *International Journal of Production Economics, 135*(1), 882–898.
46. Knemeyer, A. M., Zinn, W., & Eroglu, C. (2009). Proactive planning for catastrophic events in supply chains. *Journal of Operations Management, 27*(2), 141–153.
47. Kumar, K., Tiwari, M., & Babiceanu, R. (2009). Minimisation of supply chain cost embedded risk using computational intelligence approaches. *International Journal of Production Research, 48*(13), 3717–3739.
48. Kusumastuti, R. D., Piplani, R., & Lim, G. H. (2008). Redesigning closed-loop service network at a computer manufacturer: A case study. *International Journal of Production Economics, 111*(2), 244–260.
49. Li, J., Wang, S., & Cheng, T. (2010). Competition and cooperation in a single-retailer two-supplier supply chain with supply disruption. *International Journal of Production Economics, 124*(1), 137–150.
50. Matos, S., & Hall, J. (2007). Integrating sustainable development in the supply chain: The case of life cycle assessment in oil and gas and agricultural biotechnology. *Journal of Operations Management, 25*, 1083–1102.
51. Meixell, M., & Gargeya, V. (2005). Global supply chain design: A literature review and critique. *Transportation Research Part E: Logistics and Transportation Review, 41*(6), 531–550.
52. Minner, S. (2003). Multiple-supplier inventory models in supply chain management: A review. *International Journal of Production Economics, 81–82*, 265–279.
53. Nair, A., & Vidal, J. (2010). Supply network topology and robustness against disruptions—An investigation using multi-agent model. *International Journal of Production Research, 49* (5), 1391–1404.
54. Preece, G., Shaw, D., & Hayashi, H. (2012). Using the Viable System Model (VSM) to structure information processing complexity in disaster response. *European Journal of Operational Research, 224*(1), 209–218.
55. Rao, P., & Holt, D. (2005). Do green supply chains lead to competitiveness and economic performance? *International Journal of Operations & Production Management, 25*(9), 898–916.
56. Rush, S. C., Houser, R., & Partridge, A. (2015). Rebuilding sustainable communities for children and families after disaster: Recommendations from symposium participants in

response to the April 27th, 2011 Tornadoes. *Community Mental Health Journal, 51*(2), 132–138.
57. Sahebjamnia, S., Torabi, S. A., & Mansouri, S. A. (2014). Integrated business continuity and disaster recovery planning: Towards organizational resilience. *European Journal of Operational Research, 242,* 261–273.
58. Sawik, T. (2014). Joint supplier selection and scheduling of customer orders under disruption risks: Single vs. dual sourcing. *Omega: The International Journal of Management Sciences, 43,* 83–95.
59. Schmitt, A. (2011). Strategies for customer service level protection under multi-echelon supply chain disruption risk. *Transport Research Part B: Methodological, 45*(8), 1266–1283.
60. Schmitt, A., & Singh, M. (2012). A quantitative analysis of disruption risk in a multi-echelon supply chain. *International Journal of Production Economics, 139,* 22–32.
61. Seuring, S., & Muller, M. (2008). From a literature review to a conceptual framework for sustainable supply chain management. *Journal of Cleaner Production, 16*(15), 1699–1710.
62. Sheffi, Y. (2001). Supply chain management under threat of international terrorism. *International Journal of Logistics Management, 12*(2), 1–11.
63. Sheffi, Y., & Rice, J. (2005). A supply chain view of the resilient enterprise. *MIT Sloan Management Review, 47*(1), 41–48.
64. Silbermayr, L., & Minner, S. (2014). A multiple sourcing inventory model under disruption risk. *International Journal of Production Economics, 149,* 37–46.
65. Simpson, D., Power, D., & Samson, D. (2007). Greening the automotive supply chain: A relationship perspective. *International Journal of Operations & Production Management, 27*(1), 28–48.
66. Skipper, J., & Hanna, J. (2009). Minimizing supply chain disruption risk through enhanced flexibility. *International Journal of Physical Distribution & Logistics Management, 39*(5), 404–427.
67. Son, J., & Orchard, R. (2013). Effectiveness of policies for mitigating supply disruptions. *International Journal of Physical Distribution & Logistics Management, 43*(8), 684–786.
68. Soon, Q., & Udin, Z. (2011). Supply chain management from the perspective of value chain flexibility: An exploratory study. *Journal of Manufacturing Technology Management, 22*(4), 506–526.
69. Stevenson, M., & Spring, M. (2009). Supply chain flexibility: An inter-firm empirical study. *International Journal of Operations & Production Management, 29*(9), 946–971.
70. Tang, C. (2007). Robust strategies for mitigating supply chain disruptions. *International Journal of Logistics Research and Applications, 9*(1), 33–45.
71. Tang, C., & Tomlin, B. (2008). The power of flexibility for mitigating supply chain risks. *International Journal of Production Economics, 116,* 12–27.
72. Taskin, S., & Lodree, E. J. (2010). Inventory decisions for emergency supplies based on hurricane count predictions. *International Journal of Production Economics, 126*(1), 66–75.
73. Taticchi, P., Tonelli, F., & Pasqualino, R. (2013). Performance measurement of sustainable supply chains. A literature review and a research agenda. *International Journal of Productivity and Performance Management, 62*(8), 782–804.
74. Thevenaz, C., & Resodihardjo, S. (2010). All the best laid plans conditions impeding proper emergency response. *International Journal of Production Economics, 126*(1), 7–21.
75. Thun, J., & Hoenig, D. (2011). An empirical analysis of supply chain risk management in the German automotive industry. *International Journal of Production Economics, 131*(1), 242–249.
76. Tomlin, B. (2006). On the value of mitigation and contingency strategies for managing supply chain disruption risks. *Management Science, 52*(5), 639–657.
77. Tomlin, B., & Wang, Y. (2005). On the value of mix flexibility and dual sourcing and unreliable newsvendor networks. *Manufacturing and Service Operations Management, 7*(1), 37–57.

78. Trkman, P., & McCormack, K. (2009). Supply chain risk in turbulent environments—A conceptual model for managing supply chain network risk. *International Journal of Production Economics, 119,* 247–258.
79. Vachon, S., & Klassen, R. D. (2006). Extending green practices across the supply chain: The impact of upstream and downstream integration. *International Journal of Operations & Production Management, 26*(7), 795–821.
80. Vachon, S., & Klassen, R. D. (2008). Environmental management and manufacturing performance: The role of collaboration in the supply chain. *International Journal of Production Economics, 111*(2), 299–315.
81. Van Wassenhove, L. (2006). Humanitarian aid logistics: Supply chain management in high gear. *Journal of Operational Research Society, 57*(5), 475–489.
82. Vlajic, J., van der Vorst, J., & Haijema, R. (2012). A framework for designing robust food supply chains. *International Journal of Production Economics, 137*(1), 176–189.
83. Wagner, S., & Bode, C. (2006). An empirical investigation into supply chain vulnerability. *Journal of Purchasing & Supply Management, 12*(6), 301–312.
84. Wilson, M. (2007). The impact of transportation disruptions on supply chain performance. *Transportation Research Part E: Logistics and Transportation Review, 43*(4), 295–320.
85. Wu, T., Blackhurst, T., & O'Grady, P. (2007). Methodology for supply chain disruption analysis. *International Journal of Production Research, 45*(7), 1665–1682.
86. Yu, H., Zeng, A., & Zhao, L. (2009). Single or dual sourcing: Decision-making in the presence of supply chain disruption risks, *Omega: The International Journal of Management Sciences, 37*(4), 788–800.
87. Zeng, A., & Xia, Y. (2015). Building a mutually beneficial partnership to ensure backup supply. *Omega: International Journal of Management Sciences, 52,* 77–91.
88. Zhu, Q., & Sarkis, J. (2004). Relationships between operational practices and performance among early adopters of green supply chain management practices in Chinese manufacturing enterprises. *Journal of Operations Management, 22,* 265–289.
89. Zhu, Q., Sarkis, J., & Lai, K. H. (2008). Confirmation of a measurement model for green supply chain management practices implementation. *International Journal of Production Economics, 111*(2), 261–273.

Exploring Innovation and Sustainability in the Potato Supply Chains

Gyan Prakash

Abstract This paper explores the innovations in the food consumption and production systems in India using the case study of potatoes. This paper presents a mapping of the potato supply chain and explores the input and outputs of the system. Constraints at each stage are identified and suitable recommendations are presented. Linkage between technological innovation and sustainability of the potato production system is presented. The food production and consumption system in India is undergoing rapid transformation in relation to technology, production methods, economic structure and relation between key organizations and institutions. However, agricultural markets are still inefficient and imperfect in many parts of the country. The nature of food system is powered by changes in regulations, shifts in consumption patterns, economic competition between processors and super-markets and pressures from international competitors. India is witnessing many organizational changes which are still evolving from traditional farming to co-operatives and agri-business models. The changes that take place within the food system have impact upon the actors involved in the supply chain and on the sustainability of food system in general.

Keywords Potato supply chain · Sustainability · Innovation · Food system

1 Introduction

The food industry in India is gaining importance and is currently valued at US$39.71 billion and is expected to grow at a compounded annual growth rate (CAGR) of 11% to US$65.4 billion by 2018 [36]. In India over 58% of the rural households depend on agriculture as their principal means of livelihood. Agriculture, along with fisheries and forestry, is one of the largest contributors to the gross domestic product

G. Prakash (✉)
ABV-Indian Institute of Information Technology
and Management Gwalior, Gwalior, India
e-mail: gyan@iiitm.ac.in

X. Liu (ed.), *Environmental Sustainability in Asian Logistics and Supply Chains*,
https://doi.org/10.1007/978-981-13-0451-4_6

(GDP) [36]. As per estimates by the central statistics office (CSO), the share of agriculture and allied sectors (including agriculture, livestock, forestry and fishery) has beens 16.1% of the gross value added (GVA) during 2014–15 at 2011–12 prices. During first quarter of financial year (FY) 2016, agriculture and allied sectors grew 1.9% year-on-year and contributed 14.2% of GVA. Agricultural export constitutes 10% of the country's exports and is the fourth-largest exported commodity. The agro industry in India is divided into several sub-segments such as canned, dairy, processed, frozen food to fisheries, meat, poultry and food grains. In recent past multiple factors have worked together to facilitate the growth in the Indian agricultural sector. These include growth in household income and consumption, expansion in the food processing sector and increase in agricultural exports. The food supply chain in India involves stages of farm production, industrial food processing, distribution and consumption. The food supply chain map may involve vertically integrated economic stages such as crop cultivation, industrial processing, retailing, and end consumption and may span horizontally across different industrial sectors. Supply chain perspective of food production provides insights on its underlying structure as well as associated economic stages.

The Indian food supply chains are characterised by fragmented upstream supply chains and moderately integrated downstream supply chains. The food processing involves industrialized processes which has been oriented towards mass production of convenience food and its distribution for consumption. In India not only eating habits have been changing but production and consumption patterns have also started following international trends. Food supply chains are getting nationally as well as internationally integrated. The concern for safe and healthy food is growing. The Indian government, non-profit as well as non-governmental organizations (NGOs), consumer groups and media have been increasingly concerned about the possible effects of the food system upon society, rural economy and environment. Issues such as eating habits, the link between food and health, transparency across food processing, the environmental impacts of food production, organic production and lower input farming, animal welfare and use of certifications are gaining currency. The food production and distribution processes present a number of environmental challenges, especially in relation to waste disposal, energy use, air pollution, water degradation, and impact on bio-diversity. Production and consumption across food chains are geared towards environmental, social and economic aspects of sustainability; however, impact of technology on food system sustainability is less examined. The transformation of the Indian agricultural sector has been driven by supply side factors such as policies to push growth, efficient use of resources like land and labour, introduction of new technologies and increased use of modern inputs like chemical fertilizers and expansion of irrigation infrastructure and investments in general infrastructure like roads, energy as well as demand side factors such as population, income growth, urbanization and demand from the rest of the world through gradual liberalization of international trade. Rising private participation in the Indian agriculture, growing organic farming and use of information technology are some of the key trends in the agriculture industry. However, environmental and social aspects of sustainability of the food system have been less explored and documented.

The objective of this analysis is to explore patterns of potato production and consumption in India, to map the potato supply chain, to identify areas of technological innovations and to explore conventional strategies for potato production and consumption. The study first discusses review of literature which is followed by methodology. The results and discussion have been in terms of economic structure of the potato supply chain, map of the potato supply chain, inputs and outputs that are crucial for the sustainability of the food system, innovations across potato supply chain and key changes that are taking place within potato consumption and production system and their implications for sustainability.

2 Review of Literature

Food Security and nutritional needs of society is rendered by network of actors in agro food industry [10]. Synergy of technical and non-technical competencies nurtures innovation along agro value chain [18] and results in new knowledge [3, 4]. Towards this the role of institutions, actors and activities are central to stimulate innovation in agro food industry [11]. Agro industry prosperity is based on primary antecedents [54] such as size of the firm [62], managerial networking fervour [34]; Danish et al. [20], employee skill development [27], product diversification [25] and market integration [55]. Employee skill development and information technology have been strong predictors of firm's growth [19, 46, 51] in case of both slow and fast growing firms. Therefore, In order to produce maximal growth, small sized agro based firms should follow flexible market focus strategies [2] rather than product based focus strategy.

Food processing has been relatively a low-technology intensity industry [17, 68] which leverages local food networks and its produce. Food processors rely more on in-house research for product and process innovations [12] than on external research and development (R&D) [30, 67]. In order to foster open innovation, food processors need to rely more on its in-house competencies than on external competencies [7, 13, 14]. In order to innovate majority of the small and medium sized food processors [39] rely on their industrial networks [49, 64] for enhancement in capabilities [63, 41, 45, 69]. Compared to linkages with R&D base actors (Nieto and Santamaria, [1, 37, 45, 50]) linkages with market base actors need to be very strong [21, 8, 37, 44, 72].

The level of R&D budget, number of new product developments, and successful innovation adoption and product commercialization etc. vary substantially between food processing industry [57] and tech-based industries [15, 29, 61]. In the food processing, the novelty of innovation itself increases unplanned deficiency of existing resources and capabilities [59, 65, 73]. Therefore, food processors need to focus on capabilities in upstream stages of supply chain including assimilation of novel technologies in processing including development of functional products and novel processes [33, 66] to increase its market potential [32]. Food industry suffers from the poor rate of innovations due to risk averse behaviour of customers; therefore, food processors need to create new market opportunities through collaborative arrangements with suppliers [6]. Food processors need to challenge traditional approaches [48, 60] and develop entrepreneurial and value chain competencies in order to offer unique value to the customers. Food processors need to complement their internal competencies with external knowledge, available from buyers, suppliers, competitors etc. [13, 14]. Though customer needs act as a driver [26], however, synergy between R&D with marketing results in real benefits, moreover, advances in biological sciences have been transforming supply driven value chains into demand driven chains [52].

In the Swedish context, food processors suffers from lack of user-oriented innovations [32], poor value creation [43] and absence of open innovation mind set [13, 14]. Nonetheless processors are redesigning their value chain and achieved some incremental innovations in design of their networks and cluster [24]. In the Italian context, demand and market opportunities, competition, vertical co-operation, networking systems etc. [31] and expenses incurred on R&D [47, 53] emerge as drivers of innovation. Quality of manpower, geographical context and age of the firm [28, 56] determine organizational capabilities to introduce innovation along with its strategic interventions. Cross industry innovation crosses the ambit of discrete sectors and results in mutual benefits [35]. The dominant drivers of innovation in low-tech food industry and high-tech pharmaceutical industry comprises of in-house R&D activities [9, 40]. Its pharmaceutical industry [66] is predominated by the combination of internal and external R&D activities whereas in its food processing the absorption of external knowledge [16] emerges central to innovation. Thus, everyone can be benefitted from the inter-industry relationships and research oriented collaborations [40]. In the Canadian context, highly innovative food processors rely on skilled labour, production machinery, engineering practices etc. [5] to achieve high productivity.

Changes to environmental context of food production and distribution, changes in economic development, changes in household consumption patterns, changes in technologies have been identified as factors affecting food consumption and production [23]. An innovation in one part of the food system can lead to innovation in other part of the food system, or can affect relations between organizations that belong to different part of the food system. A disruptive technological innovation may cause social or cultural change for consumers, communities and organizations in the food system. The most appropriate way of investigating sustainability implications of innovation in relation to food is by applying systems approach. Potato is considered to be a balanced food containing carbohydrates (16%), proteins (2%), minerals (1%), dietary fibers (0.6%) and is a good source of vitamin C and antioxidants. In terms of production potato produces 47.6 kg of food/hectare/day whereas wheat, rice and maize produce 18.1, 12.4 and 9.1 kg food/ hectare/day, respectively [38].

3 Methodology

The paper follows a case study approach and involves an empirical investigation of a particular potato supply chain in the setting of the Indian state of Uttar Pradesh and uses multiple sources for capturing contextual issues. The approach is in line with

[71]. Indian potato supply chain has been chosen for this research due to the significance of this vegetable product in overall production and consumption. First, potatoes represent vegetables and fruit sector, which is one of the most important sectors in the Indian food system, accounting for 12% of the total world potato production. Within vegetables and fruit sector, potatoes are the single largest product in India in value terms. Second, potatoes play an important role in the food system in terms of domestic consumption and expenditure. The potato supply chain is a good example of a food supply chain with clear system boundaries, which is defined by number of growers, packers, processors and retailers due to dominance of domestic producers. Moreover, the potato supply chain mainly sources from domestic market, therefore the system boundaries are confined within India. The objectives of this study have been to explore the configuration of supply chain of fruits and vegetables in India, identify technologies that are crucial for determining sustainability of food consumption and production system, identify to what extent the key actors promoting technological and structural changes recognize the sustainability and system implications of their actions. Data collection methods such as questionnaires, observations, interviews and document analysis have been used for primary and secondary data collection. The paper adopts a supply chain orientation to study the system of stages, which represent a sequence of activities through which resources and materials flow downstream for the production, distribution and ultimate consumption. The potato supply chain has been conceptualised as a network of organizations that have economic and social relationships with each other that enable the smooth functioning of supply chain and in turn have environmental consequences.

3.1 Data Collection Methods

The methodology adopted is qualitative in approach. The data collection methods employed include in-depth interviews with key persons in the potato supply chain; analysis of secondary data such as market reports produced by agencies such as the Indian council of agricultural research, agriculture universities, united nations development programmes and trade associations. The key person interview approach has been adopted to provide data on the organization they represent, issues and problems that relate to their processes. The data collection process aims to cover all stages of the potato supply chain along with the processes, which have been essential for the functioning of the system such as farmers, cold storages, processors and regulators. Data have been collected from the cities of Agra, Firozabad, Farukhabad, Varanasi, Aligarh in the Indian state of Uttar Pradesh. Table 1 depicts sources of data.

Informal interviews are conducted with farmers because of their convenience. Key persons from cold storages have been approached to get data about the issues they face and waste disposal. Local processing units in the Agra district have been selected to get the information about their procurement, operations and waste management. Analysis of high-tech production of potato in the Indian state of Gujrat has been done

Table 1 Sources of Data

Supply chain stage	Informants	Data source	Geographical context
Origin of resource	Seed companies, central potato research institute (CPRI)	Reports	At national level
Agricultural production	Farmers, trade associations	Interviews, reports	Firozabad, Farukhabad, Varanasi,
Storage	Cold stores	Interviews	Firozabad, Farukhabad, Varanasi
Wholesale	Merchants, wholesalers, distributors	Interviews	Firozabad, Farukhabad, Varanasi
Processing	Processing companies, trade associations	Reports, interviews	At national level
Retail	Super markets, street hawkers, vegetable vendors	Interviews	Firozabad, Farukhabad, Varanasi
Suppliers	Packaging, equipment provider	Reports	Uttar Pradesh

to do comparative study with Uttar Pradesh. The organizations that have been selected for data collection represent important stages and processes within the potato supply chain. The data collection aims to involve economic actors within each stage but technological developments have also been analyzed within the system.

4 Findings and Discussion

4.1 Economic Structure of the Potato Supply Chain

4.1.1 Industrial Structure and Key Organizations

In terms of industrial structure, the potato supply chain in India involves large number of potato growers, commission agents, whole sellers, street vendors, moderate number of packers and merchants and small number of processors. Central potato research institute (CPRI) in the city Shimla is the most important research institute in India which develops technological know-how for potato production. CPRI intervened and initiated diversification of potato consumption for avoiding situations of gluts. The inception of CPRI changed the potato crop scenario in the country. State departments of horticulture have the responsibility of providing good quality planting materials to the farmers. For the potato crop, the department purchases basic seed from CPRI, Shimla. The department of horticulture buys back the seed to distribute among the farmers. Due to price fluctuation and glut situation in the market, some institutions like national agriculture cooperative marketing federation (NAFED), different state government agencies, and co-operative societies have been intervening in the domestic market. In the case of exports the agriculture and processed food export development authority (APEDA) intervene to stabilize the prices.

4.1.2 Conventional Potato Production and Consumption

Currently, India is the second-largest producer of potatoes in the world [58]. India produced 42.34 million tons of potato using 1.86 million hectares of land with an average yield of 22.72 tons per hectares during 2010–11 [22]. The state of Uttar Pradesh produces around 39–40% of potatoes followed by state of West Bengal which produces around 35% potatoes. The annual compounded growth rate of potato is higher than any other major food crops in terms of area, production and productivity thereby, resulting in bumper yields which lead to glut situations and low prices for the farmers. To overcome this situation, the remedial measures have been taken at different levels in regard of production, marketing, processing and export. In India, potato processing industry mainly comprises four segments of potato chips, French fries, potato flakes as well as powder and other processed products such as dehydrated chips, *alu bhujia, samosa*, and *tikkis*. However, potato chips still continue to be the most common and popular processed product and presently constitute 85% of salty snack business worth around INR 25 billion and account over 60% of the total potato processing capacity of the industry. As per the directorate of economics and statistics, India exports potato, to the tune of around 184,961 tones valued at Rs. 11,503.59 lakh to countries like Sri-Lanka, Nepal, Mauritius, Singapore, UAE, and Japan. India's share in world exports of potato is insignificant and inconsistent because of water losses during transportation and poor quality standards. Figure 1 depicts production profile of potato in India. Majority of

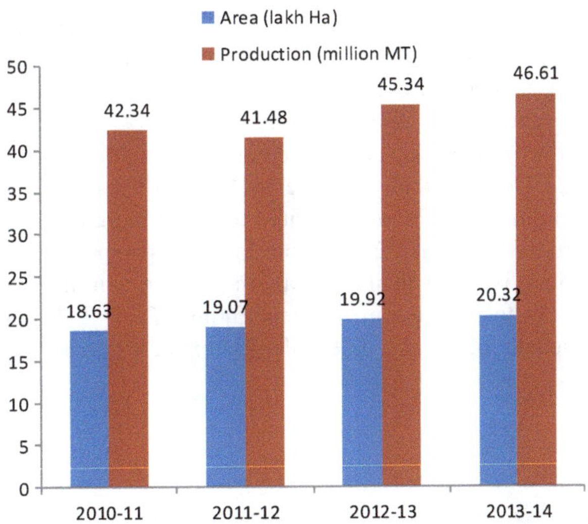

Fig. 1 Production profile of potato production in India

Table 2 Usage profile of the Indian potato

Usage	Percentage of total production
Table purpose	61.47
Seed	21
Processed	0.5
Export	0.03
Loss in post harvest, handling, marketing and storage	17

harvested potatoes are sold on fresh produce market, however, processed potatoes constitute less than 0.5% of annual production. While the consumption of processed potato products is expected to increase with increasing population and increasing disposable incomes. At present potato sector is comprised of various kinds of dehydrated potato products. The snack food sector is developing most rapidly, including potato chips. Table 2 depicts usage profile of potato in India. In India more than 95% potato is cultivated for table purposes and potato has less dry matter it is not suitable for processing. The processors had to do lots of research for development of suitable processing variety including import from Europe. The companies like Pepsi, ITC, McCain have identified varieties which are suitable for processing. The requirement of processing varieties is gradually increasing and at present estimated demand is around 6.6 lakhs ton annually. Emerging economies like India and China have tremendous potential in developing processing markets when compared to the share of processed volume in developed economies like European Union (EU) and United States of America (USA).

The overall size of the Indian snack food market is INR 45 to Rs. 50 billion (about Euro 680–750 million) per year. The market is reported to be growing at an annual rate of 7–8%. Potato chips are estimated to constitute nearly 85% of total salty snack food market and amounts to around INR 25 billion (about Euro 380 million). Frito lay has the largest market share of 45%, followed by *Haldiram* 27% and ITC at 16%. According to Euro monitor International, the branded snacks market accounted for Rs. 36 billion (about Euro 530 million) in year 2012. The development of the snack food market has created a growing demand for dehydrated potato products. The processable varieties have been generally cultivated through contract farming and currently practiced by companies like Pepsi, Mcain, Marino, Balaji, etc. keeping in view of their specific requirement at present most of the cultivation is done in states like Gujrat, Madhya Pradesh (MP), UP and WB. It is understood that climatic conditions of Gujrat are suited best and more than 30% of potato is sourced by the processors from Gujrat. From farmer's perspective as cost benefit ratio of growing potato is better than other alternative crops in the area, the cultivation of potato is likely to increase in the near future. Table 3 depicts installed potato processing capacity of India. Table 4 depicts expected potato demand and expected growth.

Table 3 Installed potato processing capacity (tons) in India

Company	Installed processing capacity (tons)		
	2006	2011	Actual in operation in 2011
Pepsico	80,000	150,000	1,30,000
ITC	20,000	50,000	33,000
Balaji	10,0000	50,000	38,000
Haldiram	–	22,000	22,000
Parle	–	50,000	15,000
Total	110,000	322,000	238,000

Table 4 Estimated potato demand and expected growth rate of processing units

SN	Name of unit	Product profile	Estimated potato demand (000'tons)	Expected growth (%)
1	Pepsi	Wafers	200	–
2	ITC	Wafers	50	–
3	Parle	Wafers	60	–
4	Balaji	Wafers	60	–
5	McCain	French fries, tikkies	50	20
6	Marino	Potato flakes	40	20
7	Others	Wafers, flakes, tikkies etc	150	15

4.1.3 Potato Supply Chain Map

The map of the conventional potato supply chain is presented in Fig. 2 and consists of stages of plant breeding for developing new varieties of potatoes, farm production in terms of potato cultivation and their harvesting, transportation of produce to distribution or processing stage, import or export of potatoes for the purpose of processing and packaging involving. These processes involves cleaning, grading, weighing, peeling, pre-cooking, cooking, seasoning, preparation of various sub-products, chilled production etc. The distribution channel involves wholesalers who acquire potatoes and potato products and distribute them amongst retailers and vendors, retail involving supermarkets and other outlets and grocers. Another channel of distribution has been through food service outlets and involves fast food service, restaurants, takeaways, work canteens etc. Final stage involves household consumption of potatoes and potato products including purchasing, storing, cooking, consuming and disposing of food. The distribution channel involves wholesalers who acquire potatoes and potato products and distribute them amongst retailers and vendors, retail involving supermarkets and other outlets and grocers. Another channel of distribution is through food service outlets and involves fast food service, restaurants, takeaways, work canteens etc. Final stage involves household consumption of potatoes and potato products including purchasing, storing, cooking, consuming and disposing of food.

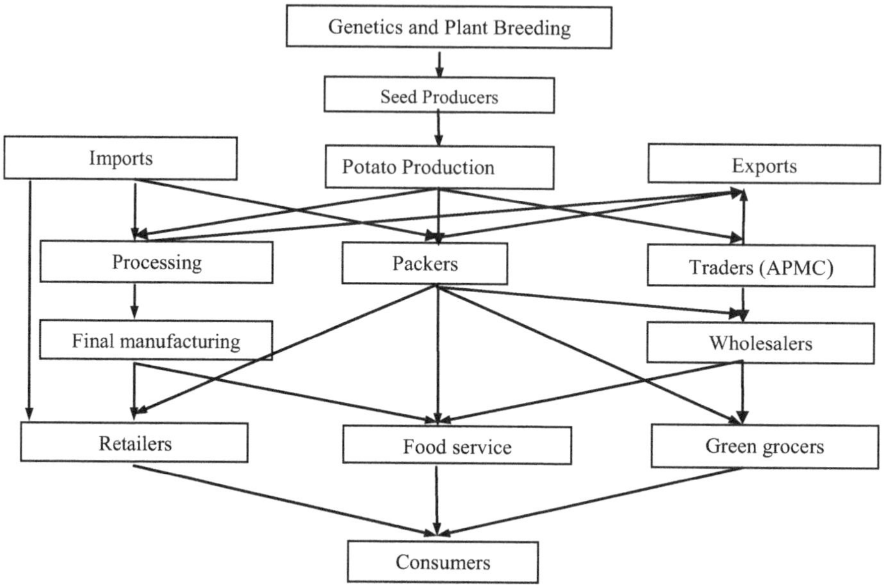

Fig. 2 The map of conventional potato supply chain

4.1.4 Marketing Channels for Potatoes in Uttar Pradesh

In Uttar Pradesh majority of the produce is sold through APMC markets to licensed wholesalers or commission agents. Potatoes are procured by farmers through auctions in APMC, farm gate and other traders. Major considerations in procurement have been price and quality by visual inspection (dryness, cleanliness, color and brightness). APMC traders procure from cold stores in the off-season. Transaction costs such as transport, packing and loading and unloading costs are borne by farmers if brought to the APMC but by traders at the farm gate (who recovered their cost by offering at lower prices). Typical channels of Potato are depicted in Fig. 3. Most traders also stored produce for 7–8 months to realize better selling prices. Supermarkets like big-bazar procure from local traders only and they don't have any direct contact with farmers. Prices are determined on the basis of market demand, quality of the produce and prevailing market prices. Large processing firms have reached agreements with state governments to procure directly from farmers rather than using the official state marketing systems. In Uttar Pradesh the processing firm Merino-vegit engages farmers in contract farming and provides them with all technical assistance required for meeting processing quality standards. The company has organized a system of contract farming for producing select variety of potatoes. About 1000 acres of land is under cultivation through contract farming method benefiting 400–500 farmers. Issues related to contract farming have been identified which encompasses exclusion of small farmers, quality standards with high rates of rejection, delayed or reduced or absent payments, and weak

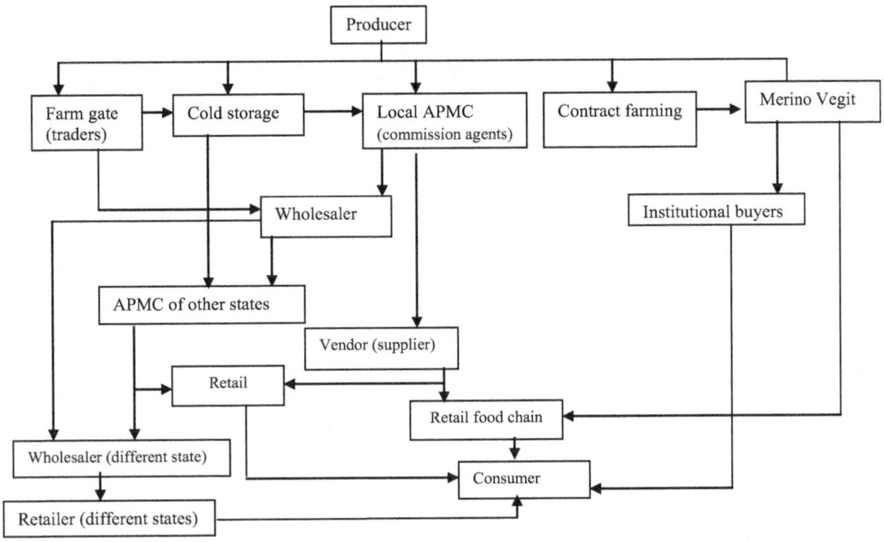

Fig. 3 Market channels of potato

bargaining power of small growers. Contract firms impose eligibility conditions for contract participants such as minimum or maximum land holdings, certification requirements etc.

The objectives of contract farming are sometimes conflicting, it is difficult to design effective public policy intervention for it and organize growers around it. Contract farming is also determined by relationship, among state, companies and farmers which interact with formal and informal institutions. Legal and institutional provisions are required to regulate and monitor contracts and facilitate their smooth functioning in order to reduce the negative effects of the system. Non-government organizations (NGO's) can intervene in contract situations as intermediaries to protect the interest of farmers and rural communities. NGO's can also play a role in information provision and in monitoring contracts.

4.1.5 Stakeholders in the Potato Supply Chain

There are various entities and actors along the potato supply chain. Following section describes the functions of various actors in the chain.

Farmers: Farmer is the most important component in the potato supply chain which make a lot of investment in terms of time and money in the processes of cultivation and harvesting. The size of operational land holdings is decreasing with every next generation which is limiting farmers to grow and earn. Potato crops require low input costs and less duration thus it is a preferred crop for the farmers.

Aggregator: An aggregator is a potato trader who acts as a collector and purchases potato from farmers at the village level and sells it either in the APMC market or stores it in the cold storage to sell it later in the off-season. Aggregators often provide credit to the farmers at the time of sowing with high interest rates.
APMC: An APMC market is a regulated market where the farmer sells its produce to the regulated agent through an open auction and the agent deducts its commission. Agents often exploit farmers by colluding with traders. A lot of agricultural produce brought to these markets is wasted due to the weak infrastructure of these markets.
Wholesalers: Wholesalers are potato traders who deal in large quantity of potatoes brought from the APMC markets or cold storages. They sell to small unorganized retailers (street vendors). Annually potatoes of estimated value of around INR 1000 billion are lost in the supply chain, around 60% of which is due to avoidable costs of wastage and rest is due to avoidable cost of storage and commissions.
Cold Storage: Cold storage plays a major role in potato supply chain since they preserve the quality of potato and store them till off season. Potato in the cold storage can remain intact for around 15 days after which the starch in the potato gets converted into sugar. Few cold storages in Agra and Firozabad districts have plants which gives FIMC treatment to potatoes which prevents starch present in potato to convert in sugar. Thus, they are called sugar free potato and can be used for processing also.
Processing units: It is estimated that about 25% of the potatoes which are spoiled due to several reasons, may be saved by processing and preservation of various types of processed products. The potatoes can be processed for preservation and value addition in the form of wafers as well as chips, powder, flakes, granules, canned slices etc. Potato powder is one of the oldest commercially processed vegetable products. It is widely used in the baking industry all over the Europe, USA, and Middle East, although its growth has not kept pace with other processed products of potato. In India it is used in baking industry and as a thickening agent in soups. Chips are the most commonly consumed first generation snack foods. This product can be safely stored for up to six months without any change in quality. In rural areas of Uttar Pradesh people produce different products of potato in small and cottage industries and sell them in local markets. Due to scarcity of potato based industries in the state, only 2–3% of potato is processed. Producers believe that large scale production of processing varieties may cause losses due to non-procurement of potatoes by processors.

4.2 *Constraints Across the Potato Supply Chain*

4.2.1 On-Farm Constrains

Lack of quality inputs at affordable prices: the most important input in the process of potato production is the seed. Farmers often store a part of their produce in the cold storage and use them as seed at the time of cultivation. Quality of that seed is not good enough (as susceptibility to diseases increases with time) and has considerable impact on the yield of potato. Fertilizers and pesticides are also not accessible at reasonable prices. Farmers often purchase seeds from cooperative banks at high interest rates and face problems when potato price plummeted in the market. Thus, better credit should be given to small farmers from banks and micro credit institutions. Cooperative societies should be formed at village level to give financial support to farmers and ensure their easy access to markets.

Inferior farm technology: the adoption of modern technology is very low in the state of Uttar Pradesh. Farmers are shifting to diesel pumps due to shortage of electricity which increases their cost of production. Now increasing shortages of water is further aggravating their situation. Thus, new technologies should be adopted for water management and other practices like drip irrigation and government should support farmers in terms of training and subsidies. Private players like processing companies and big retailers may enter to form vertical integration which can provide and support farmers with latest technologies to improve the quality of produce and reduce wastage which would be mutually beneficial for both farmers and private players.

Lack of information and knowledge to farmers: Farmers often rely on mass media for accessing information. Agricultural workshops and trainings are conducted at very high levels in the cities which makes it difficult for farmers to reach due to transportation costs and their lack of information about it. Only few farmers are able to access such workshops. Due to lack of knowledge they often use fertilizers improperly, often in large amounts in the hope of good yield, which adversely affect their produce and land resulting in huge wastages. Thus, trainings and workshops should be conducted at village level and there should be an appropriate and reliable system of informing farmers about such events.

4.2.2 Non-farm Constraints

Inefficient markets: A significant part of the produce in Uttar Pradesh is sold through APMC markets; these markets are not efficient and have ambiguous pricing process. Collusion between agents and traders prevent farmers from getting fair prices for their produce. There is high level of physical wastage due to inefficient loading and unloading of the produce. Process of weighing produce is still used in the traditional way which often leads to the wrong results. Need for license to work as commission agents acts as an entry barrier for the entrepreneurs. This activity may be eliminated since it does not add any value in the supply chain except of agents acting as a bridge between farmers and traders. Instead other trusted organizations like collections centers and distribution center should be encouraged to ensure fair price for the farmers.

Inefficient logistics and transportation: Uttar Pradesh has the maximum number of cold storage specifically for potatoes in India. Only few cold storages have the capacity and plants for CPRI treatment and serve a very small portion of farmers who can afford to pay for the treatment of their produce. Cold storages do not have chambers and technologies to store various processing variety of potatoes. Inefficient transportation is the major cause of reduced value of potatoes. Water is the major constituent of potato which gets reduced to about 5% while in the transportation which further decrease the price and quality of potatoes. Thus, cold storages should upgrade to latest technology to keep pace with demand and try to optimize process in order to reduce cost so that it can become affordable for farmers. Efficient transportation with refrigeration can reduce wastage and protect the quality of produce.

Low level of processing: The consumption of table potato as well as requirement of seed potato is more or less stable in the state, which is about 100–105 lakh MT each year. The surplus potato is being exported and or traded out of the state as table potato and a small quantity is utilized for processing. Analysis of production, consumption and market prices during past years indicate a trend of potato prices falling every third or fourth year. Since Uttar Pradesh is the largest potato producing state in India, there is the huge opportunity in terms of potato processing. There are very few processing units in Uttar Pradesh because of entry barriers like high taxes and duties, lack of government support, inferior quality of produce. Potato producers in Uttar Pradesh believe that large scale production of processing varieties may cause losses due to non-procurement of potatoes by processors because of only a small number of potato processors existing in the state.

4.3 Inputs and Outputs in the Potato Supply Chain

The resource input and environmental outputs of the potato supply chain are depicted in Fig. 4. The stages within the potato supply chain can be grouped according to similarities in the nature of their activities into four processes.

- Agricultural production: which encompasses the stages of breeding, seed production, agricultural growing have major inputs such as water, fertilizers, machinery, energy and transport and major outputs of air emissions, waste water and waste.
- Industrial processing: it encompasses the stages of packing, processing and final manufacturing with major inputs such as water, packaging material, equipment, energy and transport and major outputs of air emissions, waste water and waste.

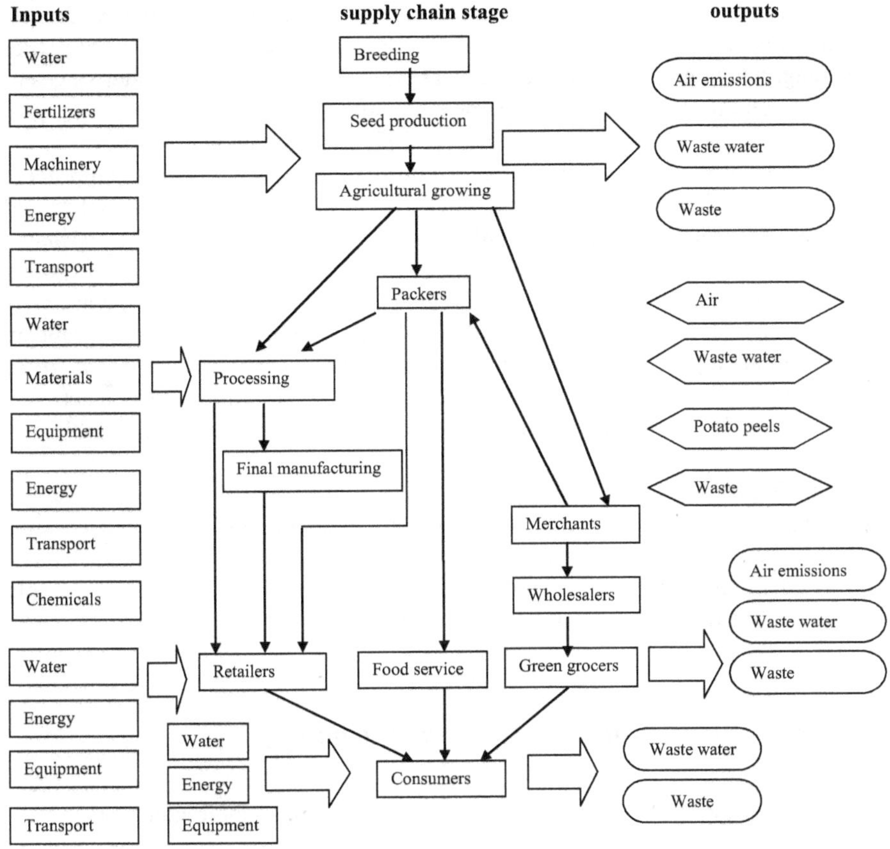

Fig. 4 Inputs and outputs in conventional potato supply chain

- Distribution: it encompasses stages of trading, wholesale, retail and food service with major inputs of water, energy, equipment and transport and major outputs of air emissions, waste water and waste.
- Domestic consumption: it has major inputs of water, energy and equipment and major outputs of waste.

The major material inputs at the stage of agricultural production include the supply of water, fertilizers, agricultural machinery, energy and transport. Despite developments in breeding, potato is still susceptible to a large number of diseases and pests and as a result potato production is one of the heaviest users of chemicals inputs for crop growing. The major environmental outputs during this stage are pollution, waste water emission, land degradation and waste generation. During the stage of potato processing the major material inputs are water, energy, materials for packaging and the like, chemicals, processing equipment and transport. Processing of potatoes involves freezing, and from this stage on, involves large energy inputs for the storage of frozen or chilled potato products. Therefore, industrial processing of potatoes is very energy and water intensive. Packaging is a very important part of processing, which greatly contributes to waste generation during the latter stages of the supply chain. The major environmental outputs of the industrial potato processing include air pollution, wastewater emission and waste generation.

A process of distribution has various inputs such as water, energy, equipment and transport. Distribution is highly intensive, because it involves display and storage of large quantities of frozen and chilled potato products. These quantifiable inputs and outputs are crucial for defining the environmental sustainability of potato production and consumption system. Conventional strategy, which incorporates freezing and chilling of potatoes, is highly resource intensive and has significant environmental impacts. Organic and sustainable production of potatoes in India presents significant opportunities which can reduce the environmental impacts to a greater extent. But organic farming of potatoes in India is almost negligible and inconsistent.

Technological design, efficiency and organization of processes in the supply chain that consume these material inputs define the quality and volume of outputs. Changes in supply chain should be technological as well as organizational merit such as changing patterns or relationship between economic actors in the supply chain or within the economic units themselves.

4.4 Innovations in the Potato Supply Chain

Innovations in the potato supply chain have taken place in three major areas:

- Agricultural developments: Many varieties of potato have been developed across the world and various technological systems have been adopted for disease and pest management of potatoes.
- Processing: the early development of potato production and consumption system is full of major process innovations at the stages of agricultural production and food storage and processing. Production of processing varieties of potatoes has been adopted with increasing number of potato processing units in India. Increasing consumer's disposable income, living standards and preference for variety of products lead to the diversification of potato consumption in India. Major potato processing players such as MCains, pepsico frito lay have entered into India looking at huge opportunities in this sector.
- Organization of the supply chain: the organizational change such as creation of organized industry for processing potatoes has been a great leap in the development of potato production and consumption system, however in many parts of the India traditional potato supply chain is dominant due to inefficient marketing channels. Various domestic processing units have also been set up to cater to the consumer's demand. Contract farming has also been adopted by foreign and private processing firms in India which has proved to be successful to an extent

but certain relationship and legal issues still needs to be addressed by forming suitable agricultural acts.

The current key innovations in the potato supply chain are depicted in Table 5. Technological change pattern within the potato supply chain indicates a shift from major process development to minor product development. New varieties of potatoes are introduced using the advanced techniques and these innovations can be considered as minor product developments.

Impact on sustainability at each stage is the major issue to consider if we look into the predictions of the rate of increase in population and climate change. In such a scenario efficiency should be given importance to meet the future challenges of resource scarcity. It has been identified that more than 90% of water is consumed at the stage of agricultural growing and other resources include diesel and chemicals to increase yield. Technological alternatives for resource optimization have already been adopted by developed countries like China, UK and USA. Waste is also identified at every stage of potato supply chain so that initiatives for resource optimization can be taken to achieve sustainability. Quantitative losses of potato at different stages in the supply chain are depicted in Table 6. Quantitative losses at processing and consumption stages are difficult to be identified. Addressing waste is a major issue in India. Currently product development is more significant for the

Table 5 Current key areas for innovation in the conventional potato supply chain

Life cycle of potato	Description	Product versus process development	Possible effect on sustainability
Seed development	New product varieties of potato	Product development	Impacts on energy use, waste generation, food miles
Seed selection	Development of new potato varieties	Product development	Increased domination of potatoes at the cost of others
Cultivation	Need based use of micro-nutrients, fertilizes and drip irrigation	Product development	Exposure of chemicals in environments, excessive water usage, loss of bio-mass in production of energy
Packing	Packaging solutions using economical products	Product development	Recycling of packaging material is energy intensive
Potato processing	Improved technology to increase shelf-life and nutrition enhancement	Product and process development	Loss of many native varieties, impact on environment due to energy use, wastage and emissions
Retail	New storage and distribution techniques.	Organizational and logistic change	Effects on economic actors within the supply chain such as small grocers and farmers
Food service	New product development	Product development	Impacts on energy use, packaging supplies and waste generation

supply chain than process development. Examples of product developments include the introduction of new potato varieties, new potato products, such as potato chips, flakes, mashed potato and new Indian ready meals. All this product development bring unavoidable changes to process development with changes in processing cycles, parts and modification of technology.

Although innovations are taking place at every stage of supply chain, technological changes in processing and distribution stages have greater effects upon the supply chain. Technological changes within the potato supply chain have significant implications in relation to time. This will involve shortening of duration of one or more stages of the supply chain such as reduction for storage, processing, transportation of products to retailers. The sourcing of materials for the consumption and production of potatoes, has witnessed an increasing degree of globalization of the supply chain. Seeds may be produced and imported from one country, grown and harvested in another country and possibly processed and consumed in third country. Moreover, food related technologies are widely exchanged between nations in the form of new products and new processes.

4.5 Case Study of Merino-Vegit

Merino Group is the largest provider of potato storage and processing facilities in the Indian market today, the group commenced this line of business in the year 1968. It then diversified its scope of activities from cold storage to farming, bio-technology and food processing. Tissue culture labs and green houses have been put up at Bhimtal (Uttaranchal) and Hapur (Uttar Pradesh). This integration is in both the directions—forward and backward and has shaped Vegit's brand initiative in the FMCG market where it launched Vegit Aloo mash as well as potato

Table 6 Quantitative losses of potato at different stages in the supply chain

Stages	Causes	Estimated losses
Harvesting	Diseased, outsize, cut potatoes. Overheating of tubers due to direct exposure to sunlight. Rough handling by laborers.	5–6%
Storage	Loss due to non-refrigerated storage (situ, heap, pit storage). Weight loss due to long time storage. Mishandling of packets while loading and unloading	3–6%
Trading	Poor infrastructure of APMC's, unhygienic surroundings of street hawkers selling potatoes, water loss and Rottage during transportation	10%
Consumers (Institutional)	Peel waste from restaurants, hotels etc.	–
Processing	Peeling, white and grey starch released while cutting and blanching potatoes	–

flakes and ready to cook snack mixes. The first of its kind potato-processing plant established in Hapur is completely automated, with minimal requirement for supervision. Since commissioning this plant, Merino group has emerged as a leading supplier of technical seed in the Indian market, raw potato through institutions (both wholesale and retail market), and potato flakes-based ready-to-cook snack mixes in the retail market, under the brand name Vegit.

To support potato flakes processing and for a consistent supply of best quality raw materials, Merino has integrated its agri-operations from tissue culture to food processing. Merino-vegit has set up tissue culture labs for development and multiplication of potato and various other seeds. Merino now produces CPRI-certified seed at its 200-acre farm in Garh Mukteswar. That enables the UP farmer to realise 12–15 tonnes per acre productivity from the current 7–8 tonnes per acre. For harvesting and producing the best variety of potatoes Merino has taken up tissue culture across 2000 acres of land. Merino provides modern farming concepts to the farmers. The storage facilities of merino are CIPC treated to keep the potatoes sugar free round the year.

Merino vegit has adopted sustainable practices by adopting various activities such as meeting a major part of electrical and heat energy requirements through agro-waste fired boilers and steam turbines. It utilizes ash and slurry as organic mass and produces bio-gas from the waste. In the process it produces more than 500 Million tons of vermi-compost using the waste from the potato processing plant. It burns all combustible waste to produce heat. It encourages plantation and development of "Green Belts" inside their premises as well as in the neighborhood.

4.5.1 Diffusion of Technology and Their Impacts

The most important trend that is taking place within the potato supply chain in India is the specialization of potato varieties for specific markets. CPRI has concentrated its efforts on the development of varieties which are short-day adapted, heat and drought tolerant, resistant to degenerative viruses, and relatively storable during hot Indian summers. A few varieties have been cited as generally popular, among them Phulwa, Darjeeling Red Round, and Gola and Kufri Jyoti, Kufri Bahar, and Kufri Sindhuri [42]. Varieties have been selected for consumption in fresh form, but a more recent objective of varietal development has been selection for processing, i.e. varieties with high dry matter content and low levels of reducing sugars. The first two processing varieties, Kufri Chipsona-1 and Kufri Chipsona-2, have been released in 1998 [42]. As the number of uses to which potatoes are put has increased, so a specialization of varieties has emerged. There are certain potato varieties, which are more suitable for boiling, others for frying, and others are more likely to end up in salads. Long tubers are preferred for French fries and round to oval potatoes are preferred for the preparation of chips. All potato varieties in India are not process able, thus a surplus in potato production does not imply a surplus in material availability for processing industry. CPRI has released five varieties that are considered suitable for processing, of which two-kufri chipsona-I and kufri chipsona-II are exclusive for processing. At present Gujrat is the major producer of processing type of potato. Cultivation of processing varieties has started taking place in other potato producing areas.

The life cycle of potato variety is relatively long; they achieve commercial success after ten years of invention. Varieties are promoted not only by seed companies, but by packers and industrial processors as well. Big potato processing players subcontract potato growers and supply them with particular varieties and provide them technical support, because the production of complex processed foods leads to increased requirements for consistency in variety, quality, shape and size of raw material. Improved agricultural techniques and use of fertilizers ensures the fulfillment of these requirements. Therefore specialization of potato processors for production of certain potato products leads to specialization of growers for production of certain potato varieties. Certain varieties of potatoes are preferred for crisping potatoes, other varieties are preferred for chipping and further varieties are best for sale on the fresh market.

5 Conclusion

The analysis of the Indian potato supply chain shows that it is affected by several major trends. The potato supply chain in India is fragmented and moving towards integration in terms of contract farming. Structural changes in the supply chain of potatoes have been occurring at a fast rate and have implications upon the actors involved in terms of social, environmental and economic sustainability. Technological developments leads to a greater number of new food products and consumer now have greater choice of products. Food consumption pattern have changed during last decades leading to consumption of more processed foods. The potato supply chain in India is highly fragmented and unorganized and needs a lot of improvement. Good agriculture practices are hardly implemented by traditional farmers which has a negative impact on overall supply chain of potato. Only few private players like Mcains and Merino industry have been working with farmers through contract farming and providing good returns to them but there are certain issues in contract farming like risk of rejection, absence of alternative markets, reduced contract prices due to low quality. Public policies and legal frameworks need to be developed in order to address these issues. Environmental issues need to be in frequent check with increasing production and processing because energy utilization and water wastage results in depletion of water table. Sustainable alternatives of potato waste needs to be identified which have already been in process in other developed countries. Sustainable potato packaging can be produced by potato starch waste which is generated by potato processing. Technological innovations in the potato supply chain take place at stages such as seed production, agriculture growing, processing and marketing. However, these innovations have largely incremental product developments. Exclusive potato supply chains of have been emerging but, these chains have been highly dependent on special clients such as processing units. If grower of crisping potatoes fails to meet the specifications of a potato crisper, the grower has limited economic alternatives for disposal of his or her harvest.

References

1. Amara, N., & Landry, R. (2005). Sources of information as determinants of novelty of innovation in manufacturing firms: Evidence from the 1999 statistics Canada innovation survey. *Technovation, 25*(3), 245–259.
2. Acquaah, M., Amoako-Gyampah, K., & Jayaram, J. (2011). Resilience in family and non-family firms: An examination of the relationship between manufacturing strategy, competitive strategy and firm performance. *International Journal of Production Research, 49* (18), 5527–5544.
3. Audretsch, D. B., & Feldman, M. P. (1996). R&D spill overs and the geography of innovation and production. *American Economic Review, 86*(3), 630–640.
4. Audretsch, D. B., & Feldman, M. P. (1996). Innovative clusters and the industry life cycle. *Review of Industrial Organization, 11*(2), 253–273.
5. Baldwin, J., & Sabourin, D. (2000). Innovative activity in Canadian food processing establishments: The Importance of engineering practices. *International Journal of Technology Management, 20,* 511–527.
6. Beckeman, M., & Skjo-ldebrand, C. (2007). Clusters/networks promote food innovations. *Journal of Food Engineering, 79*(4), 1418–1425.
7. Berchicci, L. (2013). Towards an open R&D system: Internal R&D investment, external knowledge acquisition and innovative performance. *Research Policy, 42*(1), 117–127.
8. Bigliardi, B., Colacino, P., & Dormio, A. I. (2011). Innovative characteristics of small and medium enterprises. *Journal of Technology Management & Innovation, 6*(2), 83–93.
9. Bröring, S., Cloutier, L. M., & Leker, J. (2006). The front end of innovation in an era of industry convergence: Evidence from nutraceuticals and functional food. *R&D Management, 36*(5), 487–498.
10. Caiazza, R., & Volpe, T. (2013). How Companion SME can compete in the global agro-food industry. *Journal of Food Products Marketing, 19*(5), 406–412.
11. Caiazza, R., & Volpe, T. (2014). Main rules and actors of Italian system of innovation: How to become competitive in spin-off activity. *Journal of Enterprising Communities: People and Places in the Global Economy, 8*(3), 188–197.
12. Capitanio, F., Coppola, A., & Pascucci, S. (2010). Product and process innovation in the Italian food industry. *Agribusiness, 26*(4), 503–518.
13. Chesbrough, H. W. (2003). The era of open innovation. *MIT Sloan Management Review, 44* (3), 35–41.
14. Chesbrough, H. W. (2003). *Open innovation: The new imperative for creating and profiting from technology.* Cambridge, MA: Harvard Business School Press.
15. Christensen, J. L., Rama, R., & von Tunzelman, N. (1996). *Study on innovation in the European food products and beverages industry.* Brussels: European Commission Report.
16. Cohen, W. M., & Levinthal, D. A. (1990). Absorptive capacity: A new perspective on learning and innovation. *Administrative Science Quarterly, 35*(1), 128–152.
17. Costa, A. I. A., & Jongen, W. M. F. (2006). New insights into consumer-led food product development. *Trends in Food Science & Technology, 17*(8), 457–465.
18. Das, K. (1998). Collective dynamism and firm strategy: Study of an Indian industrial cluster. *Entrepreneurship and Regional Development, 10*(1), 33–49.

19. Daneshvar, P., & Ramesh, H. N. (2010). Information technology and corporate strategy in small and medium enterprises. *International Journal of Management and Strategy, 1*(1), 1–16.
20. Danis, W. M., Chiaburu, D. S., & Lyles, M. A. (2010). The impact of managerial networking intensity and market-based strategies on firm growth during institutional upheaval: A study of small and medium-sized enterprises in a transition economy. *Journal of International Business Studies, 41*(2), 287–307.
21. Doloreux, D. (2004). Regional networks of small and medium sized enterprises: Evidence from the metropolitan area of Ottawa in Canada. *European Planning Studies, 12*(2), 173–189.
22. eands.dacnet.nic.in/…122012/Agriculture_at_a_Glance%202012/Pages242%E2%80%93316.pdf. Agricultural Statistics at a Glance—2012. Approach on May 14, 2016.
23. Fearne, A., & Hughes, D. (1999). Success factors in the fresh produce supply chain: Insights from the UK. *Supply Chain Management: An International Journal, 4*(3), 120–131.
24. Fernie, J., & Sparks, L. (2009). Retail logistics: Changes and challenges. In J. Fernie & L. Sparks (Eds.), *Logistics and retail management* (3rd ed., pp. 3–37). London: Kogan Page.
25. Foreman-Peck, J. (1983). *A history of the world economy-international economic 18 relations since 1850*. London: Harvester Wheatsheaf.
26. Fortuin, F. T. J. M., Batterink, M., & Omta, S. W. F. (2007). Key success factors of innovation in multinational agri-food prospector companies. *The International Food and Agribusiness Management Review, 10*(4), 1–24.
27. Fuller-Love, N. (2006). Management development in small firms. *International Journal of Management Review, 8*(3), 175–190.
28. Garcia Martinez, M., & Briz, J. (2002). Innovation in the Spanish food & drink industry. *The International Food and Agri-business Management Review, 3*(2), 155–176.
29. Galizzi, G., & Venturini, L. (2008). Nature and determinants of product innovation in a competitive environment of changing vertical relationships. In R. Rama (Ed.), *Handbook of innovation in the food and drink industry*. New York, NY: The Haworth Press.
30. Greco, M., Grimaldi, M., & Cricelli, L. (2016). An analysis of the open innovation effect on firm performance. *European Management Journal, 34*(5), 501–516.
31. Galende, J., & de la Fuente, J. M. (2003). Internal factors determining a firm's innovative behaviour. *Research Policy, 32*(5), 715–736.
32. Grunert, K. G., Jensen, B. B., Sonne, A. M., Brunsø, K., Byrne, D. V., Clausen, C., et al. (2008). User-oriented innovation in the food sector: Relevant streams of research and an agenda for future work. *Trends in Food Science & Technology, 19*(11), 590–602.
33. Guan, J., & Ma, N. (2003). Innovative capability and export performance of Chinese firms. *Technovation, 23*(9), 737–747.
34. Hoang, H., & Antoncic, B. (2003). Network based research in entrepreneurship: A critical view. *Journal of Business Venturing, 18,* 165–187.
35. Howells, J., Gagliardi, D., & Malik, K. (2008). The growth and management of R&D outsourcing: Evidence from UK pharmaceuticals. *R&D Management, 38*(2), 205–219.
36. IBEF. (2017). Agriculture. Available at https://www.ibef.org/download/Agriculture-February-2017.pdf. Approach on June 14, 2017.
37. Knudsen, M. P. (2007). The relative importance of inter-firm relationships and knowledge transfer for new product development success. *Journal of Product Innovation Management, 24*(2), 117–138.
38. Kumar, A., & Pandey, S. K. (2008). Potato production: Harbinger of agricultural sustainability. *Indian Farming, 58*(9), 3–7.
39. Kühne, B. (2011). *Understanding innovation capacity in food chains: The European traditional food sector*. Ghent: Ghent University.
40. Khan, R. S., Grigor, J., Winger, R., & Win, A. (2013). Functional food product development opportunities and challenges for food manufacturers. *Trends in Food Science & Technology, 30*(1), 27–37.

41. Lechner, C., & Dowling, M. (2003). Firm networks: External relationships as sources for the growth and competitiveness of entrepreneurial firms. *Entrepreneurship and Regional Development, 15*(1), 1–26.
42. Marwaha, R. S., Pandey, S. K., Kumar, D., Singh, S. V., & Kumar, P. (2010). Potato processing scenario in India: Industrial constraints, future projections, challenges ahead and remedies-A review. *Journal of Food Science Technology, 47*(2), 137–156.
43. Mascarenhas, O. A., Kesavan, R., & Bernacchi, M. (2004). Customer value-chain involvement for co-creating customer delight. *Journal of Consumer Marketing, 21*(7), 486–496.
44. Menrad, K. (2004). Innovations in the food industry in Germany. *Research Policy, 33*(67), 845–878.
45. Miotti, L., & Sachwald, F. (2003). Co-operative R&D: Why and with whom? An integrated framework of analysis. *Research Policy, 32*(8), 1481–1499.
46. Mitra, S. (2005). Information technology as an enabler of growth in firms: Empirical assessments. *Journal of Management Information System, 22*(2), 279–300.
47. Molero, J., & Buesa, M. (1996). Patterns of technological change among Spanish innovative firms: The case of Madrid region. *Research Policy, 25*(4), 647–663.
48. Morgan, K., & Murdoch, J. (2000). Organic vs conventional agriculture: Knowledge, power and innovation in the food chain. *Geoforum, 31*(2), 159–173.
49. Narula, R. (2004). R&D collaboration by SMEs: New opportunities and limitations in the face of globalisation. *Technovation, 24*(2), 153–161.
50. Nieto, M. J., & Santamaría, L. (2007). The importance of diverse collaborative networks for the novelty of product innovation. *Technovation, 27*(6–7), 367–377.
51. Olugbode, M., Elbeltagi, I., Simmons, M., & Biss, T. (2008). The effect of information system on firm performance and profitability using a case study approach. *The Electronic Journal Information Systems Evaluation, 11*(1), 11–16.
52. Omta, S. W. F., & Folstar, P. (2005). Integration of innovation in the corporate strategy of agri-food companies. In W. M. H. Jongen & M. T. G. Meulenberg (Eds.), *Innovation in agri-food systems* (pp. 223–246). Wageningen: Wageningen Academic Publishers.
53. Pavitt, K. (1984). Sectoral patterns of technical change: Towards a taxonomy and a theory. *Research Policy, 13*(6), 343–373.
54. Penrose, E. (1959). *The theory of the growth of the firm*. Oxford.
55. Pomfret, R., & Shapiro, D. (1980). Firm size, diversification, and profitability of large corporations in Canada. *Journal of Economic Studies, 7*(3), 140–150.
56. Rao, V. R., McLaughlin, E. W., & Hawkes, G. F. (1995). Supermarket buyer evaluation of hypothetical new product: An empirical analysis. *Agribusiness, 11,* 21–33.
57. Sarkar, S., & Costa, A. I. A. (2008). Dynamics of open innovation in the food industry. *Trends in Food Science & Technology, 19*(11), 574–580.
58. Scott, G. J., & Suarez, U. (2011). Growth rates for potato in India and their implications for Industry. *Potato Journal, 38*(2), 100–112.
59. Sirmon, D. G., Hitt, M. A., & Ireland, R. D. (2007). Managing firm resources in dynamic environments to create value: Looking inside the black box. *Academy of Management Review, 32*(1), 273–292.
60. Sinkula, J. M. (2002). Market-based success, organizational routines, and unlearning. *Journal of Business & Industrial Marketing, 17*(4), 253–269.
61. Steward-Knox, B., & Mitchell, P. (2003). What separates the winners from the losers in new product development. *Trends in Food Science & Technology, 14*(1), 58–64.
62. Steffens, P., Davidsson, P., & Fitzsimmons, J. (2009). Performance configuration over time: Implications for growth- and profit-oriented strategies. *Entrepreneurship: Theory & Practice, 33*(1), 125–148.
63. Street, C. T., & Cameron, A. (2007). External relationships and the small business: A review of small business alliance and network research. *Journal of Small Business Management, 45*(2), 239–266.

64. Szarka, J. (1990). Networking and small firms. *International Small Business Journal, 8*(2), 10–22.
65. Tatikonda, M. V., & Montoya-Weiss, M. M. (2001). Integrating operations and marketing perspectives of product innovation: The influence of organizational process factors and capabilities on development performance. *Management Science, 47*(1), 151–172.
66. Triguero, A., Corcoles, D., & Cuerva, M. C. (2013). Differences in innovation between food and manufacturing firms. *Agribusiness, 29*(3), 273–292.
67. Tsai, K., & Wang, J. (2009). External technology sourcing and innovation performance in LMT sectors: An analysis based on the Taiwanese technological innovation survey. *Research Policy, 38*(3), 518–526.
68. Vanhaverbeke, W., & Cloodt, M. (2006). Open innovation in value networks. In H. Chesbrough, W. Vanhaverbeke & J. West (Eds.), *Open innovation researching a new paradigm*. Oxford: Oxford University Press.
69. Wittmann, M. C., Hunt, S. D., & Arnett, D. B. (2009). Explaining alliance success: Competences, resources, relational factors, and resource-advantage theory. *Industrial Marketing Management, 38*(7), 743–756. www.ibef.org/research. Approach on April 24, 2017.
70. Yam, R. C. M., Guan, J. C., Pun, K. F., & Tang, E. P. Y. (2004). An audit of technological innovation capabilities in Chinese firms: Some empirical findings in Beijing, China. *Research Policy, 33*(8), 1123–1140.
71. Yin, R. K. (2016). *Qualitative research: From start to finish*. New York: Guildford Press.
72. Zeng, S. X., Xie, X. M., & Tam, C. M. (2010). Relationship between cooperation networks and innovation performance of SMEs. *Technovation, 30*(3), 181–194.
73. Zhou, K. Z., Yim, C. K., & Tse, D. K. (2005). The effects of strategic orientations on technology and market-based breakthrough innovations. *Journal of Marketing, 69*(2), 42–60.

The Impact of Green Supply Chain Management Practices on Competitive Advantages and Firm Performance

Xiaojing Jia and Meng Wang

Abstract This study attempts to contribute to the growing research on green supply chain management (GSCM) strategies by relying on Potter's theory of competitive advantage theory. Specifically, it investigates the relationship among GSCM practices, competitive advantages, and firm performance, using multiple linear regression analysis to analyze data from a survey of Chinese manufacturers. The results show that GSCM practices are positively correlated to competitive advantages and non-finance performance, and competitive advantage is positively related to firm performance.

Keywords Green supply chain management · Competitive advantages
Firm performance

1 Introduction

Green supply chain management (GSCM) can be generally defined as the practice of improving environmental performance along the supply chain, including product design, operations management, and customer relationships [1]. A significant number of GSCM studies have investigated whether the implementation of environmental supply chain strategies leads to enhanced firm performance [2]. Thus, GSCM is a modern management model that integrates environmental awareness and efficient resource utilization into supply chain management; it is a process in which supply chain firms incorporate environmentally sustainable practices into its

Supported by the National Natural Science Foundation of China (Grant No. 7177418).

X. Jia (✉) · M. Wang
Central University of Finance and Economics, Beijing, China
e-mail: jxjxj2005@163.com

X. Liu (ed.), *Environmental Sustainability in Asian Logistics and Supply Chains*,
https://doi.org/10.1007/978-981-13-0451-4_7

management process in order to promote both efficiency and environment benefits. Through these the entire supply chain system coordinates with environment management to optimize internally and externally.

2 Theoretical Framework and Hypothesis

Prahalad and Hamel [3] suggests that the competitive advantage of a firm comes from its core competence, and the difference in core competence results in differences in efficiency and profitability.

Potter's theory of competitive advantage (1985) states that firms mainly acquire competitive advantage in two ways. The first is through the cost driving method, which accounts for a significant proportion of the total cost of a firm. If firms can control cost drivers, they can gain a cost advantage over their competitors. The second is to reconstruct the value chain, which means to change the relative cost of firm status. Firms can implement more efficient ways of designing, producing, distributing, or selling their products, which means rebuilding the value chain to obtain cost advantages. The implementation of GSCM will increase the core competence for firms and bring corresponding advantages in terms of cost, innovations, and environmental impact. Furthermore, competitive advantages affect corporate performance, which is also the theoretical basis of this study.

Figure 1 shows our conceptual model. Building on the above two theories, this research assumes that GSCM practices are directly positively related to firm competitive advantages. This research also assumes that GSCM practices have a positive correlation with firm performance. At the same time, this research assumes that competitive advantages also directly influence firm performance.

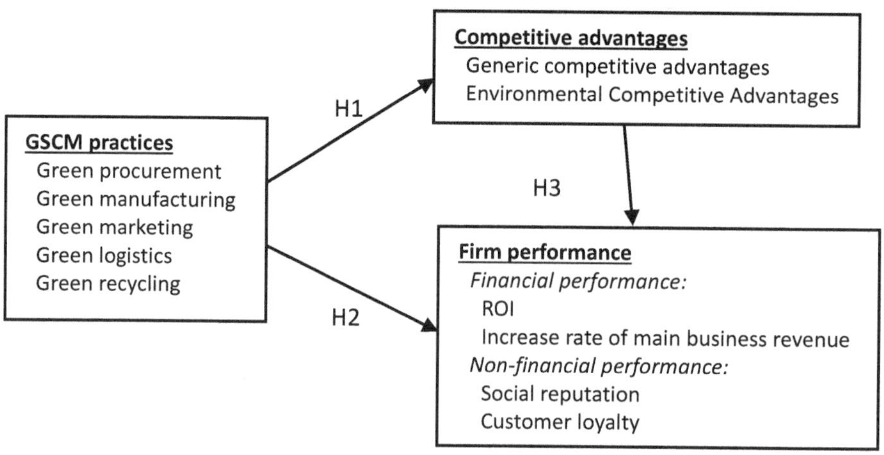

Fig. 1 Conceptual framework

Green et al. [4] has pointed out that between organizations, cooperative relationships and methods are the key to promoting, motivating, and compelling firms to achieve activities compatible with their main environmental goals. Nagel [5] suggests that GSCM involves product usage, composition, and the whole process of production. On the basis of the original supply chain emphasizes on environmental protection awareness. And during operations, technical support must be provided. Legarth [6] investigates the application of information technology in green purchasing, focusing on the communication of information in each link of the supply chain. He finds environmental awareness is of great importance to the improvement of procurement efficiency. Handfield et al. [7] states that GSCM practices largely operate under a firm-centered paradigm, focusing on environmental activities within the boundaries of a firm. Markley and Davis [8] implies that firms can develop future competitive advantage by using sustainable supply chain management and proposes that this is possible through accordance with the "triple bottom line" to improve their competitiveness. Walker et al. [9] points out the drivers of and obstacles to the implementation of GSCM, identifying the main external and internal elements of green supply chain management practices, including organization factors, management capabilities, customers, competitors, and social pressures. Albino et al. [10] suggests that although internally focused GSCM practices contribute to improved firm performance, achieving full value from GSCM programs requires a significant commitment to collaboration with various actors.

Drawing from several different theories, this research determines that GSCM practices should include green procurement, manufacturing, marketing, and logistics [11]. This study uses two important indicators of firm performance. The first is financial performance, which is one of the most common drivers for the implementation of GSCM practices. A number of studies have shown that firms that perform better environmentally are also the most successful financially [12]. The second is non-financial performance, defined as social reputation and customer loyalty. With a growing number of firms committing to creating social and environmental value, the measurement and evaluation of environmental performance are becoming more important than ever before [13, 14].

2.1 GSCM Practices and Competitive Advantages

GSCM is practiced by firms through the use of green procurement, environmental protection, and the high utilization rate of materials as raw materials. Designing and using efficient manufacturing processes in production phases reduces downtime and personnel and machine costs during production. Efficient logistics systems can improve the efficiency of transportation and reduce the cost of recycling. At the same time, efficient production processes can improve the flexibility of production and reduce the production cycle of products, enabling consumers to obtain products more quickly. Firms can use green marketing to limit resource waste in the marketing process, and can guide customers to practice environmentally friendly consumption. This can reduce packaging and recycling costs and can also improve corporate service and product quality, thus enhancing firms' social reputation and customer loyalty. In addition, the implementation of GSCM will also provide environmental cost advantages, reduce firms' emissions, reduce the cost of environmental governance, and the risk of fines.

Of course, the implementation of GSCM requires firms to not only understand the core competency of partners but also integrate all chain members of their core competence, especially in terms of green technology. The only way for the entire supply chain to adapt to the changing external marketing environment is to use mutual learning between firms to transform smoothly, increase the availability of resources, and gain competitive advantages. Each member of the supply chain has its own unique resources and capabilities. If the various elements of GSCM can be integrated, firms will be able to obtain the necessary resources, and these resources can also be used to improve overall performance. Complementary resources and capabilities are a source of power for firms in increasing performance. Thus, all the firms on the entire supply chain can share resources, jointly complete the process of value creation, enhance the ability of individual firms and the whole supply chain to provide products or services to customers, and exceed the average earnings in other supply chains [15]. Therefore, the GSCM competitive advantage is the embodiment of firm performance, and the implementation of green supply chain management can enhance a firm's competitive advantages and improve business performance. Based on the above discussion, the following hypotheses are suggested.

H1: GSCM practices are positively related to competitive advantages.

2.2 *GSCM Practices and Firm Performance*

Redesigned GSCM practices have been widely recognized as improving environmental performance, as evidenced by many empirical studies conducted with various products such as electronics [16] and disposable diapers [17]. However, despite explicit advantages from lower production costs, eco-design of GSCM practices was found to be related to poor financial performance [18]. Moreover, GSCM innovations not only improve a firm's image as environmentally friendly but also lead to higher sales growth [19]. For example, Toyota Motor Corporation introduced an LCA system called Eco-VAS (Eco-Vehicle Assessment System) to heighten the environmental performance of its vehicles [20].

It is quite difficult for a single firm to have all the information on a product and its production processes, and instead often depend on many supply chain members for their environmental activities [21]. A number of studies indicate that if firms use more environmentally friendly practices in their controlling of suppliers, customers, and recyclers, they will receive more substantial environmental and financial benefits [22]. With the development of information and communication technologies, it is now possible for firms to easily share their valuable experiences regarding

GSCM practices. For instance, LCA software packages can help firms to quantify their GSCM activities and goals, enabling them to accurately measure the potential environmental and financial consequences of their new product [23]. Based on the above discussion, the following hypotheses are suggested.

H2a: GSCM practices are positively related to financial performance.
H2b: GSCM practices are positively related to non-financial performance.

2.3 Competitive Advantages and Firm Performance

A "competitive advantage" generally signifies a firm being better than other firms in some respect. These firms can provide high quality and low prices, comprehensive services, customer satisfaction, and/or services in the most reasonable time. Improving these capabilities can enable firms to improve their performance, as such advantages can help firms to gain more market shares and increase sales [24, 25]. Timely delivery of products and comprehensive services can enhance customer satisfaction and loyalty, and improve a firm's public image, improving its competitive position. In short, through green supply chain management, firms can increase their competitive advantages and can bring superior performance. Therefore, the following assumption is made.

H3: Competitive advantages have a positive influence on firm performance.

3 Methods

3.1 Research Context

In this paper, the existing research results at home and abroad are based on the aspects of design GSCM research variables, competitive advantage, and business performance, with the relationship tested between them. In order to ensure the validity and reliability of the measurements, this study uses a scale developed according to the purpose of this study and modified as an empirical data collection tool. In this study, the three variables listed above are measured in terms of the following aspects: (1) direct reference to the project proved by empirical research at home and abroad; (2) from the existing research and by combining the purpose of the study with the actual situation of the equipment manufacturing industry to modify the measured items; (3) to communicate with experts and scholars in related fields along with interview results in order to adjust the measure items.

3.2 Control Variables

Large firms are more likely to adopt GSCM practices because they have greater resources and typically face higher environmental pressure than small or medium-sized firms. Industry type is also included as a control variable.

3.3 Sample and Procedures

The data for this study are collected from Chinese manufacturers. Our empirical setting is particularly appropriate for several reasons: First, in recent years, China has adopted many green policies as part of its national development strategy. Second, increasing global competition over the past decade has enabled Chinese firms to improve their ability to conform to global standards for green business. Third, the Chinese government now actively encourages large manufacturers to contribute their green philosophy to small and medium-sized suppliers.

Table 1 List of questionnaire items

GSCM practice factors	
Green procurement	Reproducible of materials during purchasing Recyclability and degradability of materials during purchasing Degree of sharing purchasing information between the functional departments and firms Establishment of a supplier evaluation system Cooperation between firms and suppliers in green purchasing
Green manufacturing	Decomposition and recycling of products Application and innovation of green manufacturing technology Firm resource recycling rate Raw material utilization ratio Satisfaction of product quality Discharge of "three wastes" and pollution around factory area Inspection of safety production Usage of clean energy (solar energy, wind energy, etc.) Firm production adjustment and optimization capabilities Quality difference between recycled products and manufactured products Total quality management plan
Green marketing	Degree of green marketing system standardization Guidance offered to consumers on green consumption Environmentally friendly product marketing activities Ability of after-sales service to meet the needs of green consumption Timely receipt of consumer feedback

(continued)

Table 1 (continued)

Green logistics	Degree of standardization of green logistics distribution system Warehouse efficiency or third/fourth-party logistics Use of green packaging Degree of sharing of logistical information among members in supply chain
Competitive advantages	
Generic competitive advantages	Ability to provide customers with high quality products Ability to provide customers with better price products High production flexibility and the ability to produce products that meet the unique needs of customers Regular introduction of new products or features into the market to ensure a solid competitive position
Environmental competitive advantages	Reduction of harm to the environment in order to gain a sustainable competitive advantage Avoidance of environmental risks Ability to increase environmental governance efforts
Firm performance	
Financial performance:	
ROI	
Increase rate of main business revenue	
Non-financial performance:	
Social reputation	
Customer loyalty	

In order to gather data for a comprehensive scientific analysis of firm GSCM, the present study uses a questionnaire that includes 25 questions about GSCM, 7 questions about competitive advantage, and 4 questions on firm performance, along with basic informational questions about the firm and its profits. According to the questionnaire design principle of Rong Taisheng, the questionnaire employs closed questions in order to minimize difficulty in completion, and collects personal information at the end of the questionnaire in order to improve its overall validity. By Likert scale, 5 grades are designed for each problem according to the actual conditions and effects: 1 = very dissatisfied, 2 = unsatisfied, 3 = neutral, 4 = satisfied, 5 = very satisfied. The 5 grades of firm performance evaluation design are 1 = very bad, 2 = below average, 3 = average, 4 = above average, 5 = very good (Table 1).

3.4 Data Validity

3.4.1 Cronbach's α Reliability Analysis

Reliability analysis is mainly used to scale internal reliability research, and each figure is calculated for the correlation coefficient and the simple relationship between the coefficient of a project eliminated, and internal reliability is analyzed.

Then, the reliability coefficient analysis is done for further research on internal reliability and external reliability. This paper uses Cronbach's α method to test its reliability. The higher the reliability coefficient, the more consistent, stable, and reliable the test result.

3.4.2 Regression Analysis Method

Regression analysis is mainly used for statistical analysis of the relationship between items. The number of changes between the variables is examined and described to reflect this relationship and help people grasp the degree of influence and provide a scientific basis for prediction. This paper uses GSCM as the independent variable and firm competitive advantage and firm performance as dependent variables to analyze the causal relationship between variables.

4 Results

4.1 Descriptive Statistics

		Mean	SD	1	2	3	4	5	6	7	8
1	GM	3.290	0.818	1							
2	GP	3.280	1.019	0.811**	1						
3	GS	3.376	0.820	0.809**	0.709**	1					
4	GL	3.369	0.759	0.701**	0.554**	0.586**	1				
5	GC	3.560	0.765	0.443**	0.425**	0.451**	0.340*	1			
6	EC	3.321	0.895	0.854**	0.823**	0.635**	0.661**	0.411**	1		
7	FP	3.411	0.434	0.476**	0.379*	0.356*	0.379*	0.621**	0.411**	1	
8	NFP	3.565	0.529	0.534**	0.411**	0.579**	0.379*	0.673**	0.422**	0.549**	1

$^{**}p < 0.05$, $^{*}p < 0.01$

Judging from the results of the analysis of descriptive statistics, the mean value of each factor is at a middle level and a little above the average in terms of GSCM. The highest mean is green marketing and the lowest is green procurement, which means green procurement is a weak link in GSCM and that more attention is paid to green marketing. Analysis of competitive advantage shows some firms still have better competitive advantage, and the general competitive advantage is better than the environmental competitive advantage. In terms of firm performance, the mean of non-financial performance is higher, which means that in the implementation of GSCM, some firms achieve greater non-financial performance, and the cost of investment may lead to a reduction of financial performance in the short term.

4.2 *Multiple Linear Regression Analysis*

4.2.1 Analysis of the Influence of GSCM on Firm Competitive Advantage

In this paper, the multiple linear regression model is established to consider the factors that influence GSCM on a firm's competitive advantage, with green manufacturing (GM), green procurement (GP), green marketing (GS), and green logistics (GL) the four factors used as explaining variables, with genetic competitive advantage (GC) and environmental competitive advantage (EC) as interpreted variables for regression analysis. The model can be described as follows:

$$\mathrm{NC} = \beta_0 + \beta_1 GM + \beta_2 GP + \beta_3 GS + \beta_4 GL + \mu$$

$$\mathrm{EC} = \beta_0 + \beta_1 GM + \beta_2 GP + \beta_3 GS + \beta_4 GL + \mu$$

Regression analysis of the influence of GSCM on firm competitive advantage

	β	
	NC	EC
β_0	0.471	0.957*
GM	0.320**	0.369**
GP	0.328***	0.220*
GS	0.395***	0.229*
GL	0.211*	0.250*
R^2	0.762	0.740

*$p < 0.05$, **$p < 0.01$, ***$p < 0.001$

In summary, the four factors of GSCM have a significant positive effect on general competitive advantage and environmental competitive advantage. This shows that sample firms' implementation of GSCM is conducive to the promotion of the firms' competitive advantage, thus putting the firm in a more favorable position among fierce competition. Therefore, assume that H1 is established.

4.2.2 Analysis of the Influence of GSCM on Firm Performance

This study uses a multiple linear regression model to consider the impact of GSCM practices on firm performance, using the factors of green manufacturing (GM), green procurement (GP), green marketing (GS), and green logistics (GL) as explaining variables and financial performance (FP) and non-financial performance (NP) as interpreted variables for regression analysis. The model can be described as follows:

$$FP = \beta_0 + \beta_1 GM + \beta_2 GP + \beta_3 GS + \beta_4 GL + \mu$$

$$NFP = \beta_0 + \beta_1 GM + \beta_2 GP + \beta_3 GS + \beta_4 GL + \mu$$

Regression analysis of the influence of GSCM on firm performance

	β	
	NC	EC
β_0	0.731	0.453*
GM	0.460***	0.269**
GP	0.078	0.120
GS	0.181	0.299*
GL	0.311**	0.350**
R^2	0.742	0.735

*$p < 0.05$, **$p < 0.01$, ***$p < 0.001$

Green manufacturing and green logistics have a significant positive impact on financial performance, but green purchasing and green marketing have no significant impact on financial performance. In addition, green procurement, green manufacturing, green marketing, and green logistics all have significant positive effects on non-financial performance. The results show that by implementing GSCM, sample firms improve financial performance and non-financial performance, creating more economic and social benefits for firms. Therefore, results indicate that H2b is established.

4.2.3 Analysis of the Influence of Competence Advantages on Firm Performance

This study employs a multiple linear regression model to analyze the impact of competence advantages on the performance of firms. It regards general competence advantages (GC) and environmental competence advantages (EC) as explaining variables and financial performance (FP) and non-financial performance (NP) as interpreted variables for regression analysis. The model can be described as follows:

$$FP = \beta_0 + \beta_1 GC + \beta_2 EC + \mu$$

$$NFP = \beta_0 + \beta_1 GC + \beta_2 EC + \mu$$

Regression analysis of the influence of GSCM on firm performance

	β	
	NC	EC
β_0	0.293*	0.493**
GC	0.531***	0.299*
EC	0.298*	0.520**
R^2	0.622	0.525

*$p < 0.05$, **$p < 0.01$, ***$p < 0.001$

As a result, both general competitive advantages and environmental competitive advantages have a significant positive impact on firms' financial and non-financial performance. The results show that sample firms that implement GSCM obtain high competence advantages, and indirectly promote the improvement of their financial and non-financial performance, creating more benefits. Therefore, H3 is established.

5 Discussion

5.1 *Limitations*

GSCM theory and research is becoming more and more common, but empirical studies on the performance of firms implementing GSCM are few. This study takes a single region and industry as a sample to establish the model for empirical research. Because the research content is relatively abstract and simple, it is not enough for in-depth development and application of GSCM.

At the same time, due to the 5-point Likert-scale method used to measure each index of GSCM practices, competitive advantage, and business performance, the data collection has a certain deviation. At the same time, due to the limitation of time and resources, the quantity and quality of data collection in this paper are still insufficient.

5.2 *Implications for Future Research*

In order to enrich the research framework of this thesis, further research will be conducted to make the content of each research variable more detailed. New intermediary variables will also be introduced to analyze the mechanism of GSCM on firm performance. Moreover, collection of empirical data suggests the use of a greater time span, broader geographical area, more types of supply chains, and a greater selection of firms will expand the conclusions of the study. Doing further theoretical research on GSCM, tracking the latest developments of GSCM and adding more mathematical models in the empirical investigation based on the analysis will provide results more appropriate for application by firms.

6 Conclusion

As an important new strategy, GSCM allows firms to achieve financial and market share goals by lowering their environmental costs while ensuring environmentally friendly operations. Recently, the importance of GSCM has received considerable attention. Implementing GSCM can benefit the firm as it can be a revenue driver. However, most GSCM-related studies have yet to investigate which firm capabilities are needed for the successful implementation of GSCM. This study shows that a positive relationship exists between GSCM practices and firm competence advantages, which means that the use of green manufacturing to reduce raw material consumption and waste will reduce product cost, improve product quality, and prevent environmental risks, thus enabling firms to gain general and environmental competitive advantages. Through green procurement, firms can use green materials and other measures to provide high quality products to customers, thereby satisfying customers' unique needs and ensuring a stable competitive position. Of course, the usage of green materials can also reduce the harm to the environment, thus providing another competitive advantage. Firms can use green marketing to provide competitively priced products to customers, thereby gaining a better general competitive advantage, and can also reduce waste in marketing for an environmental competitive advantage. The implementation of advanced logistics technology to reduce environmental pollution has a positive impact on the general competitive advantage and provides a strong environmental competitive advantage.

This study also implies that GSCM practices have a positive relationship with non-finance performance and partly for finance performance. Firms that implement green manufacturing by improving product quality and reducing waste to adapt to consumer demands increase their market shares and consolidate their market position. Of course, high quality products and green manufacturing systems can create a positive image for firms as well as promote sustainable development. The results show that green manufacturing can improve the financial and non-financial performance of firms and bring positive effects to all aspects of firm development. By considering the cost of green procurement, purchasing environmentally friendly materials will increase the cost of firms, and supplier assessment also requires companies to pay certain fees and costs. Because procurement, as an internal activity, is not visible to consumers, the implementation of green procurement has no obvious impact on financial and non-financial performance. Firms' green marketing is affected by business activities, which can increase their public influence and afford better non-financial performance. Perhaps due to the cost of the problem, the implementation of green logistics has no significant impact on financial performance. The logistical system is efficiency, not only reducing consumption of resources and cost, but also reducing the negative impact on the environment. This improves firms' public image, and the increase in financial performance also brings good non-financial performance. At the same time, general competence advantages and environmental competence advantages can enable firms to perform better.

References

1. Srivastava, S. K. (2007). Green supply-chain management: A state-of-the-art literature review. *International Journal of Management Reviews, 9,* 53–80.
2. Sarkis, J. (2012). A boundaries and flows perspective of green supply chain management. *Supply Chain Management: An International Journal, 17,* 202–216.
3. Prahalad, C. K., & Hamel, G. L. (1990). The core competence of the corporation. *Harvard Business Review, 68*(3), 79–91.
4. Green, K., Morton, B., & New, S. (2000). Greening organizations: Purchasing, consumption, and innovation. *Organization & Environment, 13*(2), 206–225.
5. Nagel, M. H. (2000). Environmental supply-chain management versus green procurement in the scope of a business and leadership perspective. *IEEE, 13*(3), 219–224.
6. Legarth, J. B. (2001). Internet assisted environmental purchasing. *Corporate Environmental Strategy, 8*(3), 269–274.
7. Handfield, R. B., Sroufe, R., & Walton, S. V. (2005). Integrating environmental management and supply chain strategies. *Business Strategy and the Environment, 14,* 1–19.
8. Markley, M. J., & Davis, L. (2007). Exploring future competitive advantage through sustainable supply chains. *International Journal of Physical Distribution Logistics Management, 9*(37), 763–774.
9. Walker, H., Sisto, L. D., & McBain, D. (2008). Drivers and barriers to environmental supply chain management practices: Lessons from the public and private sectors. *Journal of Purchasing and Supply Management, 14,* 69–85.
10. Albino, V., Dangelico, R. M., & Pontrandolfo, P. (2012). Do inter-organizational collaborations enhance a firm's environmental performance? A study of the largest US companies. *Journal of Cleaner Production, 37,* 304–315.
11. Zhu, Q., Sarkis, J., Cordeiro, J. J., & Lai, K. H. (2008). Firm-level correlates of emergent green supply chain management practices in the Chinese context. *Omega, 36,* 577–591.
12. Tsoulfas, G. T., & Pappis, C. P. (2008). A model for supply chains environmental performance analysis and decision making. *Journal of Cleaner Production, 16*(15), 1647–1657.
13. Kainuma, Y., & Tawara, N. (2006). A multiple attribute utility theory approach to lean and green supply chain management. *International Journal of Production Economics, 10,* 99–108.
14. Testa, F., & Iraldo, F. (2010). Shadows and lights of green supply chain management: Determinants and effects of these practices based on a multi-national study. *Journal of Cleaner Production, 18,* 953–962.
15. Guide, V. D. R. (2000). Production planning and control for remanufacturing: Industry practice and research needs. *Journal of Operations Management, 18,* 467–483.
16. Aoe, T. (2007). Eco-efficiency and eco-design in electrical and electronic products. *Journal of Cleaner Production, 15,* 1406–1414.
17. Mirabella, N., Castellani, V., & Sala, S. (2013). Life cycle assessment of bio-based products: A disposable diaper case study. *International Journal of Life Cycle Assessment, 18,* 1036–1047.
18. King, A. A., & Lenox, M. J. (2001). Lean and green empirical examination of the relationship between lean production and environmental performance. *Production and Operations Management, 10,* 244–256.

19. Chen, Y. S. (2008). The driver of green innovation and green image green core competence. *Journal of Business Ethics, 81,* 531–543.
20. Nakano, K., Nakaniwa, C., Kabeya, T., Iguchi, T., & Aoki, R. (2007). Current activities of the life cycle assessment society of Japan. *International Journal of Life Cycle Assessment, 12,* 546.
21. Nakano, K., & Hirao, M. (2011). Collaborative activity with business partners for improvement of product environmental performance using LCA. *Journal of Cleaner Production, 19,* 1189–1197.
22. González-Benito, J., & González-Benito, O. (2005). Environmental proactivity and business performance: An empirical analysis. *OMEGA International Journal of Management Science, 33,* 1–15.
23. Vallet, F., Eynard, B., Millet, D., Mahut, S. G., Tyl, B., & Bertoluci, G. (2013). Using eco-design tools: An overview of experts' practices. *Design Studies, 34*(3), 345–377.
24. Blackburn, J., Guide, V., Souza, G., & Van Wassenhove, L. (2004). Reverse supply chains for commercial returns. *California Management Review, 46,* 6–22.
25. Ilgin, M. A., & Gupta, S. M. (2010). Environmentally conscious manufacturing and product recovery (ECMPRO): A review of the state of the art. *Journal of Environmental Management, 91,* 563–591.

Studying the Effect of Ambient Temperature Exposure on Refrigerated Food Quality and Safety for Sustainable Food Cold Chains

Kune-muh Tsai and Kuo-shin Lin

Abstract The temperature of chilled or frozen foods can be easily lost and the quality of them appears worse with frequent opening and closing of insulation compartment doors of vehicles while products are distributed to storage, retail places or households. It is particularly detrimental to food quality when foods are located in an environment having temperature between 7 and 60 °C because this could trigger most microorganisms to proliferate. With proper cold chain logistics, we can maintain food quality of refrigerated foods and protect public health from food contamination. It also could protect a lot of food waste because one third of food waste is resulted from improper food cold chains. By reducing food waste amount, the CO_2 emissions for producing the food waste could be saved. The purpose of this study was to study how the quality and safety of refrigerated food are affected when the food is exposed to ambient temperatures. We designed several experiments to examine the microorganism Counts (8 kinds), water activity (WA), moisture and total volatile basic nitrogen (TVBN) of food samples—fresh (18 °C), chilled and frozen—placed at appropriate and non-compliant temperatures for different periods of time. The test results of foods stored at 25 °C show that there is no change on the test items when foods are stored at non-compliant temperatures for 3 h. The other experiment of foods stored at 25 and 37 °C both show that when foods are exposed to a longer period of time, say 12 h, many test results would go beyond the allowable range. The experimental results show that the central temperature of food does not change significantly within 3 h and thus as refrigerated foods are handled at the operational interfaces, a short period of time exposure, say 30 min, to ambient temperature, say below 15 °C, does not apparently affect food safety. However, at some extreme cases, it could affect food quality as the appearance temperature rises to −4 °C that original small ice crystals begin to thaw. Moreover, repeat exposure could also have accelerated accumulation effects on food quality.

K. Tsai (✉) · K. Lin
Department of Logistics Management, National Kaohsiung University of Science and Technology, Kaohsiung, Taiwan
e-mail: kmtsai@nkust.edu.tw

X. Liu (ed.), *Environmental Sustainability in Asian Logistics and Supply Chains*,
https://doi.org/10.1007/978-981-13-0451-4_8

Keywords Refrigerated food · Food safety and quality · Food cold chains Microorganisms · CO_2 emissions · Sustainability

1 Introduction

With the development of the economy of a society, the demand for cold and frozen foods becomes prominent. In a food cold chain, foods go through processes having temperature/humidity control to keep them fresh and non-deteriorating. Depending on the type and usage of foods, they are stored in different temperature ranges. For frozen foods such as frozen meats, frozen prepared foods, frozen fish, etc., the temperature should be maintained below −18 °C to store the foods for a long time, usually more than 6 months. For chilled foods such as milk, tofu, processed meats, etc., the temperature is maintained below 7 °C. Some chilled foods such as meats, fish, shrimps, etc., are maintained between −2 to 2 °C, just above the zone of maximum ice crystal formation, to keep them fresher. Cooled foods such as chocolates, rice balls, cold noodles, etc. are maintained at 18 °C to keep them fresh and ready-to-eat forms. Table 1 is a list of temperature ranges for temperature controlled foods [3, 18].

1.1 *Food Cold Chains Affect Food Safety and Quality*

Under the WTO framework, the market around the world is asking for a higher variety and quantity of foods; thus, global logistics faces a new challenge in handling an increasing demand for temperature-controlled foods. For example, Japanese snow crabs, salmons, grapes, peaches, etc. are welcomed in major Asian cities, like Hongkong, Taipei, Shanghai, etc. After a customer has made an order,

Table 1 Storage temperature of low-temperature foods

Categories	Storage temperature	Products
Ready-to-eat cooled foods	18 °C	Bento, sandwich, chocolates, etc.
Chilled foods	Between freezing point and 7 °C	Fresh vegetables, juice, milk, processed meats, tofu, flowers, etc.
Freezing point chilled foods	Between −2 and 2 °C	Meat products, poultry products, seafood, ice products, etc.
Frozen foods	Below −18 °C	Frozen vegetables/meats/seafood, frozen prepared foods, ice cream, etc.
Ultra-low temperature frozen foods	Below −30 °C (could be −45/−60 °C)	Fish for sashimi or to be stored longer

fresh produces from local areas would be delivered, under strict temperature control, in a short time, say 1–2 days [15]. Another example is the organic vegetables and fruits from Taiwan. They are demanded in Singapore and hence a large Taiwanese multi-temperature logistics service provider help a Singaporean EC company collect, process and package fresh produces from Taiwan after orders are received. The packaged orders are maintained at appropriate temperature and humidity to be shipped via air to Singapore. It takes about 2+ days from farms in Taiwan to tables in Singapore [16]. The above two examples shows global food cold chains are demanding and they are where global logistics players demonstrate their supreme capability compared to others. It also shows that maintaining foods during logistical processes without temperature breakage is a challenging and important task to assure food safety and quality.

Keeping perishable food in the non-desired temperature range caused by insufficient refrigeration will stimulate the growth of pathogens and spoilage microorganisms and render the product inedible [4]. Meanwhile, it may cause a significant societal cost because of unknown or unreported food safety problem where the food is consumed and induces foodborne illnesses. It is estimated that foodborne illnesses cost more than $50 billion annually in the U.S. and cause more than 120,000 hospitalizations and 3000 deaths [20, 2].

1.2 Food Waste and CO_2 Emissions

It was reported that the largest postharvest loss comes from inappropriate temperature control along the food cold chain in developing and emerging countries [24]. The annual economic impact from food waste was estimated at $218 billion in the U.S., $143 billion in Europe, and $27 billion in Canada [13]. It was estimated that by applying the same quality level of refrigeration in developing countries as that in developed ones would reduce the amount of perishable food wasted annually by more than 200 million tons, which is equivalent to around 14% of the consumption [10, 13]. With global population reaching over 8 billion in 2030 [8, 22], refrigeration is expected to play an even more important role for upgrading food demand. Thus, the need for refrigeration systems keeps rising up. For example, cold storage capacity in India grew by more than four times between 2008 and 2009, while in the US, a 14% growth in the general refrigerated warehouse capacity between 2007 and 2009 [8, 19, 23].

Despite refrigeration is important in maintaining the safety and quality of perishable foods, its operation is energy intensive. The use of refrigeration is a major contributor to global energy consumption, accounting for 15% of the electricity consumed worldwide [5, 8]. In addition, it is also a significant contributing factor to ozone depletion and global warming. This is often due to direct emissions from refrigerant leakage, as well as indirect emissions from the use of fossil fuels to produce the electrical power required to run the refrigeration equipment. It showed that irrespective of the market region and type of refrigeration system, indirect CO_2

emissions is always a major contributor to the global warming. Some food chains go through "cold chains" where continuous refrigeration is used to extend and ensure the shelf life of fresh and processed foods. Although food cold chains help keep perishable food at safety quality; however, it involves the issue of energy consumption. Smith [21] stated that it was estimated that one third of food we produce never reaches the table because it is spoiled in production and in transit or is thrown out by consumers and the amount is equivalent to 1.2 billion tons of food. The energy that goes into production, harvesting, transportation and packaging of the wasted food generates 3.3 billion metric tons of CO_2 emissions and the amount is equivalent to the CO_2 emissions of India and Japan combined or 60% of that of the U.S [17]. According to International Institute of Refrigeration, IIR [10], each year there are 360 million tons of foods being thrown away because of insufficient freezing capacity and capability and the amount is equivalent to 1/3 of food waste. In China alone, each year improper temperature control causes food loss of over RMB 100 billion the amount of food to feed 200 million capita. A well-managed food cold chain can lead to reduced loss of food due to improper refrigeration and the resultant CO_2 emission diminishing can benefit global warming and help the world achieve a more sustainable eco-system.

2 Breakage of Cold Chains and Food Safety and Quality Issues

To store foods fresh for a longer time, temperature control is the most economic ways because low temperature can slow down or freeze microorganisms to grow [1, 18]. Besides, low temperature can keep foods fresh and maintain the color and the taste [3, 18]. For most microorganisms, they grow fast between 10–40 °C and only some may grow slowly between 3–10 °C. When the temperature goes down to −12 to 0 °C, only specific microorganisms may grow and as it continues to go below −12 °C, in general, no microorganism grow [1, 18]. Thus we usually maintain foods below −18 °C as frozen foods to keep them fresh for a long period of time.

It is challenging to maintain proper temperature/humidity along the cold supply chain. Besides the facility and equipment, the breakage of cold chains could occur within processes and at the interface between processes. From farms to forks, foods are usually handled by numerous parties and even though each party can maintain proper temperature/humidity, the interfaces between any two might be neglected. Each cold chain process is performed by operators with facility, equipment and/or transporters. The breakage of cold chains could be from the incapability and/or insufficient capacity of the equipment and facility and/or transporters; it could also be from the ignorance of human operators or they do not follow the SOP (standard of operations) or that the SOP does not consider contingent situations. Many a time, the breakage is resulted from the delay at the interface of two processes due to ignorance. With so many parties involved in a food cold chain, careful management and monitoring by cooperating with people, software and hardware, etc. is necessary.

Even with the impact of food cold chain breakage on food safety, not many papers address the causes of the breakage but instead much research uses case study to describe the problem originated from food cold chain logistics [7, 25]. Little research experimented on the impacts of refrigerated food being exposed to different ambient temperatures on safety and quality issues of food, especially from the perspectives of microorganisms, WA and TVBN [1, 3, 18]. James et al. [11] studied how people use their refrigerators for the past 30 years and found that from the behavior of using refrigerators, households are the weakest spot on cold chain consciousness. The interfaces between any two processes are the most critical points in the cold chain and they affect food quality [6]. We need to be aware that the equipment used along the cold chains is different and the knowledge for proper usage of it is fundamental to the quality and safety of foods [12]. Hu [9] assessed the operational risks of cold chain logistics with a small group of experts and identified 35 failure modes resulted from manufacturers, distributors, retailers, control system and external environment. However, only a small group experts participated thus the failure modes obtained are not extensive. Chen et al. [3] implemented concept mapping with 38 industrial practitioners to study the causes of food cold chain breakage and had obtained 55 factors divided into 6 dimensions.

3 Methods

In a well-managed cold chain system, breakage of a cold chain is uncommon. However, there are places, especially during interface transitions between processes, it is unavoidable that refrigerated products could expose to ambient temperatures. In this study, we would like to investigate the effect of temperature inconformity on food quality and safety. We designed several experiments to examine the microorganism counts (8 kinds), Water Activity (AW), Moisture and Total Volatile Basic Nitrogen (TVBN) of food samples—fresh (18 °C), chilled and frozen—placed at appropriate and non-compliant temperatures for different periods of time. The examination results can be used as a reference for cold chain companies in setting their operational standards in handling food products.

3.1 The Law and Regulation on Food Safety Control in Taiwan

In recent years, food safety incidents have caused troubles and uneasiness in food consumption and daily life. According to the definition of the World Health Organization, food safety refers to the public health problem impacted by toxic and/

or hazardous substances in food on human health. It also affects the competitiveness of food manufacturers in the international market. Food safety issues have been widely concerned by the whole citizen, governments and enterprises in Taiwan.

To protect the safety and health of citizens, the Ministry of Health and Welfare (MOHW) in Taiwan legislates "Act Governing Food Safety and Sanitation" to define food additives, dosage of preservatives, inspected microorganisms, limitation in numbers of microorganism and so on in processed foods [14]. Meanwhile, the government also announced the standard examine methods of microorganisms to ensure the measurement of microorganism with the methods can be trusted and managed at all commercial products [14]. The "Good Hygiene Practice" promoted by the MOHW of Taiwan in 2013 requested that food logistics companies should follow the regulations stipulated in Chapter Four entitling "Food logistics industry." In practice, government officers require food logistics companies to obey the Article 16.8 that food logistics companies cannot arbitrarily change product storage temperature set by food manufacturers to ensure low-temperature foods are stored in defined temperature range specified by the regulation during the logistics processes at warehousing, transportation and retailing.

In fact, chilled or frozen foods could easily lose the temperature and appear worse in quality caused by frequently opening and closing the insulation compartment doors of vehicles when the products are distributed to storage, retail places or consumer homes from manufacturers. Besides, in order to manage the food quality in the market, the Council of Agriculture, Executive Yuan of Taiwan developed a system of certified agricultural standards (CAS). The limits for microorganism tests of frozen and chilled foods are displayed in Tables 3 and 4, respectively.

3.2 Experimental Design

In the experiment, we examined foods after being stored at different non-compliant temperatures for diverse periods of time. We bought samples of fresh, chilled and frozen foods from supermarkets, convenience stores and online stores having good storage facilities. Samples were first checked with an infrared thermometer on the surface temperature immediately after they were obtained. They were then placed in insulation bags that were pre-cooled to −18, 7 or 18 °C, respectively, for frozen, chilled and fresh food products. Foods were then taken back to the laboratory freezer or refrigerator to be stored for at least 12 h to make sure the central temperature of them were at −18, 7 or 18 °C. The experimental procedure is shown in Fig. 1.

We examined the physical, chemical and biological characteristics of food samples stored at non-compliant temperatures and the examinations comprise water activity, food temperature, appearance condition, Total volatile base nitrogen (TVBN) and 8 kinds of microorganism listed in Table 2. The test items, methods,

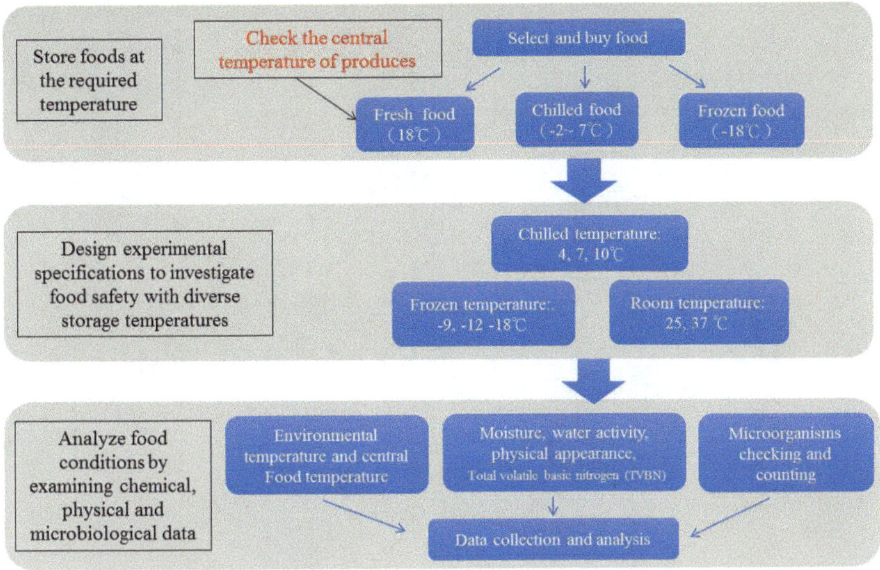

Fig. 1 The experimental procedure

and standards accord to the laws of food safety and hygiene announced by Ministry of Health and Welfare (MOHW), Taiwan and are displayed on Tables 3 and 4.

When foods are stored at ambient temperature between 7–60 °C, the microorganisms would proliferate exponentially, which could lead to food quality and safety problems. In handling and distributing food products or parcels, many a time, it is very likely for them to expose to non-compliant ambient temperatures and the experiment was to study how this exposure might affect food quality and safety and the result be referenced to be defined in the operational standards of service providers to reduce possible food waste. We designed several experiments to investigate the influence on food safety and quality.

4 Results

Experiment I

In the first experiment, chilled foods (4 °C), including juices, noodles, meats, vegetables, cakes, etc. were stored at 4, 7 and 10 °C; frozen foods (−18 °C) such as frozen chicken, frozen fish and ice creams were stored at −9, −12, and −18 °C. The tests after three hours show no significant difference on all the test items listed on Fig. 2 between those stored at 4 °C and those at 7 and 10 °C for chilled foods and −18 °C and those at −9 and −12 °C for frozen foods.

Table 2 Food items and test items

		Test items											
Storage condition	Food category	Aerobic plate count (APC)	*Escherichia coil*	*Coliform*	*Staphyloccocus aureus*	*Salmonella*	*Bacillus cereus*	*Vibrio parahaemolyticus*	*Listeria monocytogenes*	Water activity	Moisture	Mold	Total volatile basic nitrogen (TVBN)
Fresh foods (18 °C)	Hand rolls	•	•	•	•	•	•	•	•	•	•	•	•
	Bentos	•	•	•	•	•	•	•	•	•	•	•	•
	Rice dumpling	•	•	•	•	•	•	•	•	•	•	•	•
Chilled foods (7 to −2 °C)	Meats	•	•	•	•	•			•	•	•	•	
	Drinks	•	•	•	•	•			•	•	•	•	
	Vegetable	•	•	•	•					•	•	•	
	Cake	•	•	•	•	•	•		•	•	•	•	
	Noodle	•	•	•	•		•			•	•	•	
	Milk	•	•	•	•	•			•	•	•	•	
Frozen foods (−18 °C)	Seafood	•	•	•	•			•		•	•		•
	Ice cream	•	•	•	•	•		•	•		•	•	
	Meats	•	•	•	•					•	•		•

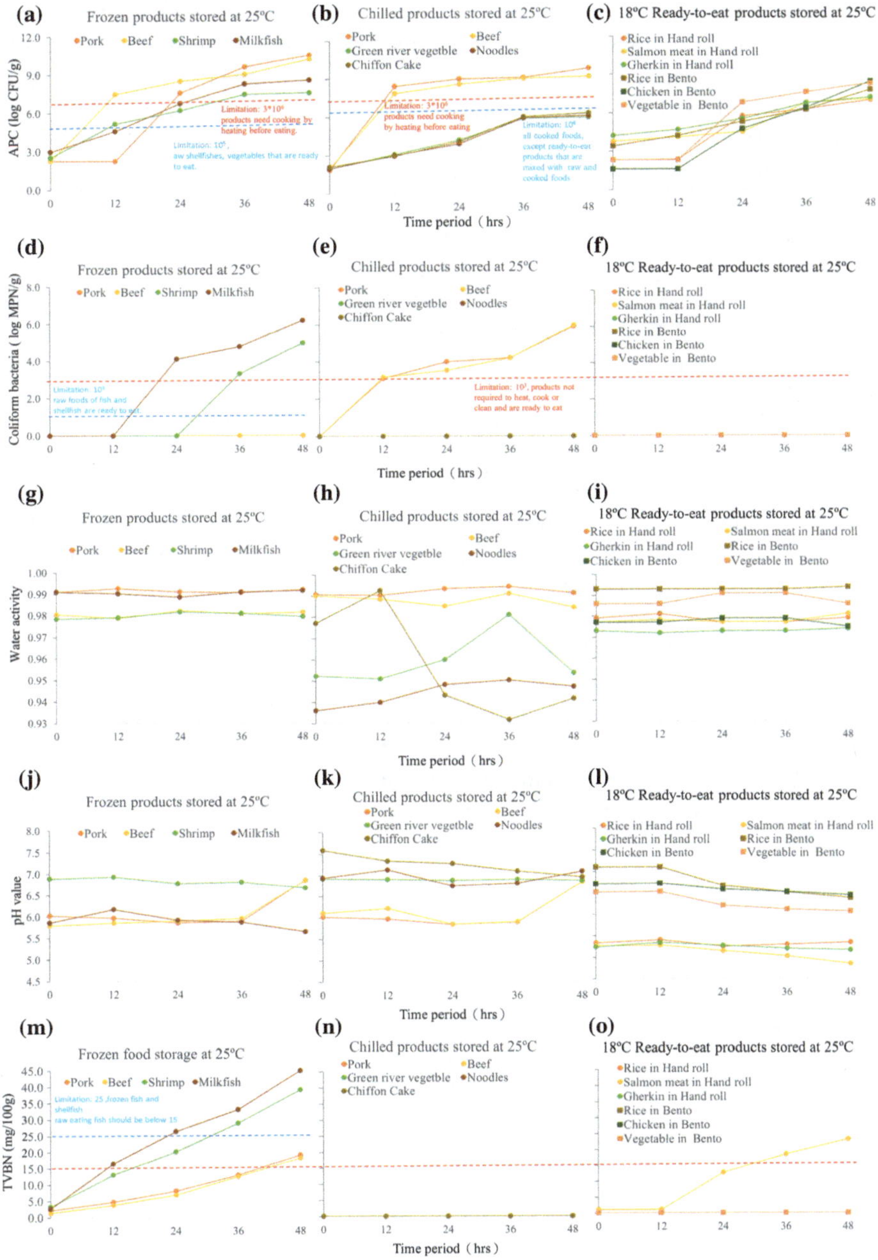

Fig. 2 Experimental results for frozen, chilled and ready-to-eat foods stored at 25 °C

Experiment II

We know that three hours cannot trigger microorganisms to grow and TVBN to increase. Thus, in the second experiment, we plan to experiment for a longer period of time, i.e., up to 48 h. In the experiment, we tested frozen pork, beef, milkfish, shrimps (−18 °C) stored at −18, 7 and 25 °C, chilled foods of pork, beef, vegetables, cakes and noodles stored at 4, 18, 25 and 37 °C as well as 18 °C of fresh foods such as lunch boxes and hand rolls stored at 18, 25 and 37 °C. Figure 3a–c shows the APC (Aerobic plate count for total bacteria) of the frozen, chilled and fresh foods after being stored at 25 °C and it shows that after 12 h, many figures go beyond the allowable range of 6 log CFU/g for APC. Other sub-figures in Fig. 3 are test results regarding coliform bacteria, water activity (WA), pH value and Total VBN. In Fig. 3, similar test results for chilled foods stored at 37 °C is displayed.

Beside microorganisms and WA, other food characteristics measured, such as pH, TVBN, Coliform bacteria and food appearance, etc. are all important conditions to discriminate foods quality. For example, the TVBN limit was 15 mg/100 g for raw-eaten fish/shellfish and foods that require cooking by heating before eating according to regulations set by MHOW. The pH value for fresh meats is about 5.8–6.4 but it could go up to over 6.7 when meat is under the decomposition process. Similar situations with different pH values during the decomposition process can be seen on products such as fish, shellfish, vegetables, fruits, etc. Thus, pH values can be one of the good methods to distinguish food quality. Other test results displayed at Fig. 3d–f have shown significant change of Coliform bacteria counts for foods store at 25 °C after 12 h. For TVBN on frozen food and 18 °C fresh chilled food stored at 25 °C, they go beyond the limit in a few hours, respectively. Others bacteria species shown in Table 2, such as *Staphyloccocus aureus*, *Salmonella*,

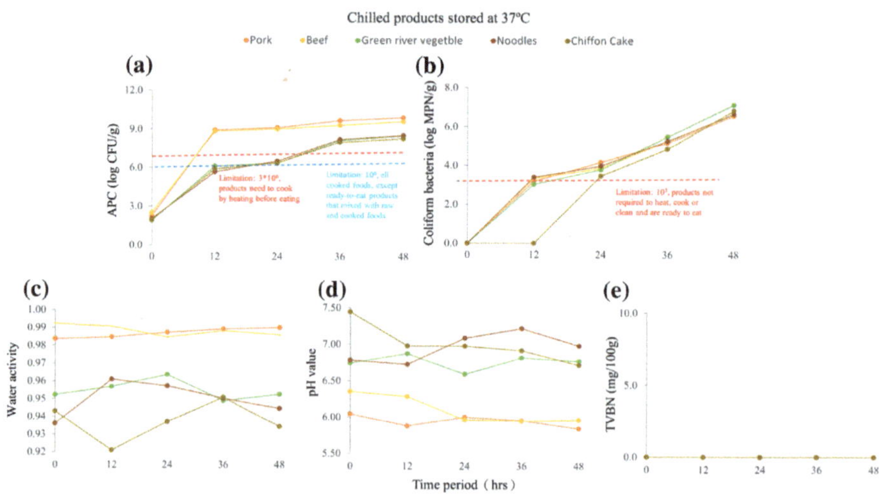

Fig. 3 Experimental results for chilled foods stored at 37 °C

Bacillus cereus, *Vibrio parahaemolyticus* and *Listeria monocytogenes* were tested but showed no response in this experiment and nor is the mold. This suggests that as the food products were manufactured following the "Act Governing Food Safety and Sanitation" and the hygiene and sanitation in the plant were under control and thus the food produced has only little bacterial contamination.

Due to global warming, even in Japan, the ambient temperature in the summer can easily goes beyond 37 °C, let alone the temperature in Taiwan and ASEAN countries in the summer. We chose chilled food to be left at ambient temperature of 37 °C for the experiment because chilled food was considered to be most sensitive to ambient temperature. Besides, most of breakage of food cold chain happens inside the processing zone of a distribution center and 37 °C is the ambient temperature set by most service providers at the loading/unloading and processing zones. From Fig. 3 we can see that APC, Coliform bacteria, WA and pH values all go beyond the limit in a shorter time than those displayed in Fig. 2. Further, Fig. 2f shows almost no data because no Coliform bacteria were found, which means those food samples were not polluted by *E. coli* during production. Figure 2n also shows almost no data because after testing, the response of TVBN was not apparent as that in seafood.

5 Conclusions and Discussions

Food Cold chains protect foods from being exposed to ambient temperature which usually are not the right temperature. From production, harvesting, transportation and packaging, foods go through many processes and one third of them never end up on the table but instead, they are thrown out. Of the wasted food, CO_2 emissions are about 3.3 billion metric tons and they are equivalent to the emission amount of India and Japan combined. If we could reduce the amount of food being thrown away, we can help diminish the CO_2 emissions and help mitigate the effects on global warming for a more sustainable society. For food cold chains, they are responsible for one third of the food wasted; thus proper cold chain services can help reduce food waste, which in turn, lowers down the CO_2 emissions.

During food cold chain operations, food goes through many processes and stages. The interfaces are where the breakage of food cold chain may occur [3]. From the study of Chen et al. [3], it was found that loading/unloading zone as well as goods processing zone for temporary goods storage are where breakage of food cold chains most likely to happen. The reasons are mainly the ignorance of operators, the scheduling of work, improper handling of operators, etc. [3, 9]. We designed several experiments to emulate the situations that might happen in the operation of food cold chains. Several different ambient temperatures were specified to emulate the situation that during handling of foods, they are left at diverse ambient temperatures for a longer period of time. Food test items, including microorganism, pH value, TVBN, etc. were defined to examine how foods respond to the breakage time intervals.

From our first experiment, there were no responses for the test items for the first 3 h. In the second experiment, as Figs. 2 and 3 show, most results deviate the limit after the first 12 h. The test items are those related to safety, i.e., they are detrimental to health if foods are consumed. The result suggests that within 3 h of exposure to ambient temperature like 25 or 37 °C, microorganisms, which determine the safety of food, do not grow in our test for most foods. This is partially true because the samples were acquired from supermarkets or convenient stores and the manufacturers are strict in hygiene and sanitation. Another observed fact is that microorganisms do not grow below 0 °C and are slow under 10 °C. The temperature of the central part of food after a few hours is usually still below zero. In an Initiative for food cold chain logistics operations of Taiwan, it stipulates that during the processing of goods as well as at loading/unloading processes, the ambient temperature should set below 15 °C and the time in these areas should be less than 30 min. Evaluating from our experiments, we can see that 30 min is quite a reasonable time period for interface operations in the food cold chain logistics. However, at some extreme cases, it could affect food quality as the appearance temperature may rise up to −4 °C so that the original small ice crystals may begin to thaw, which affect food quality.

The experiment 1 and 2 demonstrate that there is a stagnant phenomenon for microorganisms to grow, mainly due to stagnant temperature growth at the core of products. However, some other test items are necessary to holistically assure food quality such as WA, pH values, TVBN, physical appearance, the size of ice crystal, chemical reactions, etc. The latter part of the test items may affect food quality and the taste but were not included in our experiment.

Frequent high-and-low temperature change profile could have higher impacts on food safety and quality. Future study can design a suitable experimental design encompassing the scenarios of the frequency of doors opening and closing. We believe frequent high-and-low change of temperature can have severe effects on food quality and safety.

Lastly, reducing food cold chain breakage can deduce food loss and the resultant CO_2 emissions. To maintain unbreached cold chains, companies need to have complete hardware equipment and facility, software facility, process management, responsive delivery and most importantly, the knowledge and quality perception of operators. In response to external changes, companies need to have a contingency plan. Besides, in a cold distribution center, the facility needs to have quick lifting doors, proper docks, door seals, insulation plates, plastic curtains, insulated containers, warm curtains, etc. to avoid leakage of coldness when moving goods into an inconformable temperature. Moreover, consumer education about cold chain related knowledge is even more significant but challenging. Only when consumers can demand what is required can cold chain service providers perform according to regulations and initiatives to reduce food loss and to reduce the resultant CO_2 emissions.

Appendix

See Tables 3 and 4.

Table 3 Test items, methods and standards of microorganism on prepared frozen food announced by Certified Agricultural Standards (CAS)

Test items	Methods	Standards	Note
Aerobic plate count (CFU/g)	According to MOHW Food No. 1021950329 amended, 06/09/2013, Methods of Test for Food Microorganisms—Test of Standard Plate Count (Aerobic Plate Count)	Below 3×10^6	Applicable to products that are not cooked by heating before frozen
		Below 5×10^6	Applicable to frozen ground meats
		Below 10^5	Applicable to products cooked by heating before eating, or fresh-eaten fish, shellfishes, vegetables and fruits
Escherichia coli (MPN/g)	According to MOHW Food No. 1021951163 amended, 20/12/2013, Methods of Test for Food Microorganisms—Test of *Escherichia coli*	Below 50	Applicable to products that need cooking by heating before eating
		Below 10	Applicable to vegetables, fruits, fish and shellfishes except fresh-eaten fish and shellfishes
		Negative	Applicable to products that need no cooking by heating before eating, or fresh-eaten fish and shellfishes
Coliform bacteria (MPN/g)	According to MOHW Food No. 1021950329 amended, 06/09/2013, Methods of Test for Food Microorganisms—Test of Coliform bacteria	Below 10	Applicable to products that require no cooking by heating before eating and fresh-eaten fish and shellfishes
Salmonella	According to MOHW Food No. 1021951187 amended, 23/12/2013, Methods of Test for Food Microorganisms—Test of *Salmonella*	Negative	Applicable to all frozen food
Staphylococcus aureus	According to MOHW Food No. 1041901818 amended, 13/10/2015, Methods of Test for Food Microorganisms—Test of *Staphylococcus aureus*	Negative	Applicable to all frozen food

(continued)

Table 3 (continued)

Test items	Methods	Standards	Note
Vibrio parahaemolyticus	According to MOHW Food No. 1021950329 amended, 06/09/2013, Methods of Test for Food Microorganisms—Test of *Vibrio parahaemolyticus*	Negative	Applicable to all frozen seafood or processed products including seafood
Bacillus cereus (MPN/g)	According to MOHW Food No. 1021950329 amended, 06/09/2013, Methods of Test for Food Microorganisms—Test of *Bacillus cereus*	Below 100	Applicable to all frozen food that is made of rice
Listeria monocytogenes	According to MOHW Food No. 1021951354 amended, 09/01/2014, Methods of Test for Food Microorganisms—Test of *Listeria monocytogenes*	Negative	Applicable to meats that have been cooked by heating before frozen

Table 4 Test items, methods and standards of microorganism on prepared chilled food announced by Certified Agricultural Standards (CAS)

Test items	Methods	Standards	Note
Aerobic plate count (CFU/g)	According to MOHW Food No. 1021950329 amended, 06/09/2013, Methods of Test for Food Microorganisms—Test of Standard Plate Count (Aerobic Plate Count)	Below 3×10^6	Applicable to chilled products that need cooking by heating before eating
		Below 10^6	Applicable to chilled cooked foods, except chilled ready-to-eat ones
		Below 5×10^4	Applicable to dairy food
		Below 200	Applicable to vegetables or juices
Coliform bacteria (MPN/g)	According to MOHW Food No. 1021950329 amended, 06/09/2013, Methods of Test for Food Microorganisms—Test of Coliform bacteria	Below 10^3	Applicable to chilled products including raw and cooked foods and fresh-eaten vegetables, fruits, fish and shellfishes
		Below 10	Applicable to thoroughly cooked chilled foods and dairy foods
		Negative	Applicable to vegetables or juices

(continued)

Table 4 (continued)

Test items	Methods	Standards	Note
Escherichia coli (MPN/g)	According to MOHW Food No. 1021951163 amended, 20/12/2013, Methods of Test for Food Microorganisms—Test of *Escherichia coli*	Below 50	Applicable to the chilled products that need cooking by heating before eating
		Below 10	Applicable to fresh-eaten vegetables and fruits
		Negative	Applicable to thoroughly cooked chilled foods, dairy food and fresh-eaten fish with mixed raw and cooked foods
Escherichia coli O157:H7	According to MOHW Food No. 1021950329 amended, 06/09/2013, Methods of Test for Food Microorganisms—Test of *Escherichia coli* O157:H7	Negative	Applicable to fresh-eaten chilled vegetables and fruits
Salmonella	According to MOHW Food No. 1021951187 amended, 23/12/2013, Methods of Test for Food Microorganisms—Test of *Salmonella*	Negative	Applicable to all chilled seafood, meats, thoroughly cooked meats, non-thoroughly cooked meats and dairy food
Staphylococcus aureus	According to MOHW Food No. 1041901818 amended, 13/10/2015, Methods of Test for Food Microorganisms—Test of *Staphylococcus aureus*	Negative	Applicable to thoroughly cooked chilled meats
Bacillus cereus (MPN/g)	According to MOHW Food No. 1021950329 amended, 06/09/2013, Methods of Test for Food Microorganisms—Test of *Bacillus cereus*	Below 100	Applicable to all products made of cereal
Vibrio parahaemolyticus	According to MOHW Food No. 1021950329 amended, 06/09/2013, Methods of Test for Food Microorganisms—Test of *Vibrio parahaemolyticus*	Negative	Applicable to all chilled seafood or processed products including seafood

(continued)

Table 4 (continued)

Test items	Methods	Standards	Note
Mold and yeast count (CFU/g)	According to MOHW Food No. 1021950329 amended, 06/09/2013, Methods of Test for Food Microorganisms—Test of Mold and Yeast Count	Below 10	Applicable to dried fish products, processed dried meat products and vegetables or fruits juices
Listeria monocytogenes	According to MOHW Food No. 1021951354 amended, 09/01/2014, Methods of Test for Food Microorganisms—Test of *Listeria monocytogenes*	Negative	Applicable to thoroughly cooked chilled meats and dairy food

References

1. Aung, M. M., & Chang, Y. S. (2015). Temperature management for the quality assurance of a perishable food supply chain. *Food Control, 40,* 198–207.
2. Center for Disease Control and Prevention (CDC). (2016). *Burden of foodborne illness: Findings*. Retrieved from http://www.cdc.gov/foodborneburden/2011-foodborne-estimates.html on December 19, 2017.
3. Chen, M. H, Tsai, K. M., Chen, W. C., & Wu, Y. J. (2017). Applying concept mapping to explore the risk of temperature disconformity in cold chain logistics. *ICLS 2017*, Beijing.
4. Chen, C. L., Zhang, J., & Delaurentis, T. (2014). Quality control in food supply chain management: an analytical model and case study of the adulterated milk incident in China. *International Journal of Production Economics, 152,* 188–199.
5. Coulomb, D. (2008). Refrigeration and cold chain serving the global food industry and creating a better future: Two key IIR challenges for improved health and environment. *Trends in Food Science & Technology, 19*(8), 413–417.
6. Dupont, J. L. (2009). The role of refrigeration in worldwide nutrition. In *5th Informatory note on refrigeration and food*. International Institute of Refrigeration.
7. Freiboth, H. W., Goedhals-Gerber, L., Van Dyk, F. E., & Dodd, M. C. (2013). Investigating temperature breaks in the summer fruit export cold chain: A case study. *Journal of Transport and Supply Chain Management, 7*(1), 7–16.
8. Gwanpua, S. G., et al. (2015). The FRISBEE tool, a software for optimising the trade-off between food quality, energy use, and global warming impact of cold chains. *Journal of Food Engineering, 148,* 2–12.
9. Hu, K. Y. (2014). Assessment of operational risks for cold chain logistics. *Journal of Management and Systems, 21*(1), 139–160.
10. International Institute of Refrigeration (IIR). (2009). *The role of refrigeration in worldwide nutrition*. Retrieved from http://www.iifiir.org/userfiles/file/publications/notes/NoteFood_05_EN.pdf on December 19, 2017.
11. James, S. J., Evans, J., & James, C. (2008). A review of the performance of domestic refrigerators. *Journal of Food Engineering, 87*(1), 2–10.
12. Laguerre, O., Hoang, H. M., & Flick, D. (2013). Experimental investigation and modelling in the food cold chain: Thermal and quality evolution. *Trends in Food Science & Technology, 29* (2), 87–97.

13. Mercier, S., et al. (2017). Time-temperature management along the food cold chain: a review of recent developments. *Comprehensive Reviews in Food Science and Food Safety, 16*(4), 647–667.
14. Ministry of Health and Welfare (MOHW). (2017). *Act governing food safety and sanitation.* Retrieved from http://law.moj.gov.tw/Eng/LawClass/LawContent.aspx?PCODE=L0040001 on December 10, 2017.
15. Rakuten website. (2017). Retrieved from https://global.rakuten.com/zh-tw/category/110411/ on December 10, 2017.
16. RD&D website. (2017). Retrieved from http://www.roundday.com.tw on December 10, 2017.
17. Ritchie, H., & Roser, M. (2017). *CO2 and other greenhouse gas emissions.* Retrieved from https://ourworldindata.org/co2-and-other-greenhouse-gas-emissions/ on December 10, 2017.
18. Roccato, A., Uyttendaele, M., & Membre, J. M. (2017). Analysis of domestic refrigerator temperatures and home storage time distributions for shelf-life studies and food safety risk assessment. *Food Research International, 96,* 171–181.
19. Salin, V. (2010). *2010 Global cold storage capacity report.* Global Cold Chain Alliance.
20. Scharff, R. L. (2012). Economic burden from health losses due to foodborne illness in the United States. *Journal of Food Protection, 75*(1), 123–131.
21. Smith, R. (2015). How reducing food waste could ease climate change. *National Geographic.*
22. United Nations (UN). (2017). World population prospects. In *The 2017 Revision Population Database.*
23. USDA. (2016). *Capacity of refrigerated warehouses 2016.* National Agricultural Statistics Service, U.S. Department of Agriculture.
24. van Gogh, J. B., Aramyan, L. H., Sluis, A. A. van der Soethoudt, J. M., Scheer, F. P. (2013). *Feasibility of a network of excellence postharvest food losses: Combining knowledge and competences to reduce food losses in developing and emerging economies.* Rapport/ Wageningen UR—Food & Biobased Research nr. 1402.
25. Zubeldia, B. B., Jiménez, M. N., Claros, M. T. V., Andrés, J. L. M., & Martin-Olmedo, P. (2016). Effectiveness of the cold chain control procedure in the retail sector in Southern Spain. *Food Control, 59,* 614–618.

Managing Uncertainty Through Sustainable Re-engineering of the Value Chain. An Action-Research Study of the Aquaculture Industry

Ilias Vlachos and George Malindretos

Abstract Aquaculture is a constantly growing industry that provides food for the world's growing population. However, fish supply chains are not efficient and are, largely, unsustainable. As a result, without re-designing fish supply chains, aquaculture could provide solutions to feed the world's population but at the expense of the environment and global fish stocks. Uncertainty in the aquaculture value chain makes its management challenging and efficiency more difficult to achieve. Uncertainty can be found at all stages including supply, production, distribution and demand. Uncertainty largely derives from the nature of fish, as a highly perishable and price-sensitive commodity. A rule of fish price devaluation is that "*every day that fish remains unsold the average selling price decreases by at least 20%*". This study presents an action-research case study of one large aquaculture enterprise in the Mediterranean Sea. The case company executed a sustainable re-engineering of its value chain in order to reduce fish life-cycle time, bring it to market more quickly and reduce the uncertainty previously found in production and distribution processes. The findings suggest best practices to re-engineer the supply chain in a sustainable way to manage uncertainty in the aquaculture and food sector in general. Aquaculture literature has long stressed the critical reduction of global fish stocks and its huge impact on sustainability, yet few studies have provided empirically rich data on how to effectively manage uncertainty and thus increase the sustainability of the industry while also preserving fish stocks globally. Thus, this study has significant implications in global fish regions, including Asian countries, where there is stressful impact on managing the fish stocks effectively.

Keywords Aquaculture · Sustainable re-engineering aquaculture value chain
Uncertainty · Sustainable aquaculture · Supply chain re-engineering

---

I. Vlachos (✉)
University of Leeds, Leeds, UK
e-mail: I.Vlachos@leeds.ac.uk

G. Malindretos
Harokopio University, Athens, Greece
e-mail: gmal@hua.gr

X. Liu (ed.), *Environmental Sustainability in Asian Logistics and Supply Chains*,
https://doi.org/10.1007/978-981-13-0451-4_9

1 Introduction

Fish farming can be used as a solution in meeting the food needs of an increasing world population, especially with a growing middle-class that can afford to buy premium products. At the same time, fish is important in the food security of low-income populations, especially in developing countries. Thus, more than three billion people on the planet depend on seafood and, to keep pace with the growing demand for seafood, the world must increasingly rely on aquaculture.

Population growth and food scarcity—along with energy limitations—has been described as a "*daunting challenge*" that requires wider attention by engaging researchers, technical experts, management and leadership [1]. However, despite its importance, few empirical studies have provided feasible solutions to this challenge, a gap that this study seeks to address.

Uncertainty in the food supply chain can occur in all end-to-end stages, including supply, production, distribution, and demand. A large proportion of uncertainty of fish value chains is attributed to the very nature of fish, especially fresh fish, which has a limited shelf-life and it is very sensitive to temperature and humidity. The price of fresh products is directly related to their freshness, making supply chain efficiency critical in satisfying demand [2]. Recent food crises have increased consumer awareness of food safety and stimulated companies to redesign supply chains by rationalising the supplier base, increasing safety control, and becoming more flexible and agile in the face of crisis incidents [3]. Furthermore, fish supply chains are largely international since over 200 countries export fish products while, at the same time, market inefficiencies create challenges in managing the exporting process effectively [4–6].

This study is based on an action-research case study of a global supply chain of fish. The case company recently re-designed its value chain to reduce lead times and increase the market price of its fish products. Concurrently, the sustainable re-engineering of the value chain dealt with uncertainties occurring previously in production and distribution which, in turn, improved sustainable performance.

2 Literature Review

2.1 The Aquaculture Sector Global Production

Aquaculture has grown impressively over recent decades, at a pace where it has become the food sector with the highest annual growth (Fig. 1).

According to data in Fig. 2, the volume of global production increased approximately 8.6% yearly on average when compared with the relative stagnation of captured fishing. In absolute volume terms (MT-million tonnes), global production doubled within 12 years, from 32.4 MT in 2000 to 66.6 MT in 2012.

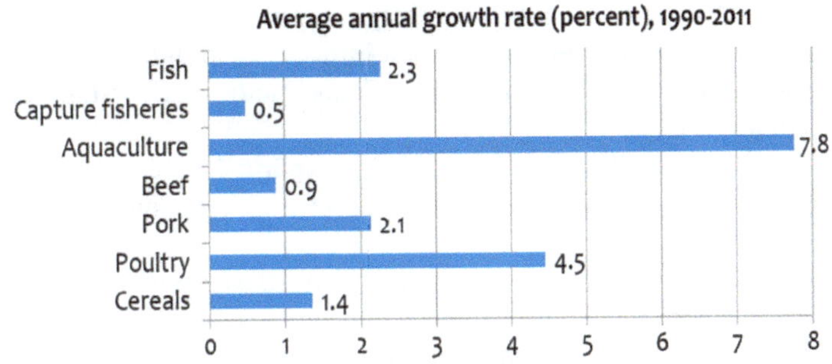

Fig. 1 Food sectors' annual growth rate. *Source* [8]

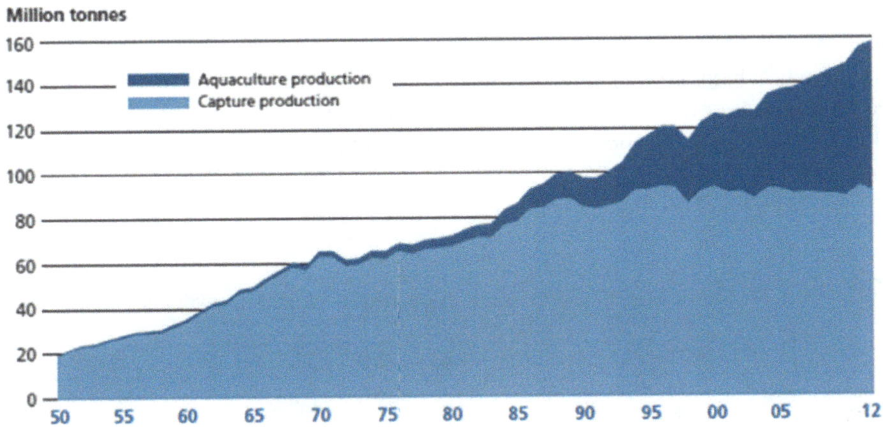

Fig. 2 World capture fisheries and aquaculture production, 1950–2012. *Source* [8]

Further analyzing global fish production, we notice that farmed fish contributed a high percentage (42.2%) of the total 158 MT of fish in captured fisheries 2012. This is a high growth if we consider that farmed fish contributed about 13% in the 1990s and 26% in the 2000s.

Fish contributes approximately 16% of all animal protein consumed globally. Fish consumption is expected to increase further as middle-class consumers increase in number and purchasing power, enabling them to seek high-quality protein [7]. It is no surprise that aquaculture's contribution to total food fish supply grew from about 10% in the 1980s to about 50% in 2011. To meet the increasing demand, the number of fish farmers is estimated to have grown from about 4 million in the 1990s to about 17 million in 2011. Another consequence of this industrial development is that retail fish prices have been kept relatively low which further reinforces the demand to a larger consumer population. Further, fish is a commodity traded in international markets. Since there are about 200 countries producing and exporting fish, the international trade of fish and fish products is highly fragmented, market inefficient, and unbalanced. A lack of a powerful mechanism to resolve these market inefficiencies in international markets, apart from intra-regional agreements (i.e., North American Free Trade Agreement NAFTA, Trans-Pacific Partnership, TPP), reinforces these inefficiencies.

It is noticeable that the flow of seafood exports between developing and developed countries is unbalanced: export from developing countries has increased to reach about 68% in value [8].

Looking across regions, we observe high fish consumption in countries like China and India where the available consumer parity is growing and expected to grow fast. However, an even higher growth in fish consumption is expected in South Asian countries (Table 1). According to World Bank projections, China will become a major contributor to international fish trade with more than 35% in production and about 38% in fish consumption (Table 2).

European aquaculture has followed a period of relative stagnation at below 1% average growth rate, compared to over seven times more for all non-EU countries combined, which corresponds to about 2% of global aquaculture production. Eight EU countries (France, UK, Italy, Greece, Spain, Denmark, Holland and Germany) account for about 80% of the Community's production.

Table 1 projected per capita fish consumption by region

	Data (kg/ person/year)		Projection (kg/person/ year)			Annual growth rate	
	2000	2006	2010	2020	2030	2000–06[a] (%)	2010–30[b] (%)
Global average	15.7	16.8	17.2	18.0	18.2	1.1	0.3
ECA	17.0	18.5	17.4	17.2	18.2	1.5	0.2
NAM	21.8	24.3	22.9	24.5	26.4	1.8	0.7
LAC	8.8	9.4	8.4	8.0	7.5	1.1	−0.6
EAP	32.1	36.5	27.1	26.1	23.8	2.2	−0.7
CHN	24.4	26.6	32.6	37.8	41.0	1.4	1.2
JAP	67.7	59.2	64.7	63.7	62.2	−2.2	−0.2
SEA	24.6	27.9	25.8	28.3	29.6	2.1	0.7
SAR	8.5	11.4	11.0	13.4	15.7	5.1	1.8
IND	4.5	5.0	5.6	6.2	6.6	1.7	0.8
MNA	83	10.2	9.3	9.4	9.4	3.5	0.0
AFR	7.1	7.5	6.8	6.1	5.6	0.8	−1.0
ROW	18.4	20.1	9.4	9.6	9.6	1.5	0.1

Sources FAO FIPS FBS and IMPACT model projections
Note: ECA Europe and Central Asia; *NAM* North America; *LAC* Latin America and Caribbean; *CHN* China; *JAP* Japan; *EAP* other East Asia and the Pacific; *SEA* Southeast Asia; *IND* India; *SAR* other South Asia; *MNA* Middle East and North Africa; *AFR* Sub-Saharan Africa; *ROW* rest of the world
[a]Based on data
[b]Based on projections

Table 2 Projected total food fish consumption by region

	Data (000 tons)	Projection (000 tons)			Share in global total		% Change
	2006	2010	2020	2030	2010 (Projection) (%)	2030 (Projection) (%)	2010–30 (%)
Global total	111,697	119,480	138,124	151,771	100.0	100.0	27.0
ECA	16,290	15,488	15,720	16,735	13.0	11.0	8.1
NAM	8151	7966	9223	10,674	6.7	7.0	34.0
LAC	5246	4900	5165	5200	4.1	3.4	6.1
EAP	3866	2975	3068	2943	25	1.9	−1.194
CHN	35,291	44,094	52,867	57,361	36.9	37.8	30.1
JAP	7485	8180	7926	7447	6.8	4.9	−9.0
SEA	14,623	14,175	17,160	19,327	111.9	12.7	36.3
SAR	4940	5063	7140	9331	4.2	6.1	84.3
IND	5887	6909	8688	10,054	5.8	6.6	45.5
MNA	3604	3571	4212	4730	3.0	3.1	32.5
AFR	5947	5980	6758	7759	5.0	5.1	29.7
ROW	367	179	198	208	0.2	0.1	15.7

Sources FAO FIPS FBS and IMPACT model projections
Note ECA Europe and Central Asia; *NAM* North America; *LAC* Latin America and Caribbean; *CHN* China; *JAP* Japan; *EAP* other East Asia and the Pacific; *SEA* Southeast Asia; *IND* India; *SAR* other South Asia; *MNA* Middle East and North Africa; *AFR* Sub-Saharan Africa: *ROW* rest of the world

Table 3 China: sales of fish and seafood by category: % total volume growth 2011–2016

% Total volume growth	2015/16	2011/16 Total
Crustaceans	3.8	25.8
Fish	4.2	22.3
Molluscs and cephalopods	4.1	21.7
Fish and seafood	4.1	22.5

Source Euromonitor international from official statistics, trade associations, trade press, company research, store checks, trade interviews, trade sources

Concerning China, fish and seafood experienced a total volume growth of 4.1% to reach 40.2 million tonnes in 2016. Fish enjoyed the highest volume growth due to the prevalence of fish recipes in fish restaurants (Table 3).

Retailing has become the most popular channel for fish and seafood globally, as supermarkets and hypermarkets mainly offer frozen and chilled fish and seafood that have become increasingly popular among consumers. Thus, in China, retail volume sales accounted for 58.9% of total volume sales of fish and seafood in 2016 (Table 4).

Table 4 China: distribution of fish and seafood by format: % total volume 2011–2016

% Total volume	2011	2012	2013	2014	2015	2016
Retail	55.6	55.6	56.3	57.1	58.0	58.9
Foodservice	29.4	29.4	28.7	27.9	27.8	27.6
Institutional	15.0	15.0	15.0	15.0	14.3	13.5
Total	100.0	100.0	100.0	100.0	100.1	100.0

Source Euromonitor International from official statistics, trade associations, trade press, company research, store checks, trade interviews, trade sources

Table 5 China: retail sales of organic fish and seafood: % volume growth 2012–2016

% Volume growth	2015/16	2012/16 Total
Organic fish and seafood	12.7	80.8

Source Euromonitor international from official statistics, trade associations, trade press, company research, store checks, trade interviews, trade sources

Table 6 China: % of retail sales of fish and seafood by packaged versus unpackaged

% Retail volume	2013	2014	2015	2016
Packaged	5.0	6.0	7.1	8.5
Unpackaged	95.0	94.0	92.9	91.5
Total	100.0	100.0	100.0	100.0

Source Euromonitor international from official statistics, trade associations, trade press, company research, store checks, trade interviews, trade sources

Imported organic fish and seafood has gained popularity in recent years reaching an increase of almost 81% from 2012 to 2016 in the China market (Table 5) while, in general, consumers tend to prefer packaged rather than unpackaged fish and seafood (Table 6).

2.2 *Sustainable Global Supply Chains in the Aquaculture Sector*

The huge environmental impact of aquaculture has invited increasing work by academics. Without doubt, the sustainable production and delivery of fish, while preserving natural resources and avoiding any damage to the aquatic environment, imposes huge challenges for companies and countries.

Businesses are in need of best practices which are reliable, efficient, and sustainable to meet growing market demands globally. Best practices, especially in order to re-design their supply chain in a sustainable way, offer a significant opportunity especially in developing countries which are exporting fish to developed countries and want to preserve their national fisheries industry and their natural aquatic environment. In this direction, technological evolution can offer solutions to aquaculture in order to grow in both efficient and sustainable ways in the long term.

One of the main challenges that global supply chains in the aquaculture sector face is that most of the fishers and fish companies (or enterprises) in developing countries are of small-scale (90% according to FAO) [8]. To many of these fishers, fish is both a source of nutrients and food and their only source of household income. As a result, sustainable re-designing of fish supply chains could provide a better income to these fishers, improve their livelihoods and, at the same time, ensure food security and preserve natural resources.

Understanding fish supply chains, especially issues on sustainability, uncertainty, and resilience, can help in addressing a number of policy issues on international trade, aquaculture, agriculture and environmental management [7]. Global supply chains are more difficult to manage than domestic supply chains [9] due to a number of factors such as: (i) Substantial geographical distances increase transportation costs, lead times, and complicate decisions because of tradeoffs between inventory, cost, and availability. (ii) Diversity in cultures and business practices constrain supply chain integration and inhibit demand forecasting and long-range planning. (iii) Poor infrastructural performance in developing countries and unreliable suppliers provide challenges that companies in developed countries are not often prepared to face.

Sustainability and market forces push food companies acting on a global scale towards re-design of existing chains to deal with the demand and supply uncertainty [10]. Re-design of existing chains proves more challenging than designing new supply chains since companies have been locked-in investments and business relationships. Furthermore, there is often a trade-off between efficiency and sustainability, meaning that the more efficient supply chains are less sustainable. Therefore, companies face significant issues and challenges with sustainable re-design of existing supply chains, and often decision-making is highly risky and complex [11, 12]. For example, when companies move from compliance to life-cycle sustainability, they have to alter their decision-making process to include new processes, which creates less routine and structure than before [13–15]. Hammami and Frein [16] argue that there is a need to develop effective and comprehensive models for the redesign of global supply chains. However, the literature on supply chain redesign strategies is overwhelmed with models concerning physical distribution and flow of materials [17–19] whilst overlooking design properties such as flexibility, reliability, uncertainty, and sustainability that reflect real challenges in global supply chains [16].

2.3 Decreasing Uncertainty in the Aquaculture Sector

The Design of global chains is faced by increasing uncertainties and high complexity which, in turn, can impact the firm's competitiveness [20–22].

Uncertainty in global supply chains is further increased by a number of business and political environment risk factors including: currency volatility (i.e., pound over dollar/euro) and geo-political uncertainty, i.e., Brexit, revision of existing international trade agreement [23, 24]. Sustainability has increased the pressure for environment impact control and, again, becoming more resource efficient [25].

According to the literature uncertainty is related to many issues. At first, exogenous factors not controllable by the firm include weather conditions, governmental regulations and disease increase uncertainty. For the last, even though there are many aspects of and causes for uncertainty concerning disease control, there is much knowledge and available strategies in use by fish farmers, and the industry is continuously improving [26]. Sustainable management of marine resources is also closely related to the resilience of communities to deal with natural disasters deriving from climate change [7].

Intrinsic characteristics such as fluctuating demand and the well-known bullwhip effect considerably increase uncertainty, affecting the entire industry from production through to supply chain operations. Demand forecasting is challenging especially with little visibility across the supply chain, resulting in efficiencies and uncertainty [27, 28]. In order to improve visibility, integration of information systems is critical for providing accurate, real-time information. Moreover, companies either have excess capacity or hold inventory to deal with unstable demand [29].

Supply chain structure and configuration may lead to important disruptions and delays. For example, Cavinato suggests five risks categories: physical, financial, informational, relational and innovative [30] while Sanchez-Rodrigues [31] argues that each supply chain member is heavily exposed to transportation risks which create further uncertainties on how to design and re-design supply chains.

Craighead [32] found that supply chain density is correlated with disruptions across the supply chain, especially when there are a number of critical notes. Another study [33] found that delays create further uncertainties especially when there is no collaboration or supply chain integration among the supply chain embers. For example, reverse logistics often have uncertain demand forecasting which creates a bullwhip-effect inefficiency to the supply chain and, while the literature has proposed a number of models to deal with these uncertainties, most models yet lack empirical validation [34, 35]. Natural disasters and catastrophes can create significant disruptions to supply chains. A recent study [36] found that the more exposure points existing in a supply chain, the more vulnerable the supply chain will be to unexpected disruptions and, in particular, export supply chains are more vulnerable to risks [37]. A number of solutions have been proposed to minimize exposure to vulnerability; for example, in the context of humanitarian supply chains, a recent study [38] proposed a model which intended to maximize cost effectively and the satisfaction of the population by reducing the number of shortages in the affected zones.

3 Sustainable Re-engineering of Value Chains: An Action-Research Project

This study is one of only a few empirical studies that have applied action-research to investigate the sustainable re-engineering of the fish supply chain. The case company, Greek Nireus S.A., is one of the top-10 fish companies in the world (www.nireus.com). Recently, the case company implemented a large-scale re-engineering of its value chain to improve overall supply chain efficiency while simultaneously improving its environmental performance.

The company is established in Greece, a country rich in coastline (over 17.400 km with 10,000 islands and islets covering 70% of the coastline) and a long tradition in fisheries and maritime industry. Regarding the maritime aspect, the Greek merchant fleet is the largest in the EU and one of the largest fleets globally.

The fisheries sector plays an important role in the Greek economy, employing around 38,000 people. Greece has a fishing fleet (15,693 vessels) dominated by small-scale fishing companies (94%). Mariculture activities in Greece are well-established and are the biggest in the Mediterranean Sea. Marine aquaculture farms are dispersed across all coastal areas in Greece such as Dodecanese, Euboea, and the Ionian Sea. Mariculture activities in Greece are often vertically integrated.

The case company has production facilities in Greece and Spain. It employs over 1000 employees which makes it one of the largest companies in the Greek economy. Furthermore, it is considered a dynamic company since its revenue comes from exports, which account for 80% of fish sales, a characteristic that adds more value to the company in a country suffering from economic crisis, cash restrictions and capital controls. The case company exports to over 40 countries. The main markets are located in Europe, but exports also reach remote countries in the USA, and Asia.

Nireus initially had two distribution centers in Athens and Patra, both in Greece (Map 1). The distribution centers also included packaging operations for all domestic demand. Furthermore, the Patras distribution center allowed the transportation to Italy and from there to mainland Europe. The Athens DC distribution center served the Eastern Europe and other remote markets via air (Venizelos airport).

The case company closely monitored and analyzed their supply chain in terms of efficiency and sustainability and a number of non-value adding activities have been identified. The company decided to proceed with a sustainable re-engineering of its supply chain. Two actions were decided upon (Map 2):

1. Firstly, the company decided to establish a new distribution center in Italy, in the region of Milan. By so doing, they were able to eliminate all intermediaries (especially third-party logistics providers) that were intervening in the previous process between Greece and Italy. The Milan distribution center took a pivotal, key role in servicing the European market. Nireus, with the new distribution center in Italy, is able to move fish faster to European markets, reducing lead

Map 1 supply chain structure "as it was". *Source* Nireus Aquaculture S.A., 2014

times considerably. By selling fish fresher than before, Nireus is able to sell at a better price. To achieve this efficiency, the order picking takes place at night and the Nireus fish arrive in Milan one day after harvesting in Greece at midnight.

2. The company re-engineered the routes from Greece to Italy and the new routes go the same day via the Igoumenitsa Port (Map 2, "IG") instead of Patra DC which took longer. To achieve this efficiency in lead times, the company had to revise the inbound logistics flows and fisheries located in Western Greece and send their products to Igoumenitsa instead of the Patras distribution center.
3. Domestic flows were also re-engineered. The produce from Evia Farms is now sent directly to the domestic market within 14 h of harvesting.
4. Nireus developed new software to manage all logistics operations better, to achieve better controls over operations and monitor sustainability in real-time. The new information system allows end-to-end traceability not only to Nireus company but, also, customers can track their fish from "Eggs to Selling Point".

ATH : Athens, PAT : Patra, IG : Igoumenitsa

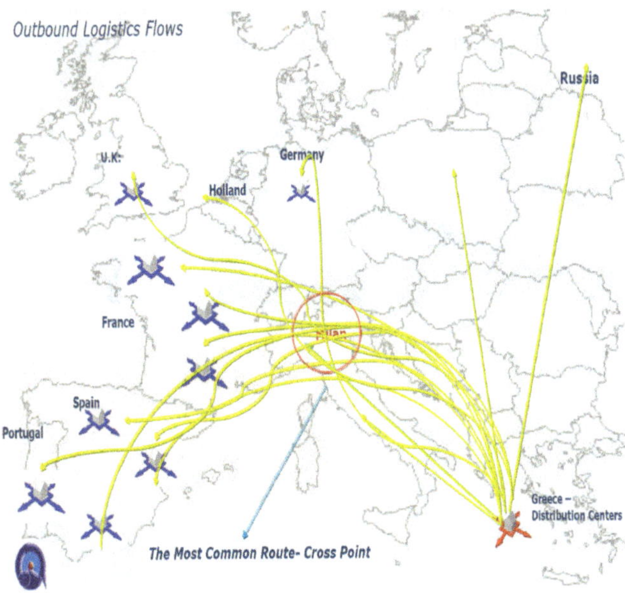

Map 2 Re-designed supply chain structure *Source* Nireus Aquaculture S.A., 2014

4 Findings

The implementation of the company's re-engineering project resulted in a significantly strengthened company with power in a fierce internationally competitive environment and considerably reduced level of uncertainty. The removal of 3PL intermediaries was a necessary step to achieve this: although 3PLs offered a number of value-added activities, there was a broken information flow between market and company operations. This created bullwhip effects in hatcheries and production operations that resulted in unsustainable practices and cost inefficiencies. In addition, mainly due to economies of scale in the new facility in Italy, the company achieved cost reductions at 17.4% to inbound logistics and 26.5% to outbound logistics compared to the previous situation.

Moreover, the decrease of total transport miles has resulted in a two-fold impact: decrease to both cost and environmental impact (CO_2 footprint). Operations turned progressively to green with personnel training and the introduction of green packaging materials. The result from the redesign process was a sustainable supply chain that was, simultaneously, agile by responding quickly to market demand and price fluctuations.

The company achieved a significant reduction in total lead time from five to two days. Product life cycle was reduced about 25%.

Thus, in addition to the fact that fish harvested in Greek coasts can reach international markets fresher, the reduction of lead times from production to market place leads to faster information flows and better management of the variability in demand, a critical inherent characteristic of uncertainty (Fig. 3).

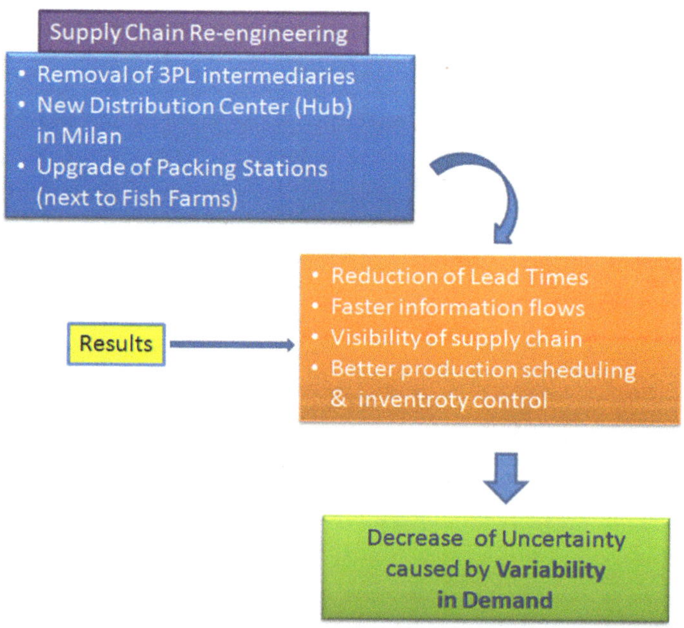

Fig. 3 Reduction of uncertainty through supply chain re-engineering

This is achieved by better production schedules and inventory control and further supported by the implementation of a new logistics information system in the packing stations, upgrading their role and providing improvements in the order cycle management. Thus, by linking production operations to market demand, production has been scheduled based on accurate market forecasts and actual sales leading to faster response to market fluctuations, reducing risk of high/low prices affecting its bottom line. By providing fresher fish value and price has increased considerably, the company's brand name has also been strengthened and market position has been less uncertain by achieving a stronger loyal consumer base. Real-time traceability has allowed total control over packaging and processing. Any quality issues or disparities are immediately identified and managed appropriately.

5 Conclusions

One important outcome of this study is, therefore, that supply chain re-engineering can contribute not only to the limitation of disruptive events—the main issue of most of papers engaged with uncertainty and supply chain—but also to increase sustainability and agility, which, when considering the bottom line, increases sales and cash flow. This study addresses the problem of uncertainty with an action project that confirms supply chain re-configuration (re-engineering) is directly connected with reduction of uncertainty caused by variability in demand (inherent characteristics). In other words, there is a combination of the two categories of supply chain uncertainty argued by Van der Vorst and Beulens, in a "cause and effect" relationship [39].

Companies have often developed their supply chains to satisfy demands for goods and services with little consideration to their impact on ecosystems, environment, and society [40]. In this respect, there must be an increasing effort from academics and practitioners to identify ways of securing the smoothest flows from production to the marketplace within the framework of sustainability.

References

1. Vlachos, I. P. (2015). Applying lean thinking in the food supply chains: A case study. *Production Planning & Control, 26*(16), 1351–1367.
2. Ivert, L. K., Dukovska-Popovska, I., Kaipia, R., Fredriksson, A., Dreyer, H. C., Johansson, M. I., et al. (2015). Sales and operations planning: responding to the needs of industrial food producers. *Production Planning & Control, 26*(4), 280–295.
3. Wang, X., Li, D., & Shi, X. (2012). A fuzzy model for aggregative food safety risk assessment in food supply chains. *Production Planning & Control, 23*(5), 377–395.
4. Anderson, J. E., & Wincoop, Van. (2003). E. Gravity with gravitas: A solution to the border puzzle. *The American Economic Review, 93*(1), 170–192.

5. Kregel, J. (2008). *Financial flows and international imbalances: The role of catching up by late-industrializing developing countries*. Working papers, The Levy Economics Institute, No. 528.
6. Barattieri, A. (2010). *Comparative advantage, service trade and global imbalances*. Boston College Economics Department.
7. The World Bank. (2013). Fish to 2030, 2013, prospects for fisheries and aquaculture. World Bank report, number 83177-GLB.
8. FAO. (2014). The State of world fisheries and aquaculture: Opportunities and challenges, Rome.
9. Olhager, J., Pashaei, S., & Sternberg, H. (2015). Design of global production and distribution networks: A literature review and research agenda. *International Journal of Physical Distribution & Logistics Management, 45*(1/2), 138–158.
10. Fahimnia, B., Sarkis, J., & Davarzani, H. (2015). Green supply chain management: A review and bibliometric analysis. *International Journal of Production Economics, 162,* 101–114.
11. Canning, L., & Hanmer-Lloyd, S. (2001). Managing the environmental adaptation process in supplier–customer relationships. *Business Strategy and the Environment, 10*(4), 225–237.
12. Lewis, G. J., & Harvey, B. (2001). Perceived environmental uncertainty: The extension of Miller's scale to the natural environment. *Journal of Management Studies, 38*(2), 201–234.
13. Aurich, J. C., Fuchs, C., & Wagenknecht, C. (2006). Life cycle oriented design of technical Product-Service Systems. *Journal of Cleaner Production, 14*(17), 1480–1494.
14. Linder, M., & Williander, M. (2017). Circular business model innovation: inherent uncertainties. *Business Strategy and the Environment, 26*(2), 182–196.
15. Song, W., & Sakao, T. (2017). A customization-oriented framework for design of sustainable product/service system. *Journal of Cleaner Production, 140,* 1672–1685.
16. Hammami, R., & Frein, Y. (2014). Redesign of global supply chains with integration of transfer pricing: Mathematical modeling and managerial insights. *International Journal of Production Economics, 158,* 267–277.
17. Bing, X., Bloemhof-Ruwaard, J., Chaabane, A., & Van der Vorst, J. (2015). Global reverse supply chain redesign for household plastic waste under the emission trading schem. *Journal of Cleaner Production, 103,* 28–39.
18. Neto, J. Q. F., Bloemhof-Ruwaard, J. M., van Nunen J. A. E. E., & Heck, E., & Spengler, T. (2009). A methodology for assesssing eco-efficiency in logistics networks. *European Journal of Operational Research, 193*, 670–682.
19. Validi, S., Bhattacharya, A., & Byrne, P. J. (2014). A case analysis of a sustainable food supply chain distribution system—A multi-objective approach. *International Journal of Production Economics, 152,* 71–87.
20. Khatami, M., Mahootchi, M., & Farahani, R. Z. (2015). "Benders' decomposition for concurrent redesign of forward and closed-loop supply chain network with demand and return uncertainties. *Transportation Research Part E: Logistics and Transportation Review, 79,* 1–21.
21. Fang, Y., & Shou, B. (2015). Managing supply uncertainty under supply chain Cournot competition. *European Journal of Operational Research, 243*(1), 156–176.
22. Pantouvakis, A., Vlachos, I., & Zervopoulos, P. D. (2017). Market orientation for sustainableperformance and the inverted-U moderation of firm size: Evidence from the Greek shipping industry. *Journal of Cleaner Production, 165,* 705–720.
23. Guillén-Gosálbez, G., Mele, F. D., & Grossmann, I. E. (2010). A bi-criterion optimization approach for the design and planning of hydrogen supply chains for vehicle use. *AIChE Journal, 56*(3), 650–667.
24. Almaraz, S. D. L., Azzaro-Pantel, C. (2017). Design and optimization of hydrogen supply chains for a sustainable future. In *Hydrogen Economy* (pp. 85–120).
25. Yadav, S. R., Mishra, N., Kumar, V., & Tiwari, M. K. (2011). A framework for designing robust supply chains considering product development issues. *International Journal of Production Research, 49*(20), 6065–6088.

26. Osmundsen, T., Almklov, P. G., & Bjelland, H. V. (2013). *Uncertainty and multilevel coordination in fish farming disease control*. NTNU Social Research, SINTEF Fisheries and Aquaculture.
27. Lee, D. H., & Dong, M. (2009). Dynamic network design for reverse logistics operations under uncertainty. *Transportation Research Part E: Logistics and Transportation Review, 45*(1), 61–71.
28. Stevens, G. C., & Johnson, M. (2016). Integrating the supply chain… 25 years on. *International Journal of Physical Distribution & Logistics Management, 46*(1), 19–42.
29. Govindan, K., & Chaudhuri, A. (2016). Interrelationships of risks faced by third party logistics service providers: A DEMATEL based approach. *Transportation Research Part E: Logistics and Transportation Review, 90,* 177–195.
30. Cavinato, J. L. (2004). Supply chain logistics risks: From the back room to the board room. *International journal of physical distribution & logistics management, 34*(5), 383–387.
31. Sanchez-Rodrigues, V., Potter, A., & Naim, M. M. (2010). Evaluating the causes of uncertainty in logistics operations. *The International Journal of Logistics Management, 21*(1), 45–64.
32. Craighead, C. W., Blackhurst, J., Rungtusanatham, M. J., & Handfield, R. B. (2007). The severity of supply chain disruptions: Design characteristics and mitigation capabilities. *Decision Sciences, 38*(1), 131–156.
33. Lee, D. H., Dong, M., & Bian, W. (2010). The design of sustainable logistics network under uncertainty. *International Journal of Production Economics, 128*(1), 159–166.
34. Vlachos, I. P. (2016). Reverse logistics capabilities impact on firm performance and the mediating role of business strategy. *International Journal of Logistics: Research and Applications*, 424–442.
35. Govindan, K., Soleimani, H., & Kannan, D. (2015). Reverse logistics and closed-loop supply chain: A comprehensive review to explore the future. *European Journal of Operational Research, 240*(3), 603–626.
36. Stecke, K. E., & Kumar, S. (2009). Sources of supply chain disruptions, factors that breed vulnerability, and mitigating strategies. *Journal of Marketing Channels, 16*(3), 193–226.
37. Vlachos, I. P., & Bourlakis, M. (2006). Supply Chain Collaboration between retailers and manufacturers: Do they trust each other? *Supply Chain Forum: An International Journal, 7* (1), 70–78.
38. Bozorgi-Amiri, A., Jabalameli, M. S., & Al-e-Hashem, S. M. (2013). A multi-objective robust stochastic programming model for disaster relief logistics under uncertainty. *OR Spectrum, 35* (4), 905–933.
39. Van der Vorst, J. G., & Beulens, A. J. (2002). Identifying sources of uncertainty to generate supply chain redesign strategies. *International Journal of Physical Distribution & Logistics Management, 32*(6), 409–430.
40. Vlachos, I. P., & Malindretos, G. (2015). *Markets, business and sustainability*. Sharjah, UAE: Bentham Science Publishers.

Part II
Math Modeling Research

A Simulated Annealing Heuristic for the Heterogeneous Fleet Pollution Routing Problem

Vincent F. Yu, A. A. N. Perwira Redi, Parida Jewpanya, Artya Lathifah, Meilinda F. N. Maghfiroh and Nur Aini Masruroh

Abstract Public consciousness on environmental sustainability and industry impact on environment has been increasing for the last few decades. As a result, more and more companies are taking pollution factor into account when planning their logistic activities. Pollution Routing Problem (PRP) is an extension of the classical Vehicle Routing Problem with Time Windows by determining a set of optimal routes and vehicle speed on each route segment for a fleet of vehicles serving a set of customers within specific time windows. In practice, many vehicle routing problems are addressed by a fleet of heterogeneous vehicles with different capacities and travel costs. Emission levels vary by vehicle type due to differences in curb weight and capacity. Therefore, Heterogeneous Fleet Pollution Routing Problem (HFPRP) has been proposed as an extension of Pollution Routing Problem (PRP). Its goal is to minimize the total costs of fuel, greenhouse gas (GHG) emissions, and vehicle variable cost put together in a more comprehensive objective function. This research developed a mathematical model and proposed a

V. F. Yu (✉) · A. A. N. P. Redi · P. Jewpanya · A. Lathifah · M. F. N. Maghfiroh
Department of Industrial Management, National Taiwan University of Science and Technology, 43, Section 4, Keelung Road, Taipei 10607, Taiwan
e-mail: vincent@mail.ntust.edu.tw

A. Lathifah · N. A. Masruroh
Department of Mechanical and Industrial Engineering, Gadjah Mada University, Yogyakarta 55281, Indonesia

M. F. N. Maghfiroh
Department of Transdisciplinary Science and Engineering, Tokyo Institute of Technology, Ookayama 2-12-1, Meguro-Ku, Tokyo 152, Japan

A. Lathifah
Department of Logistics Engineering, Universitas Internasional Semen Indonesia, Gresik 61122, Jawa Timur, Indonesia

A. A. N. P. Redi
Department of Logistics Engineering, Universitas Pertamina, Jakarta 12220, Indonesia

P. Jewpanya
Department of Industrial Engineering, Rajamangala University of Technology Lanna, 41 Moo 7 T. Mai-Ngam, Muang, Tak 63000, Thailand

X. Liu (ed.), *Environmental Sustainability in Asian Logistics and Supply Chains*,
https://doi.org/10.1007/978-981-13-0451-4_10

Simulated Annealing (SA) heuristic for HFPRP. The performance of the proposed SA heuristic was first verified using benchmark data of the Pollution Routing Problem. The result shows that SA performs better for 7 instances than previous method. SA was then used to solve HFPRP and the results were compared to those obtained by CPLEX. We found that the consideration of a heterogeneous fleet reduces total costs for all instances.

Keywords Pollution routing problem · Heterogeneous fleet · Time window Simulated annealing

1 Introduction

A greater awareness of some environmental problems has triggered some organizations to consider green principles in their company. Some of them use environmental-friendly raw materials, reduce their consumption of petroleum energy resources, use alternative energy sources, and apply recycled packaging for their products. One other important aspect to consider is transportation. Transportation indeed is an important aspect in the supply chain, carrying millions of tons freight and passenger every day. Figure 1 illustrates the movement of goods from supplier to end consumers. Every movement of the goods within the supply chain system uses transportation.

Bektaş and Laporte [1] reiterated that transportation has hazardous impacts on the environment, such as resource consumption, land use, acidification, toxic effects on ecosystems and humans, noise, and the effect induced by greenhouse gases (GHG) emissions. One of the most commonly used transportation modes is road transportation, which is a significant emitter of carbon dioxide (CO_2). In the United Kingdom, shipment transportation is responsible for 21% of CO_2 emissions from the transport sector, totaling to 6% of CO_2 emission in the country. In the United States, the percentage of total GHG emissions from transportation rose from 24.9 to 27.3% in 15 years from 1990 to 2005, with road transportation making up 78% of the emissions produced by all transportation modes [2]. Growing concerns about such hazardous effects from transportation on the environment have motivated companies to consider improvements in road transportation in order to lessen such a negative impact. This problem area belongs to Vehicle Routing Problem (VRP).

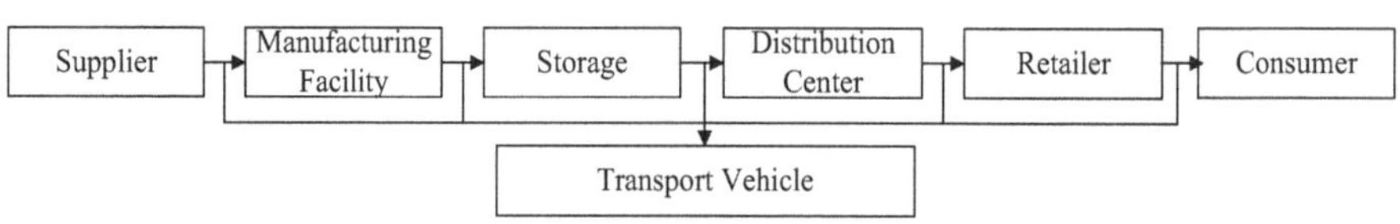

Fig. 1 Flow of the goods within supply chain system

The traditional logistics model is concerned about minimizing total cost in a network. This is where the concept of Vehicle Routing Problem (VRP) is best applied. VRP was first proposed by Dantzig and Ramser [3] when they formulated a mathematical programming model for it. Lin et al. [4] classified 284 VRP research papers into two big groups: Traditional VRP and Green Vehicle Routing Problem (GVRP), as shown in Fig. 2. Logistical activities also have a significant impact on the environment. Green supply chain management (GSCM) is a similar concept to that of classical SCM, focusing on the influences and relationships between players in the supply chain and the environment [5, 6]. Green logistics is known in coordinating logistical activities to reduce any negative impact on the environment. The purpose of green logistics is not only about their economic benefits, but at the same time, to protect the environment. Therefore, logistics target both economic and social benefits. Nowadays a green logistics strategy is becoming a high priority for many firms as a theory of sustainable development. This theory formed the relationship of promotion and constraint between logistics and the environment and is introduced as the modern logistics [7].

Freight transportation is one of the most generally used types of transportation. The planning of freight transportation mainly focuses on how to save money or

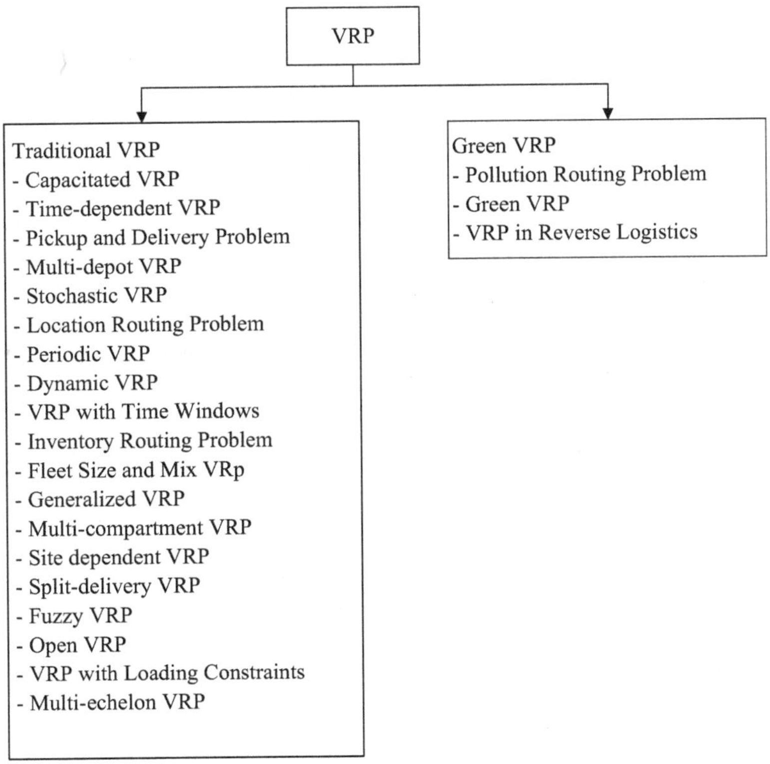

Fig. 2 Classification of VRP researches

increase profitability by considering internal transportation costs only. Green freight transportation considers other factors such as GHG and fuel cost [8]. Bauer et al. [9] investigated the minimization of GHG in inter-modal freight transportation, with an objective to minimize environmental-related costs of freight transportation aside from travel or time-related costs.

Traditional VRP focuses on the economic impact of vehicle routes and consists of 19 groups. On the other hand, GVRP is a variant of VRP combining environmental and economic impacts. This group consists of 3 sub-groups: Green-VRP (G-VRP), Polluting Routing Problem (PRP), and VRP in Reverse Logistics (VRPRL). G-VRP is concerned with energy consumption, including the use of alternative-fuel powered vehicles and alternative fuel stations. PRP takes the attention in choosing a vehicle-dispatching scheme with less pollution (i.e. carbon emissions). Meanwhile, VRPRL focuses on the distribution aspect of reverse logistics [4]. This present study tackles the issue under the sub-group PRP.

In this study, pollution costs consist of fuel and emission cost and variable cost (maintenance and driver costs). Road transportation is a significant emitter of carbon dioxide (CO_2), as such, the volume of its emissions is equal to its fuel consumption [10]. Fuel consumption itself depends on various factors such as vehicle speed, acceleration, distance, and load [11].

In practice, many vehicle routing problems are addressed by a non-homogeneous vehicle fleet where vehicles of different capacities are used. Heterogeneous fleets VRPs (HVRPs) are consider a limited or an unlimited fleet of capacitated vehicles, with problem consist of determining the fleet composition and vehicle routes [12]. Two major HVRPs are the Fleet Size and Mix Vehicle Routing Problem which works with an unlimited heterogeneous fleet, and the Heterogeneous Fixed Fleet Vehicle Routing Problem (HF) in which the fleet is predetermined. Brandão [13] solved a VRP problem with a fixed heterogeneous fleet, followed by Jiang et al. [14] whose team solved Vehicle Routing Problem with Heterogeneous Fleet and Time Windows. Demir et al. [15] showed that fuel consumption is influenced by the types of vehicle used. Therefore, for capturing the real logistic practice, this study also considers a heterogeneous fleet—hence, Heterogeneous Fleet Pollution Routing Problem (HFPRP). HFPRP extends the typical PRP with an added consideration on vehicle types and variable cost (maintenance and driver costs). Since the vehicles have different curb weights and capacities, their levels of emission also differ. Several studies suggested that light-duty vehicles should be preferred over medium and heavy-duty vehicles for routes with the same load [15].

Solving PRP is computationally expensive as it is categorized as NP-Hard [1]. Metaheuristics approach is necessary to solve this problem within considerable computational time. Compared to the classical heuristic, metaheuristics carry out a more thorough search of the solution space. Thus, they are notably capable of consistently producing high quality solutions, despite the greater computational time than early heuristics [16].

As one of metaheuristic methodology, Simulated Annealing (SA) is often used to address both discrete and continuous optimization problems [17]. SA has some attractive advantages such as its ability to deal with non-linear models, chaotic and noisy data, and many constraints. SA has been used extensively in solving VRP problems. Tavakkoli-Moghaddam et al. [18] and Van Breedam [19] employed SA to solve Capacitated Vehicle Routing Problem (CVRP) and VRP, respectively. SA performed well for large-scale real-world VRPTW problems [20]. Yu et al. [21] utilized SA to solve another variant of VRP, called Capacitated Location Routing Problem (CLRP), and it showed better results compared to other algorithms. In this study, we solved HFPRP using SA algorithm.

The use of different vehicle types produces different levels of emission. Combinations of these vehicle types generate not only cost-efficient transportation, but environmentally efficient transportation as well. Thus we propose Heterogeneous Fleet Pollution Routing Problem (HFPRP) by extending the typical PRP with a consideration of different types of vehicles. The objective is to determine the optimal vehicle type-route combination in order to minimize the level of emissions in road transportation. The three types of vehicles used in this research are: Light-Duty Vehicle Class 1 (Vehicle Type 1), Light-Duty Vehicle Class 2 (Vehicle Type 2), and Light-Duty Vehicle Class 3 (Vehicle Type 3). Light-Duty Vehicle Class 3 has been used in previous PRP research.

In summary, HFPRP aims to minimize the total pollution cost, which consists of fuel and emission cost and variable cost (maintenance and driver costs). Furthermore, this research considers time windows and capacity constraints for each vehicle. Table 1 shows this study's state of the art.

The objectives of this study are as follows:

a. To develop a mathematical model for the Heterogeneous Fleet Pollution Routing Problem (HFPRP).
b. To solve HFPRP using SA algorithm.

The contributions of this research are as follows:

a. Develop a new mathematical model for PRP with a heterogeneous fleet in consideration of vehicle type and variable cost. By modeling as well as solving the HFPRP, the optimal vehicle type-route combination can be determined in order to minimize the level of emission in road transportation.
b. Implement SA heuristic as a solution for HFPRP.

The rest of this paper is organized as follows. The problem is formulated in Sect. 2 and the solution approach is described in Sect. 3. Section 4 presents computational result and analysis about the problem. Section 5 draws conclusions and possible future research.

Table 1 State of the art

No	Aspect of review	Bektaş and Laporte [1]	Demir et al. [22]	Kwon et al. [23]	Demir et al. [15]	Koç et al. [24]	Kopfer et al. [25]	Kumar et al. [26]	Proposed research
1	Topic	Introducing pollution routing problem	Minimization pollution cost	Minimization emission cost	Minimization pollution cost by considering two objectives	Minimization pollution by considering light and heavy duty vehicle	Minimization on emission cost by considering vehicle category	Minimization pollution cost by considering multiple time horizon	Minimization pollution cost by considering different type of light duty vehicles
2	Objective function	Minimize the total cost of pollution	Calculate total fuel consumption	Minimize emission cost	Minimize pollution cost	Minimize Pollution cost	Minimize emission based on fuel consumption	Minimize pollution cost and operational cost including inventory and production cost	Minimize pollution cost with consider load carried
3	Decision variable	Vehicle travel from vertex i to j or not	Vehicle travel from vertex i to j or not, and in which speed	Vehicle travel from vertex i to j or not and using which m type vehicle	Vehicle travel from vertex i to j or not	Vehicle travel from vertex i to j or not by using which m vehicle	Vehicle travel from vertex i to j or not by vehicle with Q_k load	Production takes place at plant in period t, vehicle k traverses arc (i,j) with speed level r in period t	Vehicle travel from vertex i to j or not by using which type m vehicle and in which r speed
4	Method/ solver	CPLEX 12.1	Adaptive large neighborhood search and CPLEX 12.1	Tabu search	CPLEX 12.1 and Adaptive large neighborhood search	Hybrid evolutionary algorithm	CPLEX	A self-learning particle swarm optimization	CPLEX 12.6 and simulated annealing
5	Vehicle type	1 Type	1 Type	3 Types	1 Type	3 Types	1 Type, 4 scenarios	1 Type	3 Types
6	Additional cost	–	Driver wage	–	Driver wage	Fixed cost	–	Operational cost such as production cost and inventory cost	Variable cost

2 Problem Definition

In practice, many types of vehicles are being used to transport goods, within or out of the city depending on the goods freight and road capacity. As different types of vehicles produce different emission levels, we intend to use a heterogeneous fleet of vehicles in this study. HFPRP extends the typical PRP with additional rich constraints and a comprehensive objective function. The goal of HFPRP is to find the minimum total cost of pollution caused by the fleet deployed. Figure 3 illustrates this problem.

Heterogeneous Fleet Pollution Routing Problem (HFPRP) can be applied by companies or agencies having a fleet with different vehicle types serving customers or other entities located over a wide geographical region. We attempt to determine which type of vehicle to deploy and the corresponding speeds at each arc while minimizing pollution cost. These limitations are made: tours should start and end at the depot, each customer must be visited exactly once, vehicle capacities, time windows, and total tour duration $T_{\max}$ should be respected. The sum of all the demand cannot exceed the capacity of each vehicle type used.

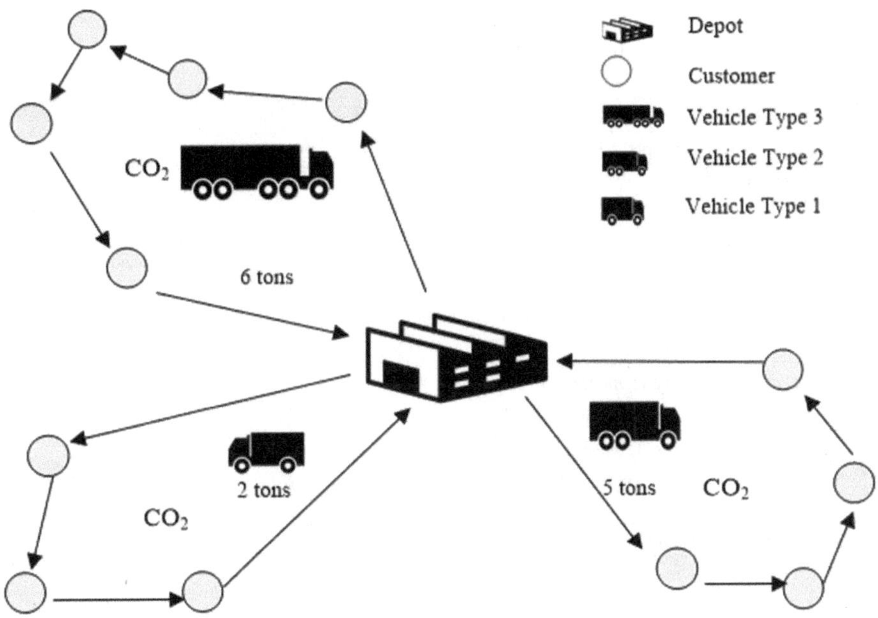

Fig. 3 Illustration of HFPRP

2.1 Assumptions

The assumptions of this study are as follows:

1. The same levels of speed r are applied to all vehicle types.
2. The depot has a demand equal to zero.
3. T_{max} is 9 h.

2.2 Mathematical Formulation

In the graph, HFPRP is defined as a complete graph $G = (N, A)$, where $N = \{0, \ldots, n\}$ is the set of nodes, 0 is the depot, and $A = \{(i, j){:}i,j \in \text{N and } i \neq j\}$ is the set of arcs. Distance from node i to j is denoted as d_{ij}, and M_m is the set of vehicle with m types. Each vehicle in the fleet has capacity of Q_m. Customer set is denoted by $N_0 = N\backslash\{0\}$, and each member has a non-negative demand q_i. The time window denoted as $[a_i, b_i]$ should be respected for each node. The set a_i is the opening time, while the set b_i is the closing time. The service time for a customer is denoted by t_i. Early arrival is allowed, but service should always start within a customer's time window. The vehicle speed and level are denoted as v and r, respectively.

Notations used in formulating HFPRP are defined as follows.

Sets and indices	
i,j	Nodes (customers), $i,j = 1,2,3,4,\ldots,N$
0	Depot
m	Vehicle types, $m = 1,2,\ldots,Mk$
r	speed levels, $r = 1,2,\ldots,R$
Decision variables	
x^r_{ijm}	One if a type m vehicle travels from node i to j at a speed level of r; otherwise zero
Parameters	
Q_m	Capacity of a type m vehicle
M_m	M total available vehicles
q	Demand at node (customer)
K	Large number of type m vehicles that travel from i to j, in order to fullfil the time window restrictions
T_{max}	Maximum available time
y_j	Time arrival in node j
a_i	Time to start the time window at node i
b_i	Time to end the time window at node i
d_{ij}	Distance between node i and j
t_i	Service time needed in node i
s_j	Total travel time

(continued)

(continued)

v^r	Available speed level (r)
x^r_{ijm}	Travel from i to node j using speed level r with type m vehicle
z_{ijm}	Vehicle of type m traveling from i to j
f_{ijm}	Amount carried using type m vehicle from i to j

Other parameters	
w_m	Curb-weight (kilogram) of a type m vehicle
k	Engine friction factor (kJ/rev/l)
N	Engine speed (rev/s)
V	Engine displacement (l)
g	Gravitational constant (m/s^2)
Cd_m	Coefficient of aerodynamic drag of a type m vehicle
ρ	Air density (k/m^3)
A	Frontal surface area (m^2)
Cr	Coefficient of rolling resistance
η_{tf}	Vehicle drive train efficiency
η	Efficiency parameter for diesel engines
C	Fuel and CO_2 emission cost per liter (£)
κ	Heating value of a typical diesel fuel (kJ/g)
ψ	Conversion factor (g/second to liter/s)
v^r	Speed level, r = 1,2,3,…,R
λ	$\lambda = \xi/\kappa\psi$
γ_m	$\gamma = 1/1000\ \eta_{tf}\eta$ of a type m vehicle
α_m	$\alpha = \tau + g \sin\theta + gC_r \cos\theta$ of a type m vehicle
β_m	$\beta = 0.5C_d\rho A$ of a type m vehicle
Vc_m	Variable cost for each vehicle m (£/m)

The mathematical formulation of HFPRP is as follows.

Objective Function:

Minimize

$$\sum_{m=1}^{M}\sum_{i=0}^{N}\sum_{j=0}^{N} k_m N_m V_m \lambda C d_{ij} \sum_{r=1}^{R} x^r_{ijm} \Big/ v_r \tag{1}$$

$$+\sum_{m=1}^{M}\sum_{i=0}^{N}\sum_{j=0}^{N} w_m \gamma_m \lambda \alpha_{ijm} d_{ij} z_{ijm} C \tag{2}$$

$$+\sum_{m=1}^{M}\sum_{i=0}^{N}\sum_{j=0}^{N} \gamma_m \lambda \alpha_{ijm} d_{ij} f_{ijm} C \tag{3}$$

$$+\sum_{m=1}^{M}\sum_{i=0}^{N}\sum_{j=0}^{N} C\beta_m\gamma_m\lambda d_{ij}\sum_{r=1}^{R} x_{ijm}^{r}(v^r)^2 \quad (4)$$

$$+\sum_{m=1}^{M}\sum_{i=0}^{N}\sum_{j=0}^{N} Vc_m d_{ij} z_{ijm} \quad (5)$$

Constraints:
Vehicle Routing

$$\sum_{j=1}^{N} z_{0jm} \leq M_m \quad \forall m \in M_m \quad (6)$$

$$\sum_{m=1}^{M}\sum_{j=0}^{N} z_{ijm} = 1 \quad \forall i \in N_0 \quad (7)$$

$$\sum_{m=1}^{M}\sum_{i=0}^{N} z_{ijm} = 1 \quad \forall j \in N_0 \quad (8)$$

$$\sum_{r=1}^{R} x_{ijm}^{r} = z_{ijm} \quad \forall (i,j) \in A, \ \forall m \in M_m \quad (9)$$

Capacity

$$\sum_{m=1}^{M}\sum_{j=0}^{N} f_{jim} - \sum_{m=1}^{M}\sum_{j=0}^{N} f_{ijm} = q_i \quad \forall i \in N_0 \quad (10)$$

$$q_i z_{ijm} \leq f_{ijm} \leq (Q_m - q_i) z_{ijm} \quad \forall (i,j) \in A \ \forall m \in M_m \quad (11)$$

Time Windows

$$y_i - y_j + t_i + \sum_{r=1}^{R} d_{ij} x_{ijm}^{r} \Big/ v^r \leq K(1 - z_{ijm}) \quad \forall i \in N, \ \forall j \in N_0, \ \forall m \in M_m, \text{ and } i \neq j \quad (12)$$

$$y_i + y_j - s_j + \sum_{r=1}^{R} d_{j0} x_{j0m}^{r} \Big/ v^r \leq K(1 - z_{j0m}) \quad \forall j \in N_0 \quad (13)$$

$$a_i \leq y_i \leq b_i \quad \forall i \in N_0 \quad (14)$$

$$0 \leq s_j \leq T_{\max} \quad \forall j \in N_0 \tag{15}$$

$$x^r_{ijm} \in \{0, 1\} \quad \begin{array}{l} \forall(i,j) \in A,\ \forall r \in R, \\ \text{and } \forall m \in M_m \end{array} \tag{16}$$

$$z_{ijm} \in \{0, 1\} \quad \begin{array}{l} \forall(i,j) \in A \text{ and} \\ \forall m \in M_m \end{array} \tag{17}$$

$$f_{ijm} \geq 0 \quad \begin{array}{l} \forall(i,j) \in A \ \text{ and} \\ \forall m \in M_m \end{array} \tag{18}$$

$$y_i \geq 0 \quad \forall i \in N_0 \tag{19}$$

This model works with discretized speed level. It is defined by R non-decreasing speed levels $v^r = (r = 1, \ldots, R)$, with $v = \{15.33, 16.44, 17.48, \ldots, 25\}$ m/s. Binary variables x^r_{ijm} take the value of 1 if arc (i, j) appears in the route using vehicle m at speed r; otherwise zero. Binary variables z_{ijm} take the value of 1 if vehicle m makes the visit from node i to node j; otherwise zero. Objective functions (1)–(4) are total pollution cost implied by variation at lower speed, total vehicle curb weight cost, total load carrier cost, and variation at high speed, respectively. The vehicle variable cost caused by distance travelled is indicated in (5).

This model has several constraints related to VRPTWs. Constraint (6) defines the maximum number of available vehicles M_m; it considers an unlimited number of vehicles for each vehicle type m. Constraints (7) and (8) ensure that nodes can only be visited once in a route. Constraint (9) guarantees only one vehicle m and only one vehicle speed level r in each arc. Constraints (10) and (11) state the restrictions for the amount of demand and capacities. Constraints (12)–(15) are the time window restrictions, where K is a large number to deal with time windows.

3 Methodology and Solutions

3.1 Solution Representation

The network considered in HFPRP consists of n nodes represented by a permutation of n customers denoted by the set $\{1, 2, 3, \ldots, n\}$. In this research, we employed 10 levels of speed, denoted as $r = 1, 2, 3, \ldots, 10$. The corresponding values for the speed level will be $v = \{15.33, 16.4, 17.48, \ldots, 25\}$. Figure 4 illustrates the feasible routes for 18 customers. These routes are restricted by time window and vehicle capacities. There are five routes to serve all customers.

Vehicle type 1 serves Customers 5, 3, and 15 in route 1. Vehicle type 1 serves customers 6, 10, and 12 in route 2. Vehicle type 2 serves customers 1, 14, 4, and 8

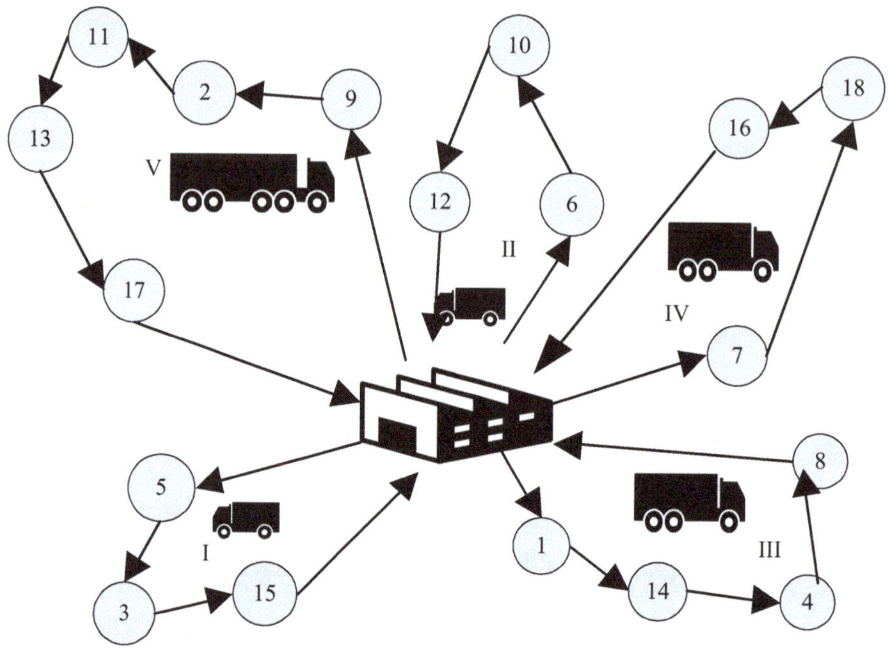

Fig. 4 Feasible solution illustration for 18 customers

in route 3. Vehicle type 2 serves customers 7, 18, and 16 in route 4. Finally, vehicle type 3 serves customers 9, 2, 11, 13, and 17 in route 5.

Figure 5 shows the solution representation of the routes. Figure 5a demonstrates the solution representation of vehicle type and speed at each arc, consisting of n nodes. The solution representation explains the choices of vehicle type when total demand is fully satisfied, which is also depicted in Fig. 5a.

Figure 5b shows the solution representation on the choices of the vehicle speed levels at each arc. To explain, for example, route 1 uses vehicle type 1 and travels from the depot (node 0) to node 5 using speed $r = 8$, then from node 5 to 3 using

(a)

Node	5	3	15	6	10	12	1	14	4	8	7	18	16	9	2	11	13	17
Vehicle Type	Vehicle 1			Vehicle 1			Vehicle 2				Vehicle 2			Vehicle 3				
Route	Route I			Route II			Route III				Route IV			Route V				

(b)

Arc	0-5	5-3	3-15	15-0	6-10	10-12	12-0	….	0-9	9-2	2-11	11-13	13-17	17-0
Value	8	10	10	6	7	8	9	…..	8	9	10	8	10	10

Fig. 5 **a** Solution representation for original routes **b** solution representation for speed each arc

speed $r = 10$, then from node 3 to 15 using $r = 10$, and then back to the depot from node 15 using speed $r = 6$.

3.2 Simulated Annealing Algorithm

Simulated Annealing (SA) consists of two parts: initial phase and improvement phase. In the initial phase, the Nearest Neighbor (NN) algorithm is used to make all the routes feasible. After the initial phase, the algorithm continues to improvement phase. This phase tries to improve the results from the initial phase by randomly choosing different improvement moves, such as swap, insertion, reverse move, change vehicle, and change speed. The algorithm begins by setting current temperature T, which is T_0, and randomly generates an initial solution X. The current best solution, X_{best}, and the best objective function of X, denoted by F_{best}, are set to be X and *objective* (X), respectively. Figure 6 illustrates the proposed SA heuristic.

The new solution Y is generated from the neighborhood of current solution X, $N(X)$, and its objective function value is evaluated. We let $\Delta = obj(Y) - obj(X)$. If Δ is less than or equal to zero, then it means that Y is better than X, and therefore X is replaced by Y; otherwise, the probability of replacing X with Y is $\exp(\Delta/KT)$. Here, X_{best} and F_{best} record the current best solution and the best objective function value, correspondingly. The current temperature T_0 decreases after $I_{iteration}$ using formula $T = \alpha T$. The algorithm terminates when the current temperature T_0 is lower than T_{final} or the current best solution X_{best} does not further improve within $N_{non-improving}$ consecutive temperature reductions.

3.3 Initial Solution

The initial solution is constructed following the Nearest Neighbor (NN) method. In this algorithm, the rule is to move to the next nearest unvisited customer subject to the following restrictions: vehicle capacity, maximum travel time, and time windows. The route starts by choosing a vehicle; then the vehicle travels from the depot, visiting exactly one customer vertex while checking capacity and time window; and finally it goes back to the depot. The next routes are constructed using the same procedure. The algorithm terminates when all customers are visited [27].

3.4 Move Procedure

In order to improve the quality of the routes and to minimize total pollution cost in HFPRP, it is necessary to perform a move procedure. The common standard SA

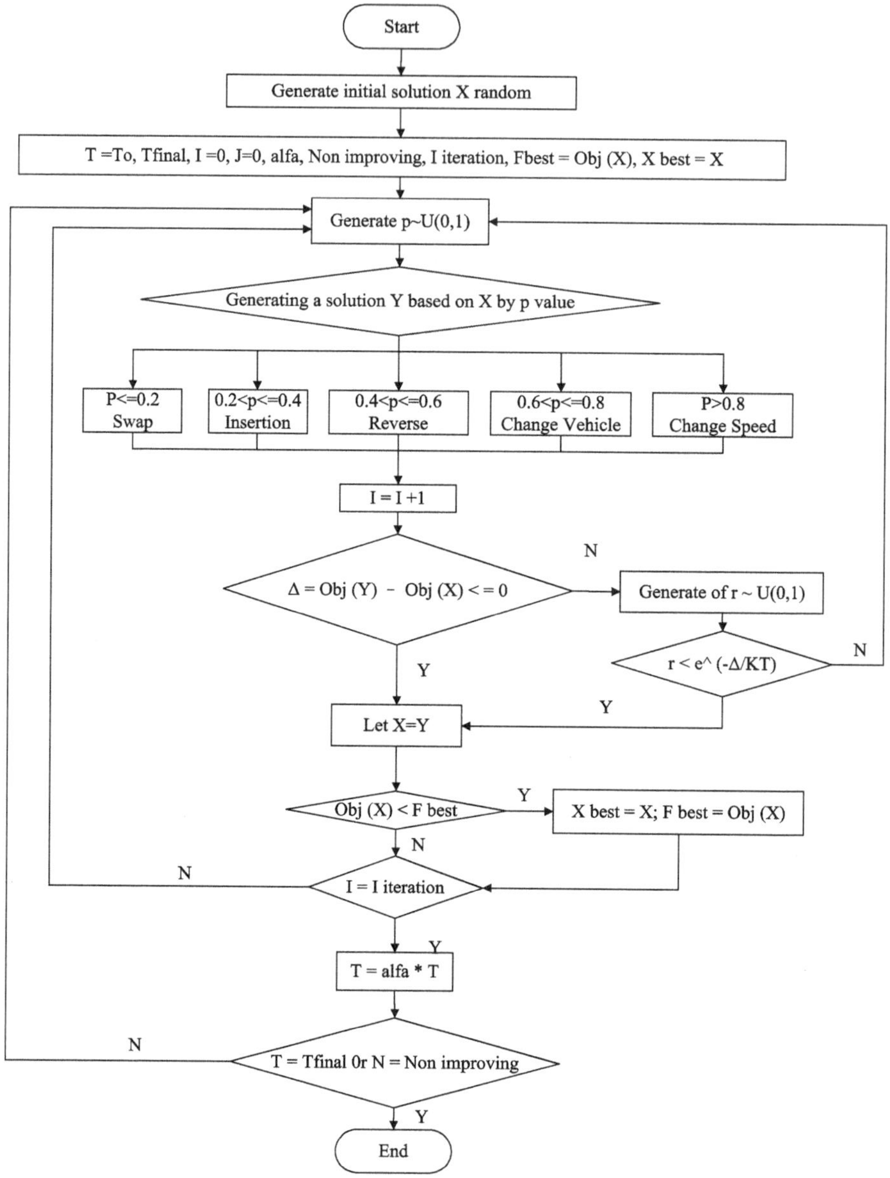

Fig. 6 Flow chart of simulated annealing algorithm for HFPRP

procedure with a random neighborhood structure that features a move includes swap and insertion [28, 29]. The neighborhood moves in this solution include swap, node insertion, reverse, change vehicle, and change speed.

(a)

Node	5	3	15	6	10	12	1	14	4	8	7	18	16	9	2	11	13	17
Vehicle	Vehicle 1			Vehicle 1			Vehicle 2				Vehicle 2			Vehicle 3				
	Route I			Route II			Route III				Route IV			Route V				

(b)

Node	5	3	4	6	10	12	1	14	15	8	7	18	16	9	2	11	13	17
Vehicle	Vehicle 1			Vehicle 1			Vehicle 2				Vehicle 2			Vehicle 3				
	Route I			Route II			Route III				Route IV			Route V				

Fig. 7 Illustration of swap **a** original route **b** new route

3.4.1 Swap

In *swap*, two nodes are picked randomly from two different routes. These two nodes then will swap their position. Figure 7 illustrates *swap* procedure. The original route is shown in Fig. 7a, where route I is 5–3–15, and route III is 1–14–4–8. In order to get a better result, a node from route I (node 15) is swapped with a node from route III (node 4). The new route is then shown in Fig. 7b.

3.4.2 Insertion

The procedure of *node insertion* is done by randomly picking a node from one route and then inserting the nodes in other route. The position for the insertion is also randomly picked. For example, node 14 is picked from route III and inserted into route V before the 15th node (customer 2). This procedure is depicted in Figs. 8a and 7b.

(a)

Node	5	3	15	6	10	12	1	14	4	8	7	18	16	9	2	11	13	17
Vehicle	Vehicle 1			Vehicle 1			Vehicle 2				Vehicle 2			Vehicle 3				
	Route I			Route II			Route III				Route IV			Route V				

(b)

Node	5	3	15	6	10	12	1	4	8	7	18	16	9	14	2	11	13	17
Vehicle	Vehicle 1			Vehicle 1			Vehicle 2			Vehicle 2				Vehicle 3				
	Route I			Route II			Route III			Route IV				Route V				

Fig. 8 Illustration of node insertion **a** original route **b** new route

(a)

Node	5	3	15	6	10	12	1	14	4	8	7	18	16	9	2	11	13	17
Vehicle	Vehicle 1			Vehicle 1			Vehicle 2				Vehicle 2			Vehicle 3				
	Route I			Route II			Route III				Route IV			Route V				

(b)

Node	5	3	15	6	10	12	1	14	4	8	7	18	16	13	2	11	9	17
Vehicle	Vehicle 1			Vehicle 1			Vehicle 2				Vehicle 2			Vehicle 3				
	Route I			Route II			Route III				Route IV			Route V				

Fig. 9 Illustration of reverse tour **a** original route **b** new route

3.4.3 Reverse

In the reverse tour, two random numbers are picked from the route. We then reverse the route based on the picked nodes. Figure 9 shows an example of a reverse procedure, showing (a) the original route and (b) the resulting route.

3.4.4 Change Vehicle

Change vehicle is performed by changing the vehicle that will be used by the route. The route is simultaneously changed if the demand exceeds the capacity of the vehicle. For example, if the vehicle is changed from 1 to 2 as shown in Fig. 10, then there will be some changes in the routes due to capacity.

(a)

Node	5	3	15	6	10	12	1	14	4	8	7	18	16	9	2	11	13	17
Vehicle	Vehicle 1			Vehicle 1			Vehicle 2				Vehicle 2			Vehicle 3				
	Route I			Route II			Route III				Route IV			Route V				

(b)

Node	5	3	15	6	10	12	1	14	4	8	7	18	16	9	2	11	13	17
Vehicle	Vehicle 1				Vehicle 1			Vehicle 2				Vehicle 2			Vehicle 3			
	Route I				Route II			Route III				Route IV			Route V			

Fig. 10 Illustration of change vehicle **a** original vehicle and the route **b** new vehicle and the route

(a)

Arc	0-5	5-3	3-15	15-0	6-10	10-12	12-0	….	0-9	9-2	2-11	11-13	13-17	17-0
Value	8	10	10	6	7	8	9	…..	8	9	10	8	10	10

(b)

Arc	0-5	5-3	3-15	15-0	6-10	10-12	12-0	….	0-9	9-2	2-11	11-13	13-17	17-0
Value	10	8	8	6	7	8	9	…..	8	9	10	8	10	10

Fig. 11 Illustration of change speed **a** original speed **b** new speed

3.4.5 Change Speed

In *change speed,* the speed will be randomly changed between $r = 1\text{–}10$ for each arc. We use ten levels of speed. The value for each level is $v = \{15.33, 16.4, 17.48, 18.55, 19.63, 20.7, 21.78, 22.85, 23.93, 25\}$ m/s. As in Fig. 11a, if $r = 10$ with the corresponding v value of 25 m/s, then as in Fig. 11b, the resulting speed could be $r = 8$ with the corresponding v value of 22.85 m/s.

4 Computational Result

Simulated Annealing (SA) was coded in Microsoft Visual Studio C++ 2012 and performed on a laptop computer with Intel (R) Core (TM) i5-2520M at 2.50 GHz (4 CPUs) processor, 4096 MB of RAM, running on a 32-bit platform under Windows 7 Operating System.

4.1 Test Problem

In order to explain how the model works, a small instance was generated with 1 depot, 5 customers, and 3 types of vehicles. The capacity of vehicle type 1 is 1000, vehicle type 2 is 2000, and vehicle type 3 is 3650. Table 2 shows the parameters for each vehicle.

The instances were solved using CPLEX version 12.6. Table 3 presents the corresponding values for the distance matrix (in meters), demand, opening time, closing time, and service time. Table 4 shows the results of this problem. To serve all customers, 3 vehicles are needed. Two vehicles are type 1 and one vehicle is type 2. The total cost for this example is £59.251, which consists of £19.429 for the cost of low speed, £5.379 for the cost of vehicle curb weight, £1.155 for vehicle load, £5.713 for the cost of high speed, and £27.575 for the variable cost.

As shown in Table 4, Route I is 0–5–4–3–0. The distance between the depot and customer 5 is 22,500. The variable cost, V_{c2}, is 3.375 ($22{,}500 \times 0.00015$) and will

Table 2 Vehicle specification

Notation	Description	Typical values of a type of m vehicle		
		Vehicle type 1	Vehicle type 2	Vehicle type 3
w_m	Curb-weight (kg) of a type of m vehicle	2700	4500	6350
Q_m	Capacity each type m vehicle	1000	2000	3650
ξ	Fuel-to-air-mass ratio	1	1	1
k	Engine friction factor (kJ/rev/l)	0.4	0.3	0.2
N	Engine speed (rev/s)	33	33	33
V	Engine displacement (l)	4	4.5	5
g	Gravitational constant (m/s^2)	9.81	9.81	9.81
Cd_m	Coefficient of aerodynamic drag of a type of m vehicle	0.25	0.35	0.7
r	Air density (kg/m^3)	1.2041	1.2041	1.2041
A	Frontal surface area (m^2)	2.1	3	3.912
Cr	Coefficient of rolling resistance	0.0062	0.009	0.01
η_{tf}	Vehicle drive train efficiency	0.6	0.5	0.4
η	Efficiency parameter for diesel engines	0.9	0.9	0.9
C	Fuel and CO_2 emission cost per liter (£)	1.4	1.4	1.4
κ	Heating value of a typical diesel fuel (kJ/g)	44	44	44
ψ	Conversion factor (g/second to liter/s)	737	737	737
v^r	Speed level, $r = 1,2,3,\ldots,R$	$v = \{15.33, 16.44, 17.48, \ldots, 25\}$ m/s		
λ	$\lambda = \xi/\kappa\psi$	3.08E−05	3.08E−05	3.08E−05
γ_m	$g = 1/1000\ h_{tf}h$ of a type of m vehicle	0.001852	0.002222	0.002777
α_m	$\alpha = \tau + g \sin\theta + gC_r \cos\theta$	0.060822	0.088291	0.098100
β_m	$\beta = 0.5C_d rA$ of a type of m vehicle	0.316076	0.632153	1.648653
Vc_m	Variable cost each vehicle m (£/m)	0.0001	0.00015	0.0002

Table 3 Parameters for the small problem size

	D	C1	C2	C3	C4	C5	Demand	a_i	b_i	t_i
D	0	4,1150	2,5680	23,000	32,450	22,500	0	0	22,400	0
C1	40,660	0	51,980	40,000	23,000	32,000	900	752	21,289	200
C2	25,010	51,780	0	30,000	32,000	23,000	727	270	24,050	2000
C3	20,000	30,000	30,000	0	23,000	25,000	800	250	22,500	1500
C4	32,500	23,000	32,000	23,000	0	30,000	580	700	28,000	200
C5	22,500	32,000	23,000	25,000	30,000	0	600	300	27,000	300

Table 4 Cumulative Result of small problem size

From to	Cost low speed	Vehicle curb weight	Pay load	Vehicle load	Cost high speed	Variable cost	Velocity	Distance	Time	Type of vehicle used
0 to 5	1.731	0.85763	0.377358	1980	0.85286	3.375	25	22500	900	2
5 to 4	4.039	2.00114	0.728035	1380	1.99001	7.875	25	30,000	2400	2
4 to 3	5.8085	2.87783	0.883891	800	2.86183	11.325	25	23,000	3520	2
3 to 0	7.3472	3.64018	0.883891	0	3.61993	14.325	25	20,000	6220	2
0 to 1	11.099	4.18049	1.06399	900	4.2699	18.44	25	41,150	1646	1
1 to 0	14.807	4.71436	1.06399	0	4.91212	22.506	25	40,660	10,145.2	1
0 to 2	17.148	5.05155	1.15478	727	5.31774	25.074	25	25,680	1027.2	1
2 to 0	19.429	5.37993	1.15478	0	5.71277	27.575	25	25,010	14,172.8	1

be added for all arcs in the route. To go from the depot to customer 5, vehicle type 2 uses speed r = 10, which is 25. The arrival time is 900 ($y_j = \frac{d_{ij}}{v^r} = \frac{22500}{25}$). The arrival time will be added for all arcs in the route. The vehicle load from the depot to customer 5 is 1980, which is the total load for customers 5, 4, and 3. The vehicle then proceeds from customer 5 to customer 4 with a load equal to 1380 (1980–600). From customer 3 and back to the depot, the load is reduced to 0.

Route II is 0–1–0. The distance between the depot and customer 1 is 41,150. The variable cost, V_{c1}, is 4.115 (41,150 × 0.0001), and this value will be added to the total variable cost of Route I. To go from the depot to customer 1, vehicle type 1 uses speed r = 10, which is 25. The arrival time is 1646 ($y_j = \frac{d_{ij}}{v^r} = \frac{41150}{25}$). The vehicle load from the depot to customer 1 is 900, which is the total load for a delivery to customer 1. The vehicle then goes back to the depot with the load reduced to 0.

Route III is 0–2–0. The distance between the depot and customer 2 is 25,680. The variable cost, Vc_1, is 2.568 (25,680 × 0.0001), and this value will be added to the total variable cost of Route II. To go from the depot to customer 2, vehicle type 1 uses speed r = 10, which is 25. The arrival time is 1027.2 ($y_j = \frac{d_{ij}}{v^r} = \frac{25680}{25}$). The vehicle load from the depot to customer 2 is 727, which is the total load for a delivery to customer 2. The vehicle then goes back to the depot with the load reduced to 0. The cumulative values for the vehicle curb weight, payload, and high speed cost are also shown in the table. Figure 12 itemizes the components of pollution cost at each arc for the test problem.

4.2 Parameter Setting

The parameters for SA are I_{iter}, T_0, T_f, $N_{non\text{-}improving}$, and α. I_{iter} denotes the number of inner iterations at a particular temperature. T_0 represents the initial temperature, and T_f represents the final temperature. $N_{non\text{-}improving}$ denotes the maximum allowable number of consecutive temperature reductions having no improvements in the objective function value. Finally, α is the cooling rate to control the cooling schedule. We performed the parameter setting using *the two-level* (2^k) *factorial design*. The best parameter combination is $N_{non\text{-}improving}$ = 200,000.000, T_o = 20, T_f = 0.001, I_{iter} = 150, and α = 0.999.

4.3 Algorithm Verification

The SA performance was then compared to the results from that of Demir et al. [22] and also to the optimal solution of the small problem size generated by CPLEX. The benchmark instances consist of datasets for PRP proposed by Demir et al. [22] for datasets having 10 nodes, 15 nodes, 20 nodes, 25 nodes, and 50 nodes, as shown

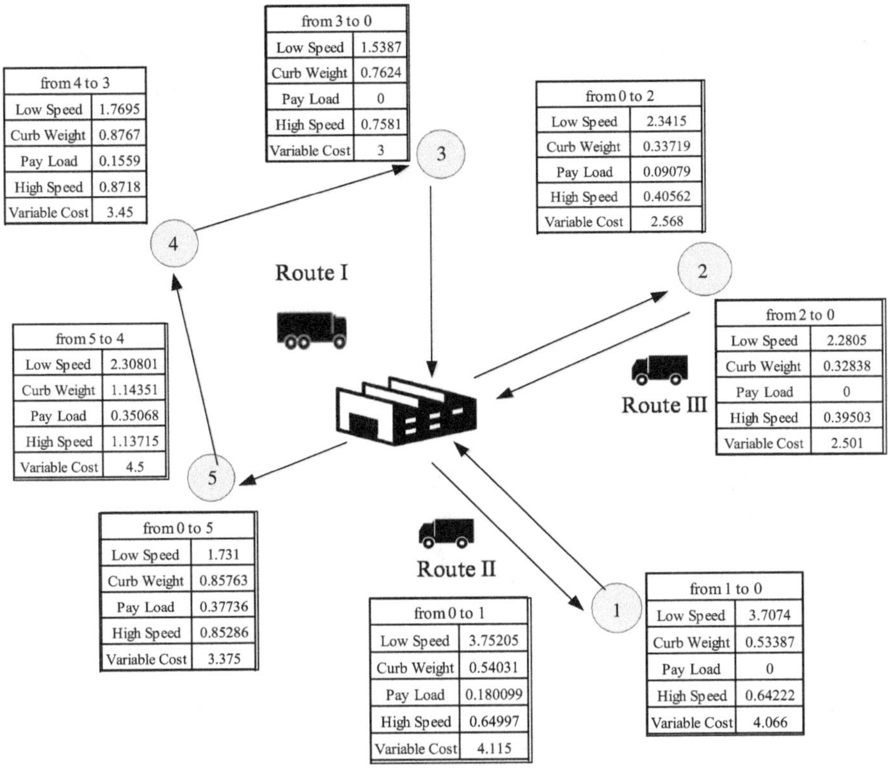

Fig. 12 Itemized pollution cost for each arc

in Table 5. Table 6 lists the average of each set of instances. The datasets are taken from http://www.apollo.management.soton.ac.uk/prplib.htm.

In terms of objective function values, SA performs at par with the optimal solution given by CPLEX for the problem size having 5 nodes, as shown in Table 7. Moreover, SA performs better when compared to the benchmark problem by a difference of 0.384% on average for large instances. In terms of computational time, in some problem sizes SA can performs better. Regardless the less of computational speed, the value is still within acceptable time constraint. Therefore, the proposed SA algorithm can be used to solve HFPRP.

4.4 *Numerical Experiment for a Heterogeneous Fleet*

The numerical experiment was conducted for 7 problem sizes: 10 nodes, 15 nodes, 20 nodes, 25 nodes, 50 nodes, 75 nodes, and 100 nodes. Each problem size consists of 20 instances totaling 140 instances. We refer to the problem size with 10 customers as small instances, 50 customers as medium instances, and 100 customers as

Table 5 Comparison proposed SA and CPLEX result

No	Instances	CPLEX	SA	Gap (%)	Number of vehicle needed		
					Type 1	Type 2	Type 3
1	5_1	39.559	39.559	0.000	2	0	0
2	5_2	39.638	39.638	0.000	2	0	0
3	5_3	80.261	80.261	0.000	3	0	0
4	5_4	56.811	56.811	0.000	0	1	0
5	5_5	55.467	55.467	0.000	2	0	0
6	5_6	46.435	46.435	0.000	3	0	0
7	5_7	79.283	79.283	0.000	2	0	0
8	5_8	29.787	29.787	0.000	1	0	0
9	5_9	59.251	59.251	0.000	2	1	0
10	5_10	36.935	36.935	0.000	2	0	0
11	5_11	130.659	130.659	0.000	2	0	0
12	5_12	34.179	34.179	0.000	2	0	0
13	5_13	203.377	203.377	0.000	0	1	0
14	5_14	37.255	37.255	0.000	2	0	0
15	5_15	67.602	67.602	0.000	0	1	0
16	5_16	43.735	43.735	0.000	2	0	0
17	5_17	22.455	22.455	0.000	1	1	0
18	5_18	26.271	26.271	0.000	0	1	0
19	5_19	26.167	26.167	0.000	2	1	0
20	5_20	31.382	31.382	0.000	0	1	0
Average				0.000			

large instances. The numerical experiment was conducted in two parts. The first part was the solution obtained using the SA algorithm with all vehicle types available. The second part was the sensitivity analysis looking at the availability scenarios of different vehicle types. Specifically, the first part uses scenario V123, which means all types of vehicles 1, 2, and 3 are available. The second part of the numerical experiment is for small, medium, and large instances and uses seven scenarios: V1, V2, V3, V12, V13, V23, and V123.

4.4.1 Impact of Heterogeneous Fleet in Pollution Routing Problem

This part shows the use of different available types of vehicles in every set of instances. We then determined the minimum pollution cost due to the vehicle types chosen. Table 8 shows the highest pollution cost in each set of instances. It also shows a comparison between the CPLEX (truncated after 14,400 s) and the SA results.

Tables 9, 10 and 11 demonstrate the number of vehicle types needed in small instances (10 nodes), medium instances (50 nodes), and large instances (100 nodes). In small instances, vehicle type 3 is not needed as often as vehicle

Table 6 Benchmarking proposed SA with previous research Demir et al. [22]

Instances	CPLEX		ALNS		SA		Improvement		
	Solution £	Time (s)	Solution £	Time (s)	Solution £	Time (s)	CPLEX versus ALNS (%)	CPLEX versus SA (%)	ALNS versus SA (%)
UK10_01	170.66	163	170.64	2.1	170.64	0.859	0.01	0.01	0.00
UK10_02	204.87	114	204.88	2.3	204.88	0.797	0.00	−0.01	0.00
UK10_03	200.33	926	200.42	2	200.48	0.817	−0.04	−0.08	−0.03
UK10_04	189.94	397	189.99	2.2	189.99	0.813	−0.03	−0.03	0.00
UK10_05	175.61	1254	175.59	2.3	175.6	0.786	0.01	0.01	−0.01
UK10_06	214.56	348	214.48	2.2	214.49	0.869	0.04	0.03	−0.01
UK10_07	190.14	191	190.14	2.9	190.14	0.818	0.00	0.00	0.00
UK10_08	222.16	140	222.17	2.1	222.17	0.79	0.00	−0.01	0.00
UK10_09	174.53	54	174.54	2.2	174.54	0.802	−0.01	−0.01	0.00
UK10_10	189.83	76.9	190.04	2.6	189.82	0.799	−0.11	0.01	0.12
UK10_11	262.07	50.5	262.08	2.2	262.07	0.87	0.00	0.00	0.00
UK10_12	183.18	1979	183.19	2.2	183.18	0.802	−0.01	0.00	0.01
UK10_13	195.97	1235	195.97	2.2	195.97	1.004	0.00	0.00	0.00
UK10_14	163.17	84.1	163.28	2.4	163.2	0.811	−0.07	−0.02	0.05
UK10_15	127.15	433	127.24	2.4	127.27	0.766	−0.07	−0.09	−0.02
UK10_16	186.63	681	186.73	1.9	186.38	0.82	−0.05	0.13	0.19
UK10_17	159.07	27	159.03	2.3	159.03	0.798	0.03	0.03	0.00
UK10_18	162.09	522	162.09	2.2	162.09	0.806	0.00	0.00	0.00
UK10_19	169.46	131	169.59	4.1	169.66	0.993	−0.08	−0.12	−0.04
UK10_20	168.8	1366	168.8	2	168.8	0.788	0.00	0.00	0.00
UK50_01	600.47	10,800[a]	593.77	29.7	588.41	25.17	1.12	2.01	0.90
UK50_02	614.18	10,800[a]	599.43	60.3	596.55	30.12	2.40	2.87	0.48

(continued)

Table 6 (continued)

Instances	CPLEX		ALNS		SA		Improvement		
	Solution £	Time (s)	Solution £	Time (s)	Solution £	Time (s)	CPLEX versus ALNS (%)	CPLEX versus SA (%)	ALNS versus SA (%)
UK50_03	640.28	10,800[a]	626.21	53.4	617.3	27.23	2.20	3.59	1.42
UK50_04	754.78	10,800[a]	740.92	35.8	723.82	29.36	1.84	4.10	2.31
UK50_05	644.53	10,800[a]	636	35.3	634.27	27.12	1.32	1.59	0.27
UK50_06	603.35	10,800[a]	584.61	54.6	584.65	28.12	3.11	3.10	−0.01
UK50_07	552.08	10,800[a]	541.07	25.7	534.62	26.33	1.99	3.16	1.19
UK50_08	573.49	10,800[a]	560.27	39.5	561.81	28.24	2.31	2.04	−0.28
UK50_09	697.26	10,800[a]	687.79	21.4	692.29	40.25	1.36	0.71	−0.65
UK50_10	698.01	10,800[a]	670.92	25.6	665.58	27.12	3.88	4.65	0.80
UK50_11	638.25	10,800[a]	618.94	25.1	615.22	30.13	3.03	3.61	0.60
UK50_12	589.59	10,800[a]	571.42	40.7	568.33	28.36	3.08	3.61	0.54
UK50_13	596.75	10,800[a]	589.11	52.1	584.58	27.33	1.28	2.04	0.77
UK50_14	663.99	10,800[a]	660.17	35	658.47	28.37	0.58	0.83	0.26
UK50_15	618.8	10,800[a]	584.13	26.2	584.37	29.36	5.60	5.56	−0.04
UK50_16	590.89	10,800[a]	585.16	51	582.43	30.24	0.97	1.43	0.47
UK50_17	480.85	10,800[a]	456.56	20	451.75	26.22	5.05	6.05	1.05
UK50_18	707.33	10,800[a]	681.72	26.4	677.53	28.36	3.62	4.21	0.61
UK50_19	613.7	10,800[a]	597.95	21.2	606.83	29.33	2.57	1.12	−1.48
UK50_20	680.44	10,800[a]	678.56	28.9	674.15	30.26	0.28	0.92	0.65
Average							1.18	1.43	0.25

[a]Not solved optimally after 10,800 s

Table 7 Average of the benchmark of proposed SA

Instances	CPLEX		ALNS		SA		Improvement of objective function		
	Solution £	Time (s)	Solution £	Time (s)	Solution £	Time (s)	CPLEX versus ALNS	CPLEX versus SA	ALNS versus SA
10	185.511	508.515	185.545	2.34	185.520	0.830	−0.019	−0.007	0.013
15	252.052	10,800[a]	280.89	3.725	249.839	5.65	0.066	0.883	0.816
20	319.219	10,800[a]	317.369	6.46	314.589	7.760	0.534	1.394	0.864
25	340.163	10,800[a]	337.345	10.025	334.763	11.152	0.879	1.665	0.794
50	627.951	10,800[a]	613.236	35.395	610.648	28.850	2.370	2.750	0.384

[a]Not solved optimally after 10,800 s

Table 8 Instances with the Largest Pollution Cost in each set

No	Instances	Time	CPLEX	SA	Time (s)	GAP	Number of vehicle needed		
							Type 1	Type 2	Type 3
1	UK10_11	14,400[a]	242.619	239.13	5.348	1.44	3	1	0
2	UK15_12	14,400[a]	312.068	305.89	7.89	1.98	1	4	0
3	UK20_14	14,400[a]	438.11	406.695	11.521	7.17	2	2	2
4	UK25_17	14,400[a]	557.92	472.206	14.652	15.36	1	5	1
5	UK50_04	14,400[a]	X	824.96	34.723	X	4	4	4
6	UK75_17	14,400[a]	X	1028.39	59.538	X	6	9	4
7	UK100_15	14,400[a]	X	1475.51	110.948	X	0	12	9

[a]Not solved optimally after 14,400 s, *X*—could not find feasible solution after 14,400 s

Table 9 Number of vehicle needed in small instances

Instances	Time	Solution £		Time (s)	GAP	Vehicle needed		
		CPLEX	SA			Type 1	Type 2	Type 3
UK10_01	14,400[a]	160.251	149.063	5.156	6.98	2	2	0
UK10_02	14,400[a]	179.604	178.661	5.067	0.53	1	2	0
UK10_03	14,400[a]	171.036	156.365	5.949	8.58	0	3	0
UK10_04	14,400[a]	156.898	154.507	5.094	1.52	1	2	0
UK10_05	14,400[a]	150.608	146.323	5.057	2.85	1	2	0
UK10_06	14,400[a]	180.701	172.857	5.075	4.34	3	1	0
UK10_07	14,400[a]	165.548	161.991	5.054	2.15	3	1	0
UK10_08	14,400[a]	217.988	217.618	4.982	0.17	0	3	0
UK10_09	14,400[a]	153.384	144.718	4.871	5.65	0	2	0
UK10_10	14,400[a]	189.165	188.881	4.998	0.15	2	2	0
UK10_11	14,400[a]	242.619	239.13	5.348	1.44	3	1	0
UK10_12	14,400[a]	154.64	144.833	5.328	6.34	4	1	0
UK10_13	14,400[a]	172.265	161.699	4.906	6.13	0	2	0
UK10_14	14,400[a]	172.154	164.517	5.066	4.44	1	2	0
UK10_15	14,400[a]	129.349	124.63	4.675	3.65	0	2	0
UK10_16	14,400[a]	187.963	187.963	5.077	0.00	0	1	1
UK10_17	14,400[a]	169.921	165.177	4.941	2.79	3	1	0
UK10_18	14,400[a]	151.628	137.21	3.62	9.51	2	2	0
UK10_19	14,400[a]	164.39	149.237	5.22	9.22	3	1	0
UK10_20	14,400[a]	142.237	134.999	5.036	5.09	0	3	0
Average		170.6175	164.019	5.026	4.08			

[a]NOT solved optimally after 14,400 s

Table 10 Number of vehicle needed in medium instances

Instances	CPLEX		SA		Vehicle		
	Time	Solution £	Time	Solution £	Type 1	Type 2	Type 3
UK50_01	14,400[a]	X	644.77	38.061	2	5	4
UK50_02	14,400[a]	X	647.87	36.829	1	3	5
UK50_03	14,400[a]	X	675.89	37.412	3	7	3
UK50_04	14,400[a]	X	824.96	34.723	4	4	4
UK50_05	14,400[a]	X	677.48	35.995	4	5	3
UK50_06	14,400[a]	X	588.24	36.627	2	8	3
UK50_07	14,400[a]	X	560.71	35.064	1	4	4
UK50_08	14,400[a]	X	567.92	36.57	5	4	3
UK50_09	14,400[a]	X	745.43	35.478	3	2	5
UK50_10	14,400[a]	X	737.93	36.119	4	1	6
UK50_11	14,400[a]	X	664.67	36.715	6	0	5
UK50_12	14,400[a]	X	571.98	35.841	1	4	5
UK50_13	14,400[a]	X	563.25	37.455	4	6	3
UK50_14	14,400[a]	X	722.68	35.054	1	6	3
UK50_15	14,400[a]	X	621.74	35.866	2	3	4
UK50_16	14,400[a]	X	626.77	33.465	1	4	4
UK50_17	14,400[a]	X	424.4	34.649	1	13	0
UK50_18	14,400[a]	X	741.24	35.158	3	7	3
UK50_19	14,400[a]	X	641.69	37.14	9	3	3
UK50_20	14,400[a]	X	720.27	34.875	1	6	4
Average			648.5	35.9548			

[a]X could not find feasible solution after 14,400 s

Table 11 Number of vehicle needed in large instances

Instances	CPLEX		SA		Vehicle		
	Time	Solution £	Time	Solution £	Type 1	Type 2	Type 3
UK100_01	14,400[a]	X	1376.5	115.009	2	9	9
UK100_02	14,400[a]	X	1338.3	119.041	0	13	6
UK100_03	14,400[a]	X	1234.8	115.965	3	8	8
UK100_04	14,400[a]	X	1178.9	112.022	0	9	10
UK100_05	14,400[a]	X	1108	115.811	0	0	15
UK100_06	14,400[a]	X	1311.3	110.237	0	0	15
UK100_07	14,400[a]	X	1188.3	112.079	1	7	8
UK100_08	14,400[a]	X	1235.1	112.185	0	0	13
UK100_09	14,400[a]	X	1031.3	104.676	0	7	9

(continued)

Table 11 (continued)

Instances	CPLEX		SA		Vehicle		
	Time	Solution £	Time	Solution £	Type 1	Type 2	Type 3
UK100_10	14,400[a]	X	1168.6	116.56	6	11	5
UK100_11	14,400[a]	X	1323.7	113.22	13	0	12
UK100_12	14,400[a]	X	1169.8	114.104	0	0	13
UK100_13	14,400[a]	X	1283.8	110.558	1	13	6
UK100_14	14,400[a]	X	1415.2	105.254	1	9	9
UK100_15	14,400[a]	X	1475.5	110.948	0	12	9
UK100_16	14,400[a]	X	1077.3	103.985	0	24	0
UK100_17	14,400[a]	X	1467.9	110.073	0	1	15
UK100_18	14,400[a]	X	1175.7	112.385	2	6	9
UK100_19	14,400[a]	X	1108	107.477	0	24	0
UK100_20	14,400[a]	X	1378.2	111.225	0	2	13
Average			1252.3	111.641			

[a]X could not find feasible solution after 14,400 s

types 1 and 2. The vehicles used differ in each instance. For example, instance UK10_08 needs three units of vehicle type 2. As the size of the instances increases, units of vehicle type 3 also increase. For example, UK100_14 needs one unit of type 1, nine units of type 2, and nine units of type 3 vehicles.

4.4.2 Impact of Using Different Types of Vehicles

This part shows the sensitivity analysis for each availability scenario of different vehicle types. We used seven different scenarios where available vehicle types are specified as follows:

(a) Scenario 1—vehicle type 1 only (V1)
(b) Scenario 2—vehicle type 2 only (V2)
(c) Scenario 3—vehicle type 3 only (V3)
(d) Scenario 4—vehicle types 1 and 2 (V12)
(e) Scenario 5—vehicle types 1 and 3 (V13)
(f) Scenario 6—vehicle types 2 and 3 (V23)
(g) Scenario 7—vehicle types 1, 2, and 3 (V123).

The average cost for all instances is obtained for each scenario. Using Scenario 3 as a benchmark, we then computed the difference in the average cost for each scenario. For example, Scenario 1 for small problem instances is −3.36 $\left(\frac{(200.814-194.074)}{200.814} \times 100\%\right)$, which would mean a 3.36% reduction of total costs if only vehicle type 1 is available compared to Scenario 3.

The results of all instances are summarized in Tables 12, 13 and 14, respectively. For cases of small instances, as shown in Table 12, all scenarios provide

Table 12 Impact of using different type of vehicle in small instances

No	Instances	V1	V2	V3	V12	V13	V23	V123
1	UK10_01	219.755	155.544	176.202	149.063	171.198	155.544	149.063
2	UK10_02	195.62	194.399	224.978	178.661	195.62	194.399	178.661
3	UK10_03	205.59	157.25	213.295	156.365	205.59	156.407	156.365
4	UK10_04	202.219	158.974	203.888	154.507	187.867	158.933	154.507
5	UK10_05	152.578	154.953	188.396	146.323	152.578	154.953	146.323
6	UK10_06	195.209	196.895	245.164	172.857	195.209	196.546	172.857
7	UK10_07	180.726	181.621	211.839	161.991	180.726	181.621	161.991
8	UK10_08	240.832	218.734	243.128	217.618	240.832	217.937	217.618
9	UK10_09	181.884	144.718	193.705	144.718	181.884	144.718	144.718
10	UK10_10	225.171	199.11	206.743	188.881	225.171	188.734	188.881
11	UK10_11	255.04	245.111	310.118	239.13	255.04	244.368	239.13
12	UK10_12	164.725	150.746	194.83	144.833	164.725	150.485	144.833
13	UK10_13	163.083	161.699	218.014	161.699	163.083	161.699	161.699
14	UK10_14	177.057	170.203	177.966	164.517	172.073	169.182	164.517
15	UK10_15	148.975	124.63	125.854	124.63	148.975	124.63	124.63
16	UK10_16	287.136	224.971	190.625	212.585	190.625	190.625	187.963
17	UK10_17	194.906	169.95	166.763	165.177	170.296	169.95	165.177
18	UK10_18	147.833	140.993	169.051	137.21	147.833	140.993	137.21
19	UK10_19	179.21	171.217	178.43	149.237	179.21	171.217	149.237
20	UK10_20	163.933	134.999	177.29	134.999	163.933	135.104	134.999
Average		194.0741	172.83585	200.81395	165.25005	184.6234	170.40225	164.01895
Percentage		−3.36	−13.93	0.00	−17.71	−8.06	−15.14	−18.32

Table 13 Impact of using different type of vehicle in medium instances

No	Instances	V1	V2	V3	V12	V13	V23	V123
1	UK50_01	905.891	679.721	705.173	679.721	684.302	679.721	644.771
2	UK50_02	954.582	692.641	687.565	692.641	676.598	649.379	647.87
3	UK50_03	984.428	702.592	696.664	702.592	688.816	677.049	675.892
4	UK50_04	1233.99	902.908	864.7	902.908	831.72	864.7	824.96
5	UK50_05	828.063	691.589	715.832	691.589	678.807	677.485	677.482
6	UK50_06	876.093	643.774	642.448	643.774	607.898	602.486	588.24
7	UK50_07	778.965	572.718	587.419	572.718	584.377	560.641	560.71
8	UK50_08	722.855	609.998	633.296	609.998	610.401	570.495	567.92
9	UK50_09	994.151	747.901	751.262	747.901	750.041	747.901	745.433
10	UK50_10	1060.05	789.551	746.205	786.26	746.205	755.913	737.933
11	UK50_11	909.184	725.487	725.655	707.497	708.967	673.527	664.673
12	UK50_12	783.15	624.222	647.864	624.222	632.715	595.039	571.98
13	UK50_13	734.593	597.352	606.338	592.208	593.723	597.352	563.248
14	UK50_14	1015.7	735.551	834.812	735.551	804.724	735.551	722.681
15	UK50_15	824.129	640.318	671.738	640.318	664.415	640.318	621.738
16	UK50_16	928.164	659.446	670.483	659.446	638.742	643.163	626.77
17	UK50_17	586.828	424.401	468.282	424.401	464.794	424.401	424.401
18	UK50_18	1027.7	793.988	785.728	793.988	765.871	754.837	741.242
19	UK50_19	837.806	663.411	678.618	663.411	649.273	663.411	641.686
20	UK50_20	1020.26	777.862	881.406	777.862	775.611	734.108	720.27
Average		900.3291	683.77155	700.0744	682.4503	677.9	662.37385	648.495
Percentage		28.60	−2.33	0.00	−2.52	−3.17	−5.39	−7.37

Table 14 Impact of using different type of vehicle in large instances

No	Instances	V1	V2	V3	V12	V13	V23	V123
1	UK100_01	1983.45	1454.07	1393.38	1454.07	1384.21	1381.18	1376.47
2	UK100_02	1778.46	1355.25	1374.37	1355.25	1342.83	1338.29	1338.29
3	UK100_03	1835.59	1301.23	1240.58	1301.23	1240.58	1240.58	1234.79
4	UK100_04	1687.36	1240.65	1211.52	1240.65	1211.52	1178.88	1178.88
5	UK100_05	1578.88	1145.42	1107.95	1145.42	1107.95	1107.95	1107.95
6	UK100_06	1988.03	1456.87	1311.28	1456.87	1311.28	1311.28	1311.28
7	UK100_07	1672.39	1203.85	1219.19	1203.85	1219.19	1188.53	1188.29
8	UK100_08	1693.37	1282.01	1288.78	1282.01	1235.08	1235.08	1235.08
9	UK100_09	1504.83	1070.05	1088.47	1070.05	1074.7	1031.33	1031.33
10	UK100_10	1575.89	1215.57	1201.51	1215.57	1201.51	1198.67	1168.55
11	UK100_11	2001.63	1467.77	1335.89	1415.27	1323.68	1335.89	1323.68
12	UK100_12	1682.59	1239.73	1169.83	1239.73	1169.83	1169.83	1169.83
13	UK100_13	1824.52	1331.42	1335.74	1331.42	1335.74	1283.81	1283.81
14	UK100_14	2093.05	1555.76	1458.48	1555.76	1443.67	1443.67	1415.24
15	UK100_15	2183.62	1595.78	1553.66	1595.78	1529.65	1475.51	1475.51
16	UK100_16	1355.08	1077.28	1089.1	1077.28	1089.1	1077.28	1077.28
17	UK100_17	2091.68	1487.03	1477.7	1487.03	1477.7	1467.93	1467.93
18	UK100_18	1719.08	1253.1	1246.6	1253.1	1246.6	1214.57	1175.69
19	UK100_19	1547.09	1107.99	1150.1	1107.99	1124.35	1124.35	1107.99
20	UK100_20	2128.39	1480.53	1429.58	1480.53	1404.18	1378.2	1378.2
Average		1796.249	1316.068	1284.1855	1313.443	1273.6675	1259.1405	1252.3035
Percentage		39.87	2.48	0.00	2.28	−0.82	−1.95	−2.48

significant pollution cost reductions. The highest pollution cost reduction is provided by Scenario 7 (18.32%), while the lowest pollution cost reduction is provided by Scenario 1(3.36%).

The results for medium instances are shown in Table 13, of which all scenarios are able to reduce the total pollution cost, except Scenario 1. The highest pollution cost reduction is provided by Scenario 7 (7.37%), while the lowest pollution cost reduction is provided by Scenario 2 (2.33%). Scenario 1 provides an inferior solution compared to Scenario 3. However, when vehicle type 1 is combined with other vehicle types, they produce better results.

Table 14 presents the results for large instances. Only Scenarios 5, 6, and 7 are able to reduce the total pollution cost, with Scenario 7 (2.48%) being the highest and Scenario 5 (0.82%) being the lowest. Other scenarios such as 1, 2, and 3 provide inferior solutions when compared to Scenario 3.

5 Conclusions

The objectives of this research are to develop a mathematical model for HFPRP and to use the SA algorithm to solve the problem. In terms of total pollution cost, the results of the computational study indicate that SA outperforms ALNS in all instances of each problem size. SA also performs better when compared to the benchmark problem by a difference of 0.384% on average for large instances. Moreover, the SA algorithm also produces the same optimal solutions given by CPLEX for small instances.

A sensitivity analysis has been conducted to determine the effects of different types of vehicles on total pollution costs. Generally, the analysis shows that using different types of vehicles provides total pollution cost reductions ranging from 0.82 to 18.32%. In large instances, only three scenarios are able to reduce the total pollution cost with the highest at 2.38 and 0.82% at the lowest. Other scenarios provide inferior solutions compared to scenario 3.

The Heterogeneous Fleet Pollution Routing Problem can be applied by companies or agencies deploying a transportation fleet consisting of different types of vehicles to serve customers or other entities located over a wide geographical region. Using the proposed model, it is possible to choose an optimum vehicle combination in order to minimize both route cost and the pollution cost.

References

1. Bektaş, T., & Laporte, G. (2011). The pollution-routing problem. *Transportation Research Part B: Methodological, 45*(8), 1232–1250.
2. Ohnishi, H. (2008). Greenhouse gas reduction strategies in the transport sector: preliminary report. In *Tech. Rep., OECD/ITF Joint Transport Research Centre Working Group on GHG Reduction Strategies in the Transport Sector, OECD/ITF, Paris*. http://www.internationaltransportforum.org/Pub/pdf/08GHG.pdf. Accessed February 11, 2008.

3. Dantzig, G. B., & Ramser, J. H. (1959). The truck dispatching problem. *Management Science, 6*(1), 80–91.
4. Lin, C., Choy, K., Ho, G., Chung, S., & Lam, H. (2014). Survey of green vehicle routing problem: Past and future trends. *Expert Systems with Applications, 41*(4), 1118–1138.
5. Aksoy, A., Küçükoğlu, İ., Ene, S., & Öztürk, N. (2014). Integrated emission and fuel consumption calculation model for green supply chain management. *Procedia-Social and Behavioral Sciences, 109,* 1106–1109.
6. Srivastava, S. K. (2007). Green supply-chain management: A state-of-the-art literature review. *International Journal of Management Reviews, 9*(1), 53–80.
7. Ping, L. (2009). Strategy of green logistics and sustainable development. In *International conference on information management, innovation management and industrial engineering 2009* (pp. 339–342). IEEE Computer Society.
8. Forkenbrock, D. J. (2001). Comparison of external costs of rail and truck freight transportation. *Transportation Research Part A: Policy and Practice, 35*(4), 321–337.
9. Bauer, J., Bektaş, T., & Crainic, T. G. (2010). Minimizing greenhouse gas emissions in intermodal freight transport: an application to rail service design. *Journal of the Operational Research Society, 61*(3), 530–542.
10. Kirby, H. R., Hutton, B., McQuaid, R. W., Raeside, R., & Zhang, X. (2000). Modelling the effects of transport policy levers on fuel efficiency and national fuel consumption. *Transportation Research Part D: Transport and Environment, 5*(4), 265–282.
11. Demir, E., Bektaş, T., & Laporte, G. (2011). A comparative analysis of several vehicle emission models for road freight transportation. *Transportation Research Part D: Transport and Environment, 16*(5), 347–357.
12. Koç, Ç., Bektaş, T., Jabali, O., & Laporte, G. (2016). Thirty years of heterogeneous vehicle routing. *European Journal of Operational Research, 249*(1), 1–21.
13. Brandão, J. (2011). A tabu search algorithm for the heterogeneous fixed fleet vehicle routing problem. *Computers and Operations Research, 38*(1), 140–151.
14. Jiang, J., Ng, K. M., Poh, K. L., & Teo, K. M. (2014). Vehicle routing problem with a heterogeneous fleet and time windows. *Expert Systems with Applications, 41*(8), 3748–3760.
15. Demir, E., Bektaş, T., & Laporte, G. (2014). A review of recent research on green road freight transportation. *European Journal of Operational Research, 237*(3), 775–793.
16. Cordeau, J.-F., Gendreau, M., Laporte, G., Potvin, J.-Y., & Semet, F. (2002). A guide to vehicle routing heuristics. *Journal of the Operational Research society,* 512–522.
17. Gendreau, M., & Potvin, J.-Y. (2010). *Handbook of metaheuristics* (Vol. 2). Springer, Berlin.
18. Tavakkoli-Moghaddam, R., Safaei, N., & Gholipour, Y. (2006). A hybrid simulated annealing for capacitated vehicle routing problems with the independent route length. *Applied Mathematics and Computation, 176*(2), 445–454.
19. Van Breedam, A. (1995). Improvement heuristics for the vehicle routing problem based on simulated annealing. *European Journal of Operational Research, 86*(3), 480–490.
20. Chiang, W.-C., & Russell, R. A. (1996). Simulated annealing metaheuristics for the vehicle routing problem with time windows. *Annals of Operations Research, 63*(1), 3–27.
21. Yu, V. F., Lin, S.-W., Lee, W., & Ting, C.-J. (2010). A simulated annealing heuristic for the capacitated location routing problem. *Computers & Industrial Engineering, 58*(2), 288–299.
22. Demir, E., Bektaş, T., & Laporte, G. (2012). An adaptive large neighborhood search heuristic for the pollution-routing problem. *European Journal of Operational Research, 223*(2), 346–359.
23. Kwon, Y.-J., Choi, Y.-J., & Lee, D.-H. (2013). Heterogeneous fixed fleet vehicle routing considering carbon emission. *Transportation Research Part D: Transport and Environment, 23,* 81–89.
24. Koç, Ç., Bektaş, T., Jabali, O., & Laporte, G. (2014). The fleet size and mix pollution-routing problem. *Transportation Research Part B: Methodological, 70,* 239–254.
25. Kopfer, H. W., Schönberger, J., & Kopfer, H. (2013). Reducing greenhouse gas emissions of a heterogeneous vehicle fleet. *Flexible Services and Manufacturing Journal, 26*(1), 221–248.

26. Kumar, R. S., Kondapaneni, K., Dixit, V., Goswami, A., Thakur, L. S., & Tiwari, M. K. (2015). Multi-objective modeling of production and pollution routing problem with time window: A self-learning particle swarm optimization approach. *Computers & Industrial Engineering*.
27. Pop, P. C., Sitar, C. P., Zelina, I., Lupse, V., & Chira, C. (2011). Heuristic algorithms for solving the generalized vehicle routing problem. *International Journal of Computers Communications & Control, 6*(1), 158–165.
28. Yu, V. F., Jewpanya, P., & Redi, A. A. N. P. (2016). Open vehicle routing problem with cross-docking. *Computers & Industrial Engineering, 94,* 6–17.
29. Yu, V. F., Redi, A. A. N. P., Hidayat, Y. A., & Wibowo, O. J. (2017). A simulated annealing heuristic for the hybrid vehicle routing problem. *Applied Soft Computing, 53,* 119–132.

A Multi-objective Model for Location-Allocation Problem with Environmental Considerations

Malika Nisal Ratnayake, Voratas Kachitvichyanukul and Huynh Trung Luong

Abstract The paper presents a multi-objective model for solving location-allocation problem (LAP) which considers the greenhouse gas. It involves the determination of the best strategy to distribute the product in a distribution network by selecting proper locations of plants and distribution centers as well as the allocation of products from plants to warehouses and from warehouses to customers. Two objective functions are considered simultaneously. The first objective is to minimize the total logistics costs and the second objective is to minimize the total amount of greenhouse gases generated by the activities. The model is validated using the test data that were derived from published benchmark test data set. The mathematical model was solved using CPLEX by converting one objective into a constraint with slack. The set of trade-off solutions is generated by solving the model repeatedly with varying slack values.

Keywords Location-allocation problem (LAP) · Multiple objective optimization Greenhouse gas

1 Introduction

Supply chain network design is a strategic decision which plays an important role in ensuring the efficiency of the supply chain. In the recent decades, many research works have been conducted to improve the performance of supply chain by optimizing the distribution network design. Most of these research works have been focused mainly on reducing the cost associated with the supply chain to improve the profit margins.

But since the dawn of the 21st century there has been an increased concern in improving the sustainability of businesses. Sustainability consists of three main

M. N. Ratnayake · V. Kachitvichyanukul (✉) · H. T. Luong
Industrial and Manufacturing Engineering, School of Engineering and Technology, Asian Institute of Technology, Pathumthani, Thailand
e-mail: voratas@ait.asia

X. Liu (ed.), *Environmental Sustainability in Asian Logistics and Supply Chains*,
https://doi.org/10.1007/978-981-13-0451-4_11

aspects. They are economic aspect, environmental aspect and the social aspect. Concerns raised by environmentalists and world organizations over the emission of greenhouse gases (GHG), increase in global warming prompted countries to force the regional governmental organizations and world organizations to introduce legislation (e.g.: European WEEE directive, carbon tax) to reduce the adverse environmental impacts. With the increased concerns over environment, many businesses have taken initiatives to improve the environmental friendliness in different aspects of the business. Reducing the emissions of GHG by the distribution network is one such initiative.

The environmental aspect was included in previous network designs in the form of single objective and multi-objective. Several studies have used single objective optimization to optimize the economic impact and the environmental impacts by including the environmental impact as a financial cost. These studies convert the environmental impacts to a monetary value by using carbon tax [1], carbon credits [2] or pollution related costs [3].

Several studies have implemented multi-objective optimization to design distribution networks which optimize economic and environmental impacts simultaneously. Shaw proposed a supplier selection model where GHG emissions, total costs and late deliveries were minimized simultaneously. This model was solved using a fuzzy LP approach [4]. Several studies have used MILP as a solution technique for multi-objective green supply chain problem. A study conducted on hydrogen supply chains minimized the environmental impacts using a life cycle assessment based approach [5]. In another study related to green supply chains, the dangerous gas emissions and total costs were minimized simultaneously for a five-echelon supply chain [6]. Normalized constrained method is used to design a supply chain which accounted for costs, CO_2 emissions and environmental protection levels [7]. MILP approach is also used to solve a Bioethanol supply chain model which considers profit and GHG emissions as objective functions [8].

Among the reviewed literature related to green supply chains, no research has considered capacity level of facilities and product groupings in the mathematical model of distribution centers. Therefore, this study attempts to bridge this gap in literature by proposing a mathematical model for a four-echelon, multi-commodity, multi-objective distribution network which minimizes the total costs and GHG simultaneously. The proposed mathematical model is then solved as Mixed Integer Linear Programing (MILP) using constraint with slack approach.

The rest of the paper is organized as follows. The mathematical model is proposed in Sect. 2. In Sect. 3 the mathematical model is solved and analyzed using a published numerical example and Sect. 4 gives conclusions and recommendations for future research.

2 Mathematical Model

The multi-objective mathematical model was developed to minimize both total cost and GHG emissions simultaneously. The model spans four echelons comprising of suppliers, manufacturing plants, DCs and customers. Multiple product types and raw materials are considered. Suppliers, plants and DCs comprises of different capacity levels (CL) and product groupings for DCs are considered. The model will determine the location of facilities and the allocation of products and raw materials for minimum total costs and GHG emissions.

Mathematical model was formulated based on the single objective model proposed in [9]. The following common assumptions were considered when developing the mathematical model.

- Demand of all customers for all product types are known and deterministic.
- Consumption rate of raw material for each product is known.
- Product or raw material flow between facilities in the same echelon are not allowed.
- Back orders are not permitted.
- Raw materials can be supplied from more than one supplier and a product type can be produced from more than one manufacturing plant.

2.1 Model Notations

Indices	
i	Candidate suppliers: $i \in \{1, 2, \ldots, I\}$
j	Candidate plants: $j \in \{1, 2, \ldots, J\}$
k	Candidate DCs: $k \in \{1, 2, \ldots, K\}$
l	Customers: $l \in \{1, 2, \ldots, L\}$
p	Product types: $p \in \{1, 2, \ldots, P\}$
τ	Raw materials: $\tau \in \{1, 2, \ldots, T\}$
a	Capacity level a of candidate supplier: $a \in \{1, 2, \ldots, A\}$
b	Capacity level b of candidate plant: $b \in \{1, 2, \ldots, B\}$
c	Capacity level c of candidate DC: $c \in \{1, 2, \ldots, C\}$
g	Product group $g \in \{1, 2, \ldots, G\}$

Decision variables	
$\alpha_i^a = \begin{cases} 1, & \text{if supplier } i \text{ with capacity level } a \text{ is operated} \\ 0, & \textit{otherwise} \end{cases}$	
$\beta_j^b = \begin{cases} 1, & \text{if plant } j \text{ with capacity level } b \text{ is operated} \\ 0, & \textit{otherwise} \end{cases}$	
$\gamma_k^c = \begin{cases} 1, & \text{if DC } k \text{ with capacity level } c \text{ is operated} \\ 0, & \textit{otherwise} \end{cases}$	
X_{ij}^{τ}	Quantity of raw material τ transported from supplier i to plant j

(continued)

(continued)

Y_{jk}^{p}	Quantity of product p transported from plant j to DC k
Z_{kl}^{p}	Quantity of product p transported from DC k to customer l

Parameters		
Type		Description
Demand	θ_l^p	Demand of the customer l for product p
Consumption rate	$\omega_{\tau p}$	Consumption rate of raw material τ per unit of product p
Product grouping	ϕ_{pg}	Group g of product p
Capacity limits	$S_{i\tau}^{a}$	Maximum capacity of supplier i with capacity level a for raw material τ
	M_{jp}^{b}	Maximum production capacity of plant j with capacity level b for product p
	D_{kg}^{c}	Maximum processing capacity of DC k with capacity level c for product group g
Facility limits	$\hat{A}$	Limited number of suppliers that can be operated
	$\hat{B}$	Limited number of plants that can be operated
	$\hat{C}$	Limited number of DCs that can be operated
Distances	F_{ij}	Distance from supplier i to manufacturing plant j
	W_{jk}	Distance from manufacturing plant j to DC k
	H_{kl}	Distance from DC k to customer l
Volumes	σ_{τ}	Unit volume of raw material τ
	V_p	Unit volume of product p
Costs (facilities)	E_i^a	Fixed cost associated with opening and operating suppler i with capacity level a
	Q_j^b	Fixed cost associated with opening and operating plant j with capacity level b
	N_k^c	Fixed cost associated with opening and operating DC k with capacity level c
Costs (transportation)	R	Transportation cost of unit volume of raw mat. per unit distance
	U	Transportation cost of unit volume of product per unit distance
Emissions (facilities)	ϵ_i^a	GHG emissions associated with opening and operating suppler i with capacity level a
	η_j^b	GHG emissions associated with opening and operating plant j with capacity level b
	v_k^c	GHG emissions associated with opening and operating DC k with capacity level c
Emissions (transportation)	λ	Emissions from transporting a of unit volume of raw mat. per unit distance
	μ	Emissions from transporting a of unit volume of product per unit distance

2.2 Objective Functions

$$\min f_{Eco} = \sum_{i}\sum_{a} E_i^a \alpha_i^a + \sum_{j}\sum_{b} Q_j^b \beta_j^b + \sum_{k}\sum_{c} N_k^c \gamma_k^c + \sum_{i}\sum_{j}\sum_{\tau} F_{ij} R \sigma_\tau X_{ij}^\tau + \sum_{j}\sum_{k}\sum_{p} G_{jk} U V_p Y_{jk}^p + \sum_{k}\sum_{l}\sum_{p} H_{kl} U V_p Z_{kl}^p \tag{1}$$

$$\min f_{Env} = \sum_{i}\sum_{a} \epsilon_i^a \alpha_i^a + \sum_{j}\sum_{b} \eta_j^b \beta_j^b + \sum_{k}\sum_{c} \nu_k^c \gamma_k^c + \sum_{i}\sum_{j}\sum_{\tau} F_{ij} \lambda \sigma_\tau X_{ij}^\tau + \sum_{j}\sum_{k}\sum_{p} G_{jk} \mu V_p Y_{jk}^p + \sum_{k}\sum_{l}\sum_{p} H_{kl} \mu V_p Z_{kl}^p \tag{2}$$

The proposed mathematical model consists of two objective functions. The first objective function (1) minimizes the total cost of the supply chain. The first three terms of the equation cover the fixed cost associated with establishing and operating suppliers, plants and DCs and the last three terms of the objective function cover the variable cost associated with transporting raw materials from suppliers to plants and transporting products from plants to DCs to customers. The second objective function (2) minimizes the total greenhouse gas emissions of the supply chain. The first three terms of the equation are related to the GHG emissions caused by establishing and operating suppliers, plants and DCs. The last three terms of the objective cover the GHG emissions caused by transporting products and raw materials between different facilities.

$$\sum_{j} X_{ij}^\tau \le \sum_{a} S_{i\tau}^a \alpha_i^a \quad \forall i, \tau \tag{3}$$

$$\sum_{k} Y_{jk}^p \le \sum_{b} M_{jp}^b \beta_j^b \quad \forall j, p \tag{4}$$

$$\sum_{l}\sum_{p} V_p Z_{kl}^p \phi_{pg} \le \sum_{c} D_{kg}^c \gamma_k^c \quad \forall k, g \tag{5}$$

$$\sum_{i} X_{ij}^\tau \ge \sum_{k}\sum_{p} Y_{jk}^p \omega_{\tau p} \quad \forall j, \tau \tag{6}$$

$$\sum_{j} Y_{jk}^p \ge \sum_{l} Z_{kl}^p \quad \forall k, p \tag{7}$$

$$\sum_{k} Z_{kl}^p \ge \theta_l^p \quad \forall l, p \tag{8}$$

$$\sum_{a} \alpha_i^a \leq 1 \quad \forall i \tag{9}$$

$$\sum_{b} \beta_j^b \leq 1 \quad \forall j \tag{10}$$

$$\sum_{c} \gamma_k^c \leq 1 \quad \forall k \tag{11}$$

$$\sum_{i} \sum_{a} \alpha_i^a \leq \hat{A} \tag{12}$$

$$\sum_{j} \sum_{b} \beta_j^b \leq \hat{B} \tag{13}$$

$$\sum_{k} \sum_{c} \gamma_k^c \leq \hat{C} \tag{14}$$

$$X_{ij}^{\tau}, Y_{jk}^{p}, Z_{kl}^{p} \geq 0 \tag{15}$$

$$\alpha_i^a, \beta_j^b, \gamma_k^c = 0, 1 \tag{16}$$

In the proposed mathematical model constraints (3)–(5) are capacity constraint which states that the capacity utilized in each facility should be less than or equal to the maximum capacity of the respective facility. Constraints (6)–(8) are material balance constraints of the mathematical model. These constraints connect the echelons of the supply chain and transfers the demand of each customer to upstream members of the supply chain. Constraints (9)–(11) represents the capacity level constraints. These constraints limit the mathematical model from selecting more than one capacity level from available capacity levels at suppliers, plants and distribution centers. Moreover, number of facilities that can be selected are restricted by constraints (12)–(14). This allows the decision maker to limit the maximum number of facilities that can be opened at each echelon. Constraint (15) prevents products flowing in the reverse direction and constraint (16) is the binary constraint for the location selection decision.

2.3 *Multi-objective Optimization*

The proposed mathematical model consists of two conflicting objectives which are to be optimized simultaneously. This was done by obtaining the set of optimal Pareto solutions. A solution is considered as a Pareto-optimal solution if it is not dominated by one of the objectives. The set of Pareto-optimal solutions were obtained using a constraint with slack approach.

$$\begin{aligned} &\text{Minimize} \quad f_{Eco} \\ &\text{Subject to} \quad f_{Env} = \min(f_{Env}) + \varepsilon_m \end{aligned} \tag{17}$$

In this method, GHG emissions were considered as the constraint and the Pareto-optimal solutions were obtained by minimizing the total cost values for different slack values (ε_m) of GHG emissions.

3 Results and Discussion

A numerical example adopted from [10] was used to analyze the performance of the proposed mathematical model. The numerical example consists of 4 candidate suppliers, 5 candidate plants, 20 candidate DCs, 50 customers, 3 product types and 3 raw material types. The maximum numbers of suppliers, plants and DCs that can be selected are 2, 3 and 10 respectively. Each facility consists of two capacity levels and the products are stored under two groups in DCs. Parameters are generated using random numbers distributed in the ranges shown in Table 1.

The numerical example was solved using CPLEX Optimization Studio 12.6.1 with an Intel® Core™ i7-2630QM CPU at 2.00 GHz and 6.00 GB of DDR3 RAM. First the mathematical model was solved to find the minimum values for each objective function. Minimum value for total cost was $25,851 and minimum GHG emissions was 5949 ton. These minimum points were used as references to obtain the Pareto-optimal points with different slack values. The slack value for GHG emissions was varied with an increment of 200 ton. The Pareto frontier obtained is shown in the Fig. 1. Solutions and the distribution network set up for the solutions are shown in Table 2. The selected capacity level of each category is given with the index.

Table 1 Distribution of input data

Data type	Distribution
Consumption rate	U[0,1]
Demand[a]	U[50,100]
Unit volume of product	U[0.08,0.12]
Unit volume of raw material	U[0.08,0.1]
Distance between facilities	U[0.5,1]
Capacity of suppliers[a]	U[4000,5000]
Capacity of plants[a]	U[3000,4000]
Capacity of DCs[a]	U[100,200]
Fixed costs	U[1000,2000]
GHG emission of facilities	U[100,500]
Per volume cost	U[5,10]
Per volume GHG emission	U[1,5]

[a]For each product type/raw material

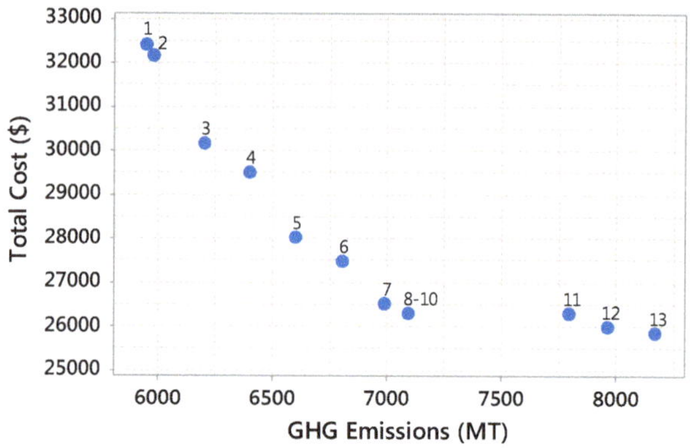

Fig. 1 Pareto-optimal solutions

Table 2 Set of Pareto-optimal solutions and network setup

Solution	Slack	Total cost ($)	GHG emissions (MT)	Suppliers	Plants	DCs
1	–	32,430	5949	$2^2,4^2$	$1^2,4^2$	$3^1,8^2,13^1,16^2,18^2$
2	6000	32,169	5980	$2^2,4^1$	$1^2,4^1$	$3^1,8^2,13^1,16^2,18^2$
3	6200	30,160	6200	$2^1,3^1$	$2^1,4^1$	$1^2,3^1,5^2,10^2,20^1$
4	6400	29,502	6400	$2^2,3^1$	$2^1,4^1$	$1^2,5^2,9^1,10^2,20^1$
5	6600	28,018	6597	$2^1,3^1$	$2^1,4^2$	$1^2,5^1,7^1,11^1$
6	6800	27,476	6800	$1^1,2^1$	$3^2,4^1$	$1^2,4^1,5^1,11^2$
7	7000	26,505	6987	$1^1,3^1$	$2^2,3^2$	$1^2,4^1,5^1,11^2$
8	7200	26,295	7093	$1^1,3^2$	$2^2,3^1$	$1^2,4^1,5^1,11^2$
9	7400	26,295	7093	$1^1,3^2$	$2^2,3^1$	$1^2,4^1,5^1,11^2$
10	7600	26,295	7093	$1^1,3^2$	$2^2,3^1$	$1^2,4^1,5^1,11^2$
11	7800	26,291	7795	$1^1,3^2$	$2^1,3^1$	$1^2,9^2,10^1,12^1,20^2$
12	8000	26,005	7962	$1^1,3^2$	$2^2,3^1$	$5^1,9^2,10^1,12^1,19^1$
13	–	25,851	8164	$1^1,3^1$	$2^2,3^1$	$9^2,10^1,12^1,14^1,19^1$

The average contribution of fixed and transportation components to total costs and GHG emissions are shown in Fig. 2. More than half of total costs and GHG emissions are related to transportation. Transportation costs and emissions are calculated based on the distance between facilities, volume of product and unit cost/emissions of transportation. From these variables, except the distance between facilities, other variables are constant for every Pareto-optimum solution.

A breakdown of total costs and GHG emissions are given in Table 3. Out of the fixed and variable components of costs and emissions, variable costs and emissions related to transportation has less percentage deviation from the mean compared to

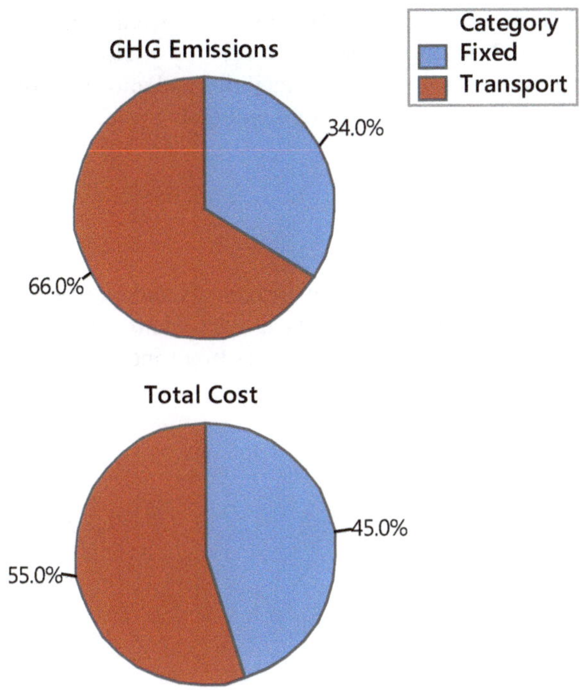

Fig. 2 Contribution of fixed and transportation costs/emissions

Table 3 Breakdown of total costs and GHG emissions

Solution	Costs ($)			GHG emissions (MT)		
	Total	Fixed	Transport	Total	Fixed	Transport
1	32,430	16,467	15,963	5949	1266	4683
2	32,169	16,206	15,963	5980	1297	4683
3	30,160	14,951	15,209	6200	1725	4475
4	29,502	14,445	15,057	6400	1977	4423
5	28,018	12,513	15,505	6597	2043	4554
6	27,476	11,806	15,670	6800	2197	4603
7	26,505	11,208	15,297	6987	2495	4492
8	26,295	10,997	15,298	7093	2602	4491
9	26,295	10,997	15,298	7093	2602	4491
10	26,295	10,997	15,298	7093	2062	5031
11	26,291	11,244	15,047	7795	3378	4417
12	26,005	10,927	15,078	7962	3537	4425
13	25,851	10,617	15,234	8164	3692	4472
% deviation	8.43	17.15	2.02	10.39	33.11	3.70

other factors. This shows that costs and emissions related to transportation are not affected by the network setup selected.

A detailed analysis on the selection of facilities and allocation of products under the different Pareto-optimal solutions is given below.

3.1 Suppliers

The supplier selection depends on the average costs and emissions associated with each supplier. A comparison of fixed costs and emissions for each supplier is given in Fig. 3a. Pareto-optimum solutions which is more inclined towards minimizing

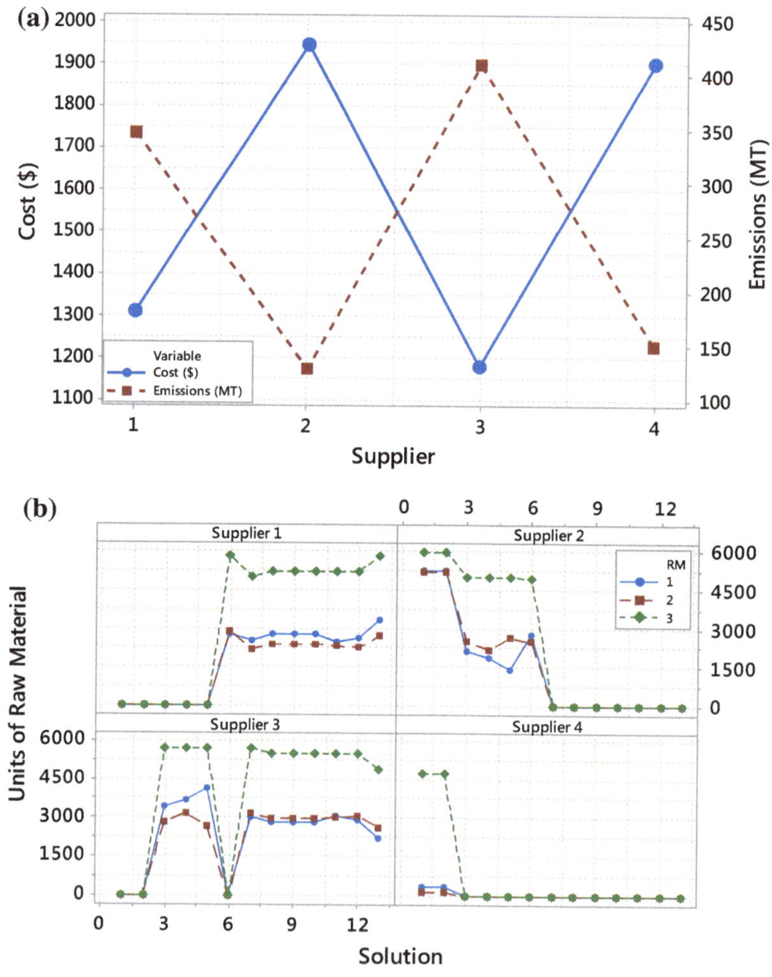

Fig. 3 **a** Comparison of costs and emissions of suppliers; **b** amount of raw materials supplied from each supplier

costs tends to select suppliers 1 and 3 since they are associated with minimum fixed cost. Similar emission sensitive solutions have selected suppliers 2 and 4 due to the less emissions associated. This phenomenon can be observed clearly through Fig. 3b which presents amount of raw materials supplied from each supplier.

3.2 Plants

Similar to supplier selection, plants selection is also dependent on the fixed costs and emissions. A comparison of fixed costs and emissions for plants are given in Fig. 4a.

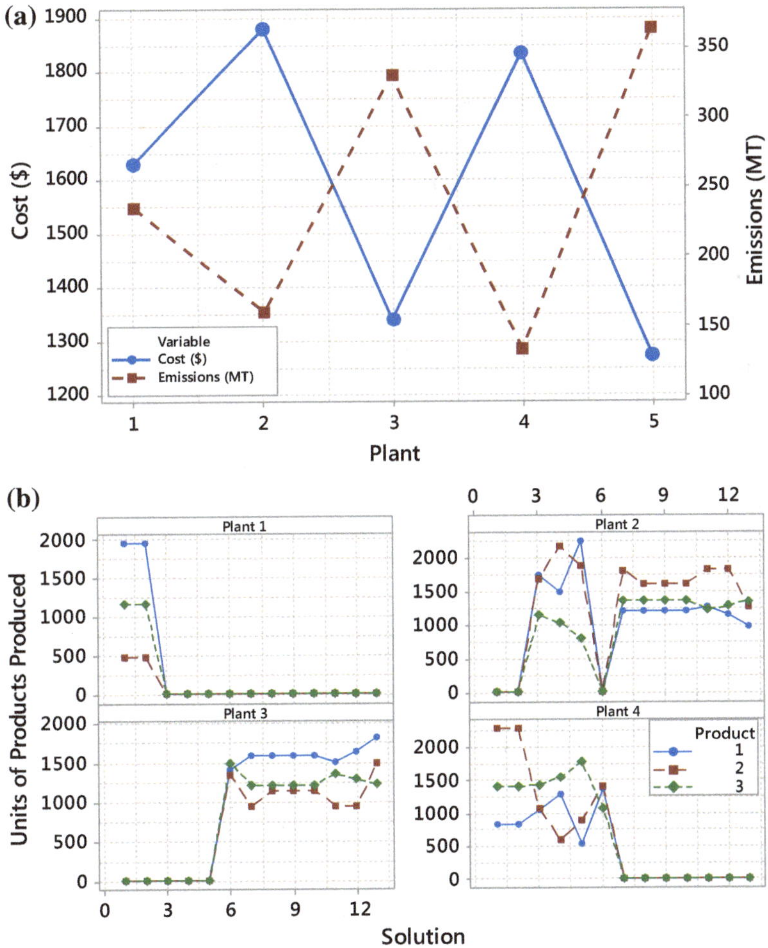

Fig. 4 **a** Comparison of costs and emissions of plants; **b** quantity of products produced from each plant

Since plants 2 and 4 has lower GHG emissions values, they are selected in Pareto-optimum solutions which has lower emissions. But it is important to note that Plant 5 is not used in any of the 13 solutions. This is because the average distance from DCs to plant 5 is higher compared to the other plants. Therefore, plant 5 was not selected even though it has a lower fixed cost value but with higher transportation cost.

3.3 Distribution centers

The same properties considered in supplier and plant selection decision were included when selecting the DCs. DC number 2, 6, 15 and 17 was not considered for any solution due to longer distance.

4 Conclusions and Recommendations

Research related to green supply chain design has grown with increased concerns over environment and climate change. But there are still many gaps in literature when it comes to mathematical models that mimics the practical scenario. This research proposed a mathematical model for four-echelon distribution network considering capacity levels of facilities and product grouping of DCs. The proposed multi-objective mathematical model was solved as MILP via a constraint with slack approach. A set of Pareto-optimal solutions were obtained for minimized total costs and GHG emissions. Costs and emissions showed a less sensitivity for the transportation component. Therefore, the costs and emissions of the distribution network mainly depends on the location decision, even though a major portion of costs and emissions are transportation related. Further analysis showed that individual cost/emission of each product does not affect the location selection or allocation decision.

For future work, this mathematical model can be extended to include the social aspect of the sustainability. The consideration of modes of transportation would also be an interesting area since much of costs and emissions are related to the allocation decision.

References

1. Abdallah, T., Diabat, A., & Simchi-Levi, D. (2010) *A carbon sensitive supply chain network problem with green procurement*. Awaji.
2. Ramudhin, A., Chaabane, A., & Paquet, M. (2010). Carbon market sensitive sustainable supply chain network design. *International Journal of Management Science and Engineering Management, 5*(1), 30–38.

3. Elhedhli, S., & Merrick, R. (2012). Green supply chain network design to reduce carbon emissions. *Transportation Research Part D: Transport and Environment, 17*(5), 370–379.
4. Shaw, K., Shankar, R., Surendra, S. Y., & Lakshman, S. T. (2012). Supplier selection using fuzzy AHP and fuzzy multi-objective linear programming for developing low carbon supply chain. *Expert Systems with Applications, 39*(9), 8182–8192.
5. Sabio, N., Kostin, A., Guillén-Gosálbez, G., & Jiménez, L. (2012). Holistic minimization of the life cycle environmental impact of hydrogen infrastructures using multi-objective optimization and principal component analysis. *International Journal of Hydrogen Energy, 37*(6), 5385–5405.
6. Jamshidi, R., Ghomi, S. M. T. F., & Karimi, B. (2012) Multi-objective green supply chain optimization with a new hybrid memetic algorithm using the Taguchi method. *Scientia Iranica, 19*(6), 1876–1886.
7. Wang, F., Lai, X., & Shi, N. (2011). A multi-objective optimization for green supply chain network design. *Decision Support Systems, 51*(2), 262–269.
8. Giarola, S., Zamboni, A., & Bezzo, F. (2011). Spatially explicit multi-objective optimisation for design and planning of hybrid first and second generation biorefineries. *Computers & Chemical Engineering, 35*(9), 1782–1797.
9. Bamrungbutr, C. (2011) *Differential evolution algorithm for the multi-commodity distribution network design problem*. Master thesis No. ISE 11-01, Asian Institute of Technology, Bangkok, Thailand.
10. Chiamchit, B. (2015). *Multi-objective differential algorithm for the multi-commodity distribution network design problem*. Bangkok, Thailand: Asian Institute of Technology.

Efficiency of Crew Assignment in Truck Freight Operation from the View of Logistics

Kuninori Suzuki, Yoji Murayama, Keizo Wakabayashi and Akihiro Watanabe

Abstract This paper firstly examines efficiency of shift scheduling of truck drivers whose number has been dramatically decreasing in recent years. In Freight Operation, burdened with a legal duty, the truck operation managers should deal with its scheduling, but it is tightly complicated, even for the qualified and experienced persons in charge. Thus, this paper analyzes the actual situations and problems on making of a crew assignment, and offers a formulation as a solution. Also, this study examines an introduction of junction transportation as the truck driver reduction measure using a computer simulation. The results showed the truck drivers' burdens could be reduced after the introduction.

Keywords Freight operation management · Crew assignment · Junction transportation

1 Introduction

In Japan, cargos are transported mostly by trucks, and truck transportation accounts for approximately 60% of all transportation on a ton-kilometer basis. Distribution and logistics have become advanced in recent years, and truck transportation has been more important than ever when a company develops its corporate strategy.

However, the number of employees in the truck transportation business is approximately 1,850,000 (2015). Of those employees, the number of transport and machine operation workers, such as drivers, was approximately 800,000, and this number has decreased for two consecutive years.

The vehicle transportation business, including the truck transportation business, depends on male workers older than 40 years, and workers younger than 40 years account only for approximately 30% of the total workers in this business. Recently,

K. Suzuki (✉) · Y. Murayama · K. Wakabayashi · A. Watanabe
College of Industrial Technology, Nihon University, Izumi-Cho 1-2-1, 285-8575 Narashino, Chiba, Tokyo, Japan
e-mail: suzuki.kuninori@nihon-u.ac.jp; QWL02764@nifty.ne.jp

X. Liu (ed.), *Environmental Sustainability in Asian Logistics and Supply Chains*,
https://doi.org/10.1007/978-981-13-0451-4_12

accidents in the vehicle transportation business caused by older drivers and over-strained driving due to prolonged work have also become a serious social problem.

To cope with the decreasing number of truck drivers and to prevent drivers from prolonged work in order to secure their safety, cargo operation management must be improved.

This study elucidates the current situation of and problems with cargo operation management; proposes a model for creating a crew assignment schedule, which is essential to increase the efficiency of operation management activities; and simulates and verifies the effect of introducing junction transportation, which is considered effective to reduce on-duty hours.

2 Operation Management of Truck Transportation [1]

2.1 Appointment of Operation Managers

The Motor Truck Transportation Business Safety Regulation was revised on May 1, 2013, and business operators are obliged to appoint operation managers to each business office in order to ensure the safety of vehicle operation.

The main duty of an operation manager is to appropriately manage operators, to secure sufficient rest and sleep time for crews, and to create a crew assignment schedule. An operation manager records and preserves a series of documents related to vehicle operation, creates a list of operators and an operation instruction sheet, manages tachographs, prevents drivers from driving under the influence of alcohol, and instructs and supervises overload-prevention measures.

An operation manager also instructs and supervises the loading and unloading of cargos and comprehends the health condition of each driver. For long-distance driving and nighttime driving, an operation manager must arrange a co-driver. When abnormal weather occurs, an operation manager must take necessary measures to secure the safety of each driver. Regarding accident-prevention measures, an operation manager also instructs and supervises crews and employees.

The number of operation managers appointed by a business operator is set by laws and ordinances, and it is calculated by the following formula (a fraction of less than 1 shall be discarded) (Table 1).

$$T_{om} = \frac{(k - kd)}{30} + 1 \quad (1)$$

here,

T_{om} the number of truck freight operation managers
K the number of vehicles belonged to the office
Kd the number of vehicle controlled by a tractor

Table 1 Number of truck operators according to that of vehicles [3]

Number of vehicles	Number of operators
Up to 29	1
30 through 59	2
60 through 89	3
90 through 119	4
120 through 149	5
150 through 179	6
180 through 209	7
210 through 39	8
240 through 269	9
270 through 299	10

2.2 *Basic Flow of an Operation Manager's Routine Work*

An operation manager's routine work is described below.

An operation manager routinely conducts visual inspections on vehicles that will be used by truck drivers based on the Road Transport Vehicle Act. When an abnormality is found in a vehicle, an operation manager arranges a suitable person to correct the abnormality or obtains a substitute vehicle.

After vehicle inspections, the operation manager "calls over" the drivers to a specified place before an operation starts. The call-over is usually performed face-to-face at a business office or a barn. An operation manager directly checks the physical condition and mental health of each driver. If an abnormality is observed in a driver, an operation manager takes necessary measures, such as cancellation of the driver's operation and arrangement of a substitute driver.

When an operation manager cannot call over drivers face-to-face beforehand, the operation manager must create an operation instruction sheet and indicate the operation route and the point when drivers should switch. Each driver must carry this operation instruction sheet. During the operation, an operation manager must call drivers via telephone (e-mail or facsimile is not allowed).

After an operation, the operation manager inspects the vehicles again. Inspections cover instantaneous velocity, driving distance, driving time, etc., and they are recorded in a tachograph. An operation manager is obliged to manage and preserve tachographs for one year. The record of an accident must be preserved for three years.

3 Working Hours of a Driver

The Japanese government takes into consideration the working condition of vehicle drivers and provides standards for on-duty hours, rest breaks, etc. The on-duty hours are the duration from the starting time of work to the ending time of work, and they indicate the total time of working hours and break time (including naps).

A rest break is the time between a duty and the next duty and is defined as the "completely free time of workers as their living hours, including sleeping hours."

In Japan, on-duty hours are limited to 293 h per month—in principle. However, when a written labor-management agreement that limits on-duty hours per month is concluded, on-duty hours per month can be prolonged, not exceeding 3516 h a year. On-duty hours are basically limited to 13 h per day and are allowed to be prolonged to a maximum of 16 h per day. A daily rest break of at least eight consecutive hours is also required. The maximum driving time per two days (48 h from the starting time of work) is nine hours a day on average.

Continuous driving time is limited to four hours. A driver must stop driving and take a rest for more than 30 min within four hours after the start of driving or immediately after four hours have passed. An operation manager must comprehend the working state of each driver and consider working hours and on-duty hours on daily, weekly, monthly, and yearly bases, in accordance with the Labor Standards Act, as well as create a vehicle operation plan. The Labor Standards Act provides that when working hours exceed six and eight hours, the driver is required to take a rest for 45 and 60 min, respectively.

4 Problems with the Creation of a Crew Assignment Schedule

An operation manager must lay down a vehicle operation plan based on the Labor Standards Act and the "standards for the improvement in working hours, etc., of vehicle drivers" by the Minister of Labor (hereinafter referred to as the "improvement standards notification"). However, it takes time to create a vehicle operation plan that does not violate the improvement standards notification and to judge whether the vehicle operation plan is in accordance with the improvement standards notification. Therefore, an operation manager, who is often pressed for time, may have difficulty coping with such tasks. Moreover, an operation manager sometimes cannot comprehend the working hours of each truck driver.

Therefore, we conducted an interview survey focusing on truck transportation networks, summarized the current problems with the creation of a crew assignment schedule as below, and examined options to solve these problems.

4.1 Work System of an Operation Manager

The Motor Truck Transportation Business Act states that a general motor truck transportation business operator shall appoint an operation manager to each business office. When the business operator does not appoint an operation manager, strict administrative measures, such as an order to cease business operations for

30 days, are taken. In the case of a business operator with fewer than 30 vehicles, to cope with the changes in the working hours of truck drivers, one operation manager must work for 24 h at a business office. However, that is actually impossible. Because an assistant to an operation manager is not allowed to perform all duties of the operation manager, shift management is required, in which an operation manager and several assistants perform operation management tasks.

4.2 *Burden of Creating a Crew Assignment Schedule on an Operation Manager*

The creation of a crew assignment schedule for truck drivers is one of the most important duties of an operation manager, but it takes quite a lot of time. An operation manager must create a crew assignment schedule for truck drivers in accordance with the Labor Standards Act and the improvement standards notification.

When on-duty hours per day are prolonged based on a labor-management agreement, on-duty hours per day must not exceed 15 h more than twice a week. For example, it is illegal to require more than 15 on-duty hours per day three times a week (for example, Monday, Tuesday, and Wednesday).

Thus, a crew assignment schedule is complicated, and even a well-experienced operation manager can have doubts about whether the crew assignment schedule is compliant. Therefore, a crew assignment schedule and a vehicle operation plan must be verified from a different perspective. To avoid human errors and to rapidly and accurately create crew assignment schedules, a certain application must be introduced.

4.3 *Environment of Long Working Hours*

Even if a business operator has cargos to be transported and vehicles to transport these cargos, he often cannot secure a sufficient number of truck drivers to comply with the Labor Standards Act. This increases the number of truck drivers who are forced to work for long periods of time. As a matter of course, this prolonged work is an illegal act. If this illegal act leads to an accident, the executive and operation manager can be severely punished.

Furthermore, if the working environment of a company is hostile, workers will avoid the corresponding duties; consequently, the work force will become further insufficient. The company will be caught in a vicious cycle. To improve the environment of long and complicated working hours, measures must be taken, such as the use of working service shifts and junction transportation. Figure 1 shows an example. Compulsory labor hours per day should be less than 15 h, except twice a week. Only once a week, a long distance round-trip transportation can be accepted.

Fig. 1 Complicated scheduling: one-week shift for a truck driver

inadequate scheduling

Mon	rest(8)	compulsory labor hours(16)
Tues	rest(8)	compulsory labor hours(16)
Wed	rest(8)	compulsory labor hours(16)
Thurs	rest(8)	compulsory labor hours(16)
Fri	rest(8)	compulsory labor hours(16)
Sat	holoday	
Sun	holoday	

appropriate scheduling

Mon	holiday	compulsory labor hours(16)	
Tues	rest(8)	compulsory labor hours(16)	
Wed	rest(8)	compulsory labor hours(15)	
Thurs	rest(9)	compulsory labor hours(13)	holiday
Fri	rest(9)	compulsory labor hours(14)	holiday
Sat	holoday		
Sun	holoday		

5 Selection of the Optimization Problem

5.1 Application of the Scheduling Problem

Together with the creation of a crew assignment schedule, the introduction of an operation management system is indispensable. To solve problems with cargo operation management, this study creates a model for rapidly, efficiently, and appropriately creating a crew assignment schedule for truck drivers.

In other words, working hours of each truck driver's every operation must be checked. For a vehicle operation plan which violates the Labor Standards Act, a draft amendment must be proposed within the scope of law. To this end, this study optimized not only driving routes but also working service shifts of truck drivers by solving the scheduling problem. This study also proposed formulae based on constraint conditions described below and performed a simulation using actual data described below on the assumption that junction transportation would be introduced.

5.2 Constraint Conditions for Truck Drivers

When the constraint conditions for truck drivers are considered from the perspective of the scheduling problem based on previous studies, a crew assignment schedule must be created under the conditions described below. The constraint conditions for truck drivers can be divided into shift and driver constraint conditions as follows:

(1) Shift constraint conditions
The conditions associated with the composition of members (satisfaction at a service level)

(a) The minimum and maximum numbers of truck drivers in each day, each time zone, each group, and each working service shift (workplace) must be kept.

(2) Driver constraint conditions
The conditions associated with the workload and duty limitations of each driver

(b) A driver is banned from continuously working more than the maximum consecutive days.
(c) The interval between duties is not allowed to exceed the maximum interval in each working service shift (workplace).
(d) A duty prohibition pattern is established, and each truck driver must abide by the pattern.
(e) The number of work attendances a month must be within the maximum and minimum numbers of work attendances in each time zone, each driver, and each working service shift (workplace).
(f) The number of Saturdays off a month must be within the maximum and minimum numbers of Saturdays and holidays of each driver.
(g) The desirable duty of each driver must be taken into consideration.

5.3 Formulae

Based on the constraint conditions described in the previous section, formulae are proposed as follows.

The objective function expressed by Formula (2) minimizes the sum of labor costs.

$$\text{Minimize} \sum_{d \in D} \sum_{h \in H} \sum_{n \in N} \sum_{b \in B} x_{dhnb} M_{hnb} \tag{2}$$

where D represents the set of days during the target period, H represents the set of time zones, N represents the set of staff members, and B represents the set of shifts (workplace). Variable x_{dhnb} is 1 when the duty assigned to each staff member n in each day d and each time zone h is b and 0 when that is not b. M_{hnb} represents the wage of truck driver n in each time zone h according to the duty.

Formula (3) indicates that each truck driver is assigned to shift s, which includes at least one rest in the duty of each day d and each time zone h.

$$\sum_{s \in S} x_{dhns} = 1, \quad d \in D, h \in H, n \in N \tag{3}$$

where S represents the set of shifts, in which a rest is added to B.

Formula (4) expresses the above-mentioned constraint condition (b) and indicates that the number of work attendances does not exceed the maximum consecutive days $c3$. Gp represents the set of truck drivers for which the maximum consecutive days must be considered.

$$\sum_{i=0}^{c3} y_{(d-i)n} \leq c3, \quad d \in D, n \in Gp \tag{4}$$

Formulae (5) and (6) indicate whether a truck driver goes to work on day n. When a truck driver goes to work or does not go, variable y_{dn} is 1 or 0, respectively.This variable is defined by Formula (17).

In Formula (5), when y_{dn} is 1, the work attendance of truck driver n on day d is restricted regardless of time zone h and shift b. In Formula (6), when y_{dn} is 1, truck driver n goes to work on day d.

In Formula (6), constant T represents the number of time zones a day.

$$y_{dn} - \sum_{h \in H} \sum_{b \in B} x_{dhnb} \leq 0, \quad d \in D, n \in N \tag{5}$$

$$Ty_{dn} - \sum_{h \in H} \sum_{b \in B} x_{dhnb} \geq 0, \quad d \in D, n \in N \tag{6}$$

Formula (7) expresses the restriction on the maximum interval $c4$ at every shift b regarding the above-mentioned constraint condition (c) and indicates that truck driver n goes to work at least once during $c4$ days.

$$\sum_{i=0}^{c4} \sum_{h \in H} x_{(d-i)hnb} \geq 1, \quad d \in D, n \in N, b \in B \tag{7}$$

Formula (8) expresses the above-mentioned constraint condition (d). This formula restricts the appearance of a shift, in which the duty in time zones $1 - T$ on day d corresponds to duty prohibition pattern p. In this formula, $k1$ represents the number of duty prohibition patterns.

$$\sum_{h \in H} x_{dhnp_{ih}} \leq T - 1, \quad d \in D, n \in N, i = 1, .., k1 \tag{8}$$

Formulae (9) and (10) express the above-mentioned constraint condition (a) and indicate the restrictions on the minimum and maximum numbers of truck drivers $c1_{dhgb}$ and $c2_{dhgb}$, respectively, in working service shift b for delivery area g on day d.

$$\sum_{n \in N_g} x_{dhnb} \geq c1_{dhgb}, \quad d \in D, h \in H, g \in G, \quad b \in B \tag{9}$$

$$\sum_{n \in N_g} x_{dhnb} \leq c2_{dhgb}, \quad d \in D\ h \in H, g \in G, \quad b \in B \tag{10}$$

Formulae (11) and (12) express the above-mentioned constraint condition (e) and indicate the restrictions on the minimum and maximum numbers of work attendances of each truck driver $c5_{hnb}$ and $c6_{hnb}$, respectively, in shift b during the target period.

$$\sum_{d \in D} x_{dhnb} \geq c5_{hnb}, \quad h \in H, n \in N, b \in B \tag{11}$$

$$\sum_{d \in D} x_{dhnb} \leq c6_{hnb}, \quad h \in H, n \in N, b \in B \tag{12}$$

Formulae (13) and (14) express the above-mentioned constraint condition (f) and indicate that for each truck driver, the number of Saturdays off a month is more than the minimum number of Saturdays and holidays $c7_n$ and the number of Sundays and public holidays off a month is more than the number of Sundays, holidays, and public holidays $c8_n$. In these formulae, *Hst* represents the set of Saturdays and *Hld* represents the set of Sundays and public holidays during the target period.

$$\sum_{d \in Hst} x_{dhn休} \geq c7_n, \quad n \in N \tag{13}$$

$$\sum_{d \in Hld} x_{dhn休} \geq c8_n, \quad n \in N \tag{14}$$

Formula (15) expresses the above-mentioned constraint condition (g). Using desirable duty L^{+}_{dhnb}, shift s of each driver n on special day d is restricted.

$$L^{+}_{dhnb} - x_{dhns} \leq 0, \quad d \in D, h \in H, n \in N, s \in S \tag{15}$$

Formula (16) expresses a night shift. This formula indicates that a duty in the final time zone on day d continues to a duty in the first time zone on the next day (d + 1); i.e., a continuous duty.

$$x_{dTnb} - x_{(d+1)1nb} \leq 0, \quad d \in D,\ n \in N,\ b \in B \tag{16}$$

The variable x_{dhnb} is 1 or 0 when the duty assigned to each staff member n in each time zone h on each day d is b or is not b, respectively. This variable is defined with Formula (17).

$$x_{dhns} \in \{0, 1\}, \quad d \in D, h \in H, n \in N, s \in S \tag{17}$$

The variable y_{dn} is 1 or 0 when each staff member n goes to work or does not go, respectively. This variable is an integer variable between two values and defined with Formula (18).

$$y_{dn} \in \{0, 1\}, \quad d \in D, \; n \in N \tag{18}$$

where all of $c1$–$c8$ are constants as follows:

c1: The minimum number of staff members in each day, each time zone, each group, and each workplace
c2: The maximum number of staff members in each day, each time zone, each group, and each workplace
c3: The maximum number of consecutive duties
c4: The maximum interval between duties
c5: The minimum number of duties of each staff member in each time zone and each workplace during the target period
c6: The maximum number of duties of each staff member in each time zone and each workplace during the target period
c7: The minimum number of Saturdays off for each staff member
c8: The minimum number of Sundays and public holidays off for each staff member

6 Measures to Cope with the Insufficient Number of Truck Drivers

6.1 *Introduction of Junction Transportation*

As discussed in the previous section, a crew assignment schedule must be rapidly, efficiently, and appropriately created. Examining the reconstruction of the framework of a vehicle operation plan is one way to cope with an insufficient number of truck drivers. A declining birthrate and the aging of truck drivers are at the root of the problem, but in addition, young people have a strong tendency to avoid being truck drivers because they are so often forced to work for long periods of time. Therefore, avoiding long-distance transportation as much as possible, which places a physical burden on truck drivers, and improving transportation efficiency are important tasks to expand the profit of transportation business operators and to cope with the insufficient number of truck drivers.

By dividing a long distance of transportation (one that requires a truck driver to work for more than two consecutive days) into several short distances, the industry can make it possible for elderly persons, women, and young people to work as truck drivers without imposing a heavy burden on them. In junction transportation, truck drivers can go and come back on the same day. A driver takes a route from a place of shipment to a trans-shipment depot, where trailers are changed or cargos are loaded or unloaded. Essentially, a long-distance transportation route previously carried out by one driver is carried out by several truck drivers. In addition, homeward cargos can be secured. Thus, junction transportation is a means to improve transportation efficiency. For this reference, Another type of the introduction of junction transportation is shown in Suzuki et al. [2].

6.2 *Verification of the Effect of Introducing Junction Transportation*

6.2.1 Outline

Truck transportation company A employs 25 truck drivers, possesses 25 trucks, and performs round-trip transportation of 850 km between Tokyo and Hiroshima (using expressways) once a day. Five truck drivers leave Tokyo every day to carry cargos to Hiroshima and return to Tokyo on the next day after loading homeward cargos. Due to the Labor Standards Act and the "standards for the improvement in working hours, etc., of vehicle drivers" notified by the Minister of Labor, a truck driver is allowed to work for more than 15 h a day twice a week. Therefore, during three days after coming back from Hiroshima, the five truck drivers deliver cargos within a 400 km range, in which they can go and come back on the same day. To reduce the burden on truck drivers due to long-distance transportation, this company has examined the introduction of junction transportation in cooperation with transportation companies B and C located in Nagoya and Osaka, respectively. With junction transportation, the distance between Tokyo and Hiroshima (850 km) is divided into the distances between Tokyo and Nagoya (340 km), between Nagoya and Osaka (180 km), and between Osaka and Hiroshima (330 km).

6.2.2 Results

Table 2 shows the results of a numerical experiment. The results consist of the number of short- and middle-distance delivery destinations (within a 400 km range), the number of long-distance delivery destinations (exceeding 400 km: 850 km between Tokyo and Osaka in this experiment), the number of truck drivers, on-duty hours, and working hours on a weekly basis. The number of delivery destinations per vehicle was set to 15–20 as the variation range of the corresponding data, random numbers were generated 300 times within the range of ±20% using the Monte Carlo method, and the actual number of delivery destinations at present was compared with the number of delivery destinations after junction transportation

Table 2 Results

Experiment	Short/ middle	Short/ middle	Long distance	Long distance	Constraint hours	Labor hours
	Number of deliveries	Number of deliveries	Number of deliveries	Number of deliveries	Average	Average
Present	460	15	25	25	57	44
Relay	850	25	25	0	52	42

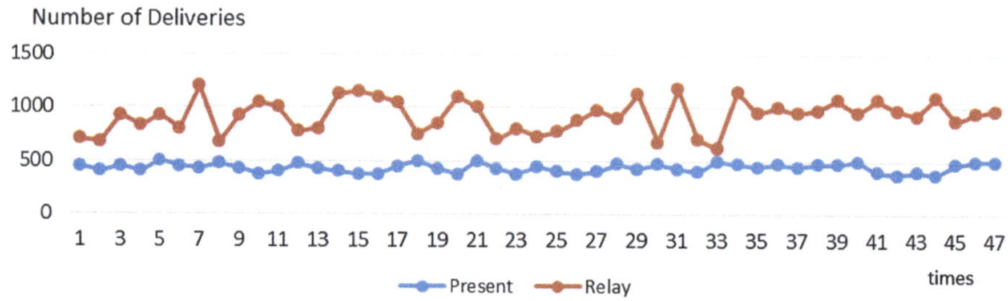

Fig. 2 Comparative simulation on the number of deliveries

using a simulation, as shown in Fig. 2. As a result, the average rate of reduction caused by the introduction of junction transportation was 55%.

6.2.3 Discussion

By introducing junction transportation, the number of short- and middle-distance delivery destinations could be increased by 45.88%, from 460 (at present) to 850, without reducing 25 long-distance delivery destinations. On-duty hours could be reduced by 9.12%, from 57 h (at present) to 52 h. In the case of five working days a week, each truck driver could reduce one on-duty hour a day.

Working hours also could be reduced by 4.55%, from 44 to 42 h. In the case of five working days a week, each truck driver could reduce by 24 min a day. The 24 min almost correspond to one loading and unloading time of a truck driver in actual practice. Therefore, junction transportation can considerably and effectively help operation managers cope with the insufficient number of truck drivers and reduce long working hours.

The simulation verified the effect of introducing junction transportation in a case with 25 vehicles and one operation manager. The effect could be larger in cases with more vehicles, drivers, and operation managers. In the future, we will simulate the introduction of junction transportation under the condition of operating and managing more than 30 vehicles. To this end, we will administer another interview survey to obtain additional data.

7 Conclusion

This study described operation management of truck transportation; elucidated the situation of and problems with the creation of a crew assignment schedule, which is the duty of an operation manager; reviewed the constraint conditions from the perspective of the scheduling problem in order to rapidly, efficiently, and appropriately create a crew assignment schedule; and proposed the reconstruction of algorithms. To cope with the insufficient number of truck drivers and to improve the environment of long working hours, this study simulated the introduction of junction transportation using actual data and verified the effect of its introduction. As a result, with junction transportation, the number of delivery destinations could be largely increased, and on-duty hours and working hours of a truck driver could be reduced.

Therefore, the results obtained in this study are useful for the trucking industry, which requires urgent measures to solve chronic and serious problems with cargo operation management.

How to cope with the insufficient number of truck drivers and how to promote safe and secure transportation management have been barely studied from the perspective of efficient and sophisticated operation management. Therefore, this study is considered to be quire meaningful.

In the future, we will examine an application for creating a crew assignment schedule and verify the validity of the application using a wide range of data. Regarding the introduction of junction transportation, we will administer interview and questionnaire surveys on actual operation management sites in detail, verify the effect of the introduction, and improve the simulation model.

References

1. Suzuki, K. (2016). Unko Kanarisha (Kamotsu) Hikkei Pocket Book, Required Pocket Book for Run Operation Managers, Nikkan Kogyo Shinbumsha, Tokyo (pp. 32–53).
2. Suzuki, K., Kawai, Y., & Wakabayashi, K. (2016). Design and analysis of the location of an online resale business distribution centre in Japan. *Production & Manufacturing Research, 4* (1), 152–174. https://doi.org/10.1080/21693277.2016.1234951.
3. Cargo Transport Business Transportation Safty Regulation, (2015). Article 18, Japan.

Combined Forecasting Method Based on Water Resources Risk Management

Hai Shen, Kin Keung Lai and Qin Liu

Abstract In water resources risk management, since water dispatching decision at the later stage lacks sufficient support, because of low accuracy, in forecasting, a combined forecasting method is put forward. The combined forecasting method constructs an angle cosine model through measurement vector, prediction vector and weight vector; upon determining variant quotient, water resources are rated "sufficient" or "insufficient" taking into account historical water resources and collected statistics, and calibration and initialization of parameters are determined by fitting goodness and dynamic approximation, switching the forecast from a solo to dual model, meanwhile comparing implications of prediction accuracies which assure the forecast supports the coordination. As the experiment demonstrates, this methodology can effectively control risks and shortcomings of a solo model of water resources risk management. Through merging various forecasting models, forecasting accuracy is improved by 20%, lowering the risk of water dispatching decisions while providing referable statistics applied in the water resources risk management.

Keywords The water resources risk management · Vector angular cosine
The dynamic variable weight · Combined forecasting

H. Shen (✉) · Q. Liu
Business School, Xi'an International Studies University, Xian, China
e-mail: xisushenhai@163.com

Q. Liu
e-mail: liuqin642@163.com

H. Shen · K. K. Lai
International Business School, Shaanxi Normal University, Xian, China
e-mail: mskklai@outlook.com

K. K. Lai
Department of Management Sciences, City University of Hong Kong,
Kowloon, Hong Kong

X. Liu (ed.), *Environmental Sustainability in Asian Logistics and Supply Chains*,
https://doi.org/10.1007/978-981-13-0451-4_13

1 Introduction

Climate change has resulted in significant threats to human beings' survival and the ecological environment. Frequent droughts and floods have made many countries emphasize the importance of tackling global climate change in their respective national development plans, including enhanced ecological protection and anti-crisis schemes, environment protection and the preservation and management of resources [1]. In this case, particularly at unfriendly climate conditions, the construction of engineering and non-engineering anti-crisis and water resources efficiency projects need to achieve harmonious development among society, economy, resource and environment has become a vital realistic issue.

Water demand forecasting is the foundation of leashing coordination, and a scientific coordination can avoid crisis to a large extent, playing a critical role in anti-flood, agricultural production safety, the full use of water resources and the utilization of water facilities [2]. The forecasting can significantly improve the accuracy of flood caution forecasts for dams, and a scientific coordination can avoid the crisis happening to a large extent, playing a critical role in the crisis management for water dams.

Currently, there are 3 models for forecasting domestic and international water demand: physical model, black box model and conceptual model. The physical model is based on continued formula and momentum equation, attaining the trend of change from time and space dimensions [3]. Typical models include SHE, NWSH and SRFCN [4]. Black box model focuses on the exchange between water system and outer world, but without considering internal properties and structure of water systems, typical models include artificial neutral network model and statistics model. Conceptual model contains few variants and bears physical implications to some extent, but can only deploy conceptual parameters in some regards [5]. Different forecasting models have diverse characteristics, and most have regional applicability, subject to weather, climate, rain, underlayer water flow and runoff concentration (especially in semi-dry, semi-humid, runoff yield under saturated storage & runoff yield under excess infiltration, the use of single model possesses limitations) [6]. A single forecasting model magnifies certain aspects and neglects other perspectives, and hence cannot provide precise forecasting requirements. Aimed at solving this issue, domestic and international scholars have put forward a combined forecasting method, mixing at least two models plus analytics, thus optimizing through a quantitative approach to increase the precision. Shamseldin [7] has used 5 water forecasting models in 11 river-runs for forecasting purposes, adopting 3 approaches (simple average, weighted average and neural network) by compositing data and generating a forecast, which is better than every other model. Xiong [8], based on previous findings, processes the data through fuzzy hybrid of Takagi-Sugeno's fuzzy system and achieves a better outcome. From the above literature review, it can be found that the current trend of water forecasting is a combined approach by selecting multiple models fit with watershed characteristics and embedding each outcome, stimulated from multi-perspective realizing the applicability and preciseness [9]. Based on this, this paper uses vector angular cosine of the combined forecasting theory, building the model by mixing measured variants, forecasted variants and weighted variants. To determine the changeable variants, water information is categorized into "abundance" and "scarcity" based on historical water data. Parameters are evaluated by goodness-of-fit and dynamic approximation, and in this way a single forecasting is transformed into a combined approach. Moreover, preciseness is guaranteed by taking into account the historical data.

2 Water Combined Forecasting

2.1 Vector Angular Cosine Model

Suppose a Q set contains m single water forecasting models, and the time gap between forecasts is τ. Within the timespan of $n\tau$, certain fraction after η measured $\{x_t, t = \tau, 2\tau, \ldots, n\tau\}$; the i single forecasting model date is $\{y_{it}, t = \tau, 2\tau, \ldots, n\tau\}$, and $i = 1, 2, .., m$, the weighed value for m forecasting is $\{w_i, i = 1, 2, \ldots, m\}$, which meets $\sum_{i=1}^{m} w_i = 1$, $w_i \geq 0$, $i = 1, 2, .., m$. According to combined forecasting theory, the combined forecasting outcome based on m single forecasting model is $\{\tilde{x}_t, t = \tau, 2\tau, \ldots, n\tau\}$, in which $\tilde{x}_t = \sum_{i=1}^{m} y_{it} w_i$, and $m = |Q|$ is seen as length. Described in vector, above information can be translated into a measured vector $X = [x_{1\tau}, x_{2\tau}, \ldots, x_{n\tau}]^T$, the I single forecasting $Y_i = [y_{i\tau}, y_{i2\tau}, \ldots, y_{in\tau}]^T$, the weighted vector $W = [w_1, w_2, \ldots, w_m]^T$, the combined forecasting vector $\tilde{X} = [\tilde{x}_\tau, \tilde{x}_{2\tau}, \ldots, \tilde{x}_{n\tau}]^T$, in which n is the length of vector. Per the definition of vector angular cosine, $\psi = AB/(|A| \times |B|)$, the vector angular cosine for single and combined forecasting data are as followed:

$$\psi_i = XY_i/(|X| \times |Y_i|) = \frac{\sum_{i=1}^{n} x_t y_{it}}{\sqrt{\sum_{t=1}^{n} x_t^2} \sqrt{\sum_{t=1}^{n} y_{it}^2}},$$

$$\psi = X\tilde{X}/(|X| \times |\tilde{X}|) \frac{\sum_{i=1}^{n} x_t \tilde{x}_{it}}{\sqrt{\sum_{t=1}^{n} x_t^2} \sqrt{\sum_{t=1}^{n} \tilde{x}_{it}^2}}.$$

Because X is the measured data, Y_i is the single forecasting outcome, which is the known variant before the forecasting, hence ψ is the function of weight value, noted as $\psi(w_1, w_2, \ldots, w_m)$. Obviously, within the timespan of $n\tau$, combined forecasting value $\tilde{X}$ approaches the measured vector X, so the vector angular cosine is smaller for $\tilde{X}$ and X, $\psi(w_1, w_2, \ldots, w_m)$ approaches the maximum "1" for angular cosine. Therefore, the combined forecasting can be transformed into $n\tau$ maximization.

$$\max\psi(w_1, w_2, \ldots, w_m)\ s.t. \sum_{i=0}^{m} w_i = 1, w_i \geq 0$$

Literature review [10] proves Y_1,Y_2,…,Y_m are linearly independent and when W is smaller than m−1, the best combined forecasting within $n\tau$ is $\max\psi(w_1, w_2, \ldots, w_m) > \max(\psi_i)$, $i = 1, 2, .., m$. This demonstrates:

(a) Y_1, Y_2,…, Y_m, linear independent; (b) W is smaller than m−1.

These 2 factors guarantee the combined forecasting $\tilde{X}$ is closer to measured X than any single forecasting Y_i, and within the timespan $n\tau$, the combined forecasting is better than single forecasting in terms of preciseness.

2.2 Calculation of Changeable Weight Value

To enable the combined forecasting system S to meet requirement (a), a filtering targeting the single models in Q set before forecasting is necessary. The forecasting by diverse models and manually breaks the connectivity, including the site choosing model of Xin An river, neural network, model, fuzzy decision-making model as single forecasting model, because the mechanism difference is big, hence the generated forecasting Y_i bears no connection. However, because of the general connectivity, the linear independence cannot be guaranteed by the model selection. Hence, when correlation exists, further amendments are needed: suppose $R \subset Q$ is the forecasting set after the correlation is confirmed, then delete one set from R altogether with its forecasting outcome, and then judge the correlation with R. Repeat the deletion process until S rests with one single model, when W is smaller than m−1, meaning the forecasting model equals to a single forecasting.

Since the water data recording begins late in China and the incompleteness of historical data, some fractions have sufficient data while some fractions have to suffer a flood. In this case, weighted values shall be different, and goodness-of-fit and dynamic approximation are needed to determine the abundance and scarcity.

(1) Goodness-of-fit: define the I single forecasting model's difference at different times is $\{z_{it}, t = \tau, 2\tau, \ldots, n\tau\}$, $z_{it} = |y_{it} - x_t|$, the maximum and minimum for z_{it} is $z_{\max}$ and $z_{\min}$. Standardized value is $z'_{it} = \sum_{j=1, j\neq i}^{m} \sum_{t=\tau}^{n\tau} z_{jt} / \sum_{j=1}^{m} \sum_{t=1}^{n} z_{jt}$. When $z_{\max} - z_{\min} \neq 0$, the defined weight is $w_i = 1 - \sum_{t=\tau}^{n\tau} z'_{it} / \sum_{i=1}^{m} \sum_{t=\tau}^{n\tau} z'_{it}$. Otherwise, each single forecasting is all correct (low possibility event), when equal weight method can be deployed making $w_i = 1/m$. Using goodness-of-fit, the weight value can be coordinated according to big or small differences, hence the forecasting outcome can have goodness-of-fit.

(2) Dynamic approximation: for easy data processing, set the length of vector n as equal to the w_i's distributed weight value w'_i with expansion $w'_i \in R$. Per literature review [11], polynomial n $w'_i(t) = f_{i1} + f_{i2}t + f_{i3}t^2 + \ldots + f_{in}t^{n-1}$ approaches, and $\tilde{x}_t$ is described as $\tilde{x}_t = \sum_{i=1}^{n} y_{it} w'_i(t) = \hat{Y}_t^T F T_t$, in which

$\hat{Y}_t = [y_{1t}, y_{2t}, \ldots, y_{nt}]^T$, $F = \{f_{in}\}$, $T_t = [1, t^1, t^2, \ldots, t^{n-1}]^T$. Applied to n continued time spots are $\tilde{x}_1 = \hat{Y}_1^T FT_1$, $\tilde{x}_2 = \hat{Y}_2^T FT_2$,..., $\tilde{x}_n = \hat{Y}_n^T FT_n$, meaning a matrix is formed $\Omega = \hat{Y}^T FT$, in which $\hat{Y} = [\hat{Y}_1, \hat{Y}_2, \ldots, \hat{Y}_n]^T$, $T = [T_1, T_2, \ldots, T_n]$, Ω equals to the n $\times$ n matrix with $\tilde{x}_t$ as its diagonal. To make the forecasting approaches the measured value, within a short timespan utilizing the sequence of forecasting, which can be applied for forthcoming forecasting, hence in the timing of F $\tilde{x}_t = x_t$, take $F = (\hat{Y}^T)^+ \Omega T^+$, in which T^+ means Matrix T generalized Moore Penrose. However, unify the F can attain $w_i'(t)$ as:

$w_i = (w' - \min(w'))/\sum_{t=1}^{n}(w_i' - \min(w'))_i$, if $\sum_{t=1}^{n}(w_i' - \min(w'))_i$ equals to zero, then put it as 1/m.

What is noticeable is, in actual application process, goodness-of-fit and dynamic approximation both cannot fully meet (b), indicating it happens when W is smaller than m−1, when combined forecasting degrades to simple forecasting, and after a time gap τ, before the next forecasting happens, weight value for W automatically updates, and system S falls to combined forecasting again.

2.3 Setting Parameters

Suppose the combined forecasting system initially runs at t_0, with only S historical data and measured data at t_0, but the measured vector X is not attained when $\eta = t_0$, so does the single forecasting Y_i. If combined forecasting needs to be done at $t = t_0 + \tau$, W is not available so historical data can be analyzed: (1) if the fractional historical data is sufficient, set p = 1 (meaning goodness-of-fit is used), set a time of flood between [λ_S, λ_E] with respective observations recorded at $X(\lambda_S, \lambda_E)$; if the data is not abundant, set p = 0 (meaning dynamic approximation is used), set n time spots smaller than t_0 as historical measured vector $X(\lambda_S, \lambda_E)$. (2) Set single model Q with a length of $m = |Q|$, forecast with τ gap during [λ_S,λ_E], historical measured data is $Y_i(\lambda_S, \lambda_E)$, and then judge the correlation $Y_i(\lambda_S, \lambda_E)$, and list the correlated data into R. With the ongoing deletion, set m = m−1. (3) when p = 1, use $z_{it} = |y_{it} - x_t|$ to calculate each single forecasting $Y_i(\lambda_S, \lambda_E)$ difference and judge if $z_{\max} - z_{\min} \neq 0$. If so, based on the computed weight value from $w_i = 1 - \sum_{t=1}^{n} z_{it}'/\sum_{i=1}^{m}\sum_{t=1}^{n} z_{it}'$, otherwise, set $w_i = 1/m$; when p = 0, forecast the n historical $X(\lambda_S, \lambda_E)$ and get $Y_i(\lambda_S, \lambda_E)$, then set $\tilde{X} = X$, with $F = (\hat{Y}^T)^+ \Omega T^+$ calculate the water forecasting weight $F = \{f_{ik}\}$, and use $w_i = (w' - \min(w'))/\sum_{t=1}^{n}(w_i' - \min(w'))_i$. The weights in both circumstances are set as W_{t_0}, which is the initial weight value after parameter setting, and it implies the historical data of fractions and available model information in S system.

To get the weighted vector to forecast $t = t_0 + 2\tau$, the middle point λ_S and its correlated data can be deleted from $X(\lambda_S, \lambda_E)$, and $t = t_0 + \tau$ is seen as historical data and compressed into historical measured vector $X(\lambda_S, \lambda_E)$ and redefined as a weight value, thus attaining the weighted vector at $t = t_0 + 2\tau$. With this cycle, historical data are gradually updated by newly available measured data to make system S approach to be optimized dynamically.

3 Experimental Analysis

3.1 Experiment

To prove the validity of this paper, we have made one forecasting about multiple fractions in Wei River. This river-run falls to the dry and semi-dry area, in a continental climate, with an average annual temperature of 6–13 °C, amount of precipitation 500–800 mm, annual evaporation at 1000–2000 mm, annual river flows at 0.32 km^3/s, and the biggest measured flood peak volume is 7.66 km^3/s. The combined forecasting adopts a length m = 3, and the set Q = {XAJ, BP, VD}, symbolizing Xin An river model, BP neural network model and fuzzy decision model, the flow unit is km^3/s, time unit is h. With the acceptable difference at 20%, the certainty coefficient of XAJ, BP and VD model of fractions excel [exceed?] 0.48, and taking into account influences of low-precise climate, terrain, geographical data and historical data, forecasting models' forecasting accuracy QR is not high; in some cases it is even lower than 50%, a non-qualified classification. To further improve the preciseness, combined forecasting has been adopted with the set n = 5 (otherwise n columns of data needs to be listed for each computation) and the time gap is τ = 2 h.

(1) Fraction A has abundant historical data, and when t_0= 2010-08-20 00:00:00, the 5 consecutive measured vectors constitute X = [2.266, 2.101, 1.978, 2.052, 2.246], and the single forecasting vectors are Y_1= [2.361, 1.696, 1.746, 2.158, 2.081], Y_2= [2.252, 2.154, 2.665, 1.879, 1.977], Y_3= [2.342, 1.769, 1.923, 1.651, 1.858]. Judging the correlation, it can be understood that Y_1, Y_2 and Y_3 are linearly independent, and because p = 1, we choose the flood with a span of $[\lambda_S, \lambda_E]$ = [2009-07-25 08:00:00, 2009-08-25 08:00:00], with a total of 488 measured data, which after computation an initial weighted vector is available at W_{t_0}= [0.558, 0.362, 0.08]. The 4 consecutive weighted vectors at τ time span are: $W_{t_0+\tau}$= [0.557, 0.362, 0.081], $W_{t_0+2\tau}$= [0.557, 0.362, 0.081], $W_{t_0+3\tau}$= [0.558, 0.361, 0.81] and $W_{t_0+4\tau}$= [0.559, 0.362, 0.079]. Using $\tilde{x}_t = \sum_{i=1}^{m} y_{it} w_{i_0}$, the combined forecasting vector is $\tilde{X}$= [2.320, 1.868, 2.093, 2.016, 2.026]. And the angular cosine for XAJ, BP and VD is 0.995, 0.988 and 0.995. The combined forecasting cosine is 0.997, which is better than any one single model. In terms of difference, the biggest and relative difference for n = 5 is 0.233 and 11.1%, which are lower than single model biggest difference at 0.401 and relative one 19.2%.

For fraction C, whose historical data is not enough, suppose n = m = 3, and forecast after t_0 = 2010-07-22 00:00:00, the forecasting at which time is 1.203, 0.795 and 1.951. For n consecutive slots before t_0 is $X(\lambda_S, \lambda_E)$ = [1.245, 1.171, 1.222], single forecasting vector of Q set $Y_i(\lambda_S, \lambda_E)$ are Y_1 = [0.852, 1.287, 1.001], Y_2 = [1.365, 1.188, 1.268], Y_3 = [1.656, 1.087, 1.225], Y_1, Y_2 and Y_3 are linearly independent. Set $\tilde{x}_t = x_t$, compute broad Moore Penrose $(\hat{Y}^T)^+$, T^+ and F:

$$(\hat{Y}^T)^+ = \begin{bmatrix} 0.583 & 3.241 & -3.665 \\ -3.702 & -4.653 & 9.123 \\ 3.355 & 2.168 & -5.642 \end{bmatrix}, T^+ = \begin{bmatrix} 2.667 & -2.000 & 0.333 \\ -2.000 & 2.500 & -0.500 \\ 0.333 & -0.500 & 0.167 \end{bmatrix},$$

$$F = \begin{bmatrix} -7.146 & 10.274 & -2.402 \\ 2.326 & -9.983 & 3.048 \\ 3.764 & 1.439 & -1.026 \end{bmatrix}$$

A weighted vector W'_{t_0} = [4.177, 2.538, −6.895] can be computed from $w'_i(t) = f_{i0} + f_{i1}t + f_{i2}t^2 + \cdots + f_{ik}t^k$, which is consolidated into W_{t_0}= [0.540, 0.460, 0], the forecasting at t_0 claims $\tilde{x}_{t_0}$= 1.015. Compared with measured data, the absolute difference for $\tilde{x}_{t_0}$ is 0.070, which is smaller than 0.258, 0.150 and 1.006; and through historical data and t_0 data, after computation, the angular cosine for XAJ, BP and VD are 0.973, 0.997 and 0.954, lower than combined forecasting cosine 0.998, and it can be seen that the combined forecasting model is more accurate than each of the single model in Q.

3.2 Accuracy Analysis

To analyze the preciseness of combined forecasting, within the span of [2010-8-12 0:00, 2010-10-17 0:00:00], fraction A and C have been analyzed for preciseness, generating a total of 180 forecasting results, 60 of them are combined ones. Figure 1 shows the forecasting outcome, measured outcome and combined forecasting model (HCF: Hydrological Combined Forecasting Model) of fraction A for XAJ, BP and VD when p = 1, QR and DC for these three are 80.0, 68.30, 51.7% and 0.832, 0.694 and 0.526, rated as B, C and unqualified forecasting, after the combination of this paper's methodology, the QR and DC become 92.0% and 0.845, with a rate B, the qualification ratio significantly increases at least for 12%. Figure 2 shows the forecasting outcome, measured outcome and combined forecasting model (HCF: Hydrological Combined Forecasting Model) of fraction A for XAJ, BP and VD when p = 0, because of the limitation of data, the qualification ratio is very low, when 20% equals to 30.0, 35.0, 23.3, 57.0%, and when 30% becomes 40.0, 45.0, 30.0 and 63.0%, the QR is better than overall single model by 1.4 times, namely an increase at 27%. Moreover, to test the effectiveness of

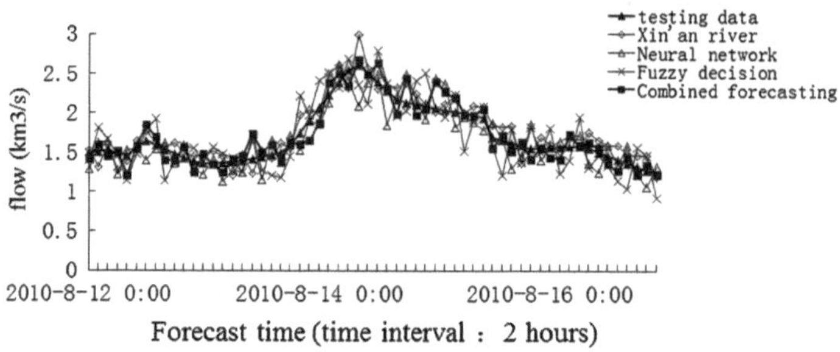

Fig. 1 $p = 1$ model comparison

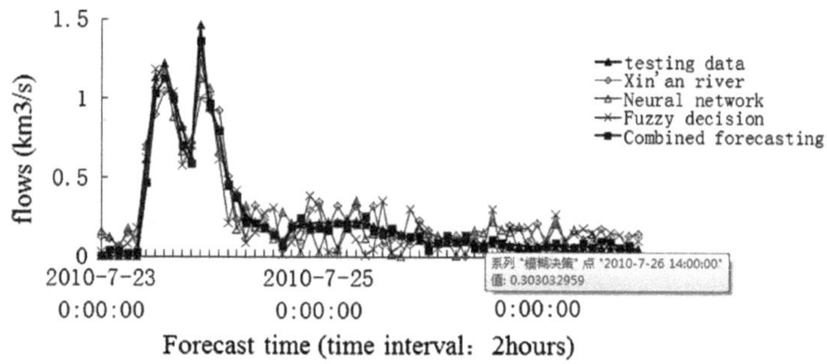

Fig. 2 $p = 0$ model comparison

Table 1 Combined forecasting comparisons of A, B, C and D

Fraction	p	Times	XAJ	BP	VD	HCF
A	1	1028	76.2%/0.741/B	60.6%/0.650/C	51.5%/0.468/N	83.1%/0.863/B
B	1	1104	82.1%/0.837/B	76.9%/0.790/B	71.7%/0.733/B	86.4%/0.908/A
C	0	976	33.8%/0.356/N	36.7%/0.399/N	29.4%/0.333/N	48.2%/0.485/N
D	0	1200	56.6%/0.450/N	58.5%/0.492/N	46.6%/0.429/N	62.7%/0.556/C

Note A, B, C and D do not represent forecasting or non-qualified ones for A, B, C and D (n for non-qualified forecasting)

multiple forecasting, we have done long-term tracking analysis to 4 fractions when n = 8 and m = 9, and in the 4308 combined forecasting, as Chart 1 shows (described as QR/DC/forecasting grade), regardless if $p = 1$ or $p = 0$, the combined forecasting at QR are all better than single ones, the preciseness increases significantly, some even upgrade to a new level (Table 1).

3.3 Parameter Analysis

In combined forecasting, the combined forecasting outcomes and parameters n and m are correlated with historical data. The parameters influence the length of vector, weight and forecasting data.

(1) Parameter n determines the length of vector, and influences the acquisition of weight indirectly. For different lengths, the combined forecasting qualification ratios are listed in Fig. 3. When n is small, the length is short, and every element plays a bigger role in influencing the angular cosine, and easily contribute to the linear connection of each single model, leading to the one or more single outcomes deleted from system S, when the preciseness is low and the system might degrade to single forecasting; when n increases gradually, the information needed to compute angular cosine increases, hence the forecasting benefits is becoming more obvious, QR increases incrementally; when n is too big, the information for angular cosine is over abundant, which is covered by the rich of data, causing QR decrease. Especially when $p = 0$, the size of n not only determines the data selection of initial weight choosing, but also sets the number of models in Q set, and hence is more obvious to the combined forecasting. With the model increases in Q elevates the forecasting preciseness, hence the increased ratio 5% is bigger than 2.44% when $p = 1$; though the big of n decrease the angular cosine validity, whereas introduced more single models into the combined model, which helps relieve the downgrading of the system effectiveness, hence the ratio 1.37% is smaller than 2.59% when $p = 1$.

Fig. 3 n impacts on QR

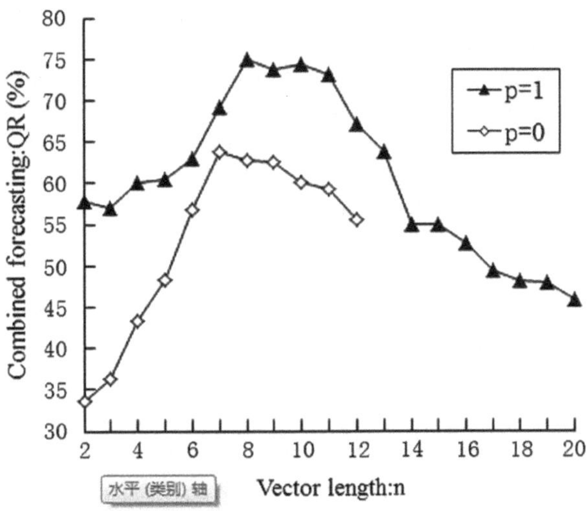

Fig. 4 m impacts on QR

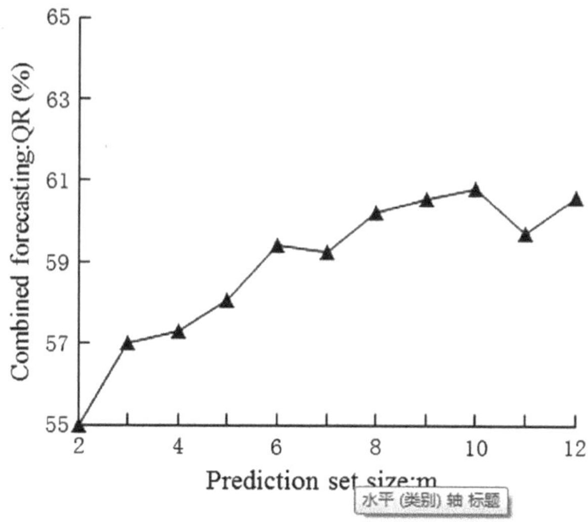

(2) Parameter m determines the length, namely the number of single models. Since the combined forecasting angular cosine must be bigger than the single model angular cosine within a designated time frame, the increase of m helps enhance system accuracy. But since the models become more and more in Q, more connections are introduced, and the generated outcomes from single models are subject to more river run elements. Hence the trend of preciseness improvement is not obvious as listed in Fig. 4, the model change from 2 to 12 only has an increase ratio of 5.53%.

(3) Historical data influence the combined forecasting when $p = 1$, the longer the time is, the more floods, the more typical, the confirmed weight can better symbolize the realistic situations of fractions, and QR is higher. Like Fig. 5, for every new historical data for a 2-month period, the QR average improves by 8.5%. In this case, when storage and computing capacity permits, the system should attain a broad water resources within a timespan, which further improves the combined forecasting level.

4 Conclusion

This paper is based on vector angular cosine and it puts forward two weight-changeable methods for combined forecasting. Parameter settings are conducted, and analysis is done through experiment on preciseness, length of vector, length of combination and historical data, effectively improves the combined forecasting outcomes through multiple single models. Tasks followed include: ① compute the weight value by dynamic approximation, demanding the length of

Fig. 5 Historical date on QR

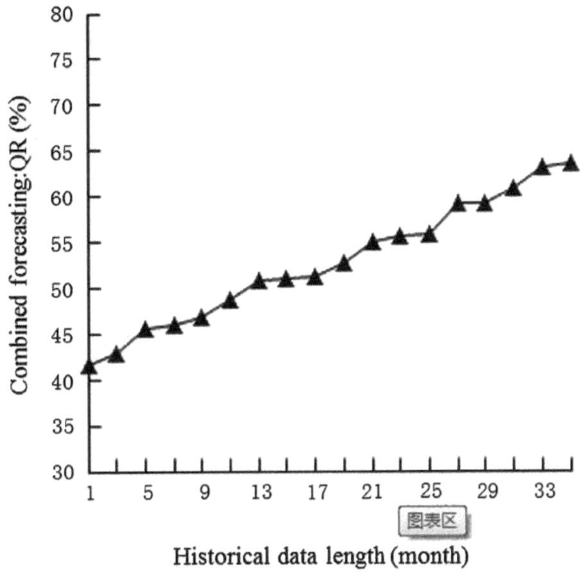

vector and set must be the same. Since the number of models is available in river run terrain, few adjacent data are incorporated into historical data for calculating purpose as a compromise, which lowers the combined forecasting's accuracy improvement, calling for a streamlining of the model; ② by further leveraging Muskingum methodology and the geographical data from RS, to improve the inwards preciseness.

References

1. Zhang, C., Zhou, H. C., Li, W., et al. (2007). Research on applications of data analysis technology to hydrological combined forecasting. *Journal of Dalian University of Technology, 47*(2), 246–251.
2. Zhang, J. Y. (2010). Review and reflection on China's hydrological forecasting techniques. *Advances in Water Sciences, 19*(7), 437–441.
3. Xie, X. M., Jiang, Y. Z., Shi, Y. B., et al. (1999). Real-time forecasting of stream flow base on artificial neural networks. *Water Resource and Hydropower Engineering, 30*(9), 1–4.
4. Xia, J. (1993). A grey correlative analysis and patter recognition applied to mid-long term runoff forecasting. *Advances in Water Sciences, 4*(3), 190–197.
5. Li, J. X., Shen, B., Xie, J. C. et al. (2010). Hydrological forecasting preferred and combination based-on multi-attribute group decision. Systems *Engineering—Theory & Practice, 30*(12), 2315–2320.
6. Wang, F. Q., & Huo, F. L. (2010). Research on method of middle and long term hydrology forecasts. *Yellow River, 32*(3), 25–27.
7. Shamseldin, A. Y., O'Connor, K. M., Liang, G. C., et al. (1997). Methods for combining the outputs of different rainfall-runoff models. *Journal of Hydrology, 19*(7), 203–229.

8. Xiong, L. H., Shamseldin, A. Y., & O'Connor, K. M. (2001). A non-linear combination of the forecasts of rainfall-runoff models by the first-order Takagi-Sugeno fuzzy system. *Journal of Hydrology, 245,* 196–217.
9. Cheng, Y. C., Wang, J., & Fan, S. X. (2009). Real-time flood forecasting method of combination forecast model. *Yellow River, 10*(31), 88–89.
10. Chen, H. Y., Sheng, Z. H., & Liu, C. L. (2006). Research on properties of combination forecasting model based on vectorial angle cosine. *Management Science & Engineering, 9*(2), 1–8.
11. Xie, K. G., & Zhou, J. Q. (2000). Research the weight changeable combination forecast model. *Systems Engineering—Theory & Practice, 20*(7), 36–40.

A Multi-objective Model for Integrated Planning of Selective Harvesting and Post-harvest Operations

Thanaphorn Sornprom, Voratas Kachitvichyanukul and Huynh Trung Luong

Abstract The paper presents an integrated planning model for selective harvesting and post-harvest processing operations with multiple objectives. A mixed integer programming model is developed to consider key operations which include harvesting, hauler assignment, processor assignment, and vehicle assignment. The first objective is to maximize profit and the second objective is to minimize the cost of lost sales. A small data set representing the operations of a company was used as the test case for model validation. The model is solved via CPLEX Optimization studio and the result of the experiment shows that the model can generate set of trade-off solutions that coordinate several related decisions in the operations, including allocation of harvesters, haulers, processors in production plant and vehicles.

Keywords Agriculture logistic optimization · Mixed integer programming
Integrated agriculture supply chain management · Multi-objective optimization

1 Introduction

Severe competition in current market and the heightened expectations of consumers have forced business enterprises to concentrate on the relationships with their customers and suppliers. The need for increasing efficiency in enterprise operations leads to the concept of collaboration among business partners to improve services for clients. Supply Chain Management (SCM) has been applied in western countries since the 1990s in the manufacturing and retailing industry [1]. Since then the interest of SCM has also been growing in agro-industry. Agro food networks play a principal role to innovate, and reduce costs while being more responsive to customers' needs [1].

T. Sornprom · V. Kachitvichyanukul (✉) · H. T. Luong
Industrial and Manufacturing Engineering, School of Engineering
and Technology, Asian Institute of Technology, Pathumthani, Thailand
e-mail: voratas@ait.asia

X. Liu (ed.), *Environmental Sustainability in Asian Logistics and Supply Chains*,
https://doi.org/10.1007/978-981-13-0451-4_14

Agriculture enterprises are the significant sources of food and revenue for many developed and developing countries. These businesses must manage various related operations such as cultivation, harvest, hauling, production, delivery, and distribution. Agricultural production starts from the planting of crops follow by harvesting of mature crops. The harvests are hauled to processing facility to be processed into products. Finally, finished products are distributed. These operations are sequentially connected. If improper decision occurs in one activity, it may affect subsequent operations, leading to such problems as dwarf crops, low product quality, delay production, insufficient workforces, machine failure, delivery postponement, or missed deadlines [2, 3]. As a result, these problems can cause poor reliability and damage reputation of the company and eventually lost customers.

Traditionally, agro-industrial operations are planned separately [3]. This practice tends to unwanted fluctuations in the production levels and inventories of finished products, intermediate goods and raw materials [4]. These challenges can be minimized or eliminated with the aid of an integrated approach to process planning [5]. In addition, a study [6] suggested that integrated planning and scheduling can enhance the performance of both functions and make the system more responsive to dynamic internal and external disturbances. Furthermore, [2] also assured that integrated planning is an important strategy for improving performance while reducing safety risks, maximizing uptimes, and making better use of resources.

According to the mentioned studies, this research addresses multi-objective problem of integrated selective harvesting and post-harvest operations in order to seek the most appropriate decisions and objective values for this particular problem. The remainder of this article is organized as follows. Section 2 provides the literature review on integrated planning. In Sect. 3, we present a mathematical model including decision variables, model parameters, constraints, and objective functions. Section 4 performs the results of model validation. In Sect. 5, some conclusions, and ideas for future studies are presented.

2 Literature Review

Integrated planning and scheduling has been adopted to improve the quality of decision making in complex operations. There are many research works related to the agricultural operations planning problems. The research study of [7] reviewed crop planning related to harvest and processing operations. The authors found three important issues. First of all, most researchers focused on either harvesting or processing planning without integration [8]. Secondly, real-life agricultural characteristics such as weather condition, uncertainties, yield perishability, and customers' demand were not often considered in existing works. Thirdly, most problems have been formulated into linear programming, mixed-integer programming, and stochastic programming for hypothetical and real cases.

Integrated approach has been applied to planning and scheduling in various industries such as machine tool production [9], job-shop [10], oil industry [11],

Table 1 Applications of integrated planning and scheduling

Name of researches	Application	No. of objectives	Objective functions
Bilgen and Celebi [13]	Dairy industry	1	Maximize benefits including pricing component, processing, set up, storage, overtime, backlogging, and transportation costs
Chu et al. [14]	Finished products	1	Minimize total holding cost, and set up cost
Fumero et al. [12]	Multi-product batch plant design	1	Maximize the net present value (NPV) of the profit
Joly et al. [11]	Oil industry	1	Minimize operating cost including raw material, inventory, and pumping costs
Liu et al. [9]	Machine tool production	2	Minimize bottleneck machines' make span and total products' tardiness
Sel et al. [15]	Perishable daily production/ yoghurt	1	Minimize total cost of loss product value including deterioration, production, inventory, changeover, waster, overtime, package, incubation operations, unmet demand, and transportation costs
Zhang and Wong [6]	Components/ parts in manufacturing	1	Minimize make span
Zhang and Yan [10]	Job-shop	2	Minimize holding cost and Maximize the earliness time

multi-product [12], dairy industries [13], and others. Most of these industries considered only single objective function. A few prior researchers which studied actual large cases applied heuristic algorithms to overcome complex combinatorial optimization problems [6, 9]. They found that heuristic algorithms could find feasible solutions that are very close to the optimal solution. The research studies are summarized in Table 1.

Based on this literature review, this research study is focusing on the development of a decision model for the creation of a plan to integrate the decisions on the allocation of various resources for the harvesting and post-harvesting operations. A mathematical model for selective harvesting will be formulated to include the decisions for harvesting, harvester assignment, hauler assignment, processor assignment. The decisions will be made in a coordinated manner to maximize profit and to minimize lost sales via Optimization programming called CPLEX.

3 Mathematical Model

Mathematical modeling approaches have been applied to help managers in making decisions to handle and prevent the conflicts that may occur in a system. The detailed assumptions, decision variables and mathematical formulations that are used in this study are described in the subsequent sections.

3.1 Assumptions of Mathematical Model Formulations

The following assumptions are required in the formulation of the mathematical model.

1. Each harvesting equipment can be used in every field.
2. Different types of harvesting equipment are allowed, and the harvesting rate may vary with equipment type.
3. Only a single crop is considered.
4. All crops that are hauled from fields to the processing plant can be used as materials in producing various products.
5. Each processor can produce more than one product.
6. Only one distribution center is considered.
7. There is no initial inventory of products in the distribution center.
8. The box of each product has the same size.
9. Different products can be delivered together.
10. Forecasted demand is used in the planning process.

3.2 Mathematical Model Formulations

There are three main stages in this study: field source, processing plant, and distribution center. Harvest, hauling, production, delivery, and distribution are five main activities of this interested supply chain. Thus, important operation decisions are related to these five main activities and the quantities of interest include:

1. Quantity of crops harvested from field.
2. Quantity of crops hauled.
3. Quantity of products finished in processing plant.
4. Quantity of products delivered from processing plant to distribution center.
5. Quantity of products sold to customers.

The mathematical formulation is given in this section. The definitions of key indices, decision variables, and model parameters are given. The objective functions are then defined along with the required constraints for relevant decisions.

Indices:

d	Day	$d \in \{1, 2, 3, \ldots, L_1\}$
f	Field	$f \in \{1, 2, 3, \ldots, L_2\}$
i	Harvesting equipment	$i \in \{1, 2, 3, \ldots, L_3\}$
j	Hauler	$j \in \{1, 2, 3, \ldots, L_4\}$
k	Processor	$k \in \{1, 2, 3, \ldots, L_5\}$
p	Product	$p \in \{1, 2, 3, \ldots, L_6\}$
r	Vehicle	$r \in \{1, 2, 3, \ldots, L_7\}$

Decision Variables for Harvest:

Q_{fd} Quantity of crop harvested from field f on day d (box)
E_{fd} Actual available quantity of crops in harvesting field f at the beginning of day d (box).

Decision Variables for Hauling:

N_{fjd} Quantity of crops hauled from field f with hauler j on day d (box)
I_{fjd} Total number of trips for hauler j to deliver material from field f on day d (trip)
A_{fd} Remaining quantity of harvested crops from field f that are not hauled on day d (box).

Decision Variables for Production:

B_{pkd} Quantity of finished product p produced from processor k on day d (box)
G_d Remaining quantity of crops that are not processed into products on day d (box).

Decision Variables for Delivery:

W_{prd} Quantity of product p delivered by vehicle r on day d (box)
K_{rd} Total number of trips for vehicle r on day d (trip)
C_{pd} Remaining quantity of product p that are not delivered on day d (box).

Decision Variables for Distribution:

U_{pd} Quantity of product p sold to customers on day d (box)
F_{pd} Remaining quantity of product p that are not sold on day d (box)
J_{pd} Shortage quantity of product p on day d (box).

Model Parameters:

D_{pd} Forecasted demand of product p on day d (box)
S_{fd} Forecasted available crops from field f on day d (box)
χ_p Quantity of crops to produce one box of product p (box)
H_i Harvesting rate of harvesting equipment i (box per hour)
θ_i Total available hours of harvesting equipment i per day (hour)
V_k Total available time of processor k (hour)
T_{pk} Time to produce a box of product p on processor k (hour)
g_j Capacity per trip of hauler j (box)
α_k Efficiency of processor k (percent)
β_r Capacity of vehicle r (box)
Z_1 Total lost sales cost
Z_2 Profit.

Cost Parameters:

ρ_p Selling cost of product p (unit cost per box)
η_j Hauling cost per trip for hauler j (unit cost per trip)
π_r Transportation cost of vehicle r (unit cost per kilometer)
λ Harvesting cost (unit cost per box)
φ_{pk} Cost of producing product p on processor k (unit cost per box)
γ_p Holding cost of product p (unit cost per box per day)
σ_p Lost sales cost of product p (unit cost per box per day).

Constraints

The constraints are organized according to relationship among parameters and decisions.

A. Harvest Constraints

Actual available crop quantity on the first day is equal to the forecasted available of crops on the first day.

$$E_{f1} = S_{f1} \quad \forall f \tag{1}$$

Actual available crop quantity for day d is equal to the actual available crop quantity of previous day subtract the quantity of harvested crops on the previous day plus the forecasted available crops for day d.

$$E_{fd} = E_{f,d-1} - Q_{f,d-1} + S_{fd} \quad \forall fd = 2, 3, \ldots \tag{2}$$

Quantity of harvested crops cannot exceed actual available quantity of crops.

$$Q_{fd} \leq E_{fd} \quad \forall f, d \tag{3}$$

Quantity of harvested crops from every fields cannot exceed the harvesting rate of harvesting equipment times the total available hours of harvesting equipment.

$$\sum_{f} Q_{fd} \leq \sum_{i} H_i * \theta_i \quad \forall d \tag{4}$$

B. Harvest and Hauling Constraints

There is no initial quantity of harvested crops on day 0.

$$A_{f,0} = 0 \quad \forall f \tag{5}$$

Quantity of hauled crops cannot exceed the sum of the remaining quantity of harvested crops from previous day that are not hauled and the quantity of harvested crops on this day.

$$\sum_{j} N_{fjd} \leq A_{f,d-1} + Q_{fd} \quad \forall f, d \tag{6}$$

Remaining quantity of harvested crops that are not hauled are equal to the sum of the remaining quantity of harvested crops on the day before that are not hauled and the quantity of harvested crops on this day subtract the quantity of hauled crops on this day.

$$A_{fd} = A_{f,d-1} + Q_{fd} - \sum_{j} N_{fjd} \quad \forall f, d \tag{7}$$

C. Hauling Constraints

Total number of hauled trips is at least the quantity of hauled crops divided by the hauler capacity.

$$\frac{N_{fjd}}{g_j} \leq I_{fjd} \quad \forall f, j, d \tag{8}$$

D. Hauling and Production Constraints

The remaining quantity of crops that are not processed into products on day 0 is equal to zero.

$$G_0 = 0 \quad (9)$$

Quantity of crops to be processed as finished products cannot exceed the sum of hauled crops on that day and the remaining quantity of crops on the previous day.

$$\sum_p \left(\chi_p * \sum_k B_{pkd} \right) \leq \sum_f \sum_j N_{fjd} + G_{d-1} \quad \forall d \quad (10)$$

Remaining quantity of unprocessed crops are equal to the sum of hauled crops and the remaining quantity that are not processed on previous day subtract the quantity of crops processed on this day.

$$G_d = \sum_f \sum_j N_{fjd} + G_{d-1} - \sum_p \left(\sum_k B_{pkd} * \chi_p \right) \quad \forall d \quad (11)$$

E. Production Constraints

The quantity of finished products produced should not be more than the forecasted demand per day divided by 0.95.

$$\sum_k B_{pkd} \leq \frac{D_{pd}}{0.95} \quad \forall p, d \quad (12)$$

Total quantity of finished products cannot exceed the multiple of processor efficiency, and total available time of processor per day.

$$\sum_p \left(\sum_d B_{pkd} * T_{pk} \right) \leq V_k * \alpha_k \quad \forall k \quad (13)$$

F. Production and Delivery Constraints

There is no remaining quantity of product that are not delivered on day 0.

$$C_{p,0} = 0 \quad \forall p \quad (14)$$

Quantity of delivered products cannot exceed the sum of the remaining quantity of products that are not delivered on the day before and the quantity of finished products on this day.

$$\sum_r W_{prd} \leq C_{p,d-1} + \sum_k B_{pkd} \quad \forall p, d \tag{15}$$

Remaining quantity of products are equal to the summation of the remaining quantity of products that are not delivered and the quantity of finished products on this day subtract the quantity of products delivered on this day.

$$C_{pd} = C_{p,d-1} + \sum_k B_{pkd} - \sum_r W_{prd} \quad \forall p, d \tag{16}$$

G. Delivery Constraints

Total number of trips are at least the quantity of delivered products divided by the vehicle capacity.

$$\sum_p \left(\frac{W_{prd}}{\beta_r} \right) \leq K_{rd} \quad \forall r, d \tag{17}$$

H. Delivery and Distribution Constraints

There is no remaining product in the distribution center on day 0.

$$F_{p,0} = 0 \quad \forall p \tag{18}$$

Quantity sold cannot exceed the forecasted demand.

$$U_{pd} \leq D_{pd} \quad \forall p, d \tag{19}$$

Quantity sold on this day cannot exceed the sum of remaining products that are not sold on the day before and the delivered products on this day.

$$U_{pd} \leq F_{p,d-1} + \sum_r W_{prd} \quad \forall p, d \tag{20}$$

Remaining quantity of products on this day are equal to the sum of the remaining products on the day before and the delivered products on this day subtract the forecasted demand on this day.

$$F_{pd} = F_{p,d-1} + \sum_r W_{prd} - U_{pd} \quad \forall p, d \tag{21}$$

I. Distribution Constraints

The shortage amount is equal to the difference of the forecasted demand and the quantities of product sold if the forecasted demand is greater than the quantities sold.

$$D_{pd} > U_{pd}; \quad J_{pd} = D_{pd} - U_{pd} \quad \forall p, d \tag{22}$$

The shortage amount is equal to zero if the forecasted demand is less than the quantities sold.

$$D_{pd} < U_{pd}; \quad J_{pd} = 0 \quad \forall p, d \tag{23}$$

In the harvesting process, it is assumed that the workers can select and harvest only the crops that meet the quality criteria. The quality constraints are therefore omitted in the mathematical model.

The constraints B, D, F, and H serve to integrate related operation decisions. Part B links between harvest and hauling operations. Part D connects the activities of hauling, and production. The coordination between production and delivery operations is in part F. Part H integrates the delivery and distribution operations.

Objective Functions

Two objective functions are paid attention in this research. The first objective is to minimize total lost sales cost. The second is to maximize profit. In calculating the total cost, only direct operating costs are considered, i.e., harvesting cost, hauling cost, processing cost, holding cost, and transportation cost. The details are given next.

Minimum: Total lost sales cost

$$\textit{Total lost sales cost} = \sum_{p} \left[\sum_{d} J_{pd} \right] * \sigma_p \tag{24}$$

Maximum: Profit

$$\textit{Profit} = \textit{Revenue} - \textit{Total direct cost} \tag{25}$$

$$\textit{Revenue} = \sum_{p} \left[\sum_{d} U_{pd} \right] * \rho_p \tag{26}$$

$$\textit{Hauling cost} = \sum_{j} \left[\sum_{f} \sum_{d} I_{fjd} \right] * \eta_j \tag{27}$$

$$Processing\ cost = \sum_{p}\sum_{k}\left[\sum_{d} B_{pkd}\right] * \varphi_{pk} \tag{28}$$

$$Harvesting\ cost = \sum_{f}\sum_{d} Q_{fd} * \lambda \tag{29}$$

$$Transportation\ cost = \sum_{r}\sum_{d}\left[\frac{\sum_{p} W_{prd}}{\beta_r} * 2\iota * \pi_r\right] \tag{30}$$

where l is the distance from processor to distribution center

$$Holding\ cost = \sum_{p}\left[\sum_{d} F_{pd}\right] * \gamma_p \tag{31}$$

$$\begin{aligned} Total\ direct\ cost = {} & Harvesting\ cost + Hauling\ cost \\ & + Processing\ cost + Holding\ cost \\ & + Transportation\ cost \end{aligned} \tag{32}$$

All the proposed model will be used to be a base structure in generating optimal decisions for harvest, hauling, production, delivery, and distribution, which will be presented in Sect. 4.

4 Model Validation

In order to validate the proposed model, test data was developed with three finished products, three fields, three harvesting equipment, three haulers, three processors, and two vehicles for a seven-day planning horizon. The model was coded and solved by using IBM ILOG CPLEX V.12.6.1 software package. All the experiments are carried out on a computer equipped with CPU Intel Core i7-6500U, up to 3.1 GHz, and 8 GB Memory.

The proposed model was validated to single and multi-objective problem. Due to the CPLEX's limitation in solving multi-objective problem, one objective is converted into a constraint as shown in Eqs. (34), and (36). Minimal value of lost sales cost, and maximal value of profit are used to limit the lost sales cost or profit in the constraints. The delta values is repeatedly adjusted by observing the generated values.

Objective function for maximization problem:

$$Profit = Revenue - Total\,direct\,cost \tag{33}$$

Constraint:

$$Lost\,sales\,cost \leq Min\,Lost\,sales + Delta \tag{34}$$

Objective function for minimization problem:

$$Lost\,sales\,cost = \sum_{p}\left[\sum_{d} J_{pd}\right] * \sigma_p \tag{35}$$

Constraint:

$$Profit \geq Max\,Profit - Delta \tag{36}$$

For the case of single objective, optimal values are presented with red color, which are displayed in Table 2. These values can be extend to five main decisions shown in Tables 3, 4, 5, 6 and 7.

Table 2 Objective values when single objective is considered

Objective	Profit ($)	Lost sales cost ($)	Computer time
Profit maximization	4275	7236.25	00:00:02:46
Total lost sales cost minimization	2260	6846.25	00:09:18:60

Table 3 An example of harvest decision

Day	Field 1 (box)		Field 2 (box)		Field 3 (box)	
	Harvested crops	Actual available crops	Harvested crops	Actual available crops	Harvested crops	Actual available crops
1	2	2	3	3	15	15
2	9	9	9	9	20	20
3	16	16	0	12	23	23
4	23	23	27	27	24	24
5	30	30	18	18	28	28
6	37	37	21	21	29	29
7	40	44	23	23	31	31

Table 4 An example of hauling decision

Day	Hauler	Field 1		Field 2		Field 3	
		Hauled crops (box)	No. of trip (trip)	Hauled crops (box)	No. of trip (trip)	Hauled crops (box)	No. of trip (trip)
1	2	2	1	3	1	4	1
2	2	9	1	9	1	31	3
3	2	16	2	0	0	23	2
4	2	23	2	27	2	24	2
5	2	30	2	18	2	28	2
6	2	37	3	21	2	29	2
7	2	40	3	23	2	31	3

Table 5 An example of production decision

Day	Processor	Finished product 1 (box)	Finished product 2 (box)	Finished product 3 (box)
1	3	3	0	0
2	2	1	0	0
	3	15	0	0
3	3	3	0	3
4	3	21	0	2
5	3	16	0	3
6	3	19	0	4
7	3	0	5	6

Table 6 An example of delivery decision

Day	Vehicle	Delivery product 1 (box)	Delivery product 2 (box)	Delivery product 3 (box)	No. of trip (trip)
1	V2	3	0	0	1
2	V2	16	0	0	1
3	V2	3	0	3	1
4	V2	21	0	2	1
5	V2	16	0	3	1
6	V2	19	0	4	1
7	V2	0	5	6	1

Table 7 An example of distribution decision

Day	Product 1		Product 2		Product 3	
	Sold product (box)	Shortage (box)	Sold products (box)	Shortage (box)	Sold products (box)	Shortage (box)
1	3	4	0	9	0	6
2	16	33	0	3	0	14
3	3	0	0	3	3	19
4	21	0	0	12	2	10
5	16	0	0	4	3	22
6	19	0	0	0	4	0
7	0	0	5	0	6	2

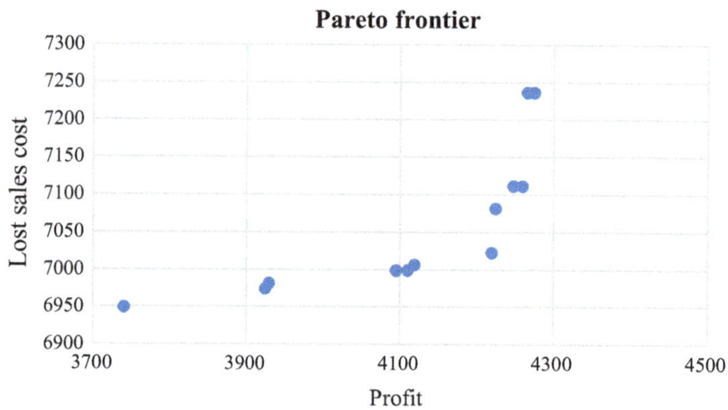

Fig. 1 Non-dominated frontier from CPLEX optimization studio

According to the Table 3, a decision plan of harvest operation shows the possible values of harvested crops, and actual available crops from limited crop yields and available equipment. From this table, the number of harvested crops in each field are unequal. This shows that the size of each field are totally different.

The generated values in harvesting stage will be used in creating decision variables in the next operations. From Tables 3, 4, 5, 6 and 7, it is evident that the decision variables of harvest, hauling, production, delivery, and distribution operations connect sequentially. The decision variables of the previous stage are applied to plan next stages as prescribed in the constraint sets and illustrated in the experimental results given in Tables 3, 4, 5, 6 and 7.

The experimental results demonstrate that the proposed model can generate five coordinated decision plans. It is clear that this model can be adopted to manage and allocate restricted resources of each operation in practical cases.

For the case of multiple objective, Fig. 1 presents non dominated points from CPLEX Optimization Studio by trial and error the value of delta. Each point in Fig. 1 represents two objective functions. X-axis presents profit value whereas Y-axis illustrates lost sales cost value. Each point contains a set of five decision plans as shown in the case of single objective. The decision makers can make the trade-off decisions based on the values of profit and total lost sales cost and also the different resource allocation scheme in the decision plans so as to choose the most effective solution set.

From all computational experiments, the capability of the proposed model in selecting the appropriate resources to perform the operations at optimal performance indicates that the proposed model is systematic and reliable.

5 Conclusions and Recommendations

The integrated planning of harvesting and post-harvesting operations deals with five decisions for harvest, hauling, production, delivery, and distribution. This study developed a mathematical model that focuses on two conflict objectives: profit maximization and total lost sales cost minimization. The proposed math model was solved with CPLEX Optimization Studio.

CPLEX Optimization software package is a powerful optimization software in solving single objective problem. Nevertheless, it cannot directly search the solutions for multiple objective problem. Therefore, one objective is considered while another objective is converted to be a constraint. The optimal values from single objective are used to restrict the possible area in inventing Pareto frontier.

According to the experimental results, the solutions can be found within short time as shown in Table 2. For the generated decisions, it is obvious that the solutions from the previous stage are continuously related to the next stages. For multi-objective problem, the non-dominated points can be found by adjusting the constrained values called delta value.

From this study, there are a plenty of rooms for future study. The limitation of CPLEX Optimization Studio in handling multi-objective problems can be the main motivation in modifying new algorithms by applying heuristic technique. Additionally, the proposed model can be concentrated more on environmental or social purposes in the future.

References

1. Vorst, J. G. v. d., Silva, C. A. d., & Trienekens, J. H. (2007). Agro-industrial supply chain management: Concepts and applications. *Agricultural Management, Marketing and Finance Occasional Paper.*

2. McCreery, J., & Phillips, E. (2013). Integrated planning: The key to upstream operational excellence. *Oil & Gas Financial Journal.*
3. Grunow, M., Gunther, H.-O., & Westinner, R. (2007). Supply optimization for the production of raw sugar. *International Journal of Production Economics, 110*(1–2), 224–239.
4. Ferreira, J. O., Batalha, M. O., & Domingos, J. C. (2016). Integrated planning model for citrus agribusiness system. *Computers and Electronics in Agriculture, 126,* 1–11.
5. Chryssolouris, G., Chan, S., & Suh, N. (1985). An integrated approach to process planning and scheduling. *CIRP Annals-Manufacturing Technology, 34*(1), 413–417.
6. Zhang, L., & Wong, T. (2016). Solving integrated process planning and scheduling problem with constructive meta-heurictics. *Information Sciences, 340–341,* 1–16.
7. Kusumastuti, R. D., van Donk, D. P., & Teunter, R. (2016). Crop-related harvesting and processing planning: A review. *International Journal of Production Economics, 174,* 76–92.
8. Ahumada, O., & Villalobos, J. (2011). Operational model for planning the harvest and distribution of persihable agricultural products. *International Journal of Production Economics, 133*(2), 677–687.
9. Liu, L.-L., Zhao, G.-P., Ou'yang, S.-S., & Yang, Y.-J. (2011). Integrating theory of constraints and particle swarm optimization in order planning and scheduling for machine tool production. *The International Journal of Advanced Manufacturing Technology, 57*(1–4), 285–295.
10. Zhang, X.-D., & Yan, H.-S. (2005). Integrated optimization of production planning and scheduling for a kind of job-shop. *The International Journal of Advanced Manufacturing Technology, 26*(7–8), 876–886.
11. Joly, M., Moro, L., & Pinto, J. (2002). Planning and scheduling for petroleum refineries using mathematical programming. *Brazilian Journal of Chemical Engineering, 19*(2), 207–228.
12. Fumero, Y., Moreno, M. S., Corsano, G., & Montagna, J. M. (2016). A multi product batch design model incorporating production planning and scheduling decisions under a multiperiod scenario. *Applied Mathematical Modelling, 40*(5–6), 3498–3515.
13. Bilgen, B., & Celebi, Y. (2013). Integrated production scheduling and distribution planning in dairy supply chain by hybrid modelling. *Annals of Operations Research, 211*(1), 55–82.
14. Chu, Y., You, F., Wassick, J. M., & Agarwal, A. (2015). Integrated planning and scheduling under production uncertainties: Bi-level model formulation and hybrid solution method. *Computers & Chemical Engineering, 72,* 255–272.
15. Sel, C., Bilgen, B., Bloemhof-Ruwaard, J., & van der Vorst, J. (2015). Multi-bucket optimization for integrated planning and scheduling in the perishable dairy supply chain. *Computers & Chemical Engineering, 77,* 59–73.

Multiple-Trip Vehicle Routing with Physical Workload

Tarit Rattanamanee and Suebsak Nanthavanij

Abstract This paper addresses the vehicle routing problem in which delivery vehicles can perform several trips within one workday. Initially, a mathematical model of the multiple-trip vehicle routing problem (MTVRP) is formulated. Its objective is to minimize a total cost that consists of the costs of vehicles, workforce, and transportation. The MTVRP assumes that vehicles and workers are heterogeneous, customer locations and demands are known, all vehicles must complete their trips within one workday, delivery workers are pre-assigned to vehicles, and all loads are unloaded from vehicles manually. For safety, a total physical workload endured by any worker must not exceed his/her working physical capacity. A numerical example is presented. The MTVRP solutions are determined using the ILOG CPLEX. The result shows that by allowing the vehicles to make several trips, the total cost can be reduced, and both vehicles and workers are better utilized. However, workers are required to work harder due to their longer working times.

Keywords Multiple-trip vehicle routing problem · Optimization
Logistics management · Manual unloading · Physical workload

1 Introduction

In today's business environment, distribution of goods is an important logistic and operational task that is faced continually by many enterprises. The capacitated vehicle routing problem (CVRP) was firstly introduced by Dantzig and Ramser [1]

T. Rattanamanee (✉)
Department of Materials Handling and Logistics Engineering, Faculty of Engineering,
King Mongkut's University of Technology North Bangkok, Bangkok 10800, Thailand
e-mail: tarit.r@eng.kmutnb.ac.th

S. Nanthavanij
School of Management Technology, Sirindhorn International Institute of Technology,
Thammasat University, Pathum Thani 12121, Thailand
e-mail: suebsak@siit.tu.ac.th

X. Liu (ed.), *Environmental Sustainability in Asian Logistics and Supply Chains*,
https://doi.org/10.1007/978-981-13-0451-4_15

as a problem to determine the best routes for a fleet of vehicles that must serve a set of customers. In their classical work, the demand and geographical locations of individual customers are known; each route starts and ends at the depot; all vehicles have the same capacity; each customer must be visited by only one vehicle; its demand must be completely fulfilled; the total demand from all customers on a route must not exceed the vehicle capacity. In some problems, the objective might be to determine a minimum number of delivery vehicles to serve all customers [2, 3]. To cope with real world constraints, many variants of the VRP were developed, e.g., VRP with simultaneous pick-up and deliveries [4, 5], VRP with time windows [6–8] and VRP with multiple compartment [9]. Recently, the state of the art classification and review for VRP presented in [10]. However, when short trips are performed by some vehicles, they will be idle for the rest of the workday. Thus, those vehicles are not economically utilized. For other vehicles that have to work all day, their delivery workers tend to be dissatisfied and the conflict among workers may arise.

In practice, vehicles can be better utilized by making another round of deliveries if the remaining working time is sufficient for the second trip. This called, the multiple-trip vehicle routing problem (MTVRP) is an extension of the classical VRP in which a vehicle may perform several routes (trips) within a given time period. Along with typical constraints, the assignment of the optimized set of routes to the available fleet is considered [11]. Multiple trips are beneficial to the logistics service provider by limiting the number of vehicles and drivers necessary for the deliveries, providing that vehicle capacities, distances, or time constraints are suitable for short routes. The operation cost can be reduced through better utilization of resources such as vehicles and workers.

Brandão and Mercer [12] studied the single-trip VRP to multiple-trip VRP with scheduling problem. The objective is to minimize the total operating costs involving travel time and over time. A tabu search algorithm is employed to solve the distribution problems that involve not only multiple trips and time windows, but also heterogeneous vehicles, restricted access between vehicles and customers, maximal legal driving time and so on. They used a real-life company's data to test the performance of their proposed algorithm. Olivera and Viera [13] proposed an adaptive memory algorithm to solve the VRP with multiple trips. The algorithm was ran over a set of benchmark problems and the solutions obtained were compared with those reported for three previously proposed algorithms. The result show that proposed algorithm obtained more feasible solutions than the previous approaches.

Furthermore, Campbell and Savelsbergh [14] propose insertion heuristics to handle vehicle routing and scheduling problems with different types of constraints including time windows and multiple trips. Azi et al. [15] propose an exact algorithm to solve the single vehicle MTVRP with time window. The solution approach exploits an elementary shortest path algorithm with resource constraints. In the first phase all non-dominated paths are calculated. Then the shortest path algorithm is applied to a modified graph. Each node represents a non-dominated route and two nodes are connected by an arc whether it is possible to serve the two routes consequently and they do not serve common customers. Solomon instances are used with different values of time horizon. 16 instances out of 54 with 100 customers are solved to optimality. Later, they address the MTVRPTW with a column generation approach embedded within a branch-and-price algorithm [16]. A set packing formulation is given for the master problem and each column represents a working day. Wassan et al. [17] studied the multiple-trip VRP with backhauls (MT-VRPB). The classical MTVRP model is extended by including the back-hauling aspect. An ILP formulation of the MT-VRPB is presented and IBM ILOG CPLEX results for small and medium size instances are reported. Moreover, a two-level variable neighbourhood search is developed for solving large size problem.

Another variant of VRP which consider physical workload when workers has to deliver a goods to customers manually is called the vehicle routing problem with manual materials handling (VRPMMH). Nanthavanij and Chalidabhongse [18] studied VRPMMH. They considered a simple problem with uniform vehicle fleet and homogeneous workers. Nanthavanij et al. [19] later studied more realistic VRPMMH covering vehicles with unequal load capacities and heterogeneous workers. They developed two mathematical models. The first model determined a number of utilized vehicles and their delivery routes to satisfy the daily work duration and recommended physical energy limit. The second model then assigned worker teams to vehicles so as to minimize a maximum percent residual energy of any worker team. Asawarungsaengkul and Nanthavanij [20] developed a model for solving the garbage collection problem which considers the garbage pick-up cost and the required physical workload. In their study, an optimal number of garbage trucks and their pick-up sites were determined such that the total travel cost was minimized while the physical workloads were equally distributed among workers.

Boonprasurt and Nanthavanij [21] studied the VRPMMH with fixed workforce assignments (VRPMMH-FXW) and flexible workforce assignments (VRPMMH-FLW). In their study, the vehicles had different load capacities and the numbers of workers per vehicle were unequal. Each vehicle had a fixed operation cost depending on the vehicle type and number of delivery workers assigned to it. A variable (fuel) cost was based on the travel distance and fuel consumption rate. The vehicles had to complete all deliveries within an 8-h workday. The problem objective was to determine an optimal number of delivery vehicles and their delivery routes. For the VRPMMH-FLW, the assignment of workers to vehicles such that their percent residual energies are minimally different was determined.

The multiple-trip vehicle routing problem with physical workload consideration (MTVRP-WL) has not yet attracted much attention from researchers. In this paper, we focus on the analysis of physical workloads among workers in the MTVRP when the workers are pre-assigned to the heterogeneous fleet of vehicles. A mathematical model is formulated to determine the minimum number of utilized vehicles and their optimal delivery routes such that the total operating cost (both fixed and variable cost) is minimized.

2 Multiple-Trip Vehicle Routing Problem with Physical Workload Consideration

The multiple-trip vehicle routing problem with physical workload (MTVRP-WL) consideration can be described as follows. Consider a city-wide logistics network with one supplier and a set of customers. Goods have to be delivered to the customers on a daily basis and all customer demands are known in advance. In an 8-h workday, delivery vehicles may perform multiple trips depending upon the number of customers assigned to them. The supplier has a set of delivery vehicles with limited load capacities. Each vehicle has one driver and a team of workers in which the number of workers for each vehicle depends on the vehicle type (size). Irrespective of the vehicle's carried load, the numbers of workers accompanying individual vehicles are unchanged. When arriving at the customer location, delivery workers unload goods from the vehicle and move them into a stock room. All load handling activities at the customer location are performed manually, possibly with the use of hand carts or dollies. When there are several workers in a worker team, all workers split the goods to be unloaded equally irrespective of their working energy capacities. The worker-vehicle assignment is pre-determined at the beginning of the workday and the pairing is fixed throughout the workday. Delivery workers are heterogeneous in terms of their physical fitness (and working energy capacity). Since the worker-vehicle pairing is known, the energy capacity of the vehicle can be determined from the energy capacities of all workers assigned to it.

Each day, all vehicles must start from the depot, visit their assign customers, perform the delivery to satisfy the daily customer demands, and return to the depot. If any vehicle has only a few customers to serve, they can be re-loaded at the depot to perform another delivery trip. The vehicles may perform several delivery trips within the given working time limit. The re-loading of goods at the depot is performed by warehouse workers, not the delivery workers who accompany the vehicles.

For each vehicle, when its delivery route(s) is (are) known, the required daily energy expenditure can be determined.

3 Energy Expenditure

Boonprasut and Nanthavanij [21] discussion on working energy capacity and energy expenditure. For better understanding and completeness, we briefly describe energy expenditure once again.

To match a person's work capacity with the requirements of a job, one needs to know the individual's energy capacity and how much the job demands from this capacity. To measure an individual's capacity, one makes the person perform a known amount of work and measures the subject's reactions. To measure the energy requirements of a given task, one lets a standardized person perform the job and again measures the person's reactions to the task [22].

The energy capacity is determined from the maximal aerobic power of the worker, which is his/her maximal oxygen uptake during the steady state (i.e., the energy capacity required in the job is the workload of the job performed by a standardized worker). Since a standardized worker is generally unavailable, the worker who actually performs the job then represents the standardized subject under an assumption that he is physically normal. Methods of measuring a worker's maximal aerobic power can be direct or indirect.

For direct measurement, the maximal oxygen uptake is the highest oxygen uptake attainable in the subject, i.e., a further increase in workload will not result in an increase in oxygen uptake. The subject will be tested until he/she cannot continue to perform the work and becomes exhausted. The workload is started at a safe, low level and is then increased either continuously or intermittently until the maximum oxygen uptake is reached. Most common physical tests representing workloads are cycling on a cycle ergometer, running on a treadmill, or stepping up and down on a step test. The heart rate at the maximum oxygen uptake is approximately a difference between 220 and the subject's age (years). This method is not generally used in industries due to its unsafe effect. However, it is more accurate and suitable for physically fit and young subjects. There are also several indirect methods of estimating the maximal oxygen uptake, for example, linear relationship between heart rate and oxygen uptake, Astrand-Astrand nomogram [23–25], step test [26, 27], Tayyari's conventional method [28, 29], and doubly labeled water [30].

A method that is frequently used is the indirect calorimetry method. In this method, a person's oxygen consumption while performing work can be used as a measure of his or her metabolic energy production. One simply measures the subject's oxygen uptake per unit time by measuring total ventilation and the oxygen content of both inspired and expired air. From this value one calculates heat content based on the principle that 1 L of oxygen required in the oxidation of nutrients equals to an energy expenditure of approximately 5.0 kcal. One can now calculate the energy conversion occurring in the body from the volume of oxygen consumed.

Another simpler method but less accurate is to classify the typical activities with known energy expenditure. For 24 h, the subject or an observer keeps a detailed diary of activities. These activities are classified according to standard semantic descriptions such as light sitting, light standing, etc. The total time spent in each category is obtained and an estimate of the total oxygen uptake made based upon values of oxygen uptake assigned to each of the semantic descriptions. The detailed tables of energy expenditure of each semantic description can be found in the ISO 8996 Standard (ISO, 1990).

Light work is associated with rather small energy expenditure (about 2.5 kcal/min, including the basal rate) and is accompanied by a heart rate of approximately 90 beats/min. For medium work, the rate of energy expenditure goes up to 5 kcal/min, where the heart rate is about 100 beats/min. The heavy work typically requires at least 7.5 kcal/min of energy expenditure. For more explanation on energy expenditure, see Kroemer et al. [22].

In this study, the NIOSH limit or 33% of maximum oxygen uptake is used as the limit of working energy capacity in an 8-h workday [31]. Since the maximum oxygen uptake of any worker must be individually identified, this limit has no bias over a group of people with differences in age, sex, or physical fitness.

4 Mathematical Model

The MTVRP-WL is formulated as a mixed integer linear programming (MILP) model. The model can consider as extended and modification combined model from MTVRP with VRPMMH. The objective of this model is to minimize total fixed and variable cost. Permission of second trip or multi-trip are allowed but the total operating time must not exceed working time limit.

4.1 Assumptions and Conditions

The mathematical formulation of the MTVRP-WL is based on the following assumptions:

- the worker's working energy capacity can be estimated,
- the average rate of energy expenditure to unload a unit of goods is known and constant,
- all delivery workers in the same vehicle split the goods to be unloaded equally,
- the vehicle's load capacity is known, and
- the daily customer demands are known.

The MTVRP-WL must satisfy the following conditions:

- the vehicle must not carry the goods more than its load capacity,
- the vehicle must not finished the deliveries (all trips) beyond pre-set time limit,
- the customer must receive its daily demand only once per day and from only one vehicle (i.e., no split delivery),
- the daily total energy expenditure of the worker must not exceed his/her working energy capacity.

4.2 Notation and Model

Notation

Indices

i, j Index for nodes; $i, j = 0,\ldots,N$ (0 represent the depot)
k Index for delivery vehicles; $k = 1,\ldots,K$
r Index for trip; $r = 1,\ldots,R$

Parameters

N Number of customers
K Number of delivery vehicles
R Number of available trips
d_{ij} Distance (km) when travel from node i to node j
q_j Demand of good (units) of customer j
W_k Number of worker(s) required for vehicle k; $l = 1,\ldots,W_k$
EC_{kl} Working energy capacity (kcal/day) of worker l assigned to vehicle k
EU Average rate of energy expenditure (kcal/min) of the worker to unload unit
s Average travel speed (km/min) for each vehicle
cf_k Fixed cost of vehicle k
cv_k Variable cost of vehicle k
C_k Capacity of vehicle k
$TMAX$ Working time limit (min) per day
TU Average unloading time (min) required by worker to unload one unit
TR Average re-loading time (min) required to reload vehicle at depot
M An arbitrary large positive number

Decision variables

X_{ijk}^r 1 if vehicle k travels from node i to node j in the rth trip
0 otherwise
Y_k 1 if vehicle k is utilized
0 otherwise
U_i Variables used to avoid sub tours, and can be interpreted as the position of node i along the route

Model

$$\text{Minimize} \quad \sum_{k=1}^{K} cf_k Y_k + \sum_{i}^{N}\sum_{j}^{N}\sum_{k}^{K}\sum_{r}^{R} d_{ij} cv_k X_{ijk}^r \tag{1}$$

subject to

$$\sum_{i=0}^{N}\sum_{k=1}^{K}\sum_{r=1}^{R} X_{ijk}^{r} = 1 \quad j = 1,\ldots,N \tag{2}$$

$$\sum_{j=1}^{N} X_{0jk}^{r} \le 1 \quad k = 1,\ldots,K;\ r = 1,\ldots,R \tag{3}$$

$$\sum_{i=1}^{N} X_{i0k}^{r} \le 1 \quad k = 1,\ldots,K;\ r = 1,\ldots,R \tag{4}$$

$$\sum_{i=0}^{N}\sum_{j=0}^{N}\sum_{r=1}^{R} X_{ijk}^{r} \le Y_k M \quad k = 1,\ldots,K \tag{5}$$

$$\sum_{i=0}^{N} X_{ihk}^{r} - \sum_{j=0}^{N} X_{hjk}^{r} = 0 \quad h = 1,\ldots,N;\ k = 1,\ldots,K;\ r = 1,\ldots,R;\ i \ne j \ne h \tag{6}$$

$$\sum_{i=1}^{N} X_{0ik}^{r} - \sum_{j=1}^{N} X_{j0k}^{r} = 0 \quad k = 1,\ldots,K;\ r = 1,\ldots,R \tag{7}$$

$$\sum_{i=0}^{N}\sum_{j=0}^{N} q_j X_{ijk}^{r} \le C_k \quad k = 1,\ldots,K;\ r = 1,\ldots,R \tag{8}$$

$$\frac{EU \times TU \sum_{i=1}^{N}\sum_{j=1}^{N}\sum_{r=1}^{R} q_j X_{ijk}^{r}}{W_k} \le EC_{kl} \quad k = 1,\ldots,K;\ l = 1,\ldots,W_k \tag{9}$$

$$\sum_{i=0}^{N}\sum_{j=0}^{N}\sum_{r=1}^{R}\left(\frac{d_{ij}}{s} + \frac{q_j TU}{W_k}\right) X_{ijk}^{r} + TR\sum_{j=1}^{N}\sum_{r=2}^{R} X_{0jk}^{r} \le TMAX \quad k = 1,\ldots,K \tag{10}$$

$$U_j \ge U_i + 1 - N\left(1 - \sum_{k=1}^{K} X_{ijk}^{r}\right) \quad i,j = 1,\ldots,n;\ i \ne j;\ r = 1,\ldots,R \tag{11}$$

$$\sum_{j=1}^{N} X_{0jk}^{r} \ge \sum_{j=1}^{N} X_{0jk}^{r+1} \quad k = 1,\ldots,K; r = 1,\ldots,R-1 \tag{12}$$

$$X_{ijk}^{r} \in \{0,1\}; Y_k \in \{0,1\} \quad i,j = 0,\ldots,N;\ k = 1,\ldots,K;\ r = 1,\ldots,R \tag{13}$$

Objective function (1) is to determine the optimal solution that minimizes the total fixed and variable (fuel) cost. Constraint (2) confirms that each customer will be visited by only one vehicle. Constraints (3)–(5) define that the vehicle being utilized must be from the given fleet of vehicles and only the utilized vehicles can deliver goods to the customers. Constraint (6) is the flow conservation constraint. Constraint (7) states that after leaving the depot, each vehicle must return to the depot. Constraint (8) requires that the total load carried by the vehicle in each trip does not exceed its load capacity. Constraint (9) states that the daily energy expenditure of any worker does not exceed his/her energy capacity. Constraint (10) does not allow the total working time (traveling, unloading and re-loading) of any vehicle to exceed the time limit. Constraint (11) prevents the sub-tours. Constraint (12) requires that for multiple trips, the sequence of trips must be from r to $r + 1$. Finally, constraints (13) define the binary decision variables of the problem.

5 Numerical Example

Consider a hypothetical city-wide logistics network with one supplier and ten customers. Tables 1, 2, 3 and 4 show the vehicle data, workers' working energy capacity and worker-vehicle assignment data, daily customer demand data, and travel distances among the supplier and all customers. All deliveries must start from the supplier and end at the supplier. They must be completed within 8 h or 480 min. Each vehicle can make more than one delivery trip per workday. An average unloading time at the customer location is 3 min/unit. For the vehicle making more than one delivery trip, an average re-loading time at the depot is

Table 1 Delivery vehicle data

	Vehicle					
	V1	V2	V3	V4	V5	V6
Load capacity (units)	60	60	60	100	100	100
Fixed cost (baht/day)	1800	1800	1800	3000	3000	3000
Variable cost (baht/km)	5	5	5	7	7	7
Worker (persons)	1	1	1	2	2	2

Table 2 Working energy capacity (EC) (kcal/day) and worker-vehicle assignment data

Worker	EC	Assignment	Worker	EC	Assignment
W1	2500	V1	W6	2600	V5
W2	2300	V2	W7	2200	V5
W3	2000	V3	W8	2300	V6
W4	2500	V4	W9	2100	V6
W5	2050	V4			

Table 3 Customer demand data (units)

Customer	C1	C2	C3	C4	C5	C6	C7	C8	C9	C10
Demand	19	36	60	24	9	15	28	42	75	65

Table 4 Supplier (S)—customer travel distance data (km)

S		Customer									
		C1	C2	C3	C4	C5	C6	C7	C8	C9	C10
S	0.0	13.0	4.0	8.0	1.0	6.0	9.0	17.0	10.0	10.0	5.0
C1	13.0	0.0	17.0	17.0	12.0	18.0	17.0	23.0	13.0	17.0	18.0
C2	4.0	17.0	0.0	5.0	5.0	2.0	6.0	20.0	14.0	13.0	8.0
C3	8.0	17.0	5.0	0.0	7.0	5.0	1.0	25.0	14.0	18.0	13.0
C4	1.0	12.0	5.0	7.0	0.0	7.0	8.0	18.0	9.0	11.0	6.0
C5	6.0	18.0	2.0	5.0	7.0	0.0	6.0	20.0	16.0	14.0	9.0
C6	9.0	17.0	6.0	1.0	8.0	6.0	0.0	26.0	15.0	19.0	14.0
C7	17.0	23.0	20.0	25.0	18.0	20.0	26.0	0.0	11.0	7.0	12.0
C8	10.0	13.0	14.0	14.0	9.0	16.0	15.0	11.0	0.0	4.0	15.0
C9	10.0	17.0	13.0	18.0	11.0	14.0	19.0	7.0	4.0	0.0	12.0
C10	5.0	18.0	8.0	13.0	6.0	9.0	14.0	12.0	15.0	12.0	0.0

60 min per vehicle. An average travel speed of vehicle is 0.33 km/min. An average rate of energy expenditure required for unloading is 8 kcal/min.

The above example is solved to optimality using the IBM ILOG CPLEX V.12.4.0 optimization software tool. The obtained solutions include delivery routes, total cost of vehicle, working time of vehicle, carried loads of utilized vehicles and percent residual energies of workers. They are presented separately below.

Delivery routes

Trip 1	Vehicle1	S → C8 → S
	Vehicle3	S → C1 → S
	Vehicle4	S → C10 → C7 → S
	Vehicle6	S → C4 → C9 → S
Trip 2	Vehicle1	S → C3 → S
	Vehicle3	S → C2 → C5 → C6 → S

Table 5 Total cost of vehicles

Vehicle	Variable cost (baht)	Fixed cost (baht)	Total cost (baht)
V1	180	1800	1980
V3	235	1800	2035
V4	238	3000	3238
V6	154	3000	3154
Total	807	9600	**10,407**

Table 6 Working times and carried loads

Vehicle	Carried loads (units)	Total working time (min)
V1	102	475
V3	79	439
V4	93	382
V6	99	364

Table 7 Percent residual energies (%) of workers

	W1	W3	W4	W5	W8	W9
Percent residual energies	2.08	5.2	55.36	45.56	48.35	43.43

Total cost of vehicle

The total cost for the utilized delivery vehicles are shown in Table 5. The total cost is 10,407 baht.

Working times and carried loads of utilized vehicles

The working times and total carried loads of all utilized vehicles over a workday are presented in Table 6.

Percent residual energies

The residual energy is defined as the remaining working energy capacity of the worker. The percent residual energy is computed as a ratio of the residual energy to the person's working energy capacity. Table 7 and Fig. 1 show percent residual energies of 6 utilized workers.

From Table 7 and Fig. 1, readers can see that workers W4, W5, W8, and W9 have light workloads since their percent residual energies are large. On the other hand, workers W1 and W3 have to work very hard during the workday since their percent residual energies are small. This is because workers W1 and W3 have to work two trips with vehicles V1 and V3. The uneven distribution of workloads is considered unfair and could result in job dissatisfaction in some workers.

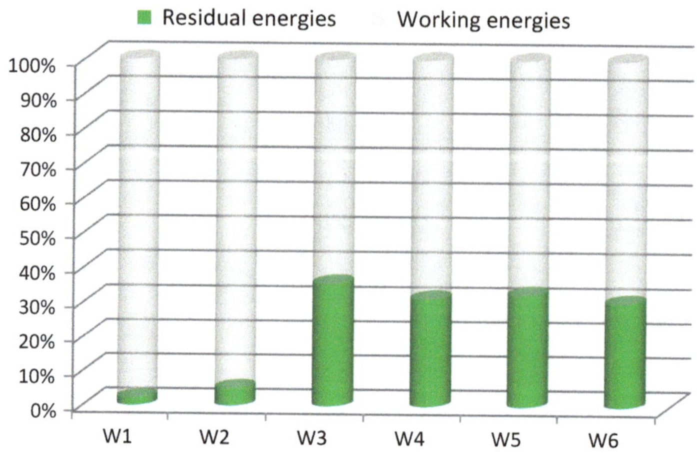

Fig. 1 Chart of percent residual energies (%) of workers

6 Conclusion

This paper introduces the multiple-trip vehicle routing problem (MTVRP) which considers the required energy expenditure of workers to perform manual unloading tasks at customer locations. Vehicles are allowed to perform more than one delivery trip per workday and the worker-vehicle assignment is pre-determined. An integer linear programming model is developed to represent the MTVRP-WL. Its objective is to minimize the total cost (fixed and variable) of vehicles. From the given numerical example, the result also shows that the percent residual energies of individual workers vary depending on their imposed workloads and number of delivery trips. While the total cost can be reduced by the multiple used of vehicles, workers are required to work harder due to the longer working time per day.

References

1. Dantzig, G. B., & Ramser, J. H. (1959). The truck dispatching problem. *Management Science, 6,* 80–91.
2. Laporte, G., Gendreau, M., Potvin, J. Y., & Semet, F. (2000). Classical and modern heuristics for the vehicle routing problem. *International Transactions in Operational Research, 7,* 285–300.
3. Toth, P., & Vigo, D. (2002). *SIAM Monographs on Discrete Mathematics and Applications. The vehicle routing problem*. Philadelphia, PA.
4. Min, H. (1989). The multiple vehicle routing problem with simultaneous delivery and pickup. *Transportation Research Part A: Policy and Practice, 23,* 377–386.
5. Tasan, A. S., & Gen, M. (2012). A genetic algorithm based approach to vehicle routing problem with simultaneous pick-up and deliveries. *Computer and Industrial Engineering, 62,* 755–761.

6. El-Sherbeny, N. A. (2010). Vehicle routing with time windows: An overview of exact, heuristic and metaheuristic methods. *Journal of King Saud University Science, 22,* 123–131.
7. Hashimoto, H., Ibaraki, T., Imahori, S., & Yagiura, M. (2006). The vehicle routing problem with flexible time windows and traveling times. *Discrete Applied Mathematics, 154,* 2271–2290.
8. Jiang, J., Ng, K. M., Poh, K. L., & Teo, K. M. (2014). Vehicle routing problem with a heterogeneous fleet and time windows. *Expert Systems with Applications, 41*(8), 3748–3760.
9. Asawarungsaengkul, K., Rattanamanee, T., & Wuttipornpun, T. (2013). A multi-size compartment vehicle routing problem for multi-product distribution: Models and solution procedures. *International Journal of Artificial Intelligence, 11*(13A), 237–256.
10. Braekers, K., Ramaekers, K., & Nieuwenhuyse, I. V. (2016). The vehicle routing problem: State of the art classification and review. *Computer and Industrial Engineering, 99,* 300–313.
11. Taillard, E. D., Laporte, G., & Gendreau, M. (1996). Vehicle routing with multiple use of vehicles. *European Journal of Operational Research, 47,* 1065–1070.
12. Brandão, J., & Mercer, A. (1997). A tabu search algorithm for the multi-trip vehicle routing and scheduling problem. *European Journal of Operational Research, 100,* 180–191.
13. Olivera, A., & Viera, O. (2007). Adaptive memory programming for the vehicle routing problem with multiple trips. *Computers & Operations Research, 34,* 28–47.
14. Campbell, A. M., & Savelsbergh, M. (2004). Efficient insertion heuristics for vehicle routing and scheduling problems. *Transportation Science, 38,* 369–378.
15. Azi, N., Gendreau, M., & Potvin, J. V. (2007). An exact algorithm for a single-vehicle routing problem with time windows and multiple routes. *European Journal of Operational Research, 178,* 755–766.
16. Azi, N., Gendreau, M., & Potvin, J. V. (2010). An exact algorithm for a vehicle routing problem with time windows and multiple use of vehicles. *European Journal of Operational Research, 202,* 756–763.
17. Wassan, N., Wassan, N., Nagy, G., & Salhi, S. (2017). The multiple trip vehicle routing problem with backhauls: Formulation and a two-level variable neighbourhood search. *Computers & Operations Research, 78,* 454–467.
18. Nanthavanij, S., & Chalidabhongse, J. (2007). Ergonomic scheduling of delivery crew for the vehicle routing problem with manual materials handling. In *Proceedings of the 2nd International Conference on Operations and Supply Chain Management, CD-ROM.*
19. Nanthavanij, S., Boonprasurt, P., Jaruphongsa, W., & Ammarapala, V. (2008). Vehicle routing problem with manual materials handling: Flexible Delivery crew—vehicle assignments. In *Proceedings of the 9th Asia Pacific Industrial Engineering and Management Systems Conference, CD-ROM.*
20. Asawarungsaengkul, K., & Nanthavanij, S. (2010). Optimal truck routing design for garbage collection with cost and physical workload consideration. In *Proceedings of the 11th Asia Pacific Industrial Engineering & Management Systems Conference, CD-ROM.*
21. Boonprasurt, P., & Nanthavanij, S. (2012). Optimal fleet size, delivery routes, and workforce assignments for the vehicle routing problem with manual materials handling. *International Journal of Industrial Engineering—Theory, Applications and Practice, 19*(6), 252–263.
22. Kroemer, K., Kroemer, H., & Kroemer-Elbert, K. (2001). *Ergonomics: How to design for ease and efficiency* (2nd ed.). Englewood Cliffs, NJ: Prentice Hall.
23. Astrand, I. (1960). Aerobic work capacity in men and women with special reference to age. *Acta Physiologica Scandinavica, 49,* 169.
24. Astrand, P. O., & Rodahl, K. (1986). *Textbook of work physiology: Physiological bases of exercise* (3rd ed.). New York: McGraw-Hill.
25. Rodahl, K. (1989). *The physiology of work.* London: Taylor and Francis.
26. American College of Sports. (1991). *Medicine guidelines for exercise testing and prescription.* London: Lea and Febiger.
27. Sigconolfi, S. F., Garber, C. E., Lasater, T. M., & Carleton, R. A. (1985). A simple valid step test for estimating maximal oxygen uptake in epidemiologic studies. *American Journal of Epidemiology, 14,* 209–223.

28. Tayyari, F. (1995). Estimation of maximum oxygen uptake: a convenient method for industry. In A. C. Bittner & P. C. Champney (Eds.), *Advances in industrial ergonomics and safety* (Vol. VII, pp. 169–172). London: Taylor and Francis.
29. Tayyari, F., & Smith, J. L. (1997). *Occupational ergonomics: Principles and applications*. London: Chapman and Hall.
30. Metabolic Solution, Inc. (2002). http://www.metsol.com.
31. National Institute for Occupational Safety and Health. (1981). *Work practices guide for the design of manual handling task*. Washington, DC.

Author Index

X. Liu (ed.), *Environmental Sustainability in Asian Logistics and Supply Chains*,
https://doi.org/10.1007/978-981-13-0451-4

FSC
www.fsc.org
MIX
Papier | Fördert
gute Waldnutzung
FSC® C083411

Kolibri 360 GmbH
Ferdinand-Jühlke-Straße 7
99095 Erfurt, Deutschland
produktsicherheit@kolibri360.de